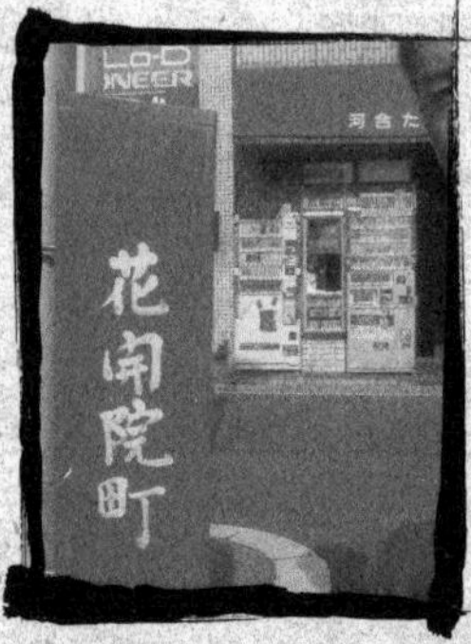
Lo-D
花園院町

Summer vacation.

Clickity clickity clickity

There were club activities every day from morning to afternoon in the hot weather, and on the way home I would go into a bookstore that was super-cool because they kept the air conditioner cranked up. The bookstore was quiet, and you could faintly hear the sound of the cicadas through the window glass. I picked up the various book fair pamphlets and wondered, which book should I read next? I visited the manga corner in the next aisle, dreaming of the day when my own manga might appear on that shelf, and then I would go home and draw...

I like summer vacation because it reminds of those days.

—HIROSHI SHIIBASHI,
2009

HIROSHI SHIIBASHI debuted in BUSINESS JUMP magazine with *Aratama.* NURA: RISE OF THE YOKAI CLAN is his breakout hit. He was an assistant to manga artist Hirohiko Araki, the creator of *Jojo's Bizarre Adventure. Steel Ball Run* by Araki is one of his favorite manga.

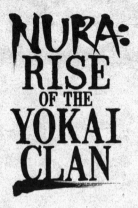

NURA: RISE OF THE YOKAI CLAN
VOLUME 6
SHONEN JUMP Manga Edition

Story and Art by HIROSHI SHIIBASHI

Translation — Yumi Okamoto
Adaptation — Mark Giambruno
Touch-up Art and Lettering — Annaliese Christman,
Gia Cam Luc
Graphics and Cover Design — Fawn Lau
Editor — Joel Enos

NURARIHYON NO MAGO © 2008 by Hiroshi Shiibashi. All rights reserved. First published in Japan in 2008 by SHUEISHA Inc., Tokyo. English translation rights arranged by SHUEISHA Inc.

The rights of the author(s) of the work(s) in this publication to be so identified have been asserted in accordance with the Copyright, Designs and Patents Act 1988. A CIP catalogue record for this book is available from the British Library.

The stories, characters and incidents mentioned in this publication are entirely fictional.

Printed in the U.S.A.

Published by VIZ Media, LLC
P.O. Box 77010
San Francisco, CA 94107

10 9 8 7 6 5 4 3 2 1
First printing, December 2011

www.viz.com   www.shonenjump.com

PARENTAL ADVISORY
NURA: RISE OF THE YOKAI CLAN is rated T for Teen and is suitable for ages 13 and up. This volume may contain fantasy and realistic violence and alcohol usage.
ratings.viz.com

NURA: RISE OF THE YOKAI CLAN

6

THE HOUSE WHERE JYAMI WANDERS

STORY AND ART BY HIROSHI SHIIBASHI

CHARACTERS

NURARIHYON

Rikuo's grandfather and the Lord of Pandemonium. He intends to pass leadership of the Nura clan—leaders of the yokai world—to Rikuo.

RIKUO NURA

Though he appears to be a human boy, he's actually the grandson of Nurarihyon, a yokai. His grandfather's blood makes him one-quarter yokai, and he transforms into a yokai at times.

KIYOTSUGU

Rikuo's classmate. He has adored yokai ever since Rikuo saved him in his yokai form, leading him to form the Kiyojuji Paranormal Patrol.

KANA IENAGA

Rikuo's classmate and a childhood friend. Even though she hates scary things, she's a member of the Kiyojuji Paranormal Patrol for some reason.

YUKI-ONNA

A yokai of the Nura clan who is in charge of looking after Rikuo. She disguises herself as a human and attends the same school as Rikuo to protect him from danger. When in human form, she goes by the name Tsurara Oikawa.

YURA KEIKAIN

Rikuo's classmate and a descendant of the Keikain family of onmyoji. She transferred into Ukiyoe Middle School to do field training in yokai exorcism. She has the power to control her shikigami and uses them to destroy yokai.

TAMAZUKI

Leader of the 88 Demons of Shikoku. Came to the Kanto region to take over the Nura clan territory. He'll do whatever it takes to achieve his goal.

KUBINASHI

A Nura clan yokai. He joined the ranks of Rikuo's guards ever since the boy became the official successor to the Supreme Commander. Handsome, but has low tolerance for alcohol.

YOSUZUME

One of the 88 Demons of Shikoku. Her black wings have the ability to deceive and blind her enemies. She acts as Tamazuki's guard.

INUGAMI

One of the 88 Demons of Shikoku. Has the ability to change hatred into power. After his defeat by Rikuo, Tamazuki killed him.

AOTABO

ZEN

MOKUGYO-DARUMA

KARASU-TENGU

STORY SO FAR

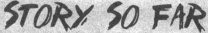

Rikuo Nura appears to be just your average seventh-grader at Ukiyoe Middle School. But he's actually the grandson of the yokai Overlord Nurarihyon and has just been promoted to become the Underboss of the Nura clan, the Tokyo region's powerful yokai syndicate! For now, he lives his days as a human boy, but eventually he is expected to take his grandfather's place as the leader of the clan.

In order to counter the aggressive advances of the Shikoku yokai, Rikuo sends his clan members Gozumaru and Mezumaru to spy on the enemy. They are successful at blending in with the enemy. But when they go further undercover and attempt to gain intel on Tamazuki's treasure, the Devil's Hammer, they are captured. Bizarrely, Tamazuki slays his own troops to get to the pair of Nura spies, but they escape with the aid of other clan members.

Meanwhile, Zen tells Rikuo he must create a Night Parade of a Hundred Demons. Rikuo hesitates, lacking the confidence to lead a yokai clan, but his friends strongly encourage him, and he ultimately holds the Rite of Brotherhood with them.

Now, at last, a full-on confrontation takes place when the Shikoku group attacks. Rikuo comes face-to-face with Tamazuki!!

TABLE OF CONTENTS

NURA: RISE OF THE YOKAI CLAN

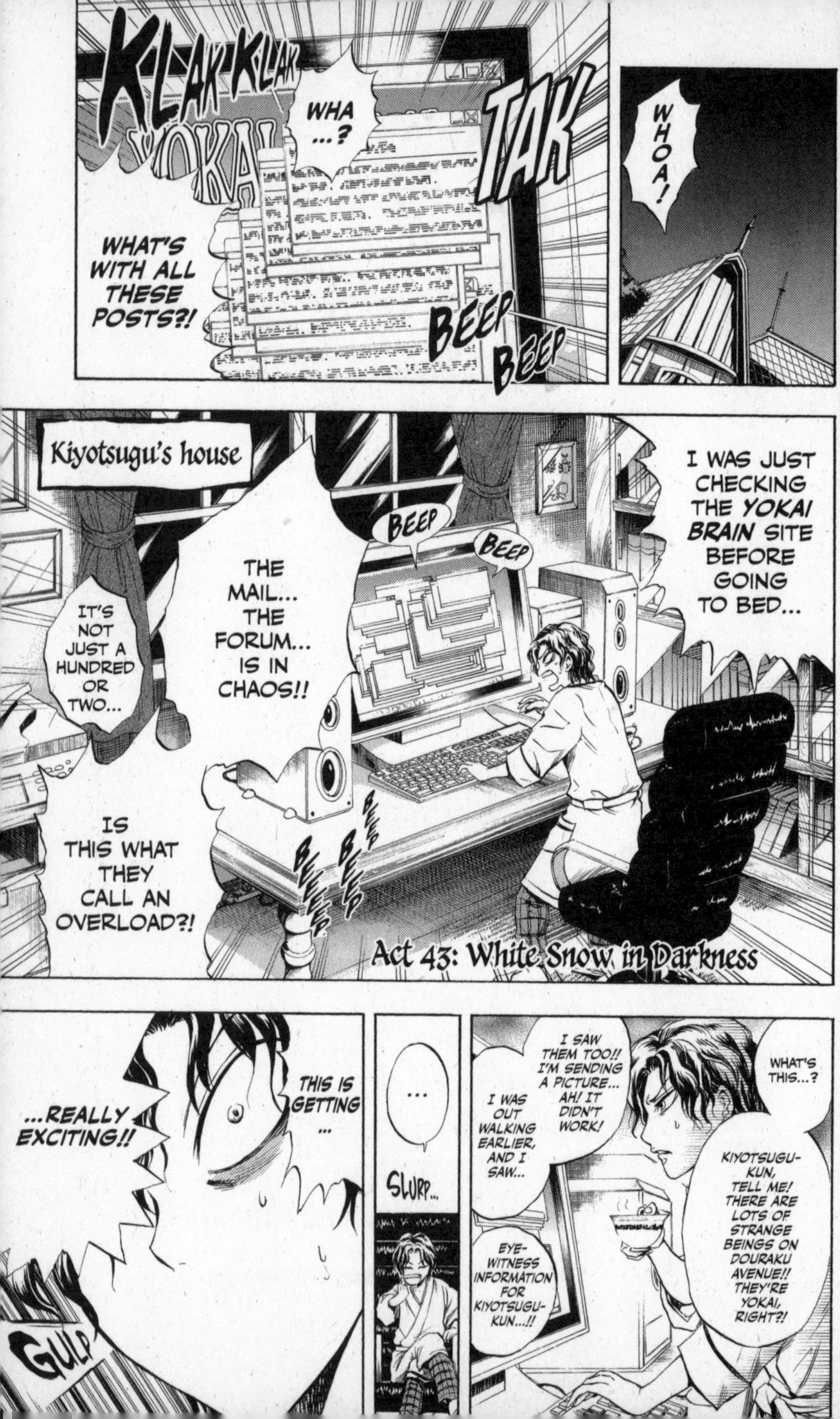
WHOA!
TAK
WHA ...?
KLAK KLAK KLAK
YOKAI
WHAT'S WITH ALL THESE POSTS?!
BEEP BEEP
I WAS JUST CHECKING THE YOKAI BRAIN SITE BEFORE GOING TO BED...
BEEP
BEEP
THE MAIL... THE FORUM... IS IN CHAOS!!
Kiyotsugu's house
IT'S NOT JUST A HUNDRED OR TWO...
IS THIS WHAT THEY CALL AN OVERLOAD?!
BEEP BEEP BEEEEP
Act 43: White Snow in Darkness
WHAT'S THIS...?
KIYOTSUGU-KUN, TELL ME! THERE ARE LOTS OF STRANGE BEINGS ON DOURAKU AVENUE!! THEY'RE YOKAI, RIGHT?!
I SAW THEM TOO!! I'M SENDING A PICTURE... AH! IT DIDN'T WORK!
I WAS OUT WALKING EARLIER, AND I SAW...
EYE-WITNESS INFORMATION FOR KIYOTSUGU-KUN...!!
...
SLURP...
THIS IS GETTING ...
...REALLY EXCITING!!
GULP

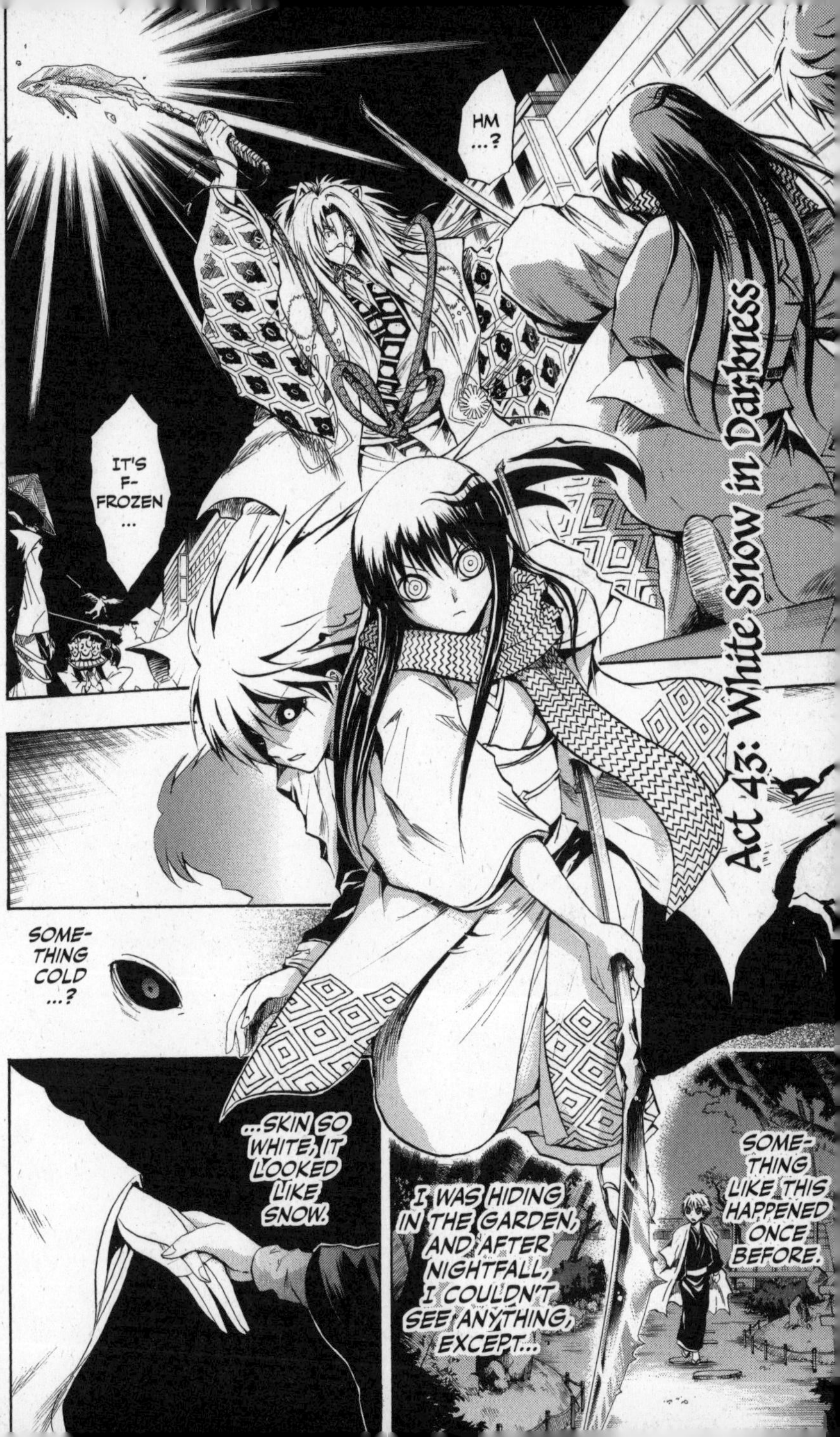
Act 43: White Snow in Darkness
HM ...?
IT'S F-FROZEN ...
SOME-THING COLD ...?
SOME-THING LIKE THIS HAPPENED ONCE BEFORE.
I WAS HIDING IN THE GARDEN, AND AFTER NIGHTFALL, I COULDN'T SEE ANYTHING, EXCEPT...
...SKIN SO WHITE, IT LOOKED LIKE SNOW.

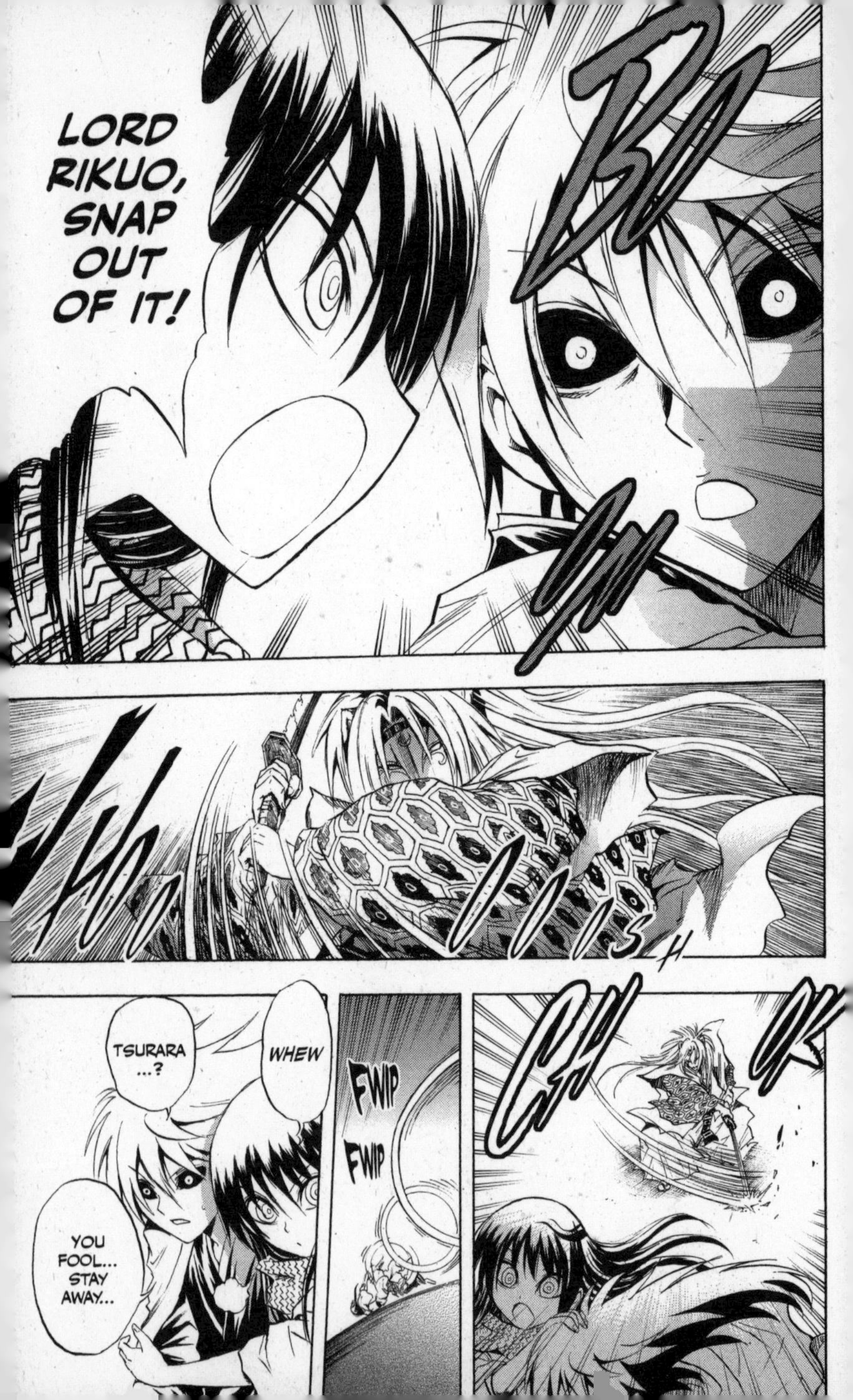
LORD RIKUO, SNAP OUT OF IT!
FWIP
FWIP
WHEW
TSURARA ...?
YOU FOOL... STAY AWAY...

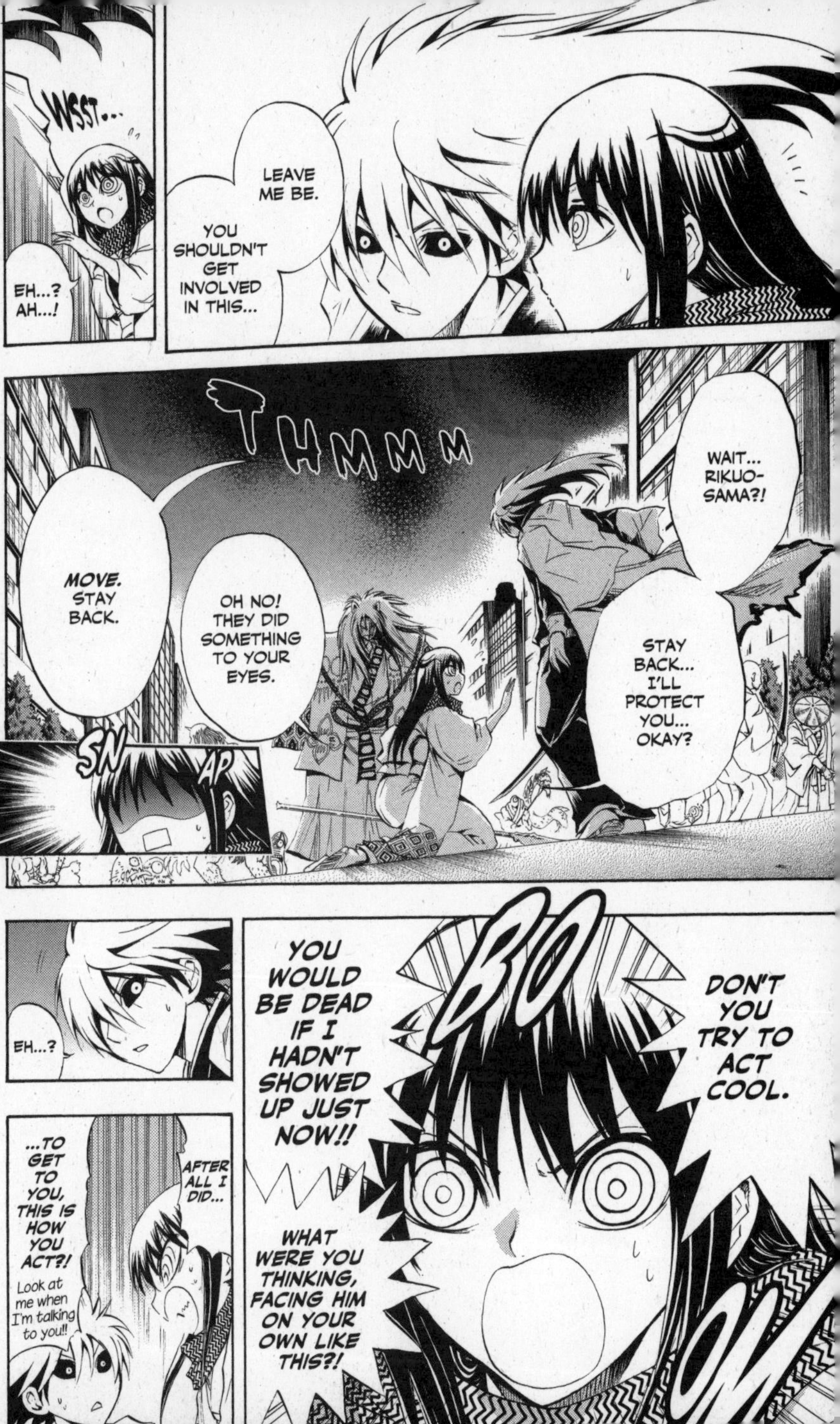
LEAVE ME BE.
YOU SHOULDN'T GET INVOLVED IN THIS...
WSST...
EH...? AH...!
WAIT... RIKUO-SAMA?!
STAY BACK... I'LL PROTECT YOU... OKAY?
THMMM
OH NO! THEY DID SOMETHING TO YOUR EYES.
MOVE. STAY BACK.
SNAP
BO
DON'T YOU TRY TO ACT COOL.
YOU WOULD BE DEAD IF I HADN'T SHOWED UP JUST NOW!!
WHAT WERE YOU THINKING, FACING HIM ON YOUR OWN LIKE THIS?!
EH...?
AFTER ALL I DID...
...TO GET TO YOU, THIS IS HOW YOU ACT?!
Look at me when I'm talking to you!!

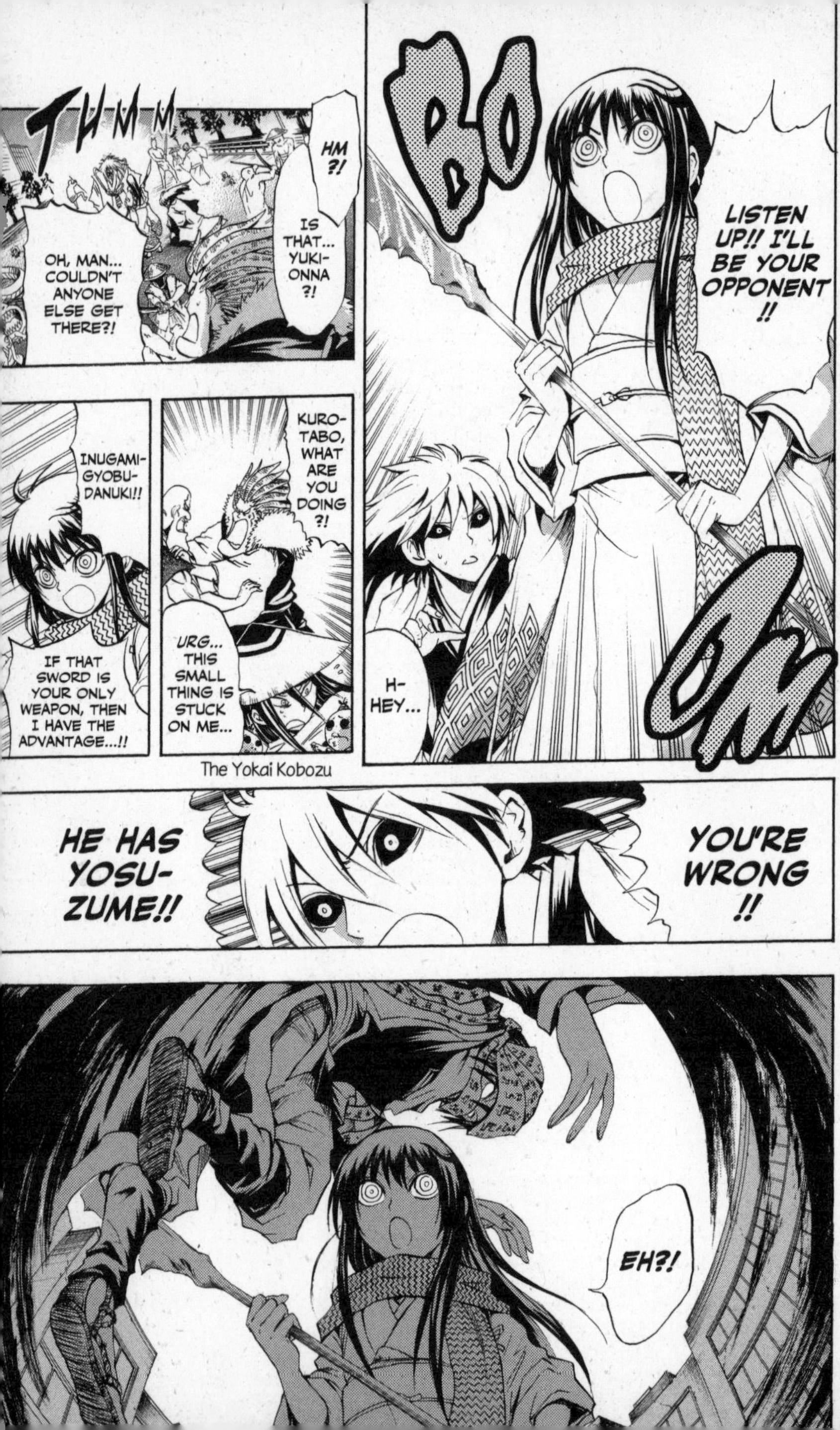
BO
OM
LISTEN UP!! I'LL BE YOUR OPPONENT!!
H-HEY...
THMM
HM?!
IS THAT... YUKI-ONNA?!
OH, MAN... COULDN'T ANYONE ELSE GET THERE?!
KURO-TABO, WHAT ARE YOU DOING?!
URG... THIS SMALL THING IS STUCK ON ME...
The Yokai Kobozu
INUGAMI-GYOBU-DANUKI!!
IF THAT SWORD IS YOUR ONLY WEAPON, THEN I HAVE THE ADVANTAGE...!!
YOU'RE WRONG!!
HE HAS YOSU-ZUME!!
EH?!

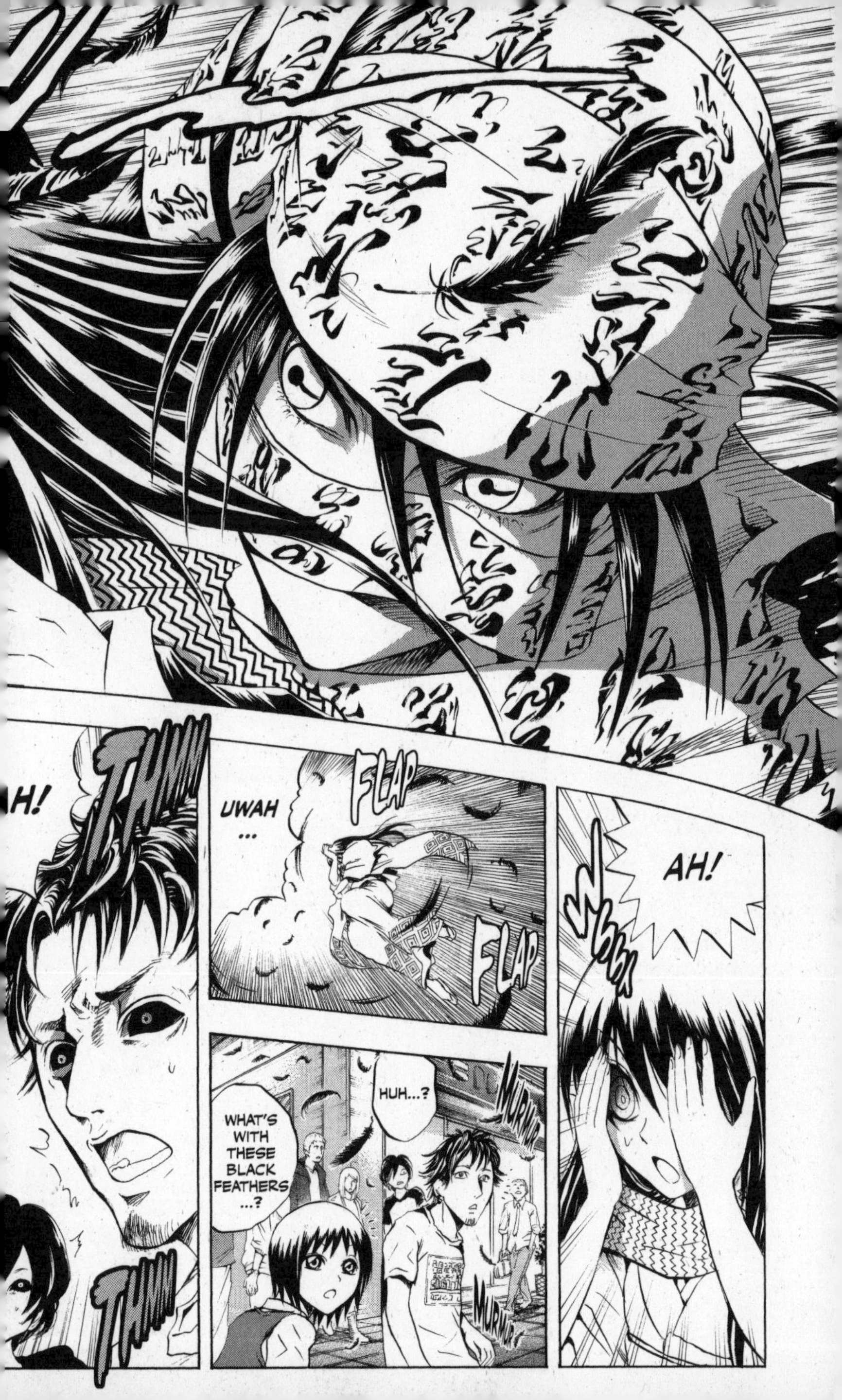
AH!
FLAP
UWAH ...
FLAP
HUH...?
WHAT'S WITH THESE BLACK FEATHERS ...?
MURMUR
MURMUR

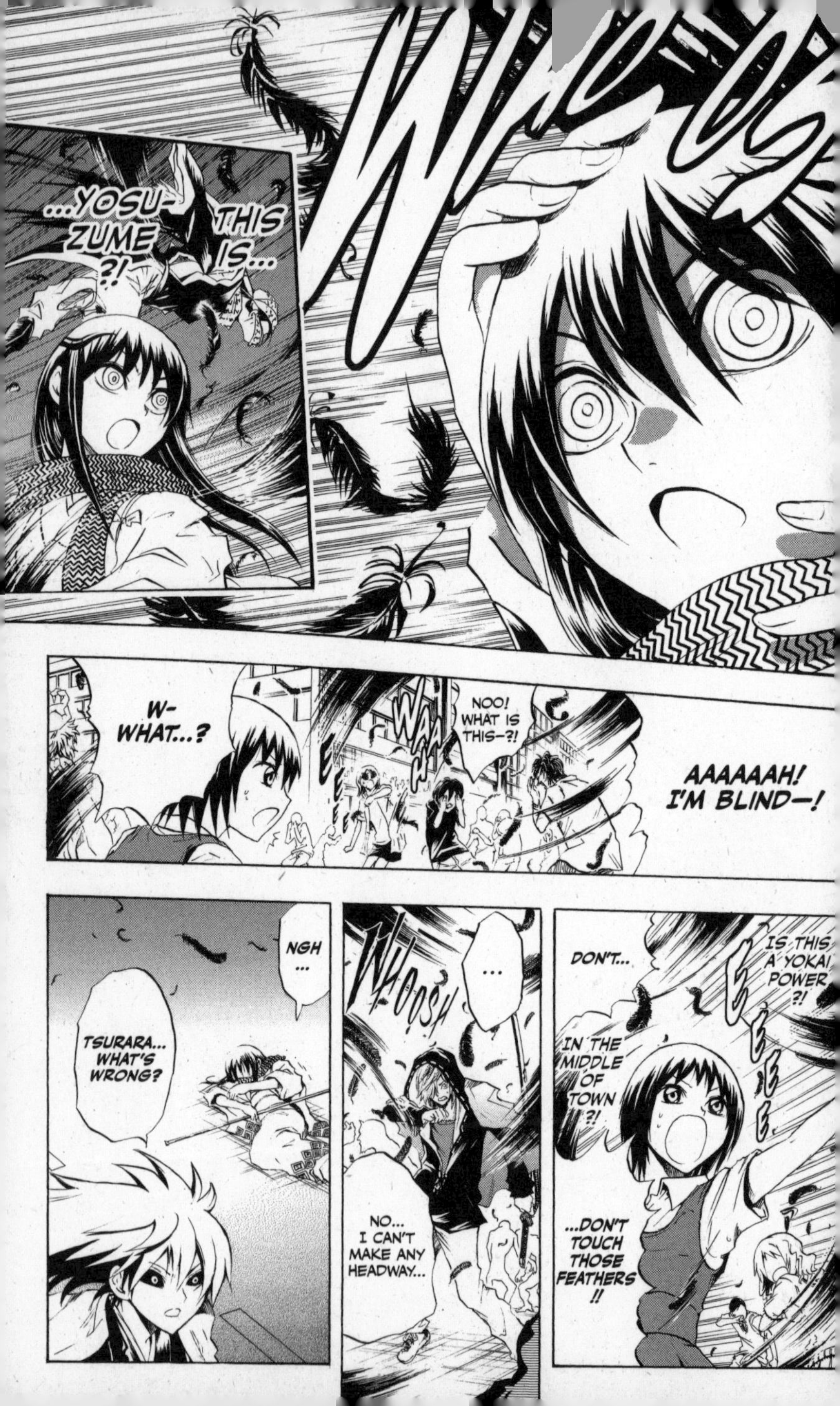

THIS IS...
...YOSU-ZUME ?!
AAAAAAH! I'M BLIND—!
NOO! WHAT IS THIS—?!
WAAH
W-WHAT...?
IS THIS A YOKAI POWER ?!
DON'T...
IN THE MIDDLE OF TOWN ?!
...DON'T TOUCH THOSE FEATHERS !!
...
WHOOSH
NO... I CAN'T MAKE ANY HEADWAY...
NGH ...
TSURARA... WHAT'S WRONG?

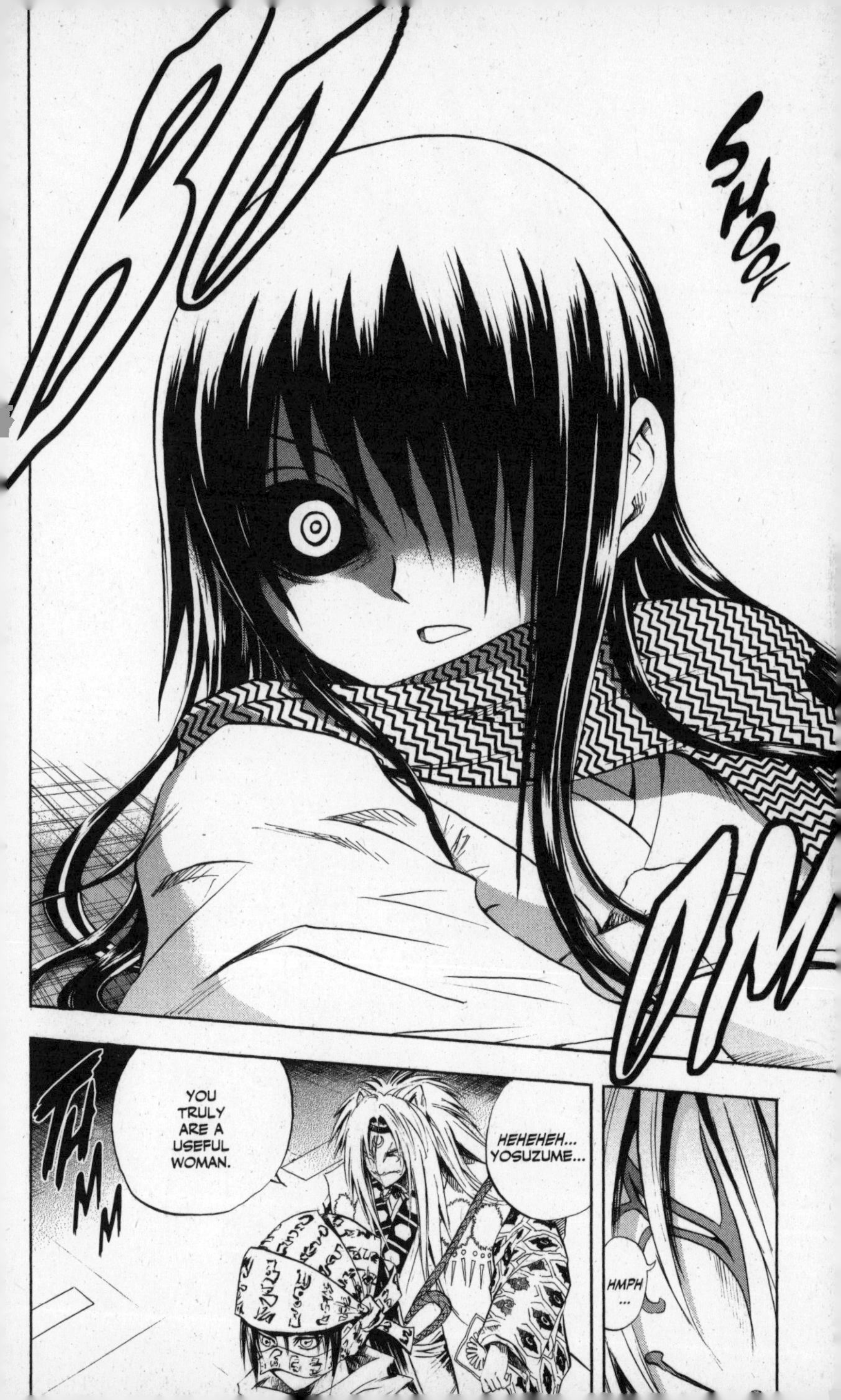
SHOOK
HMPH ...
HEHEHEH... YOSUZUME...
YOU TRULY ARE A USEFUL WOMAN.

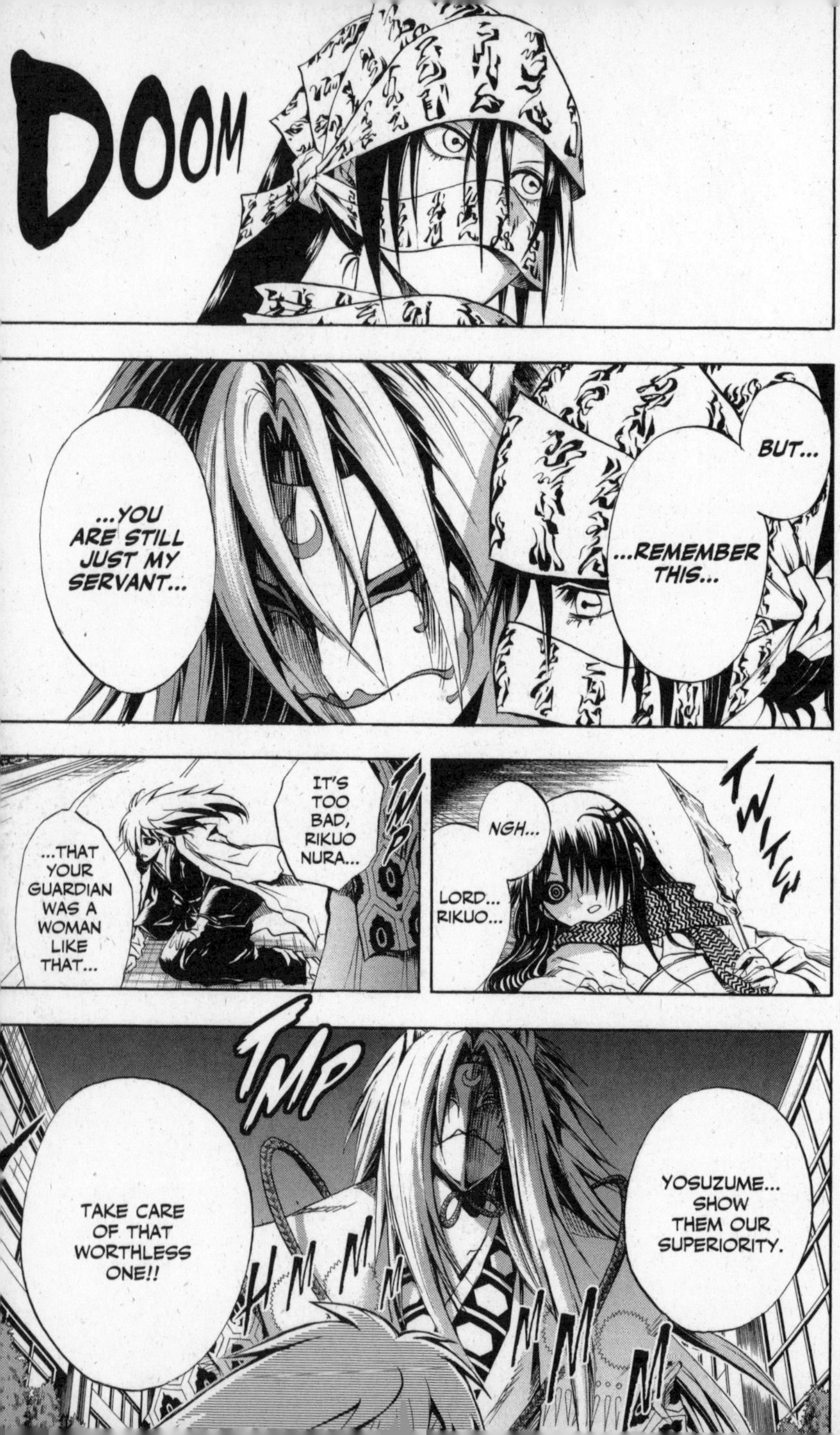

DOOM
BUT...
...REMEMBER THIS...
...YOU ARE STILL JUST MY SERVANT...
NGH...
LORD... RIKUO...
IT'S TOO BAD, RIKUO NURA...
...THAT YOUR GUARDIAN WAS A WOMAN LIKE THAT...
TMP
YOSUZUME... SHOW THEM OUR SUPERIORITY.
TAKE CARE OF THAT WORTHLESS ONE!!

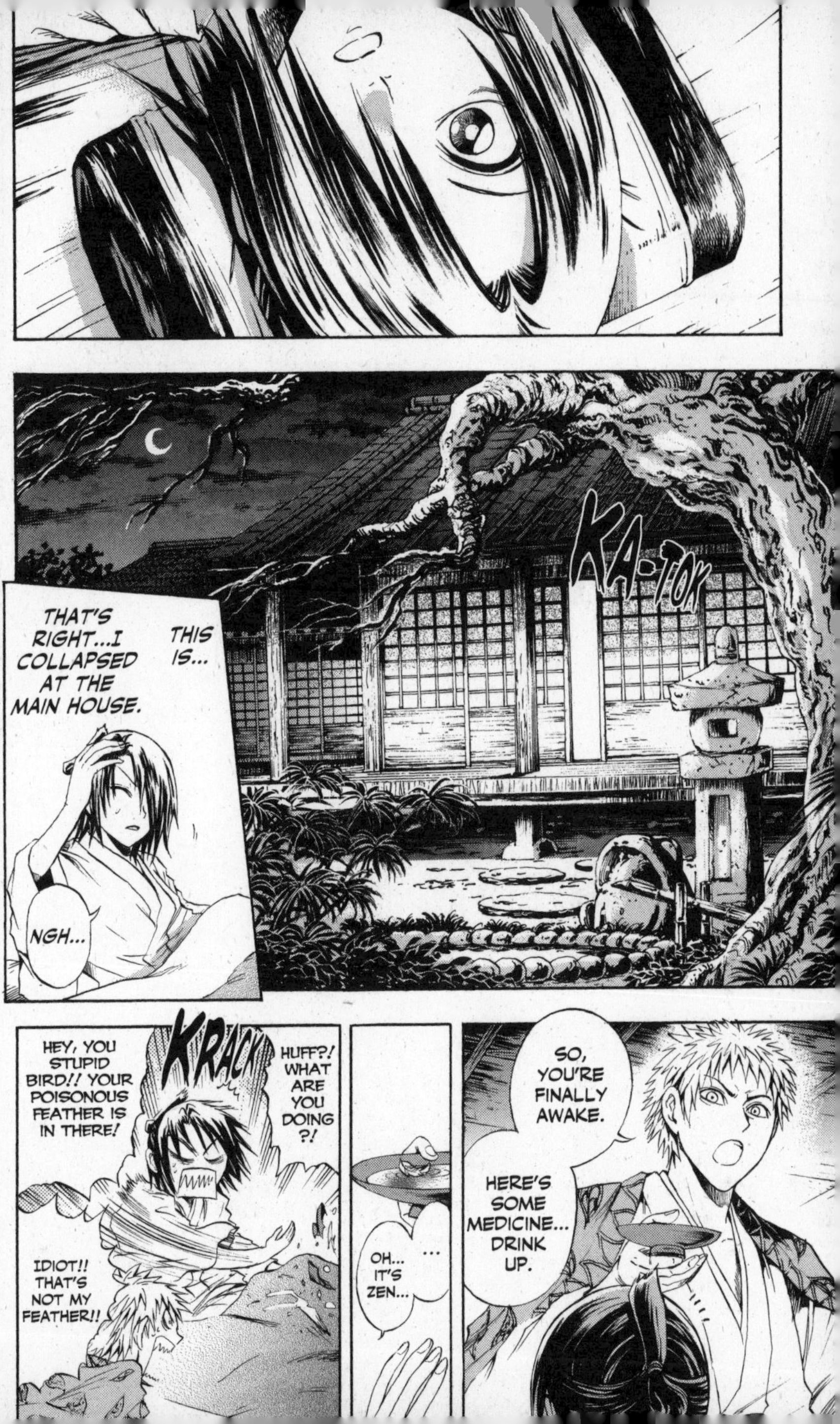

KA-TOK
THIS IS...
THAT'S RIGHT...I COLLAPSED AT THE MAIN HOUSE.
NGH...
SO, YOU'RE FINALLY AWAKE.
HERE'S SOME MEDICINE... DRINK UP.
...
OH... IT'S ZEN...
HUFF?! WHAT ARE YOU DOING?!
KRACK
HEY, YOU STUPID BIRD!! YOUR POISONOUS FEATHER IS IN THERE!
IDIOT!! THAT'S NOT MY FEATHER!!

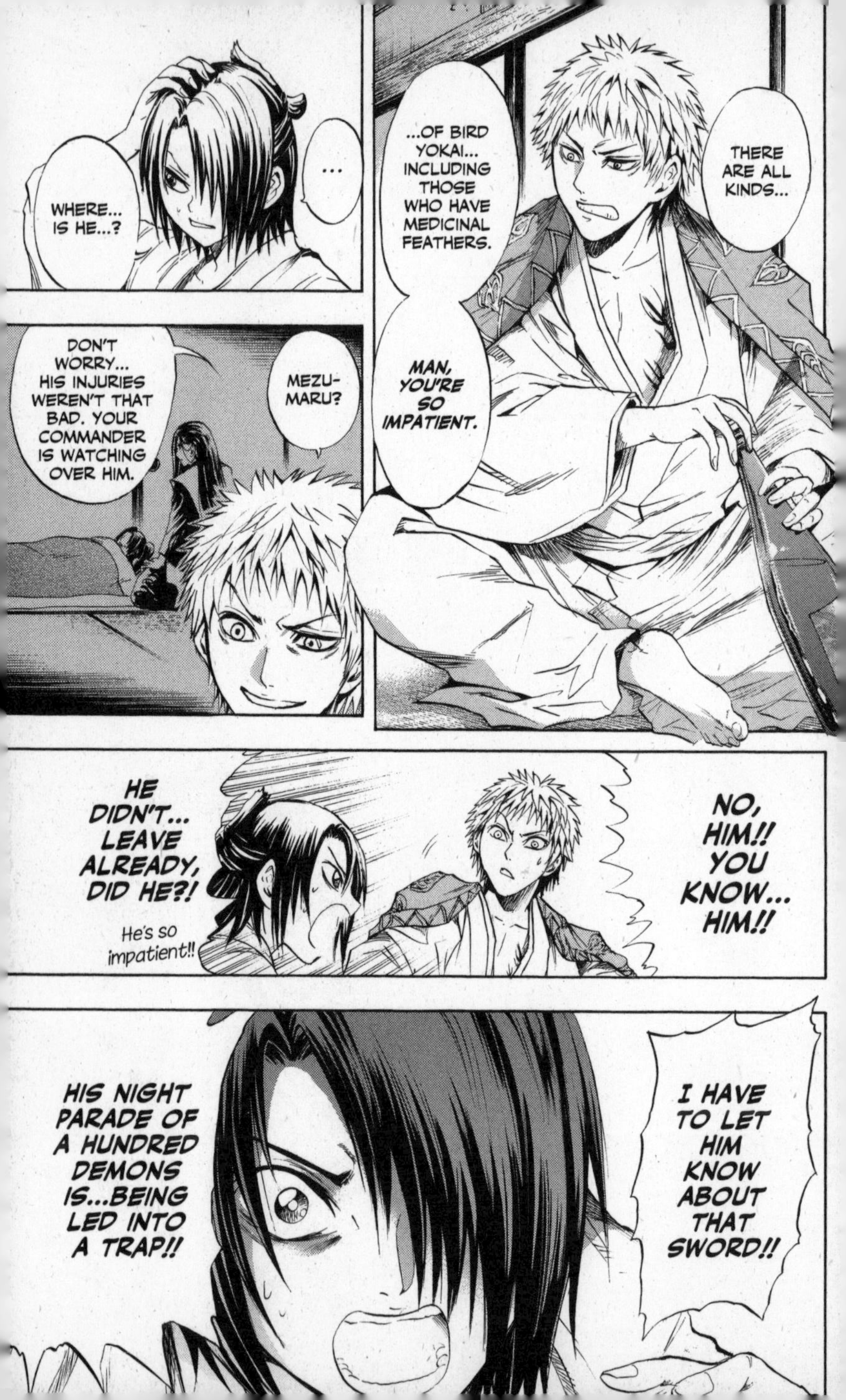
THERE ARE ALL KINDS...
...OF BIRD YOKAI... INCLUDING THOSE WHO HAVE MEDICINAL FEATHERS.
MAN, YOU'RE SO IMPATIENT.
...
WHERE... IS HE...?
MEZU-MARU?
DON'T WORRY... HIS INJURIES WEREN'T THAT BAD. YOUR COMMANDER IS WATCHING OVER HIM.
NO, HIM!! YOU KNOW... HIM!!
HE DIDN'T... LEAVE ALREADY, DID HE?!
He's so impatient!!
I HAVE TO LET HIM KNOW ABOUT THAT SWORD!!
HIS NIGHT PARADE OF A HUNDRED DEMONS IS...BEING LED INTO A TRAP!!

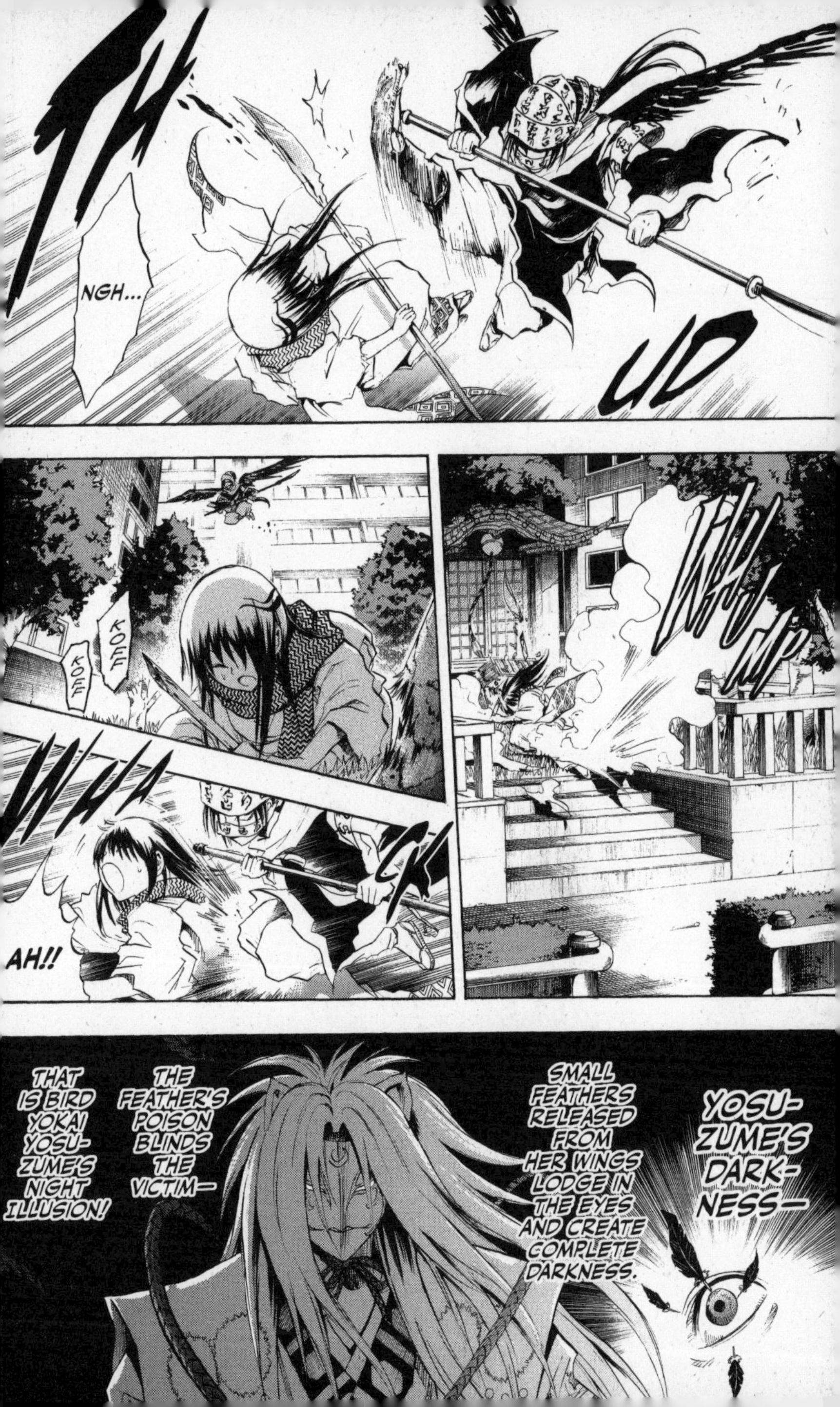
NGH...
KOFF
KOFF
AH!!
YOSU-ZUME'S DARK-NESS—
SMALL FEATHERS RELEASED FROM HER WINGS LODGE IN THE EYES AND CREATE COMPLETE DARKNESS.
THE FEATHER'S POISON BLINDS THE VICTIM—
THAT IS BIRD YOKAI YOSU-ZUME'S NIGHT ILLUSION!

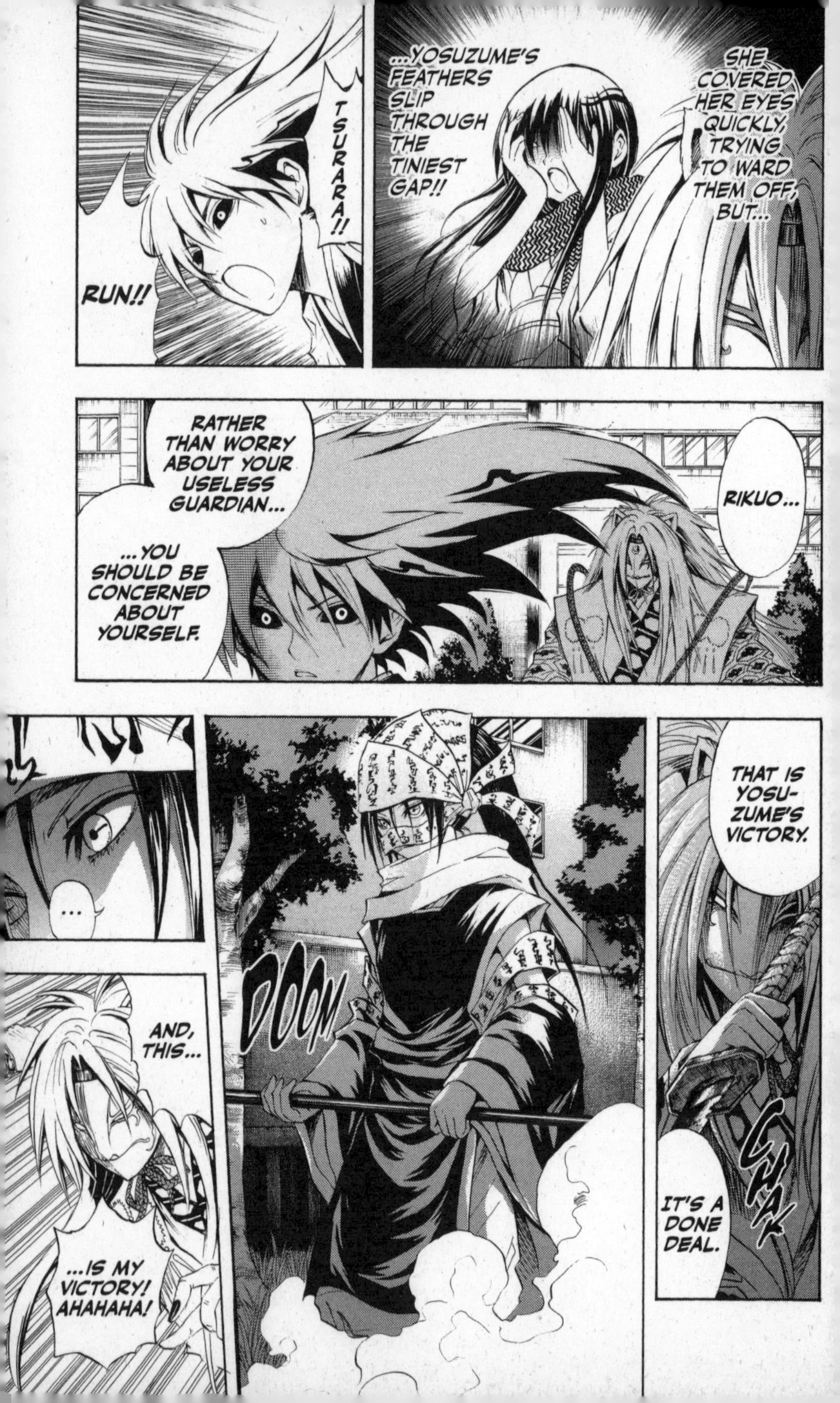
SHE COVERED HER EYES QUICKLY, TRYING TO WARD THEM OFF, BUT...
...YOSUZUME'S FEATHERS SLIP THROUGH THE TINIEST GAP!!
TSURARA!!
RUN!!
RIKUO...
RATHER THAN WORRY ABOUT YOUR USELESS GUARDIAN...
...YOU SHOULD BE CONCERNED ABOUT YOURSELF.
THAT IS YOSU-ZUME'S VICTORY.
CHAK
IT'S A DONE DEAL.
DOOM
...
AND, THIS...
...IS MY VICTORY! AHAHAHA!

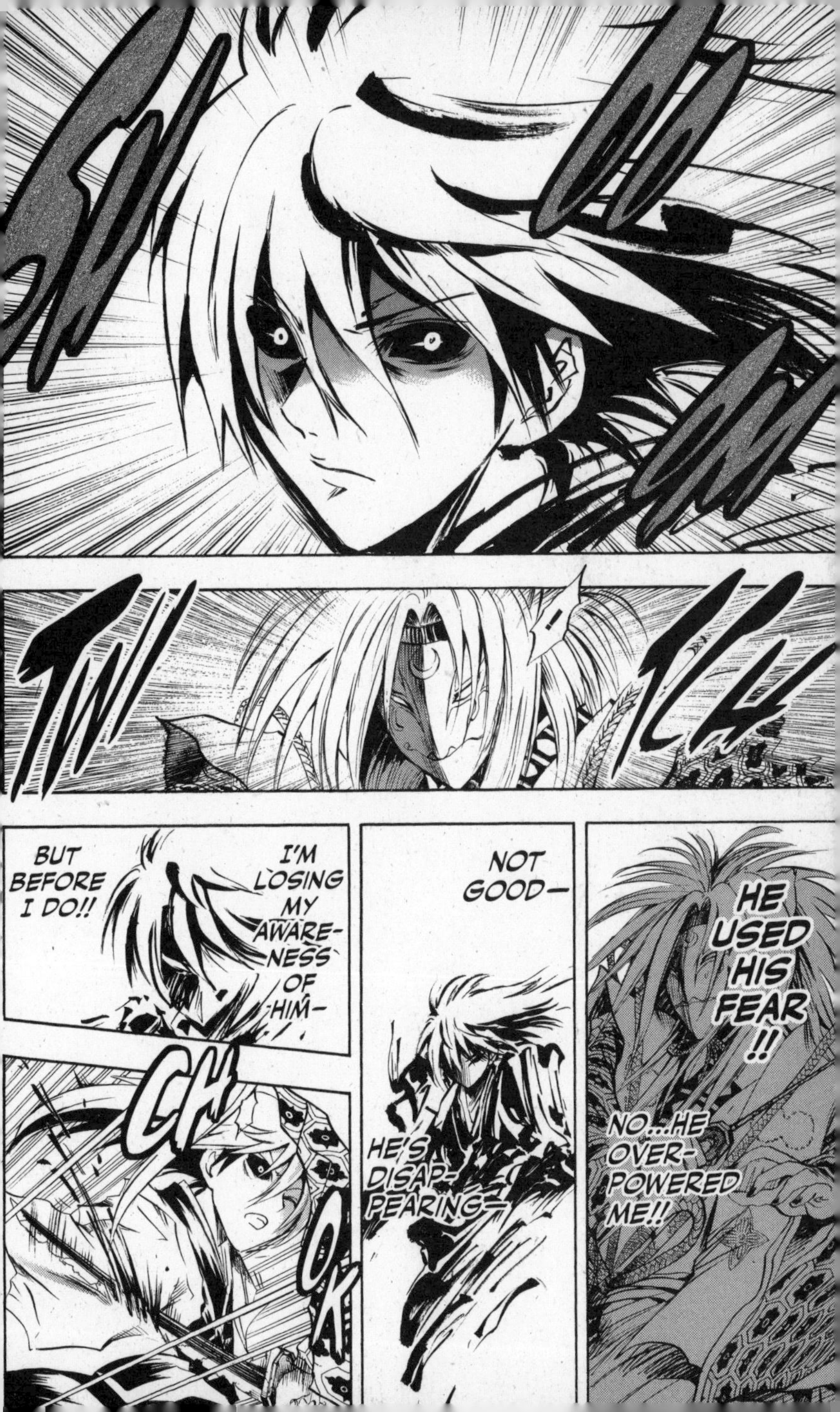
TWITCH
HE USED HIS FEAR!!
NO...HE OVER-POWERED ME!!
NOT GOOD—
HE'S DISAP-PEARING—
I'M LOSING MY AWARE-NESS OF HIM—
BUT BEFORE I DO!!

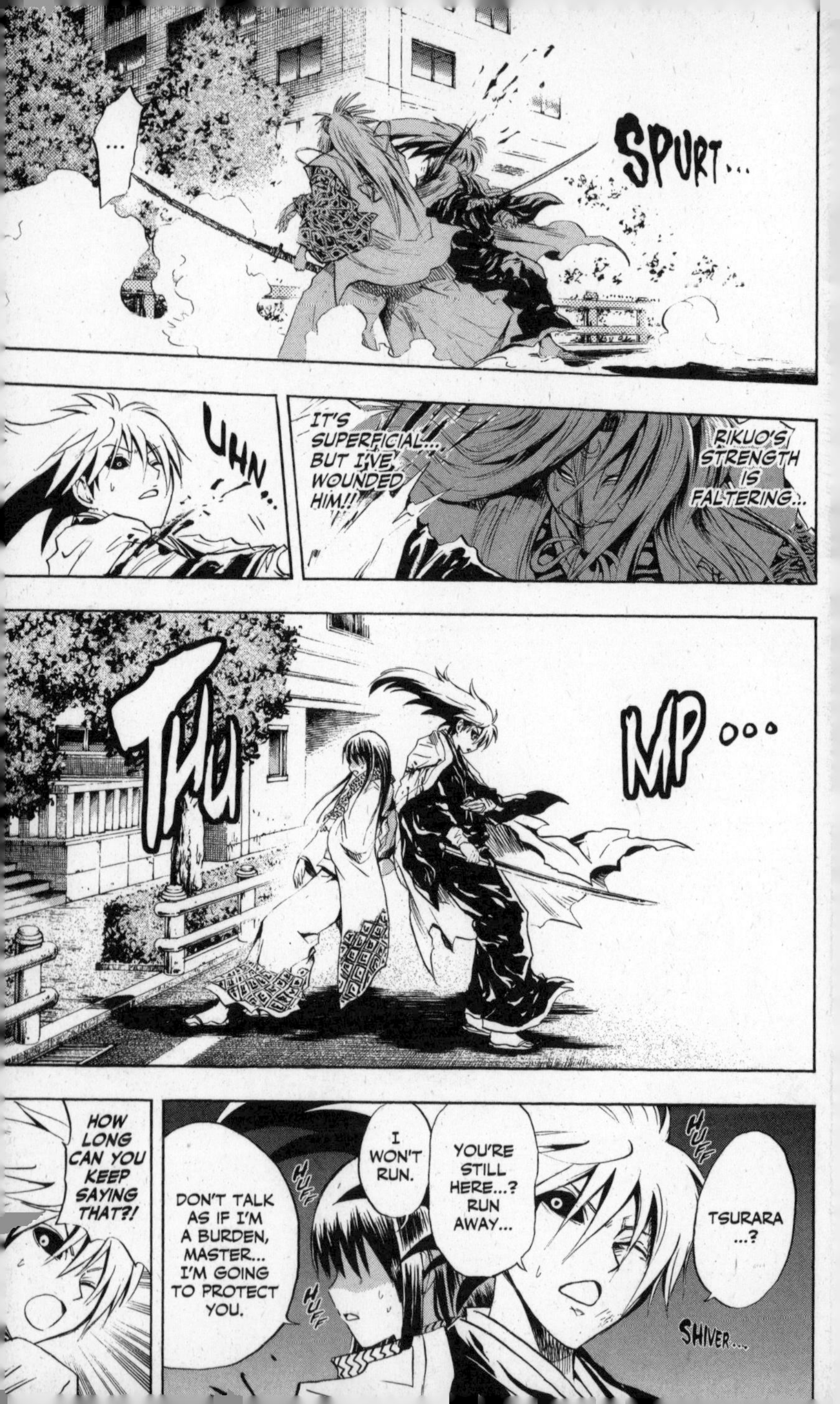
SPURT...
...
RIKUO'S STRENGTH IS FALTERING...
IT'S SUPERFICIAL... BUT I'VE WOUNDED HIM!!
UHN...
THU
MP...
HUFF
TSURARA ...?
SHIVER...
YOU'RE STILL HERE...? RUN AWAY...
I WON'T RUN.
HUFF
DON'T TALK AS IF I'M A BURDEN, MASTER... I'M GOING TO PROTECT YOU.
HUFF
HOW LONG CAN YOU KEEP SAYING THAT?!

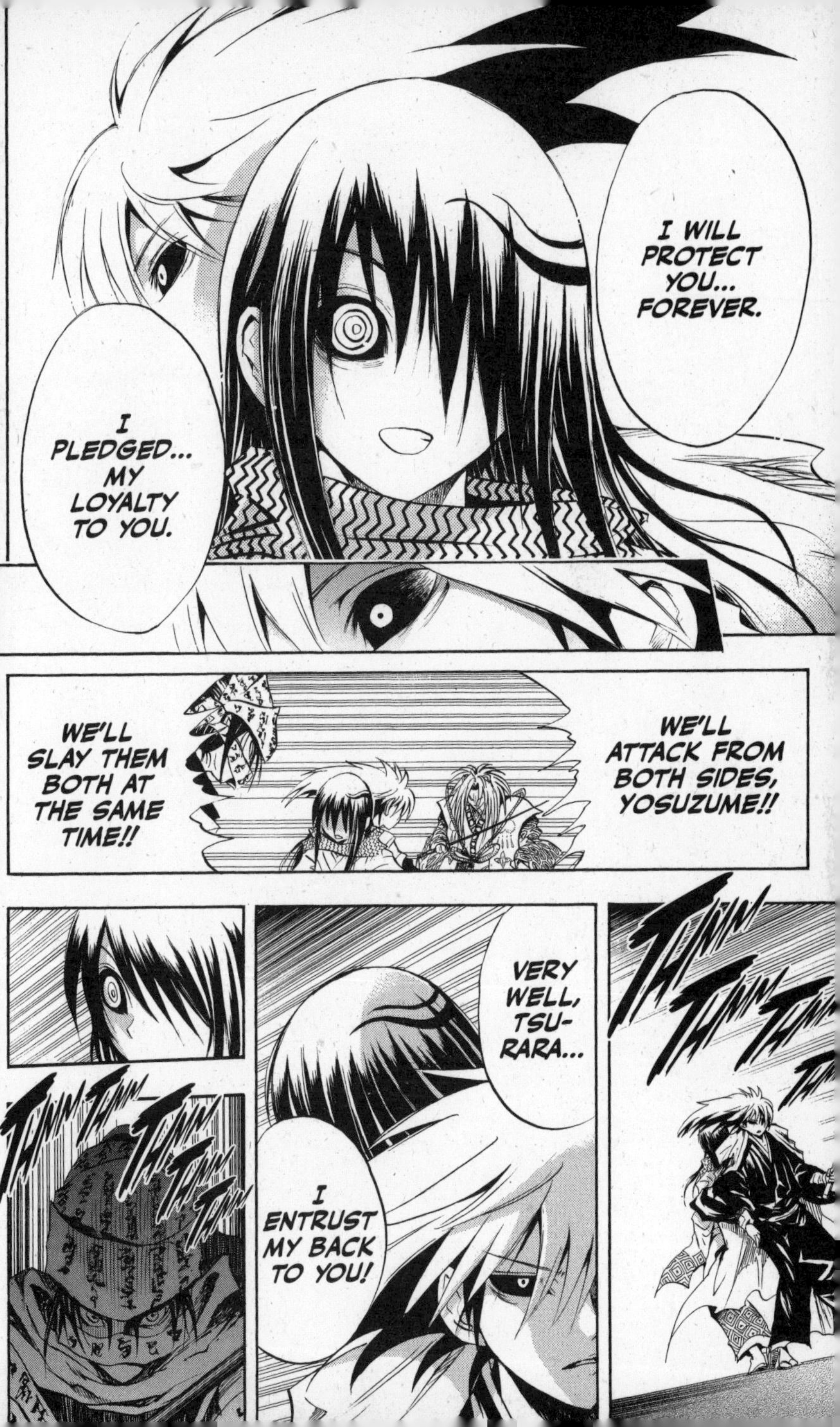
I WILL PROTECT YOU... FOREVER.
I PLEDGED... MY LOYALTY TO YOU.
WE'LL ATTACK FROM BOTH SIDES, YOSUZUME!!
WE'LL SLAY THEM BOTH AT THE SAME TIME!!
VERY WELL, TSURARA...
I ENTRUST MY BACK TO YOU!

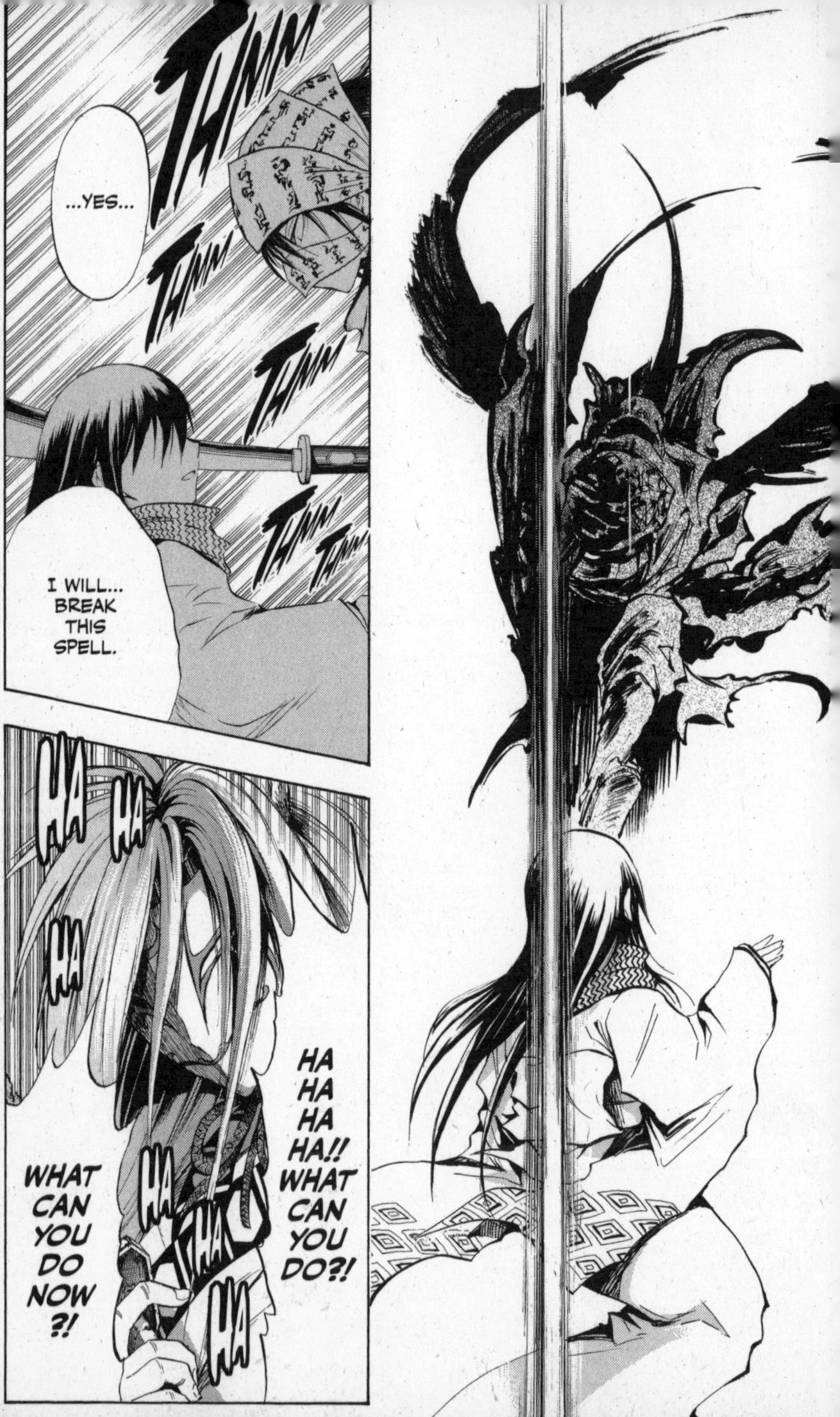
...YES...
I WILL... BREAK THIS SPELL.
HA HA HA HA!! WHAT CAN YOU DO?!
WHAT CAN YOU DO NOW?!

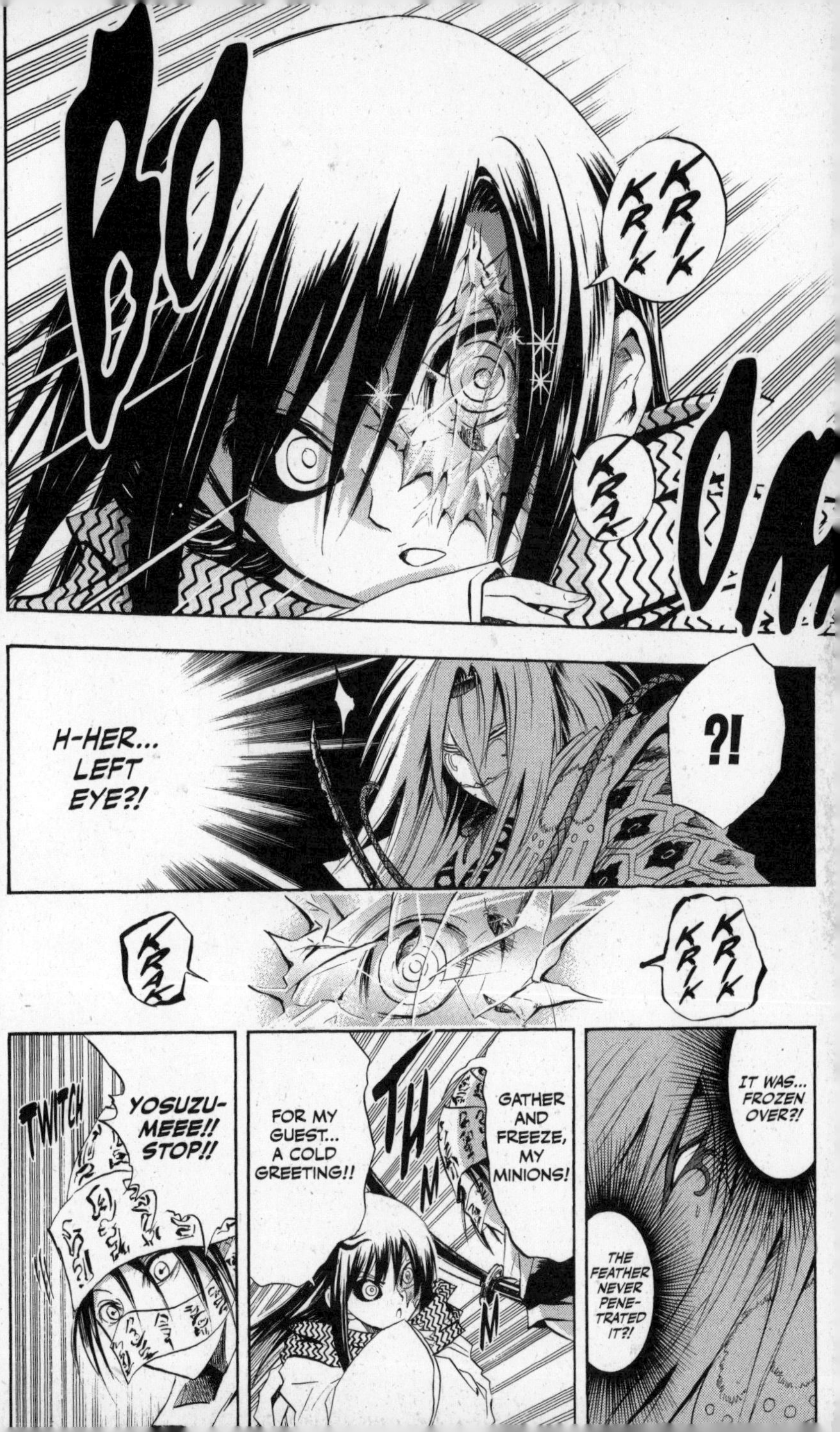
KRIK KRIK
KRAK
?!
H-HER... LEFT EYE?!
KRIK KRIK
KRAK
IT WAS... FROZEN OVER?!
THE FEATHER NEVER PENE-TRATED IT?!
GATHER AND FREEZE, MY MINIONS!
FOR MY GUEST... A COLD GREETING!!
YOSUZU-MEEE!! STOP!!
TWITCH

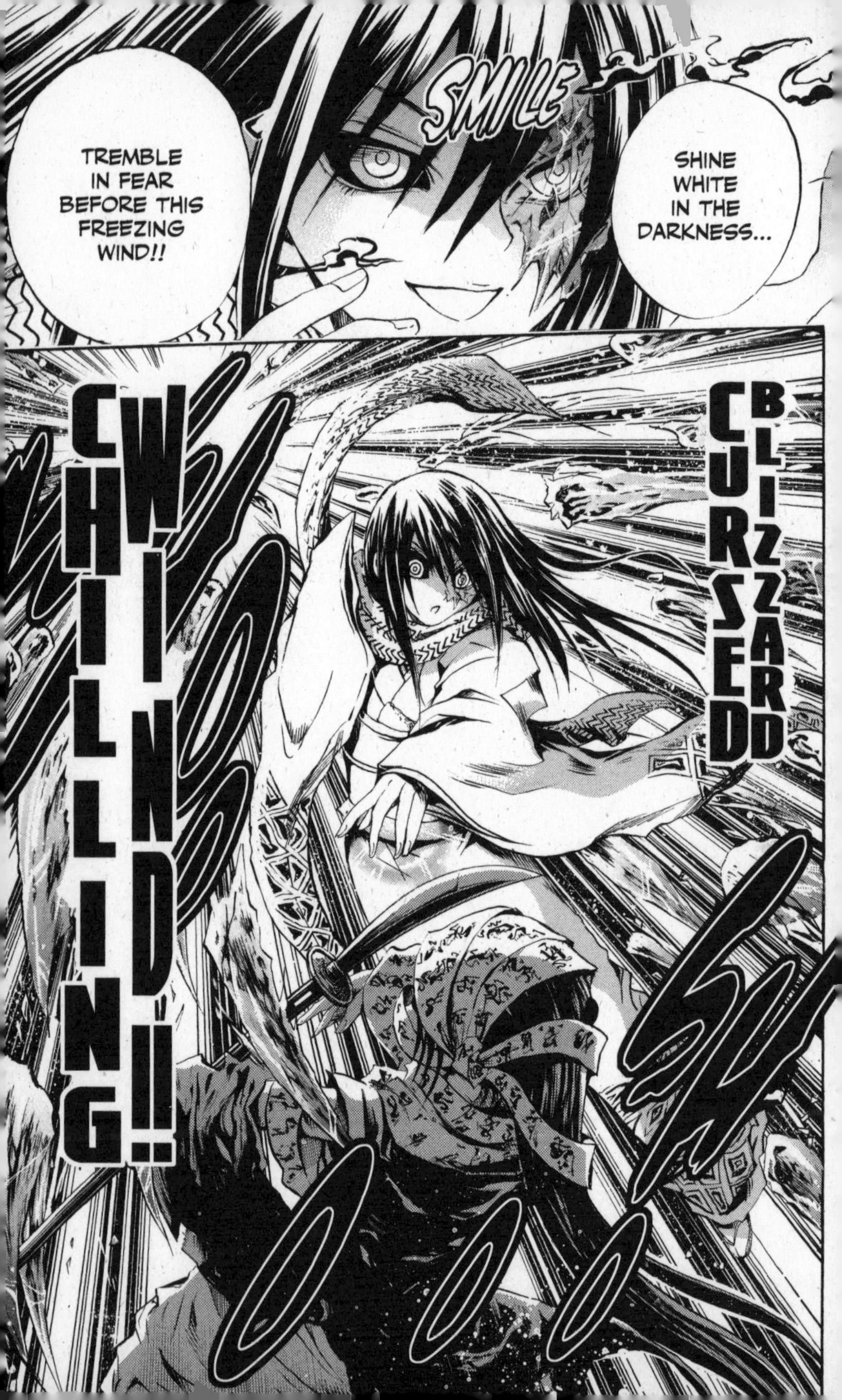
SMILE
SHINE WHITE IN THE DARKNESS...
TREMBLE IN FEAR BEFORE THIS FREEZING WIND!!
CURSED BLIZZARD
CHILLING WIND!!

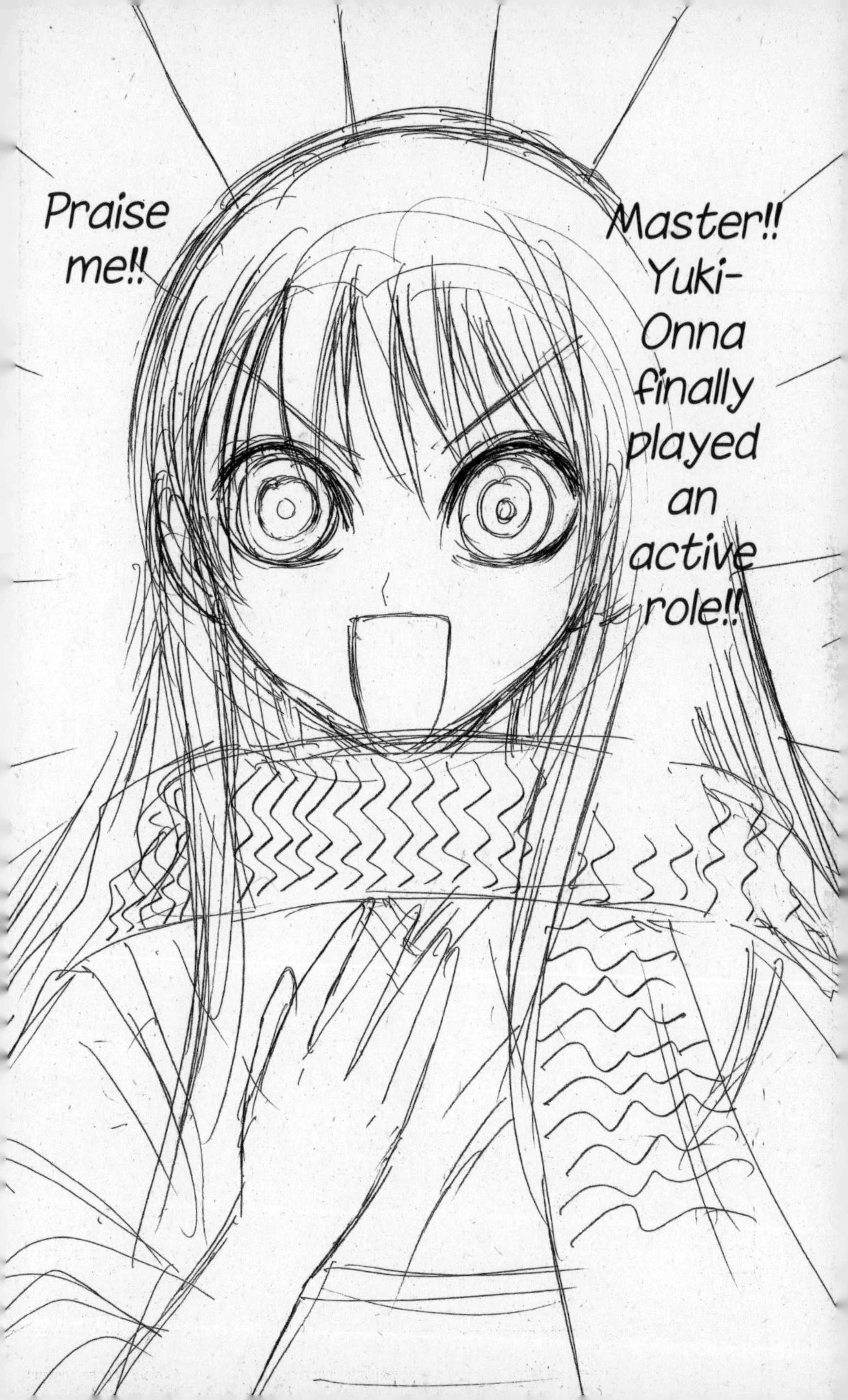
Master!! Yuki-Onna finally played an active role!!
Praise me!!

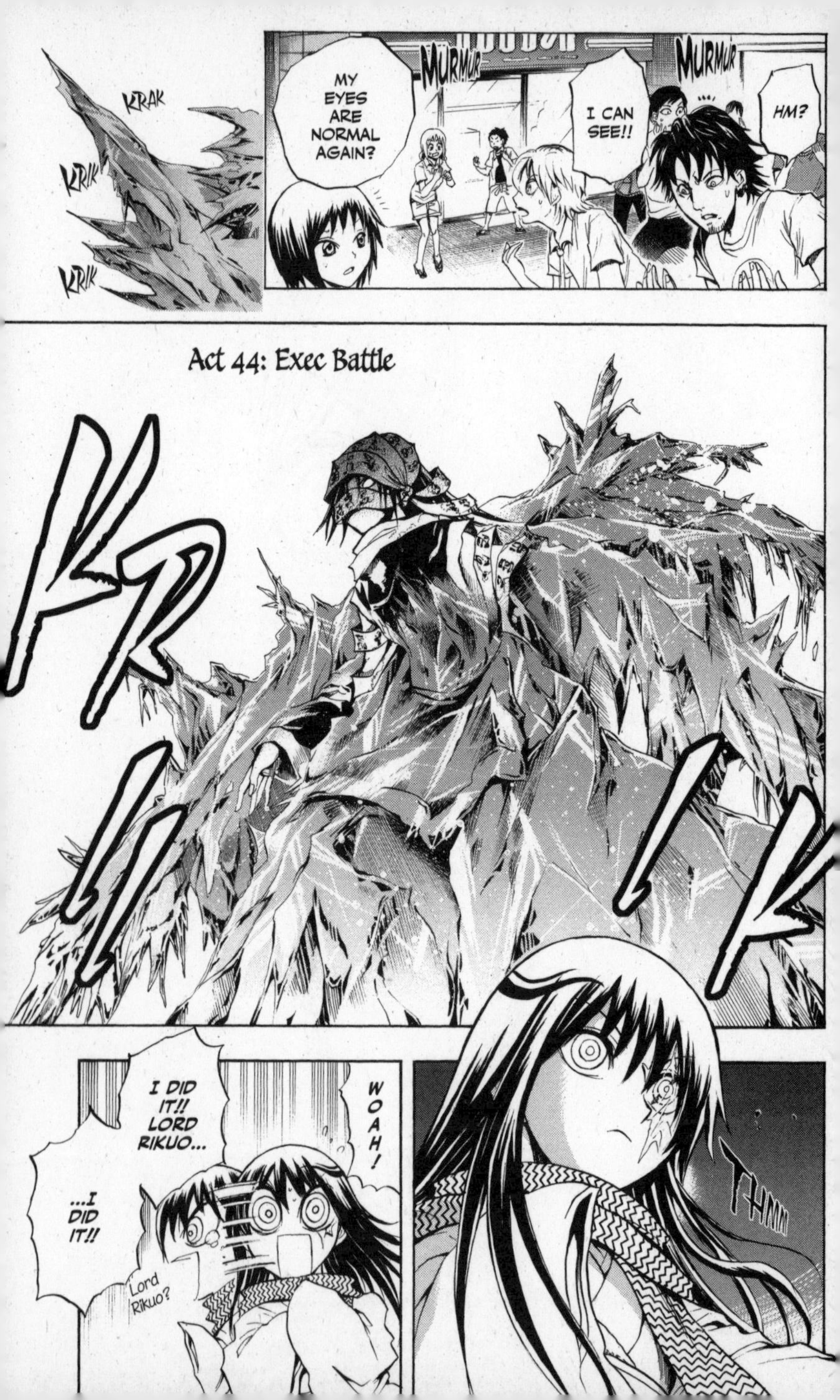
HM?
MURMUR
I CAN SEE!!
MURMUR
MY EYES ARE NORMAL AGAIN?
KRAK
KRIK
KRIK
Act 44: Exec Battle
THNN
WOAH!
I DID IT!! LORD RIKUO...
...I DID IT!!
Lord Rikuo?

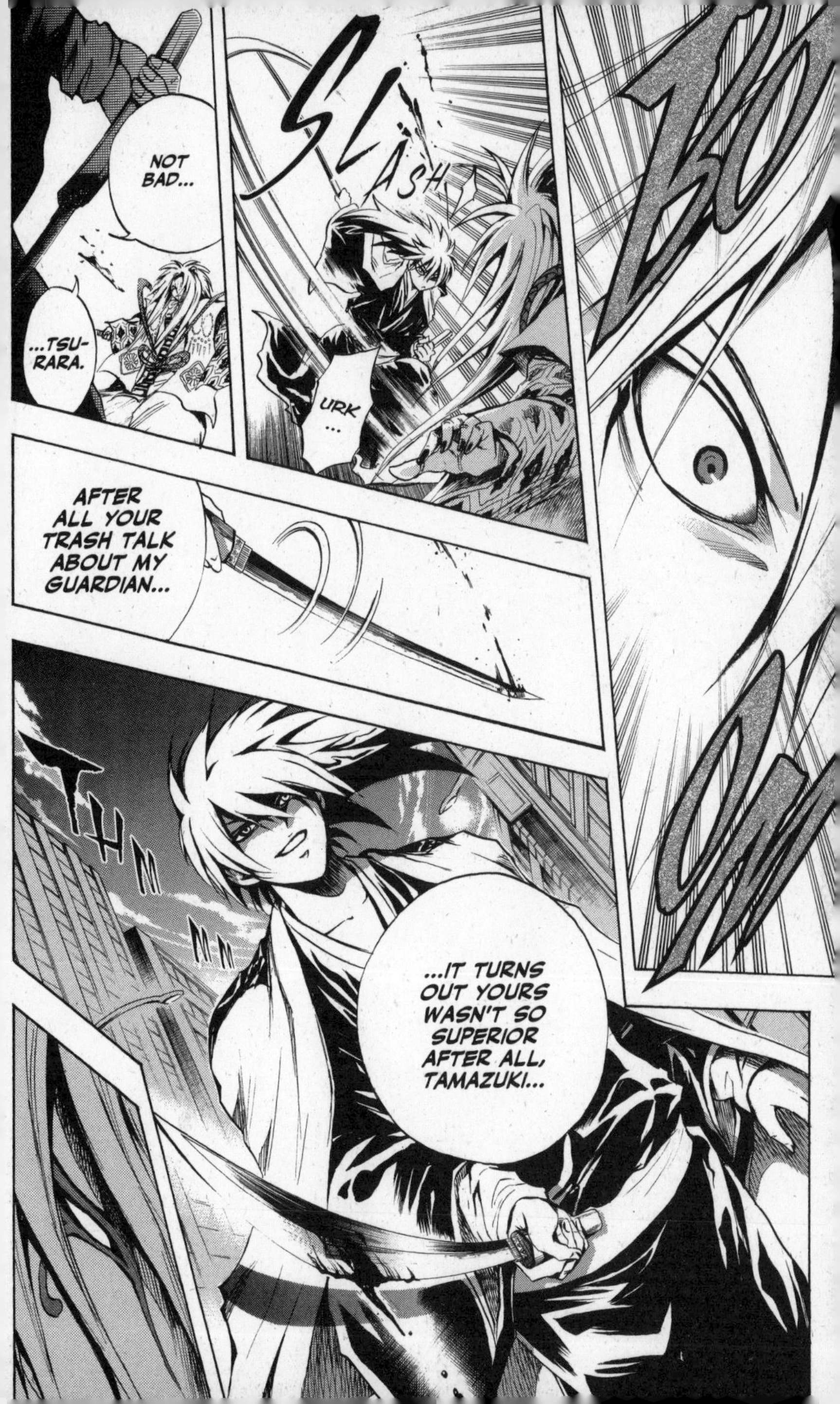
SLASH
URK ...
NOT BAD...
...TSU-RARA.
AFTER ALL YOUR TRASH TALK ABOUT MY GUARDIAN...
...IT TURNS OUT YOURS WASN'T SO SUPERIOR AFTER ALL, TAMAZUKI...

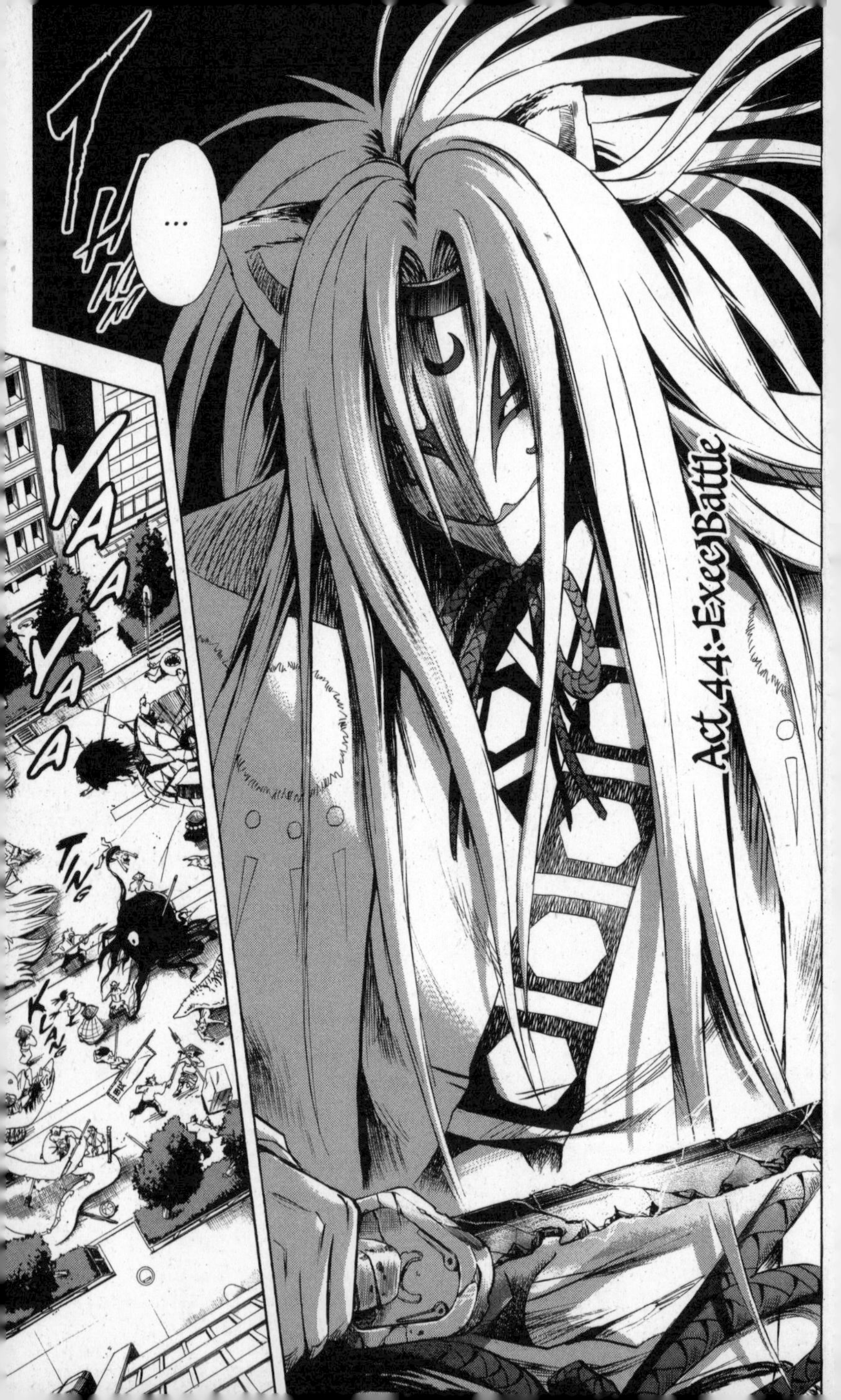
Act 44: Exec Battle
...
YAAA YAAA
TING
KLANG

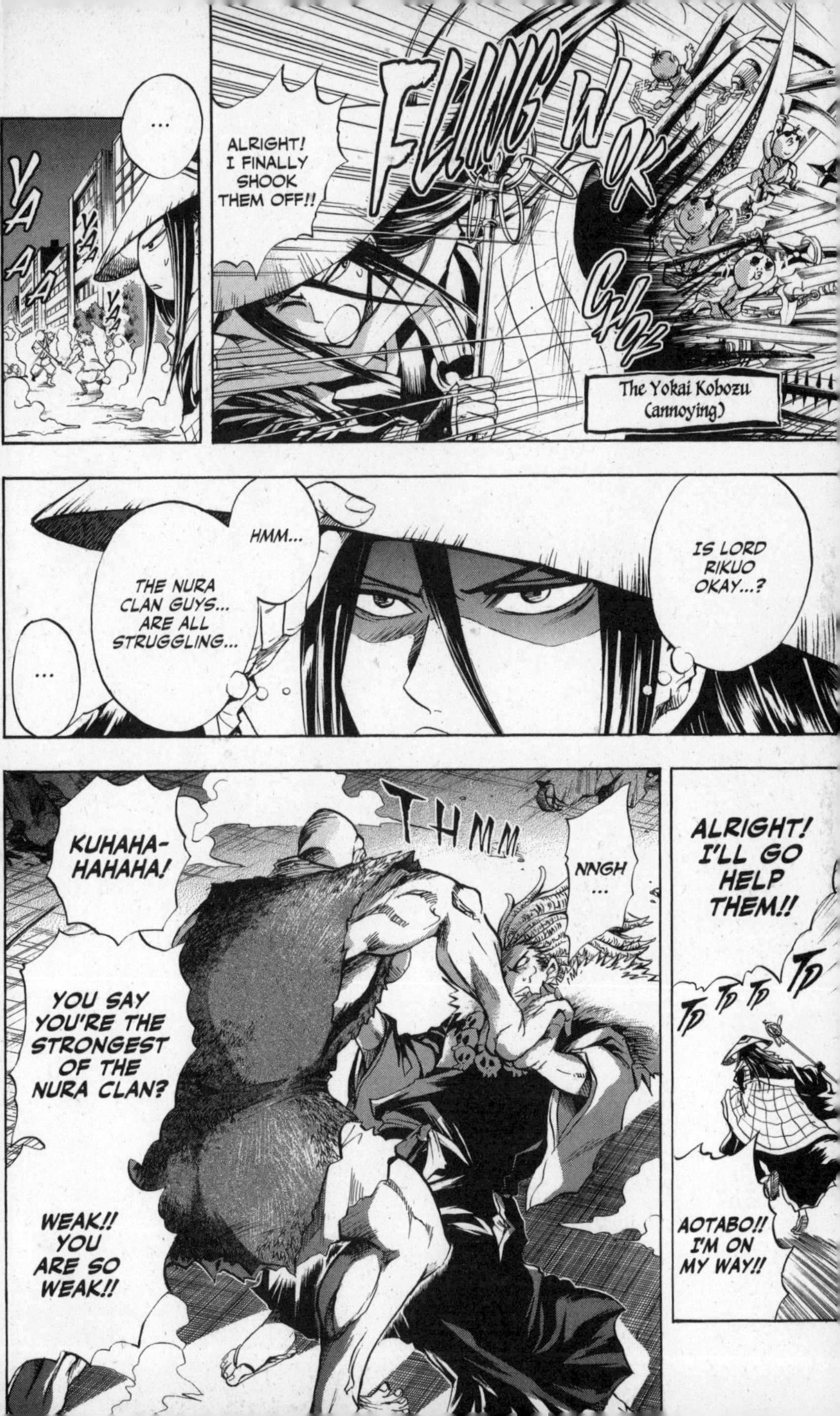
ALRIGHT! I FINALLY SHOOK THEM OFF!!
FLING
The Yokai Kobozu (annoying)
...
YAAA
YAA
YAA
IS LORD RIKUO OKAY...?
HMM...
THE NURA CLAN GUYS... ARE ALL STRUGGLING...
...
ALRIGHT! I'LL GO HELP THEM!!
Tp Tp Tp Tp
AOTABO!! I'M ON MY WAY!!
THMM
NNGH ...
KUHAHA-HAHAHA!
YOU SAY YOU'RE THE STRONGEST OF THE NURA CLAN?
WEAK!! YOU ARE SO WEAK!!

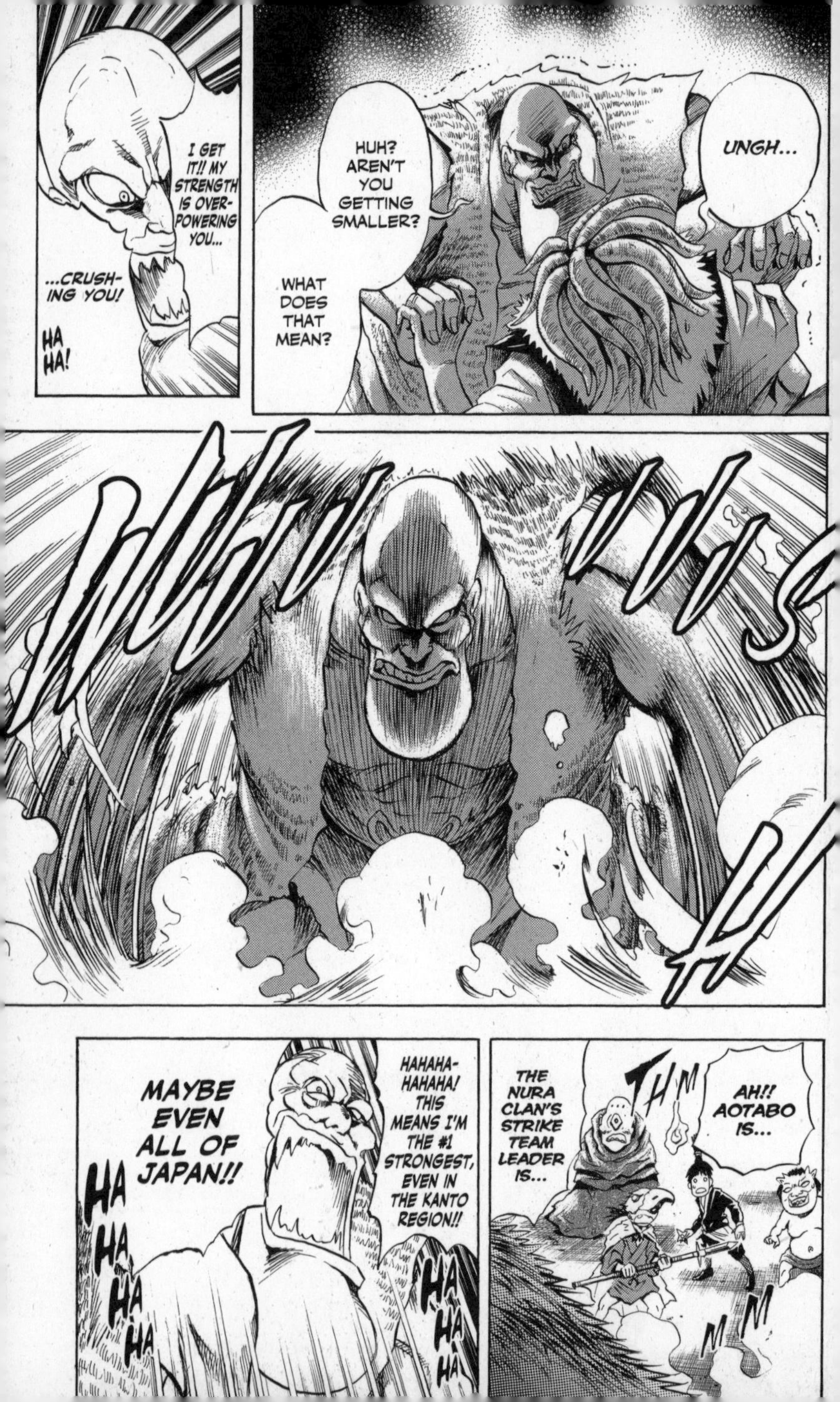
UNGH...
HUH? AREN'T YOU GETTING SMALLER?
WHAT DOES THAT MEAN?
I GET IT!! MY STRENGTH IS OVER-POWERING YOU...
...CRUSH-ING YOU!
HA HA!
AH!! AOTABO IS...
THE NURA CLAN'S STRIKE TEAM LEADER IS...
HAHAHA-HAHAHA! THIS MEANS I'M THE #1 STRONGEST, EVEN IN THE KANTO REGION!!
MAYBE EVEN ALL OF JAPAN!!

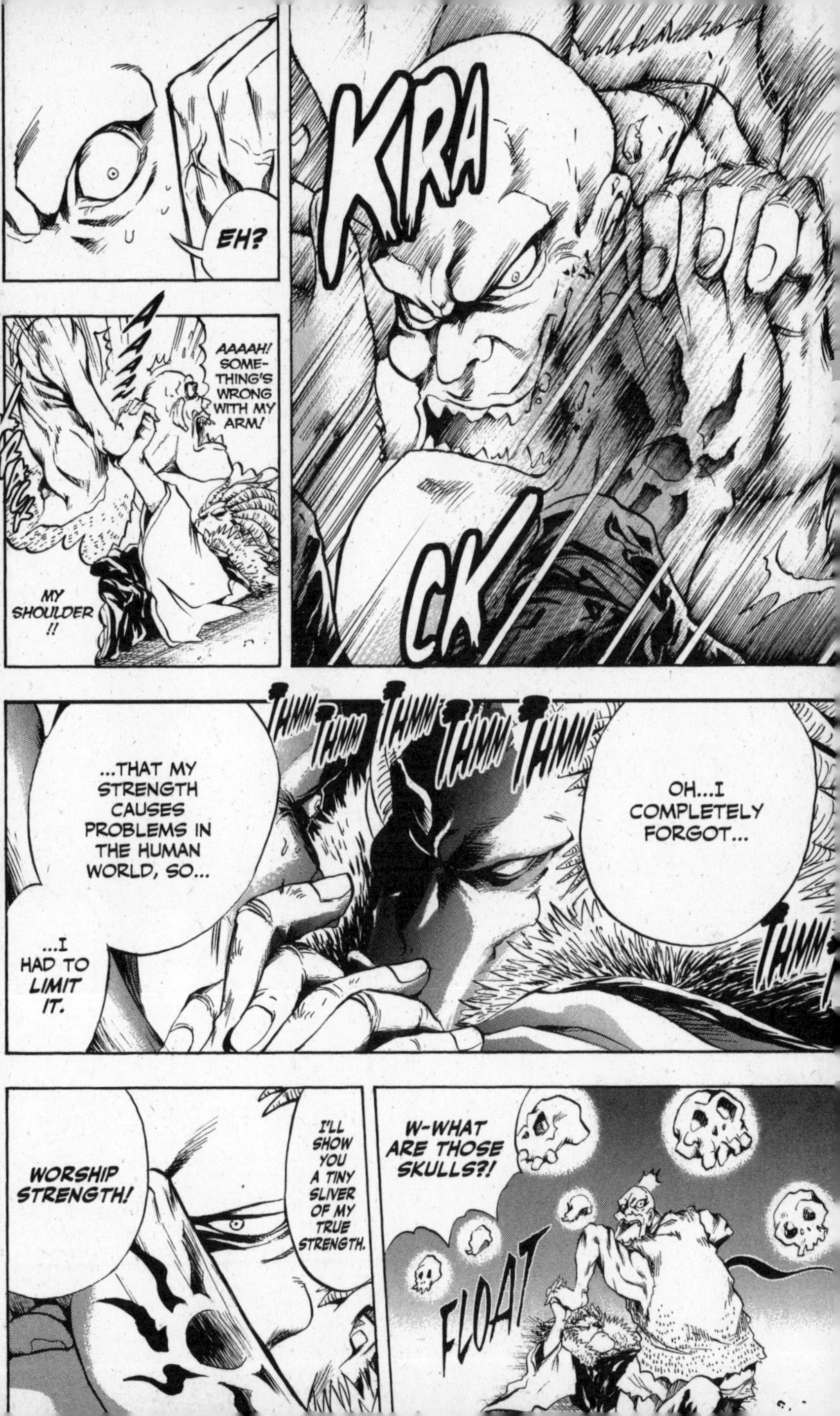
KRA
CK
EH?
AAAAAH
AAAAH! SOME-THING'S WRONG WITH MY ARM!
MY SHOULDER!!
OH...I COMPLETELY FORGOT...
THMM THMM THMM THMM THMM THMM
...THAT MY STRENGTH CAUSES PROBLEMS IN THE HUMAN WORLD, SO...
...I HAD TO LIMIT IT.
W-WHAT ARE THOSE SKULLS?!
FLOAT
I'LL SHOW YOU A TINY SLIVER OF MY TRUE STRENGTH.
WORSHIP STRENGTH!

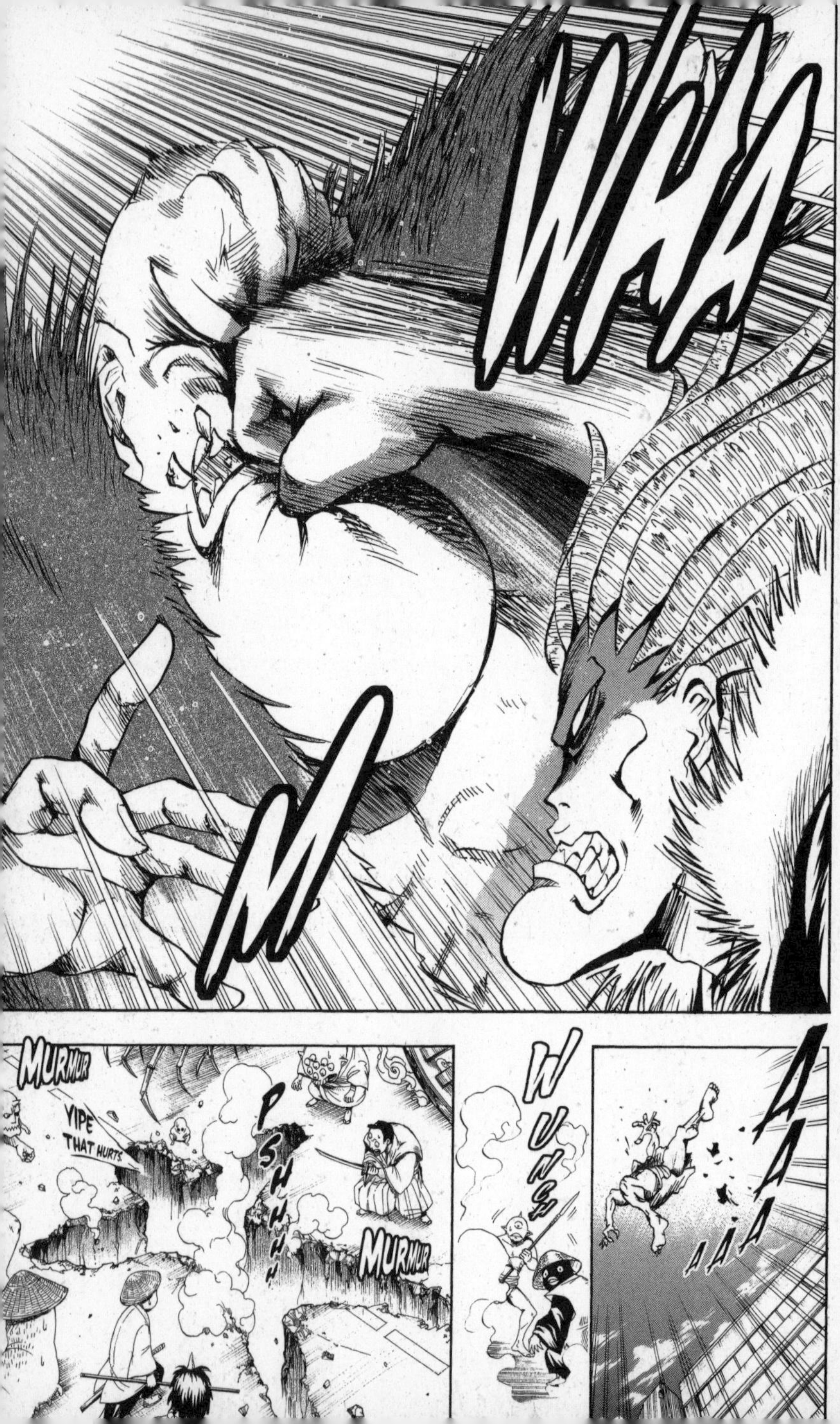
WHAM
AAAAAAA
WUNCH
PSHHHH
MURMUR
MURMUR
YIPE THAT HURTS.

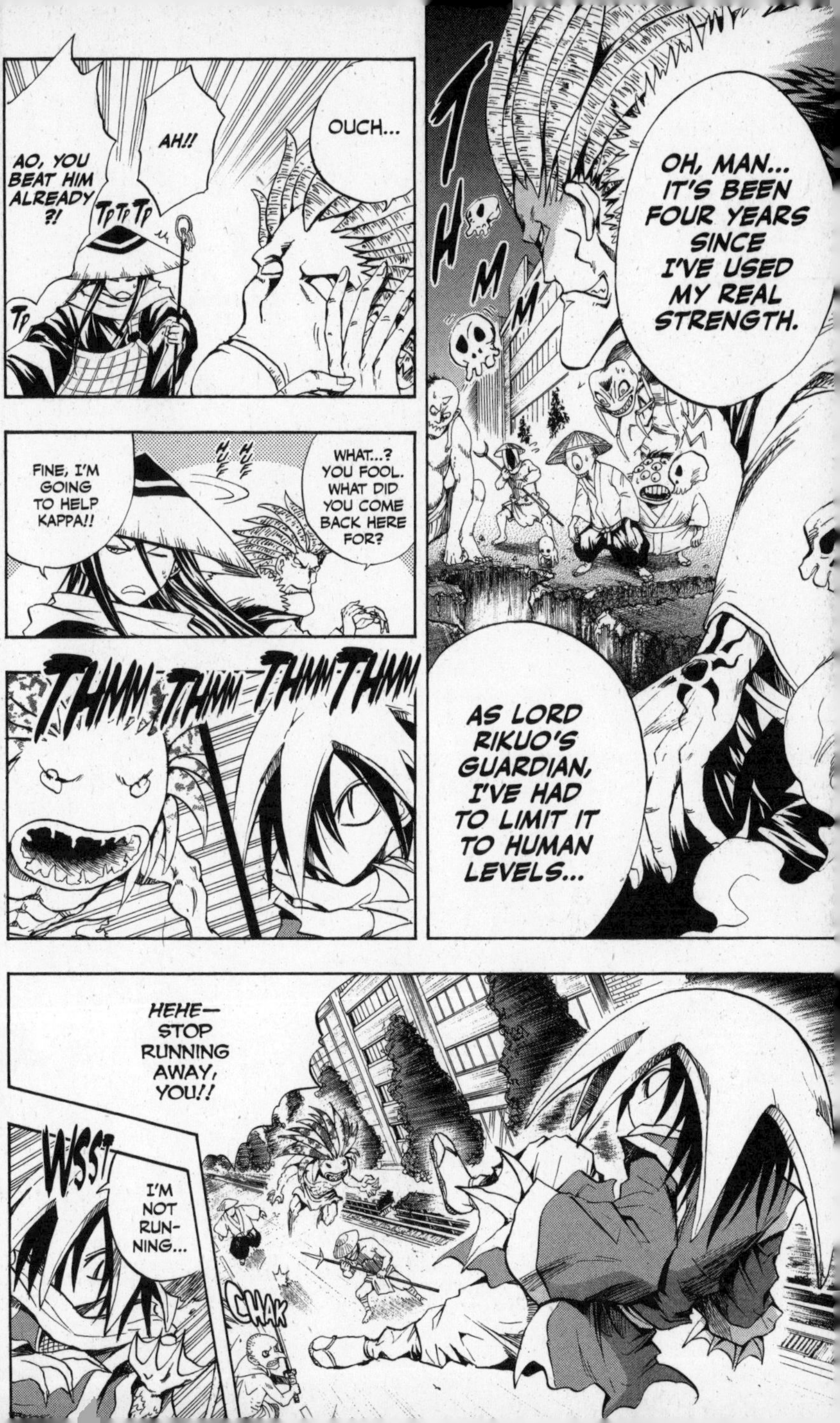
THMM
OH, MAN... IT'S BEEN FOUR YEARS SINCE I'VE USED MY REAL STRENGTH.
AS LORD RIKUO'S GUARDIAN, I'VE HAD TO LIMIT IT TO HUMAN LEVELS...
OUCH...
AH!!
AO, YOU BEAT HIM ALREADY?!
TpTpTp
Tp
HUF HUF
WHAT...? YOU FOOL. WHAT DID YOU COME BACK HERE FOR?
FINE, I'M GOING TO HELP KAPPA!!
THMM THMM THMM THMM
HEHE— STOP RUNNING AWAY, YOU!!
CHAK
WSST
I'M NOT RUN-NING...

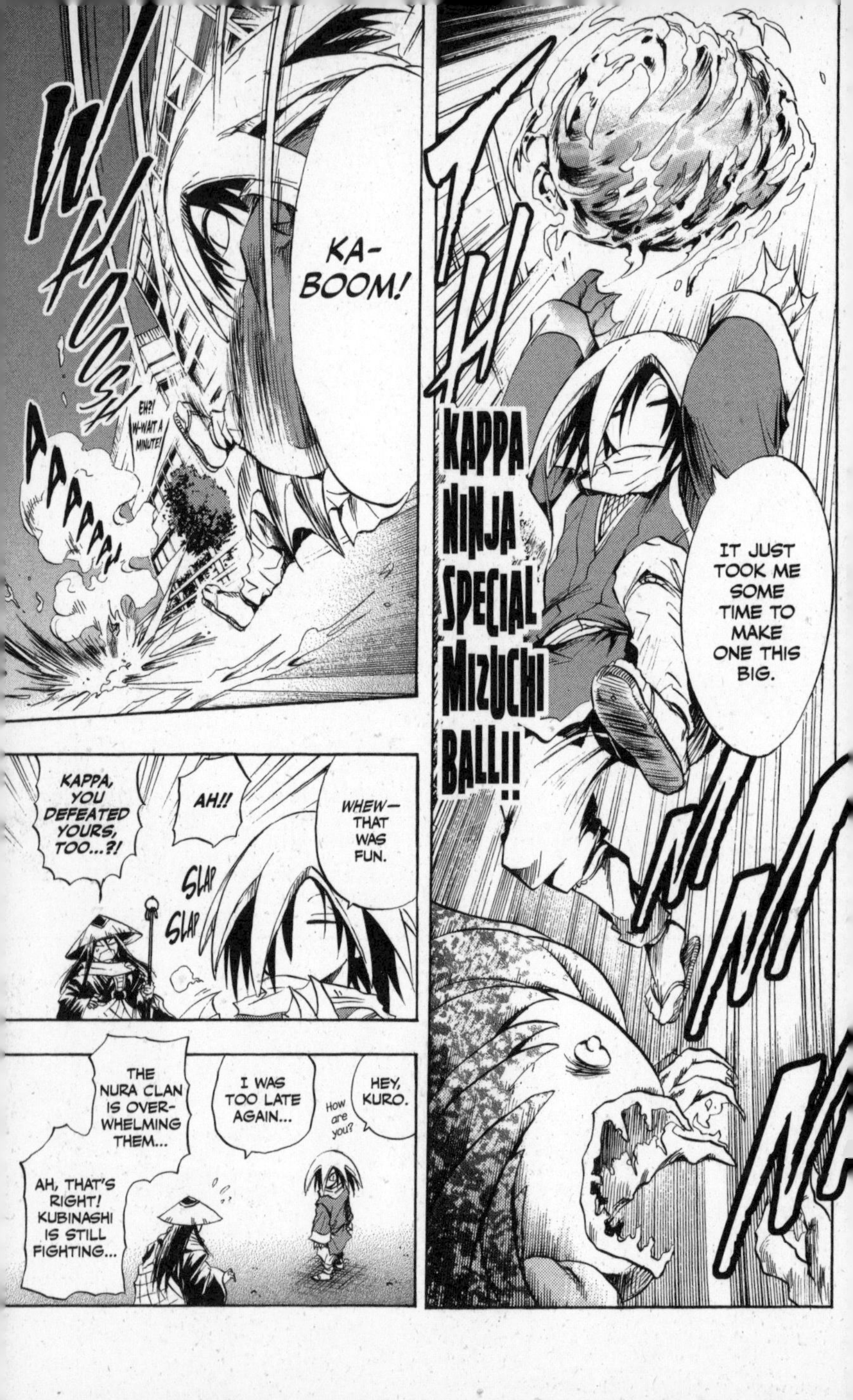
KAPPA NINJA SPECIAL MIZUCHI BALL!!
IT JUST TOOK ME SOME TIME TO MAKE ONE THIS BIG.
KA-BOOM!
EH?! W-WAIT A MINUTE!
WHEW—THAT WAS FUN.
AH!!
KAPPA, YOU DEFEATED YOURS, TOO...?!
SLAP SLAP
HEY, KURO.
How are you?
I WAS TOO LATE AGAIN...
THE NURA CLAN IS OVER-WHELMING THEM...
AH, THAT'S RIGHT! KUBINASHI IS STILL FIGHTING...

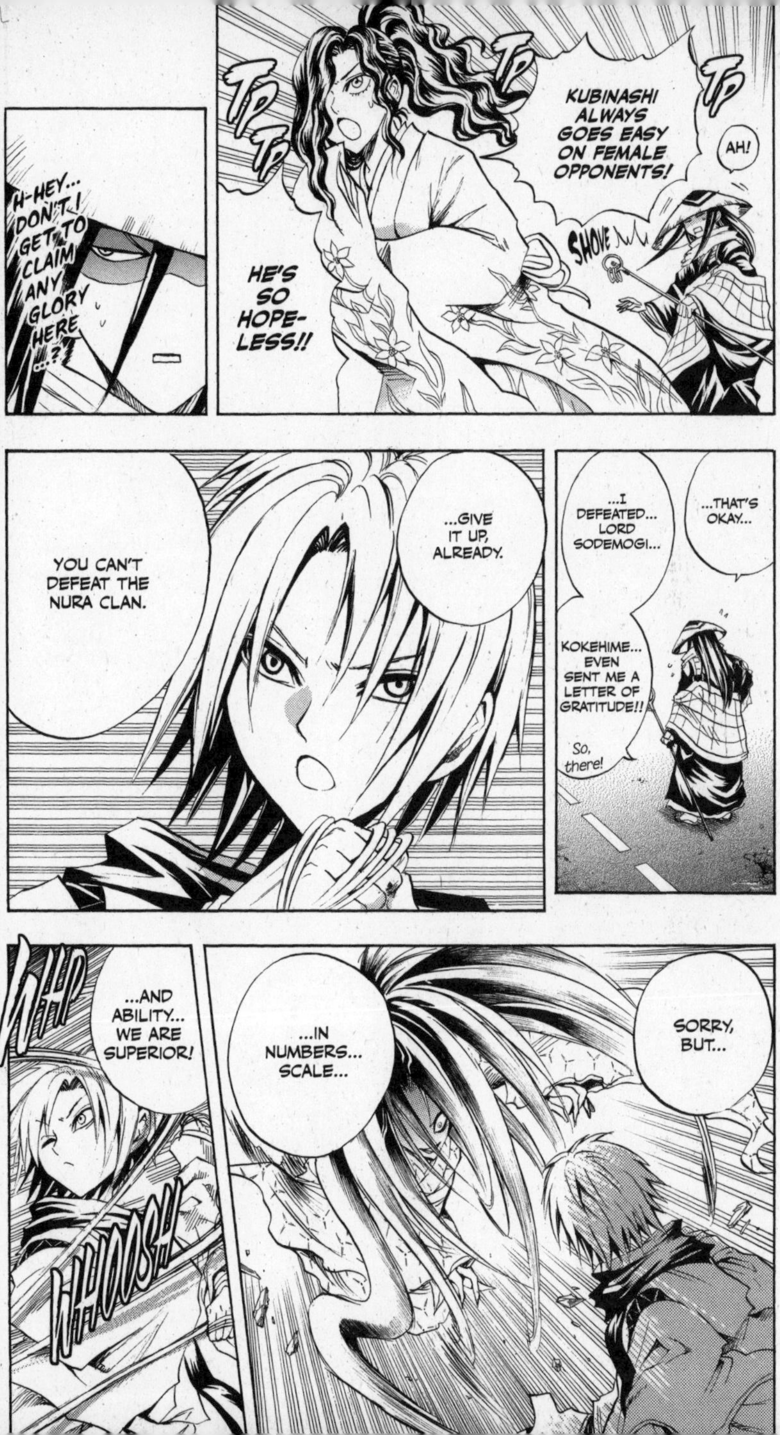
Tp Tp Tp Tp
KUBINASHI ALWAYS GOES EASY ON FEMALE OPPONENTS!
AH!
SHOVE
HE'S SO HOPE-LESS!!
H-HEY... DON'T I GET TO CLAIM ANY GLORY HERE ...?
...THAT'S OKAY...
...I DEFEATED... LORD SODEMOGI...
KOKEHIME... EVEN SENT ME A LETTER OF GRATITUDE!!
So, there!
...GIVE IT UP, ALREADY.
YOU CAN'T DEFEAT THE NURA CLAN.
SORRY, BUT...
...IN NUMBERS... SCALE...
...AND ABILITY... WE ARE SUPERIOR!
WHP
WHOOSH!

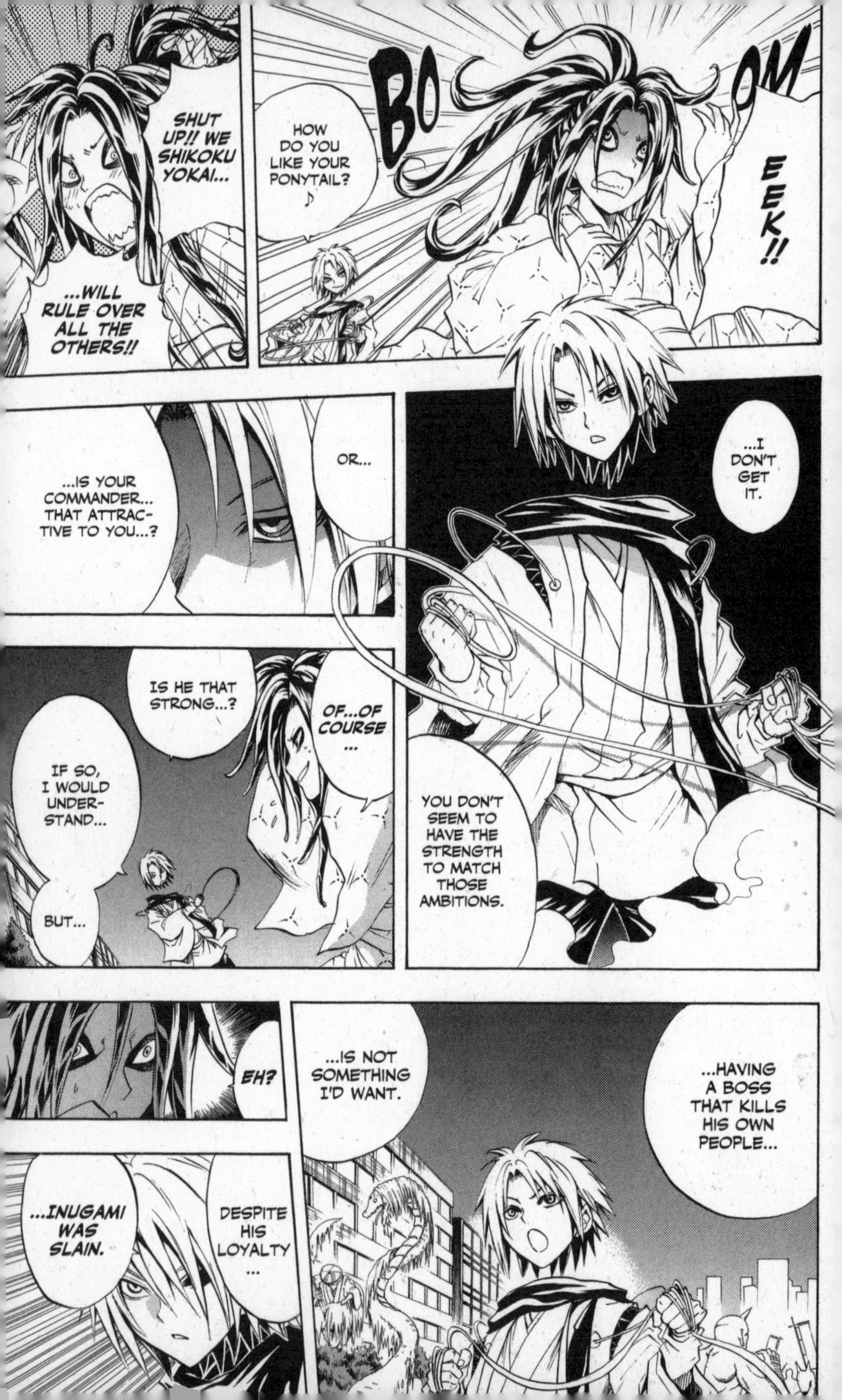
BO
OM
EEK!!
HOW DO YOU LIKE YOUR PONYTAIL? ♪
SHUT UP!! WE SHIKOKU YOKAI...
...WILL RULE OVER ALL THE OTHERS!!
...I DON'T GET IT.
YOU DON'T SEEM TO HAVE THE STRENGTH TO MATCH THOSE AMBITIONS.
OR...
...IS YOUR COMMANDER... THAT ATTRAC-TIVE TO YOU...?
OF...OF COURSE...
IS HE THAT STRONG...?
IF SO, I WOULD UNDER-STAND...
BUT...
...HAVING A BOSS THAT KILLS HIS OWN PEOPLE...
...IS NOT SOMETHING I'D WANT.
EH?
DESPITE HIS LOYALTY...
...INUGAMI WAS SLAIN.

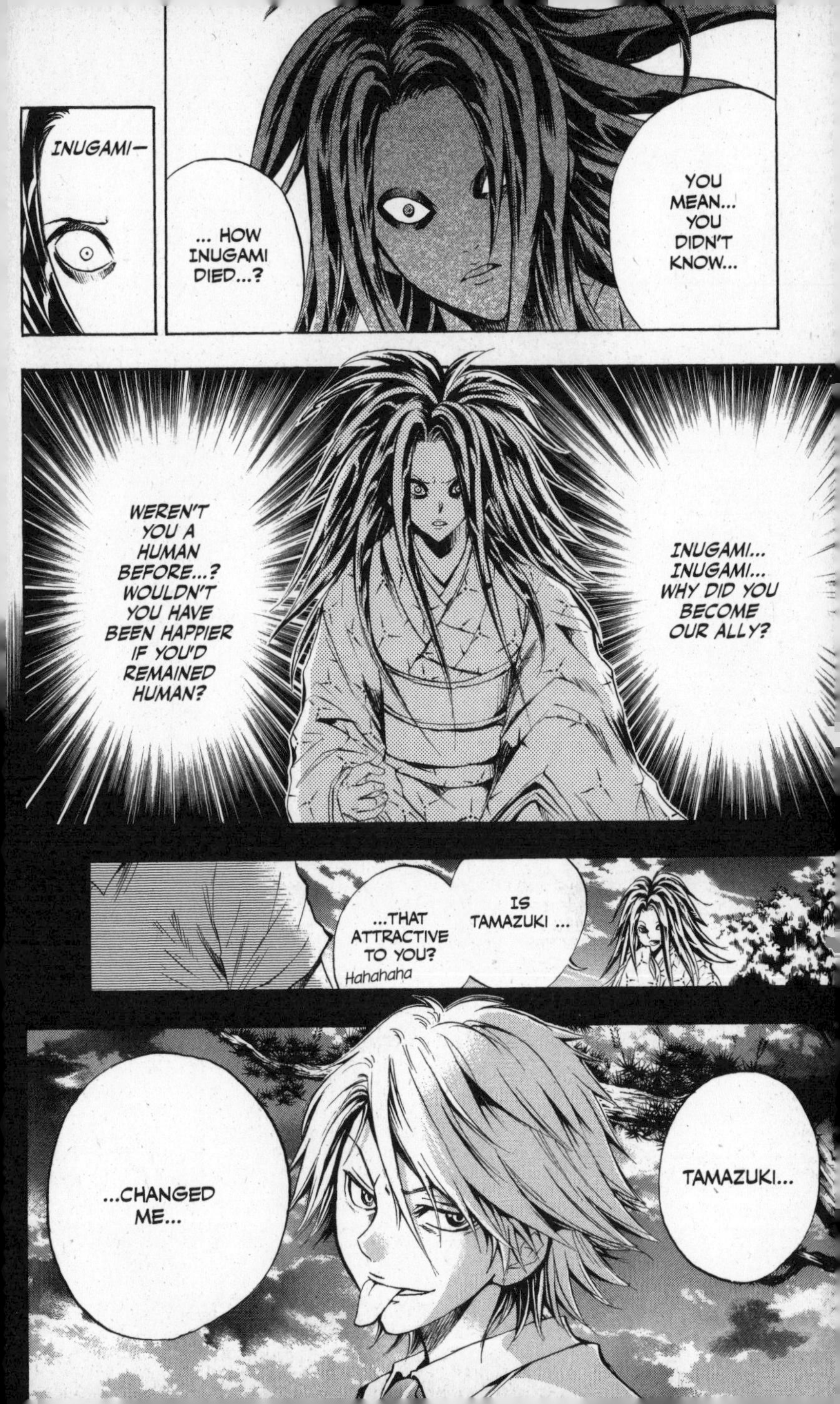
YOU MEAN... YOU DIDN'T KNOW...
... HOW INUGAMI DIED...?
INUGAMI—
INUGAMI... INUGAMI... WHY DID YOU BECOME OUR ALLY?
WEREN'T YOU A HUMAN BEFORE...? WOULDN'T YOU HAVE BEEN HAPPIER IF YOU'D REMAINED HUMAN?
IS TAMAZUKI ...
...THAT ATTRACTIVE TO YOU?
Hahahaha
TAMAZUKI...
...CHANGED ME...

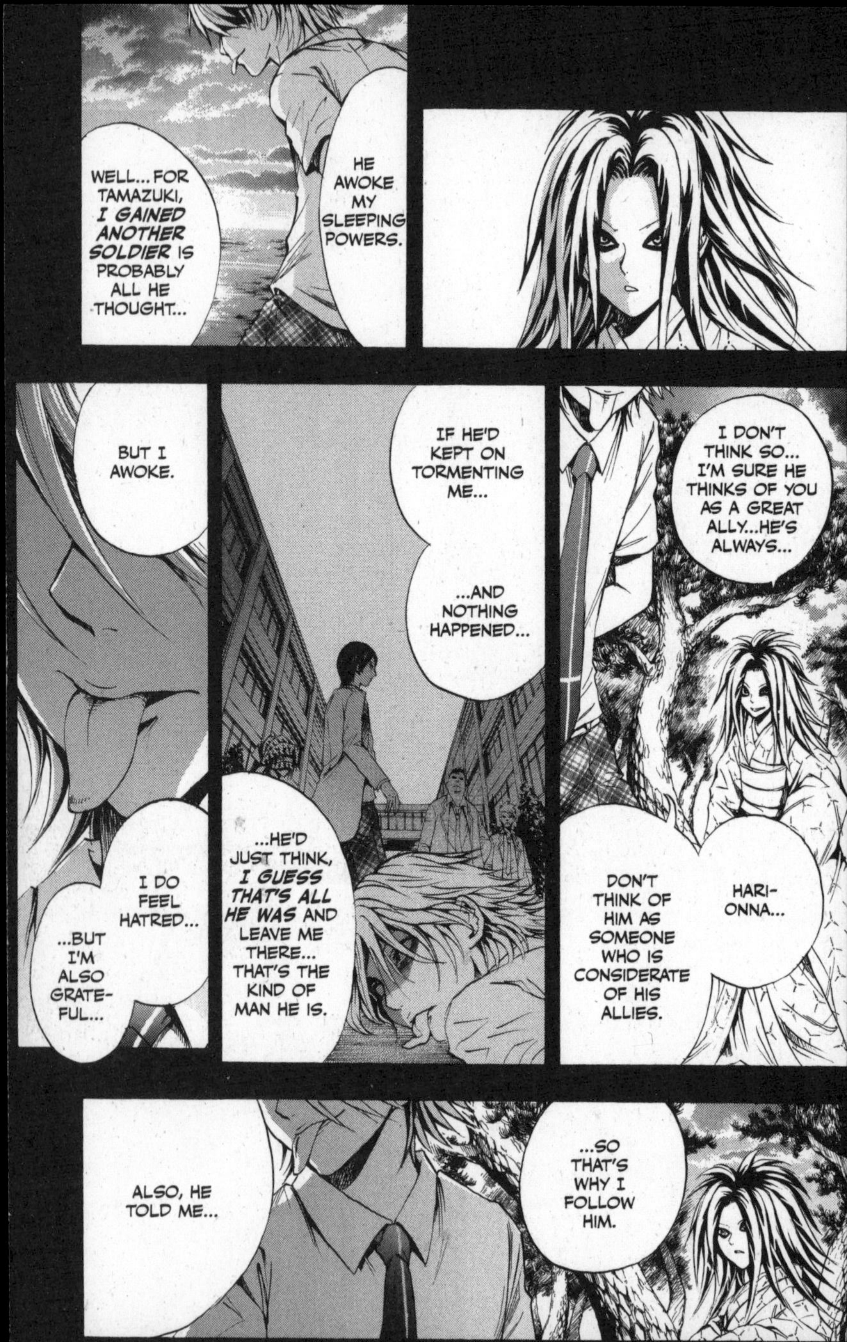
HE AWOKE MY SLEEPING POWERS.
WELL... FOR TAMAZUKI, *I GAINED ANOTHER SOLDIER* IS PROBABLY ALL HE THOUGHT...
I DON'T THINK SO... I'M SURE HE THINKS OF YOU AS A GREAT ALLY...HE'S ALWAYS...
HARI-ONNA...
DON'T THINK OF HIM AS SOMEONE WHO IS CONSIDERATE OF HIS ALLIES.
IF HE'D KEPT ON TORMENTING ME...
...AND NOTHING HAPPENED...
...HE'D JUST THINK, *I GUESS THAT'S ALL HE WAS* AND LEAVE ME THERE... THAT'S THE KIND OF MAN HE IS.
BUT I AWOKE.
I DO FEEL HATRED...
...BUT I'M ALSO GRATE-FUL...
...SO THAT'S WHY I FOLLOW HIM.
ALSO, HE TOLD ME...

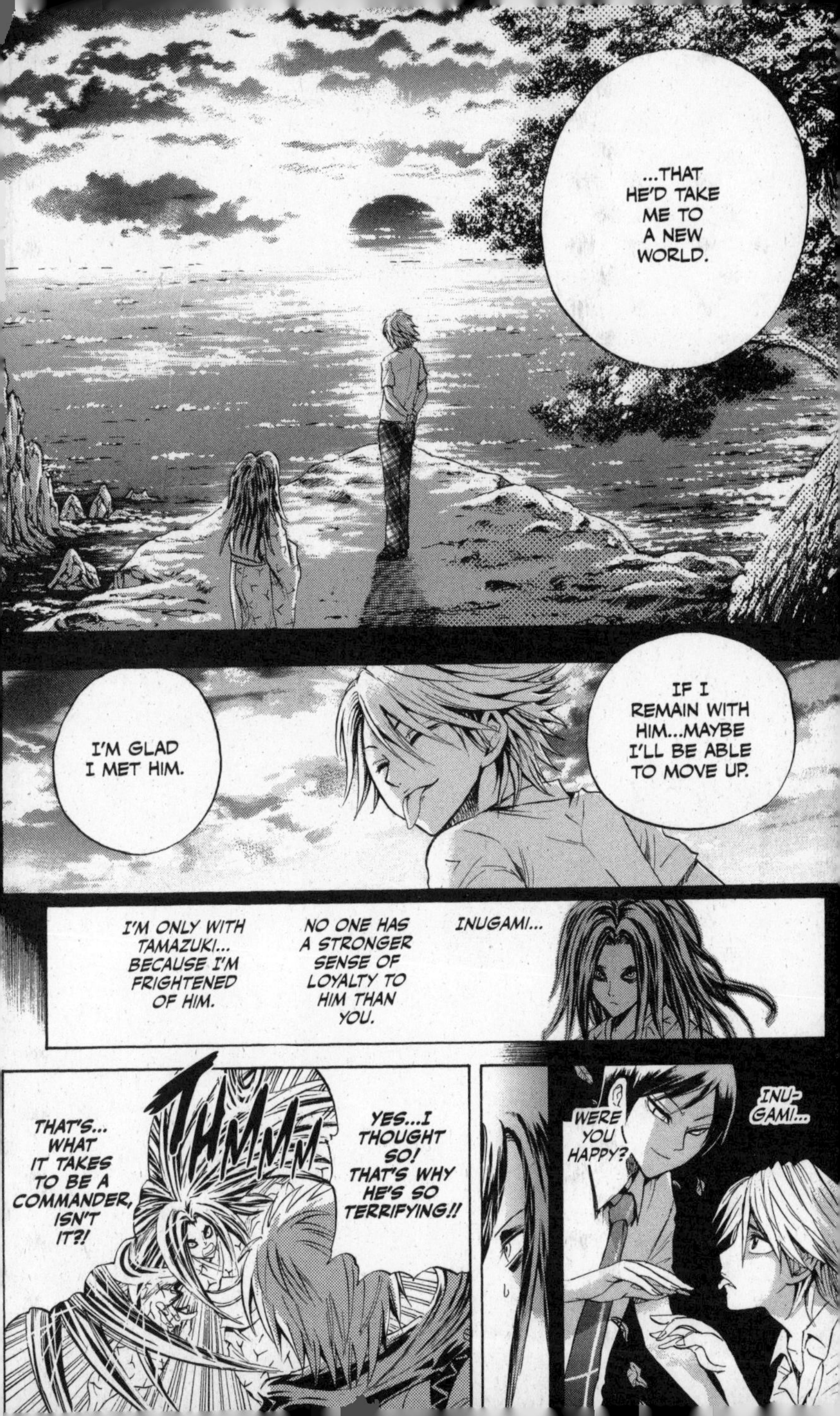
...THAT HE'D TAKE ME TO A NEW WORLD.
IF I REMAIN WITH HIM...MAYBE I'LL BE ABLE TO MOVE UP.
I'M GLAD I MET HIM.
INUGAMI...
NO ONE HAS A STRONGER SENSE OF LOYALTY TO HIM THAN YOU.
I'M ONLY WITH TAMAZUKI... BECAUSE I'M FRIGHTENED OF HIM.
INU-GAMI...
WERE YOU HAPPY?
YES...I THOUGHT SO! THAT'S WHY HE'S SO TERRIFYING!!
THMMM
THAT'S... WHAT IT TAKES TO BE A COMMANDER, ISN'T IT?!

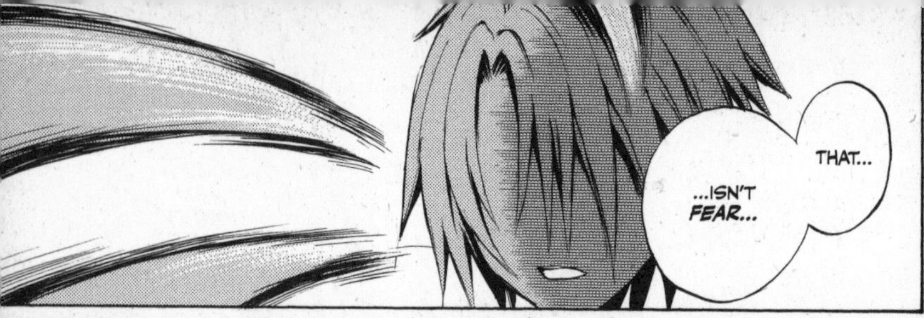
THAT...
...ISN'T FEAR...

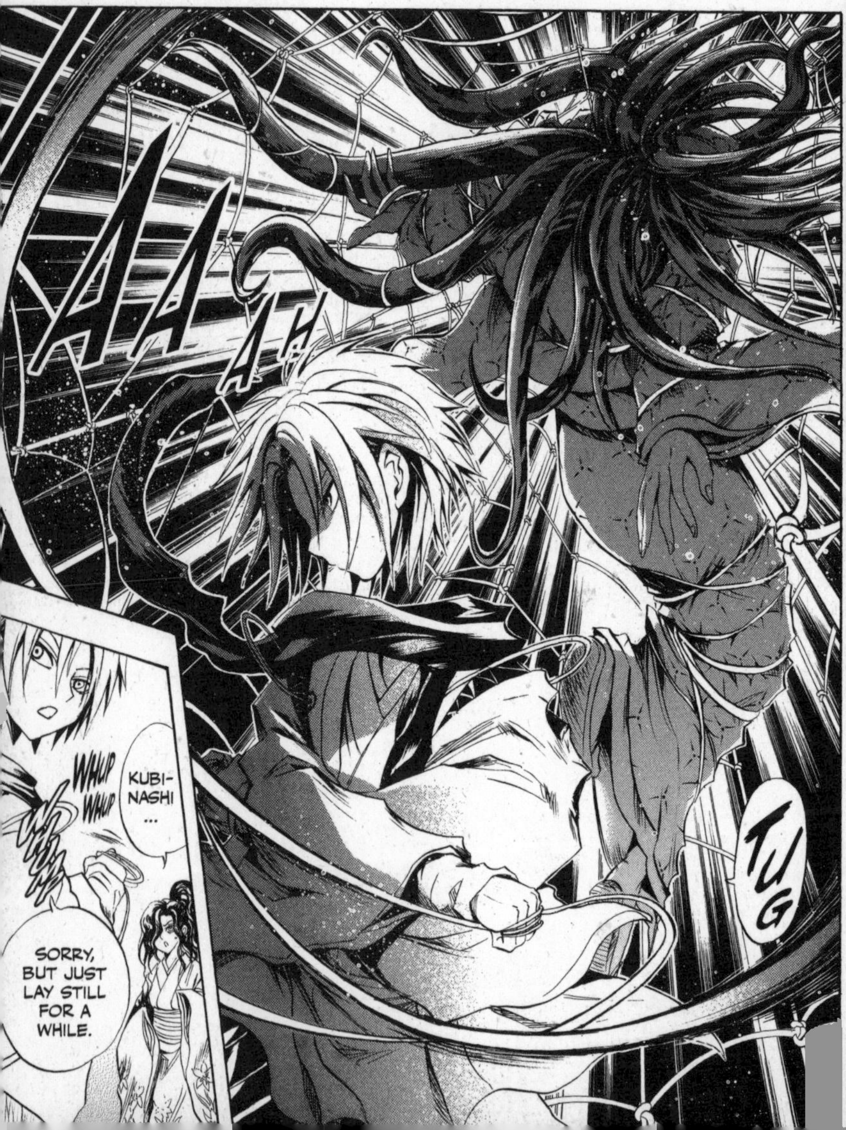
AAAAH
TUG
KUBI-NASHI...
WHUP WHUP
SORRY, BUT JUST LAY STILL FOR A WHILE.

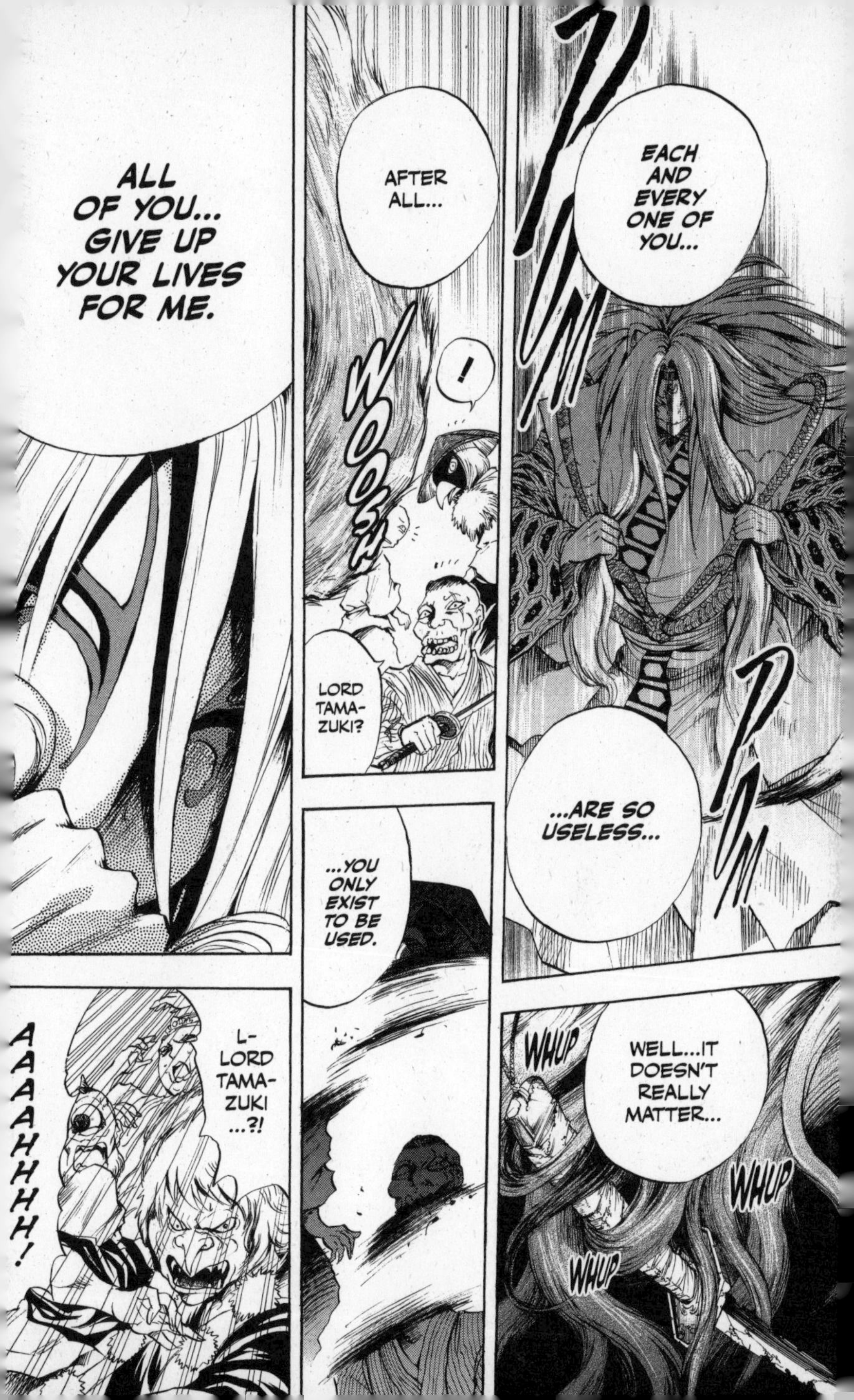
EACH AND EVERY ONE OF YOU...
...ARE SO USELESS...
AFTER ALL...
WOOOSH
!
LORD TAMA-ZUKI?
...YOU ONLY EXIST TO BE USED.
ALL OF YOU... GIVE UP YOUR LIVES FOR ME.
WHUP
WELL...IT DOESN'T REALLY MATTER...
WHUP
WHUP
L-LORD TAMA-ZUKI...?!
AAAAAHHHHH!

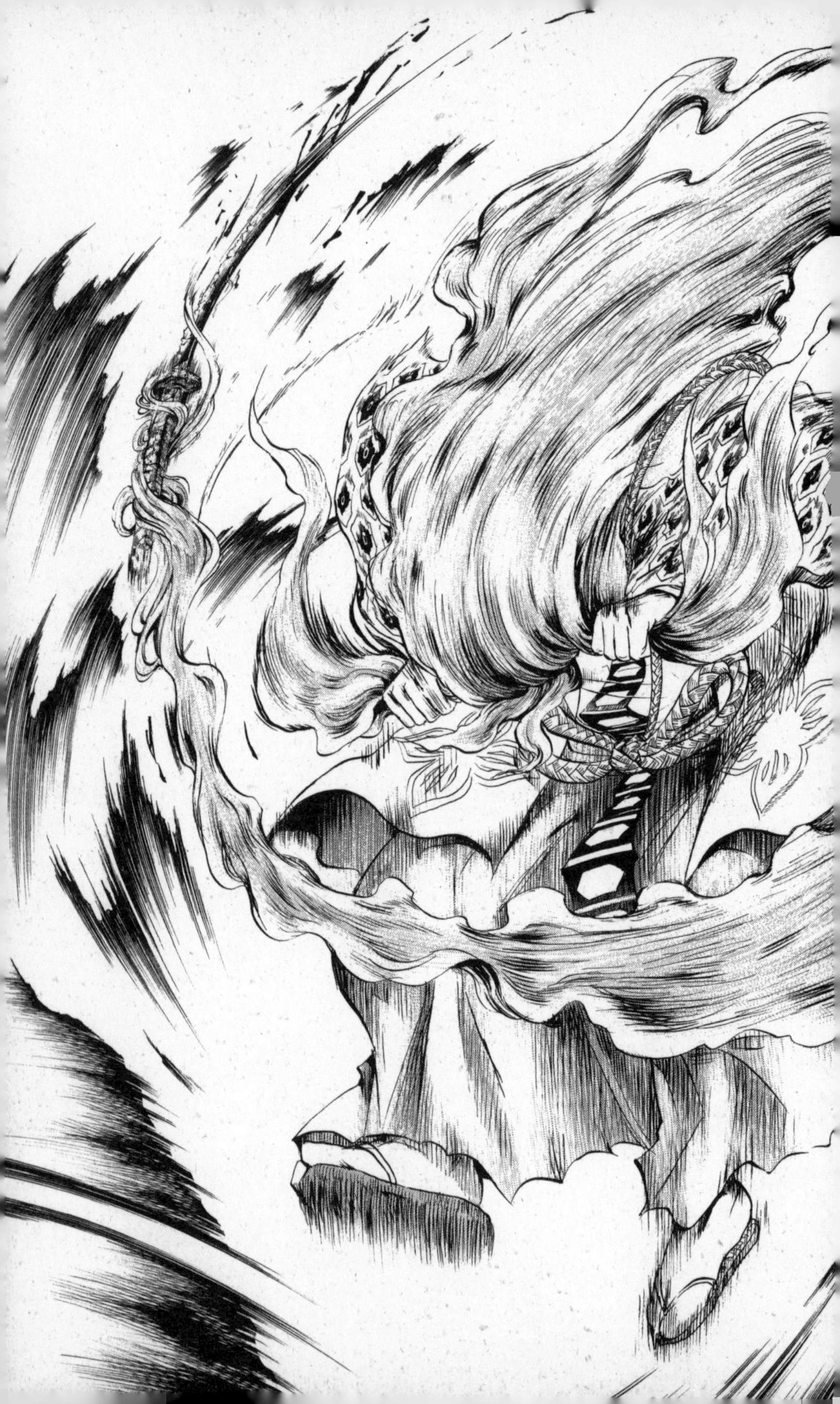

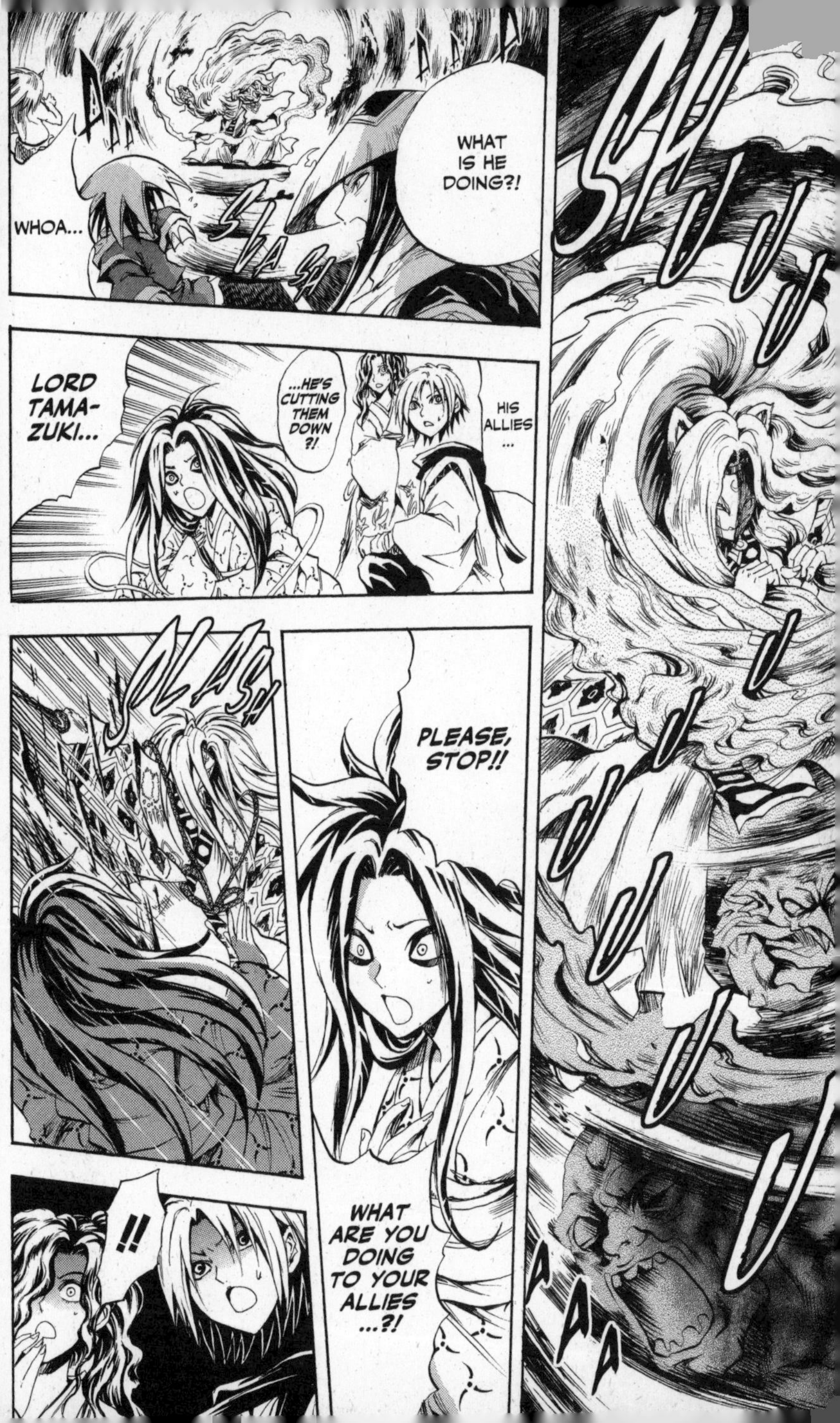
WHAT IS HE DOING?!
WHOA...
HIS ALLIES...
...HE'S CUTTING THEM DOWN?!
LORD TAMAZUKI...
PLEASE, STOP!!
WHAT ARE YOU DOING TO YOUR ALLIES...?!
!!

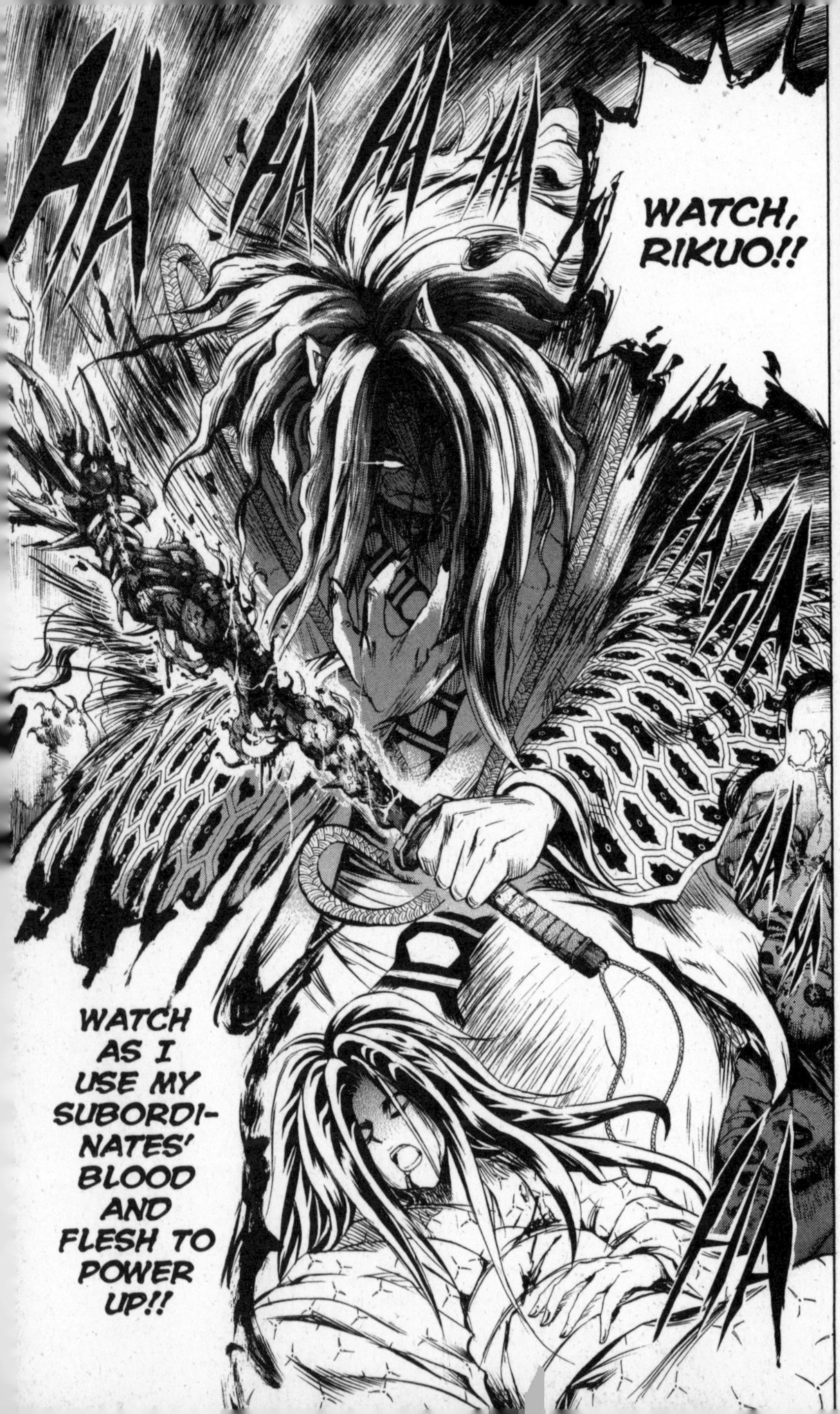
HA HA HA HA HA
WATCH, RIKUO!!
HA HA HA HA
WATCH AS I USE MY SUBORDINATES' BLOOD AND FLESH TO POWER UP!!
HA HA

NURA: RISE OF THE YOKAI CLAN

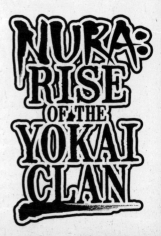

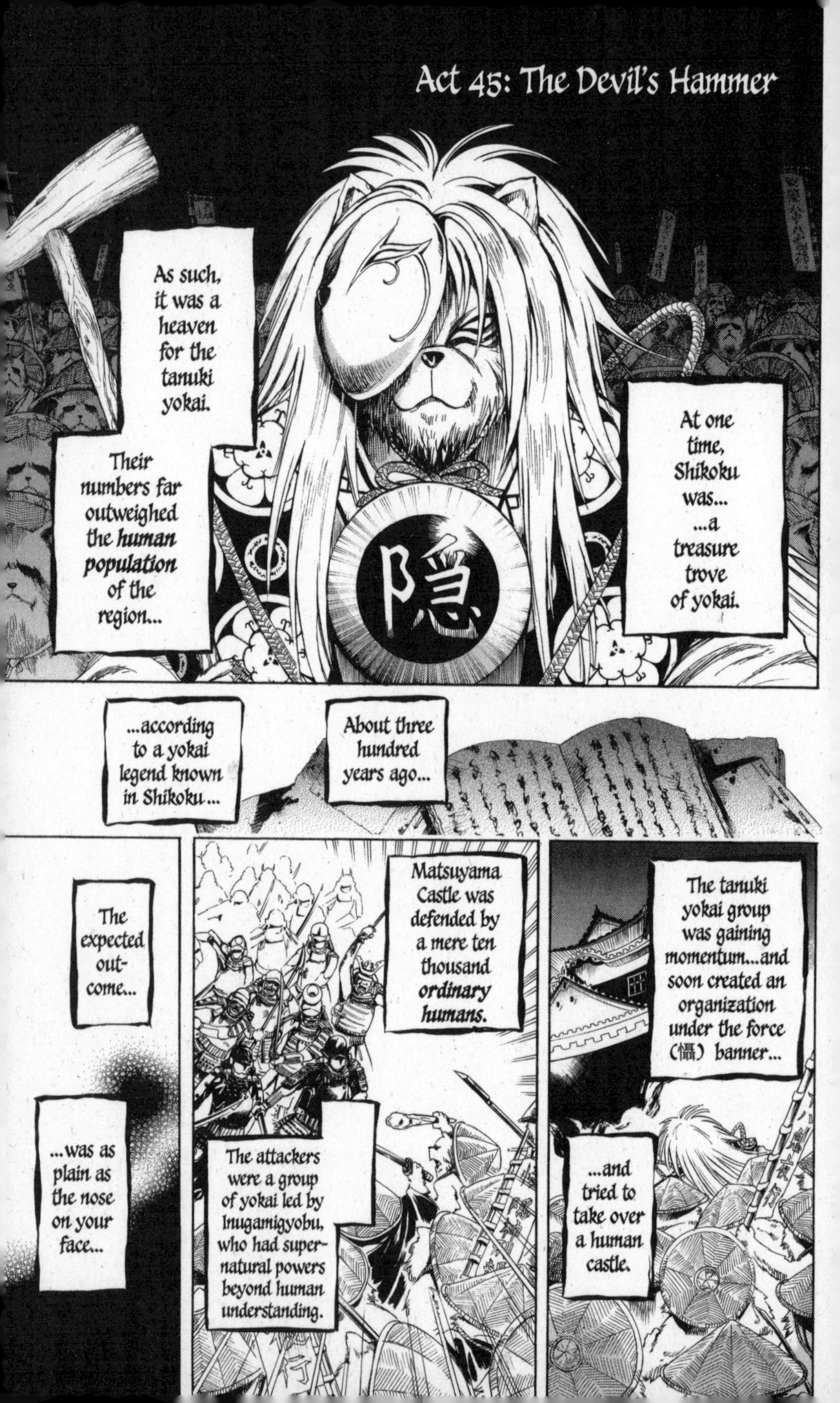
Act 45: The Devil's Hammer
At one time, Shikoku was... ...a treasure trove of yokai.
As such, it was a heaven for the tanuki yokai.
Their numbers far outweighed the *human population* of the region...
隠
About three hundred years ago...
...according to a yokai legend known in Shikoku...
The tanuki yokai group was gaining momentum...and soon created an organization under the force (懾) banner...
...and tried to take over a human castle.
Matsuyama Castle was defended by a mere ten thousand *ordinary humans*.
The attackers were a group of yokai led by Inugamigyobu, who had super-natural powers beyond human understanding.
The expected out-come...
...was as plain as the nose on your face...

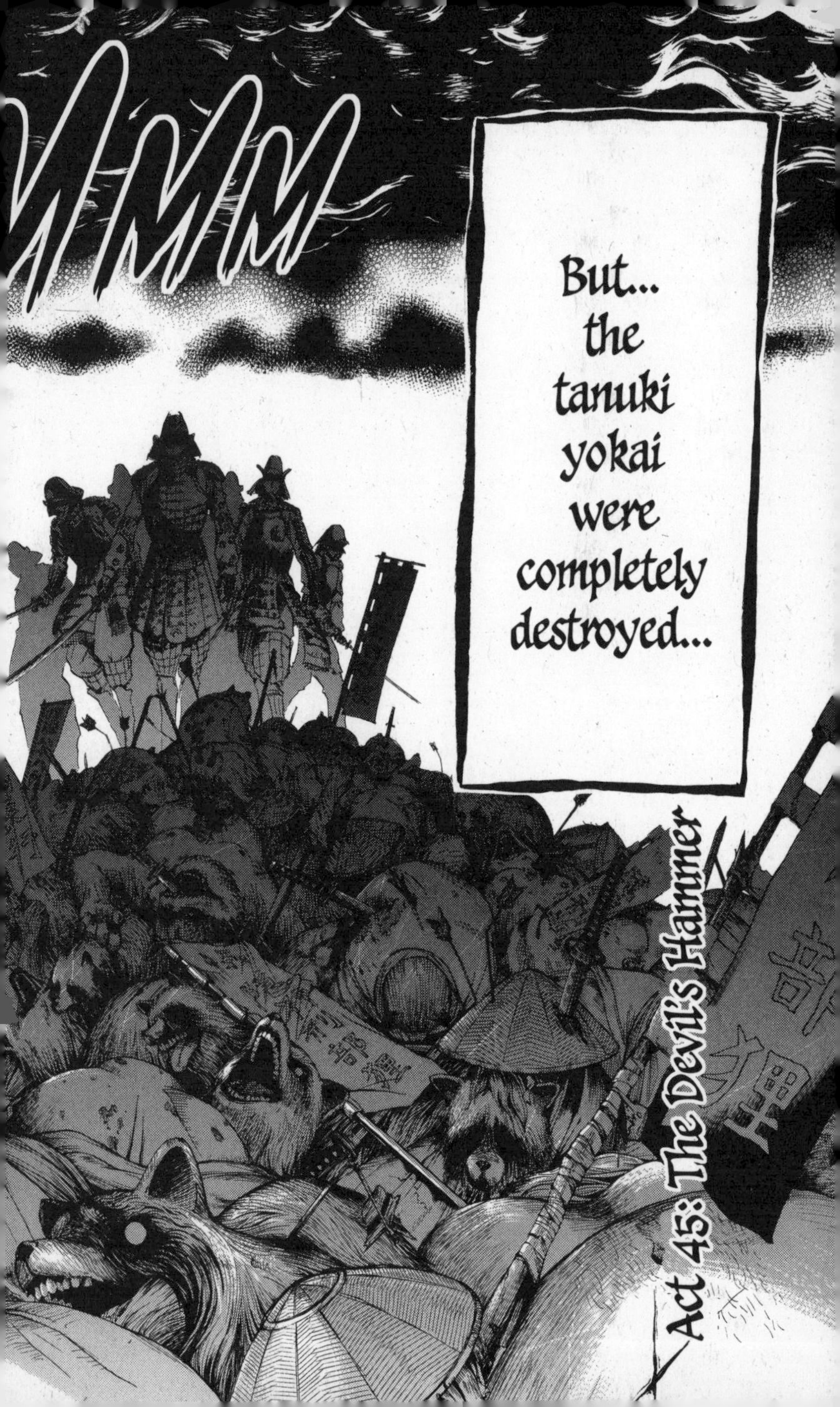
But... the tanuki yokai were completely destroyed...
Act 45: The Devil's Hammer

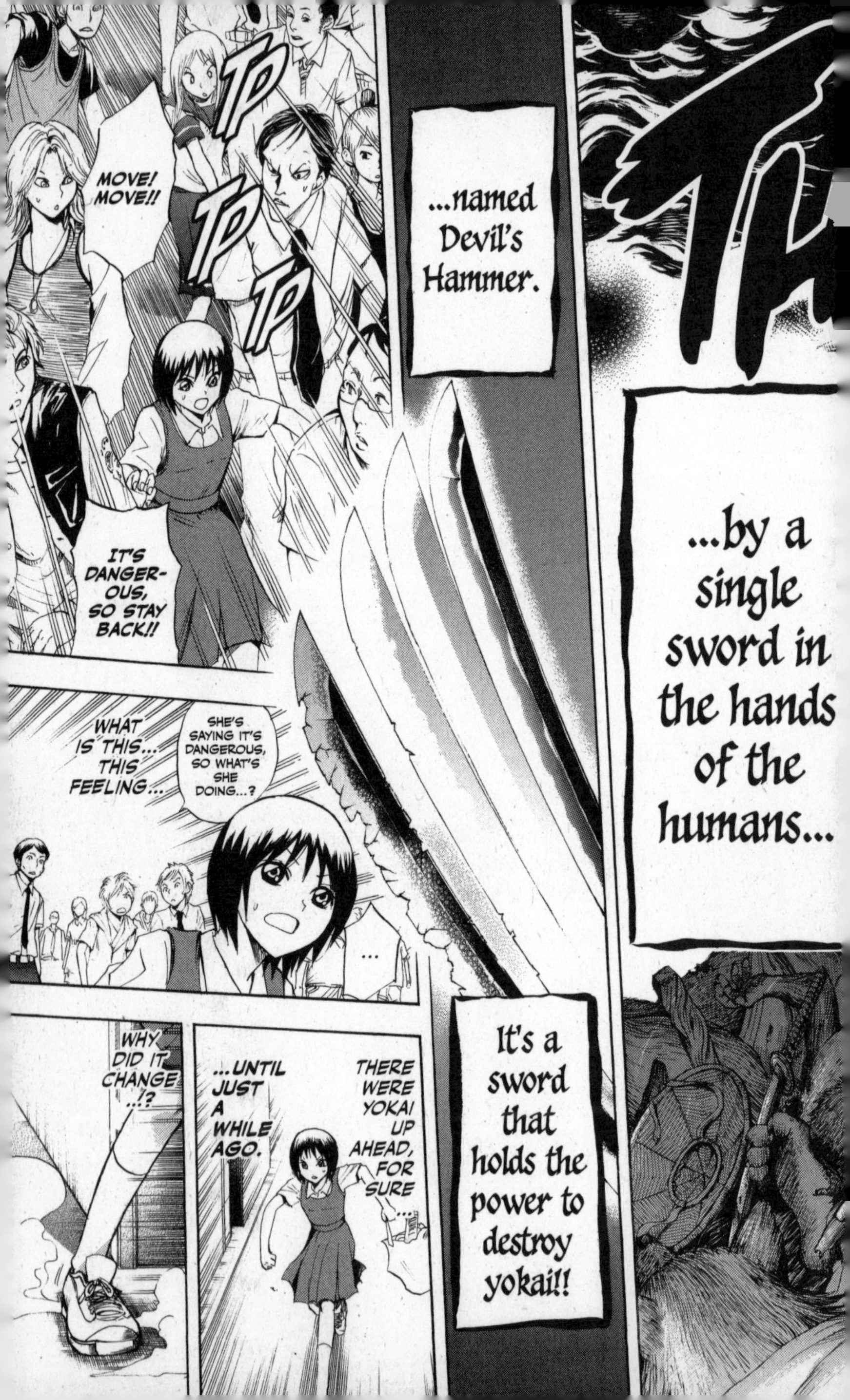

...by a single sword in the hands of the humans...
...named Devil's Hammer.
It's a sword that holds the power to destroy yokai!!
TP
MOVE! MOVE!!
TP
TP
IT'S DANGER-OUS, SO STAY BACK!!
SHE'S SAYING IT'S DANGEROUS, SO WHAT'S SHE DOING...?
WHAT IS THIS... THIS FEELING...
...
THERE WERE YOKAI UP AHEAD, FOR SURE...
...UNTIL JUST A WHILE AGO.
WHY DID IT CHANGE...!?

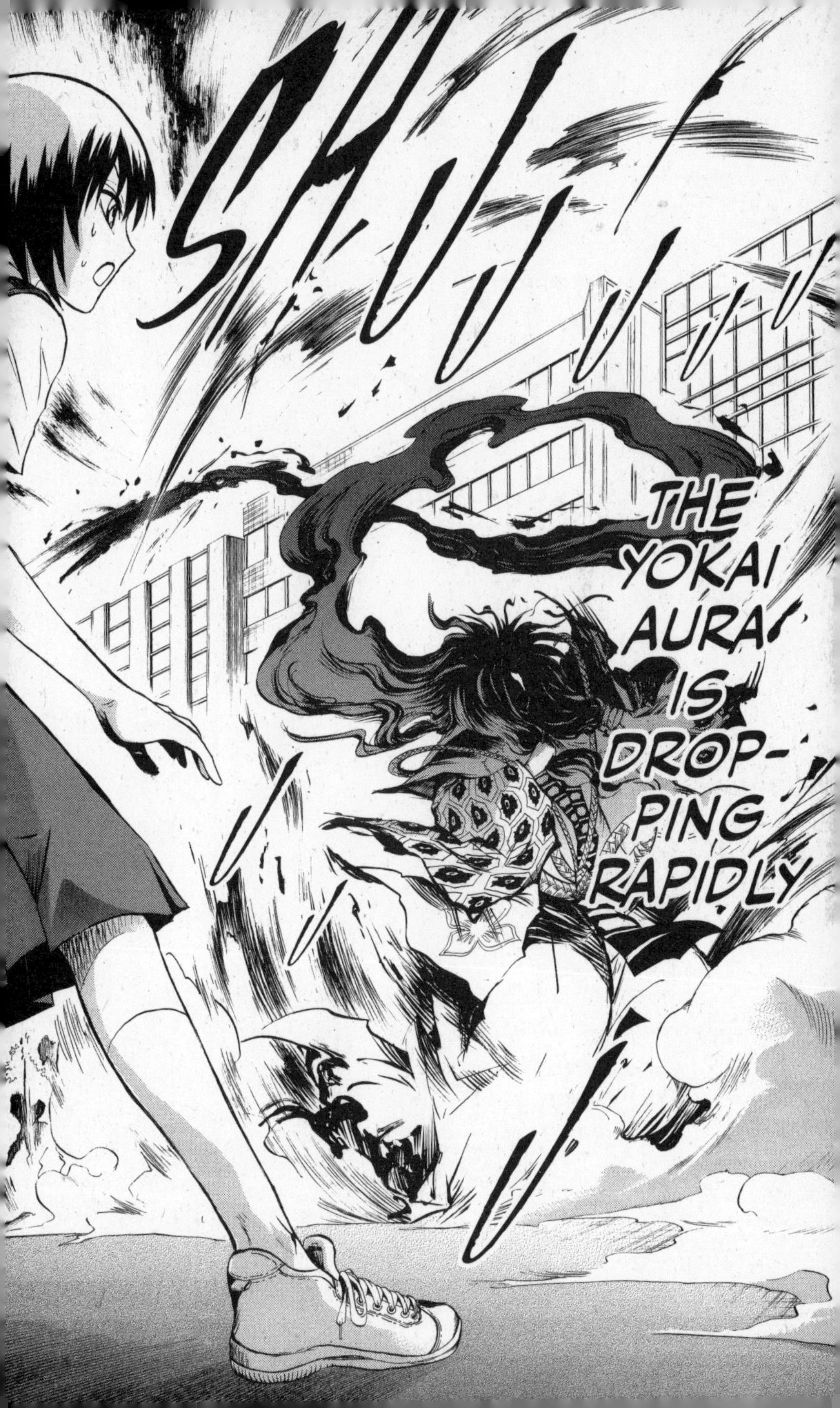
SHUU
THE YOKAI AURA IS DROP-PING RAPIDLY

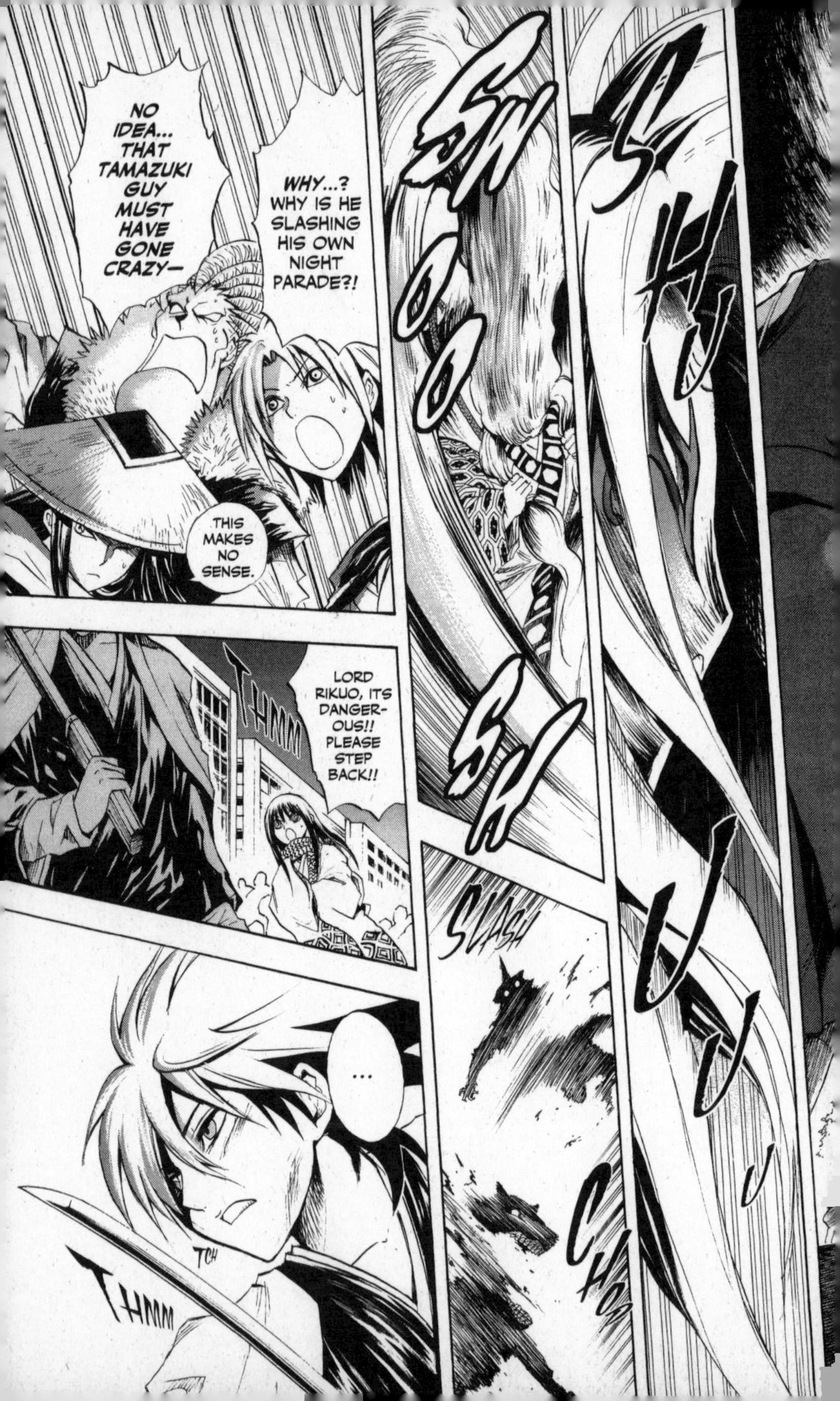
SLASH
WHY...? WHY IS HE SLASHING HIS OWN NIGHT PARADE?!
NO IDEA... THAT TAMAZUKI GUY MUST HAVE GONE CRAZY—
THIS MAKES NO SENSE.
THMM
LORD RIKUO, ITS DANGER-OUS!! PLEASE STEP BACK!!
...
TCH
THMM

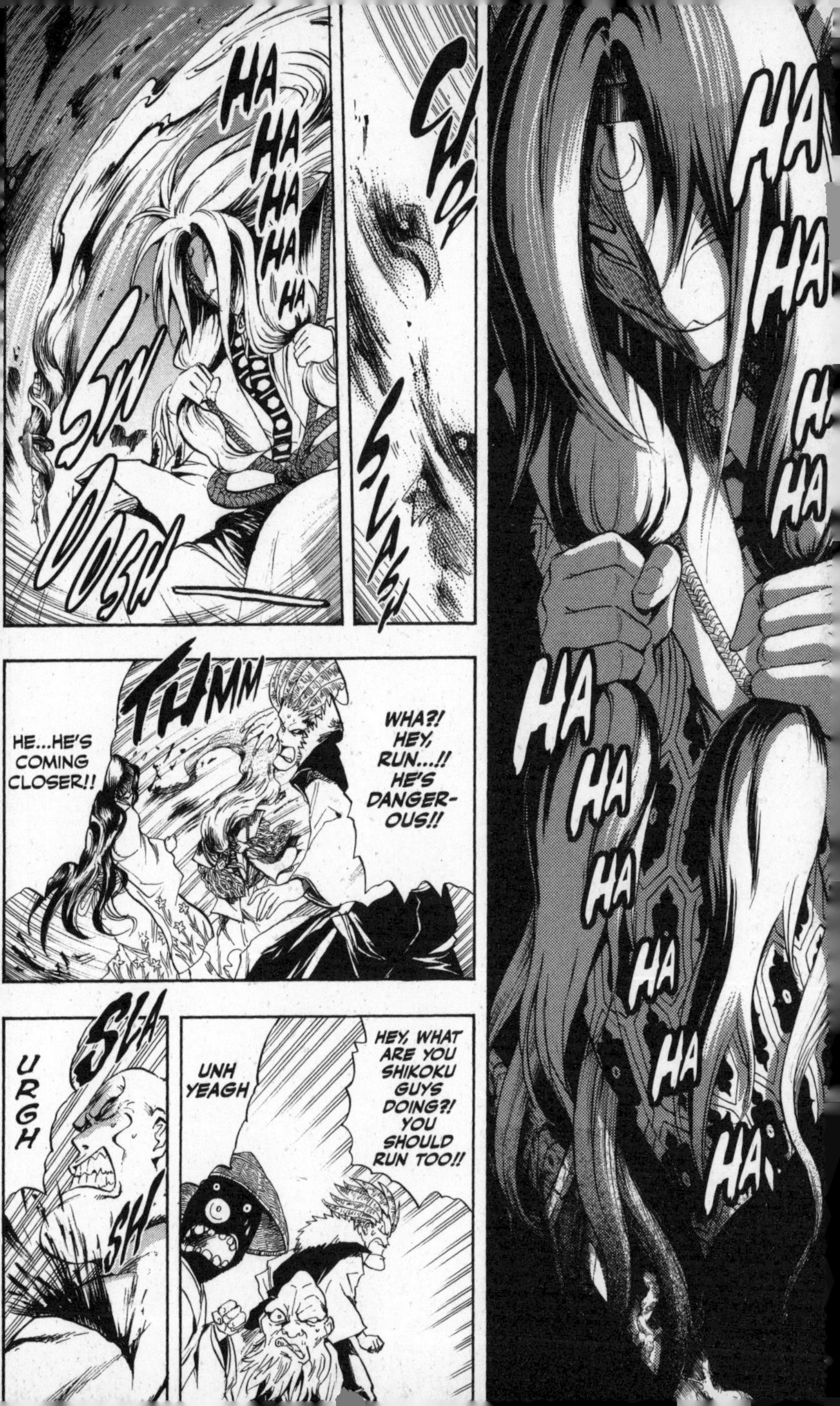
HA HA HA HA
HA HA HA HA HA HA HA
CHOK
SLASH
HA HA HA HA HA HA
SWOOSH
THMM
WHA?! HEY, RUN...!! HE'S DANGER-OUS!!
HE...HE'S COMING CLOSER!!
HEY, WHAT ARE YOU SHIKOKU GUYS DOING?! YOU SHOULD RUN TOO!!
UNH YEAGH
SLASH
URGH

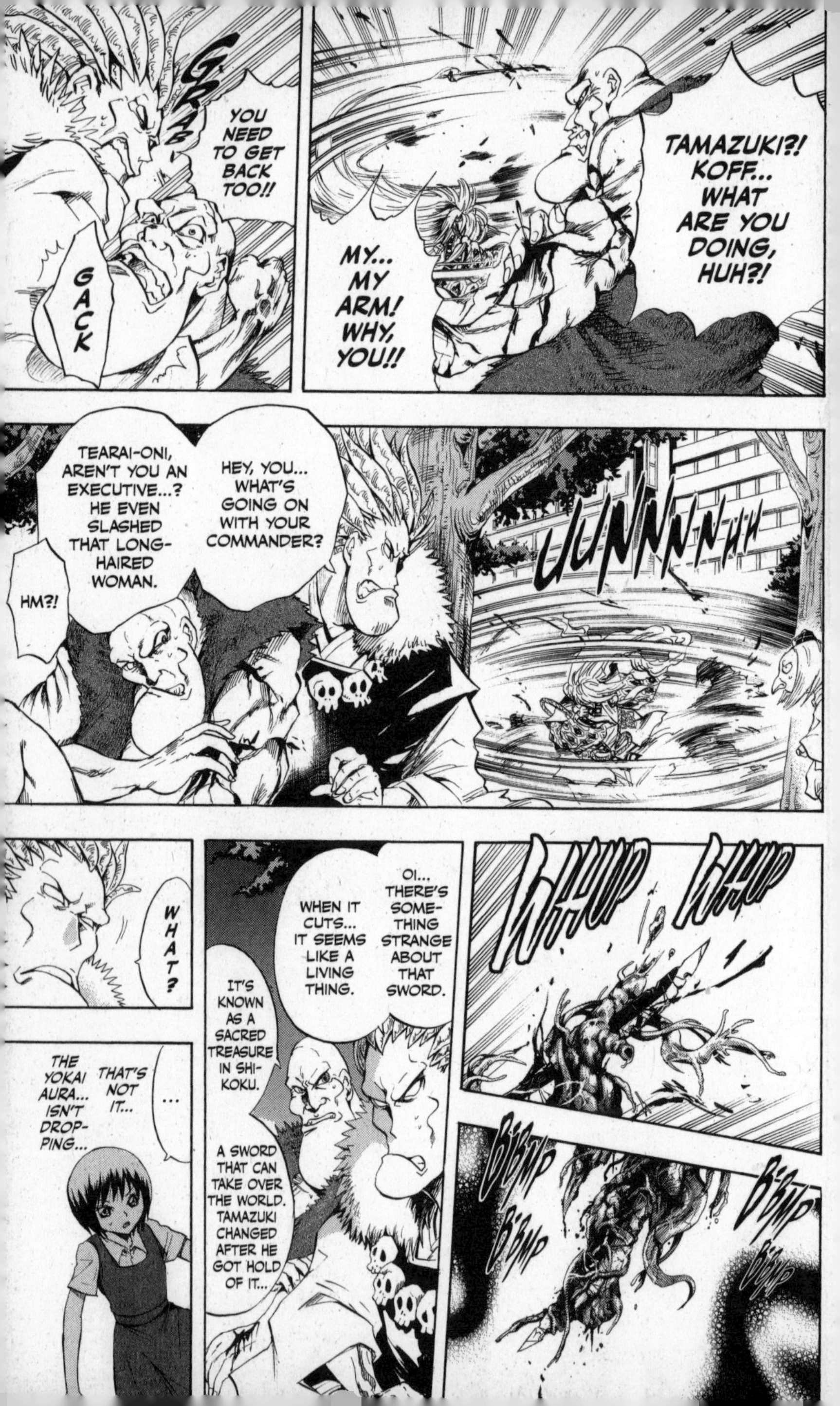
TAMAZUKI?! KOFF... WHAT ARE YOU DOING, HUH?!
MY... MY ARM! WHY, YOU!!
GRAB
YOU NEED TO GET BACK TOO!!
GACK
JUNNNNNHH
HEY, YOU... WHAT'S GOING ON WITH YOUR COMMANDER?
TEARAI-ONI, AREN'T YOU AN EXECUTIVE...? HE EVEN SLASHED THAT LONG-HAIRED WOMAN.
HM?!
WHUP
WHUP
OI... THERE'S SOMETHING STRANGE ABOUT THAT SWORD.
WHEN IT CUTS... IT SEEMS LIKE A LIVING THING.
IT'S KNOWN AS A SACRED TREASURE IN SHIKOKU.
A SWORD THAT CAN TAKE OVER THE WORLD. TAMAZUKI CHANGED AFTER HE GOT HOLD OF IT...
WHAT?
...
THAT'S NOT IT...
THE YOKAI AURA... ISN'T DROPPING...

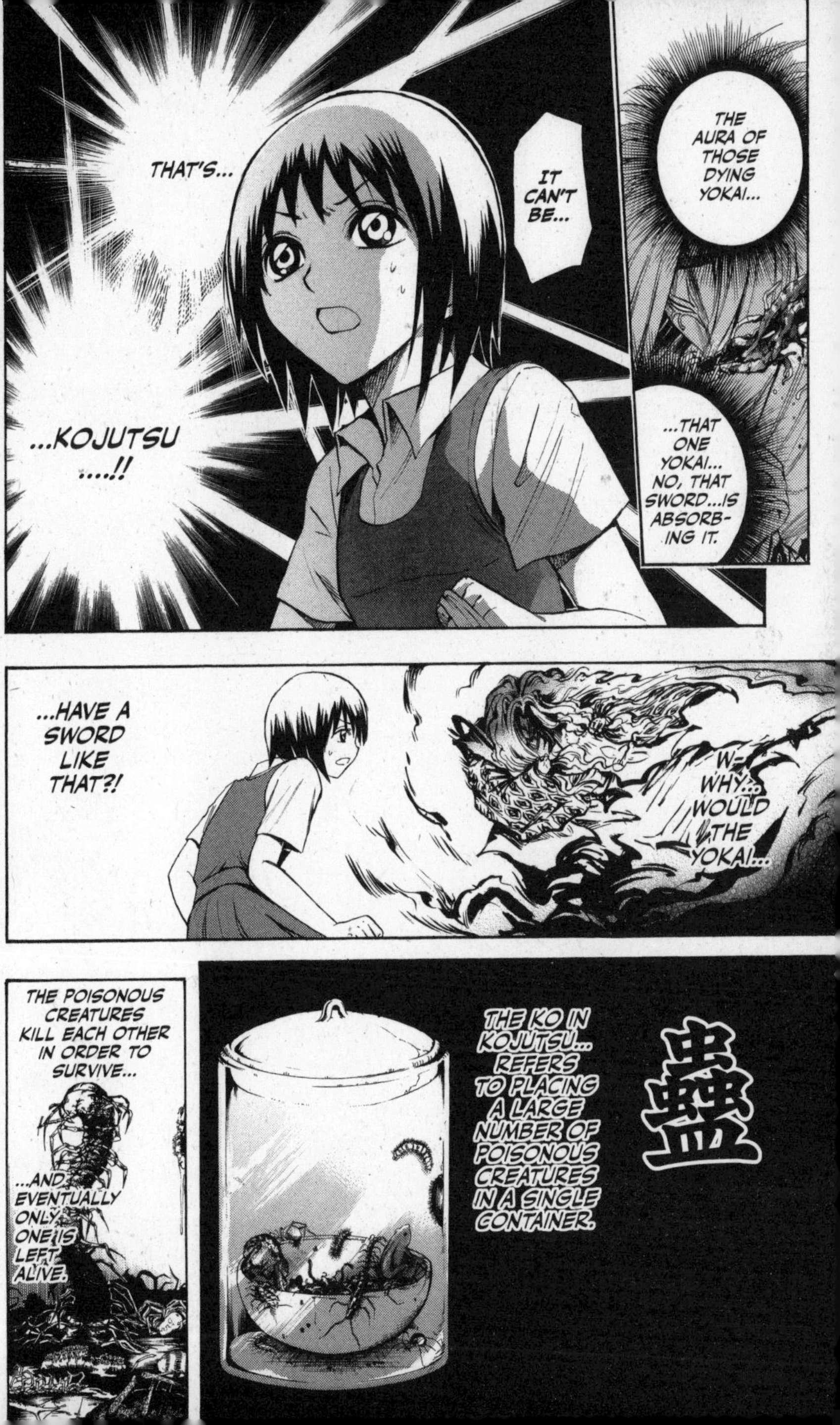
THE AURA OF THOSE DYING YOKAI...
...THAT ONE YOKAI... NO, THAT SWORD...IS ABSORBING IT.
IT CAN'T BE...
THAT'S...
...KOJUTSU ....!!
W-WHY... WOULD THE YOKAI...
...HAVE A SWORD LIKE THAT?!
蠱
THE KO IN KOJUTSU... REFERS TO PLACING A LARGE NUMBER OF POISONOUS CREATURES IN A SINGLE CONTAINER.
THE POISONOUS CREATURES KILL EACH OTHER IN ORDER TO SURVIVE...
...AND EVENTUALLY ONLY ONE IS LEFT ALIVE.

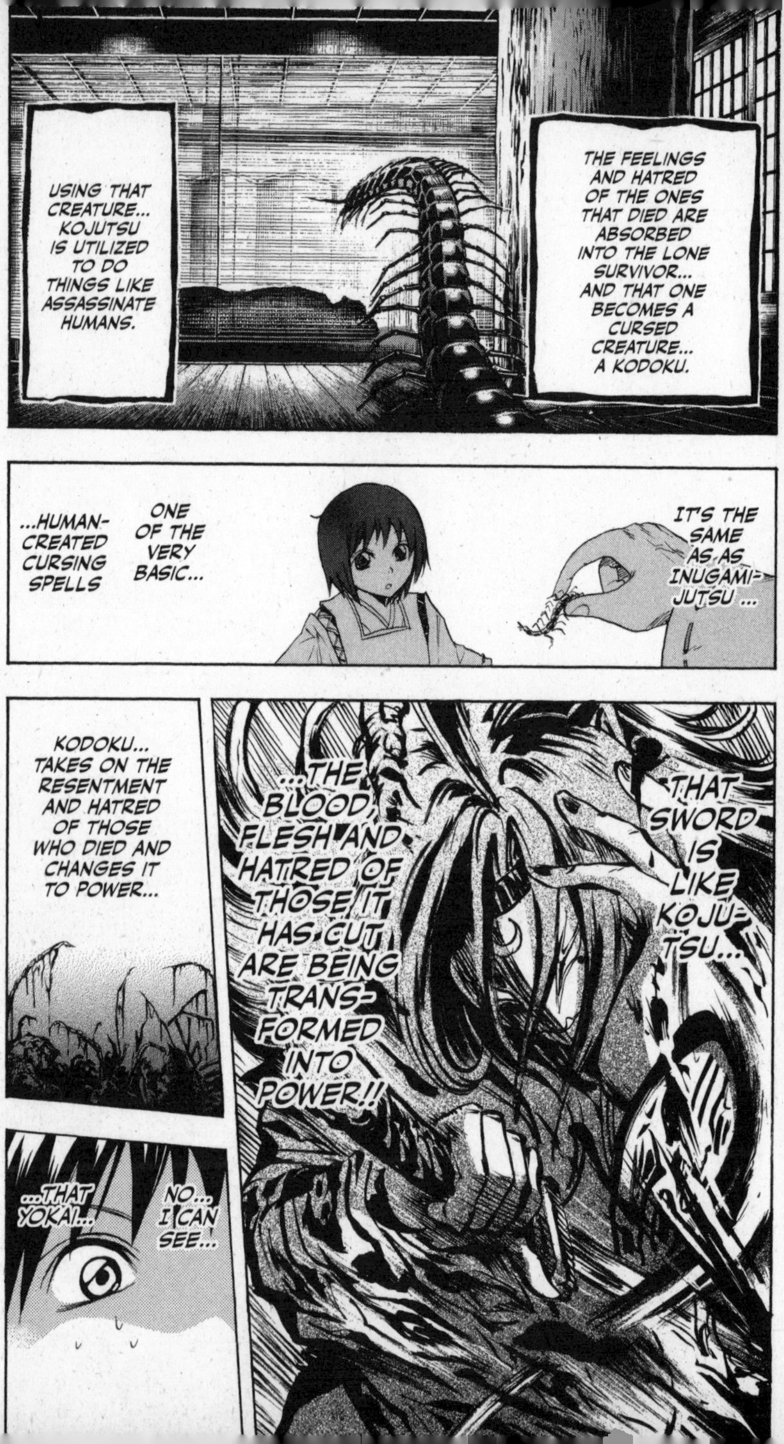

THE FEELINGS AND HATRED OF THE ONES THAT DIED ARE ABSORBED INTO THE LONE SURVIVOR... AND THAT ONE BECOMES A CURSED CREATURE... A KODOKU.
USING THAT CREATURE... KOJUTSU IS UTILIZED TO DO THINGS LIKE ASSASSINATE HUMANS.
IT'S THE SAME AS AS INUGAMI-JUTSU...
ONE OF THE VERY BASIC...
...HUMAN-CREATED CURSING SPELLS
THAT SWORD IS LIKE KOJU-TSU...
...THE BLOOD, FLESH AND HATRED OF THOSE IT HAS CUT ARE BEING TRANS-FORMED INTO POWER!!
KODOKU... TAKES ON THE RESENTMENT AND HATRED OF THOSE WHO DIED AND CHANGES IT TO POWER...
NO... I CAN SEE...
...THAT YOKAI...

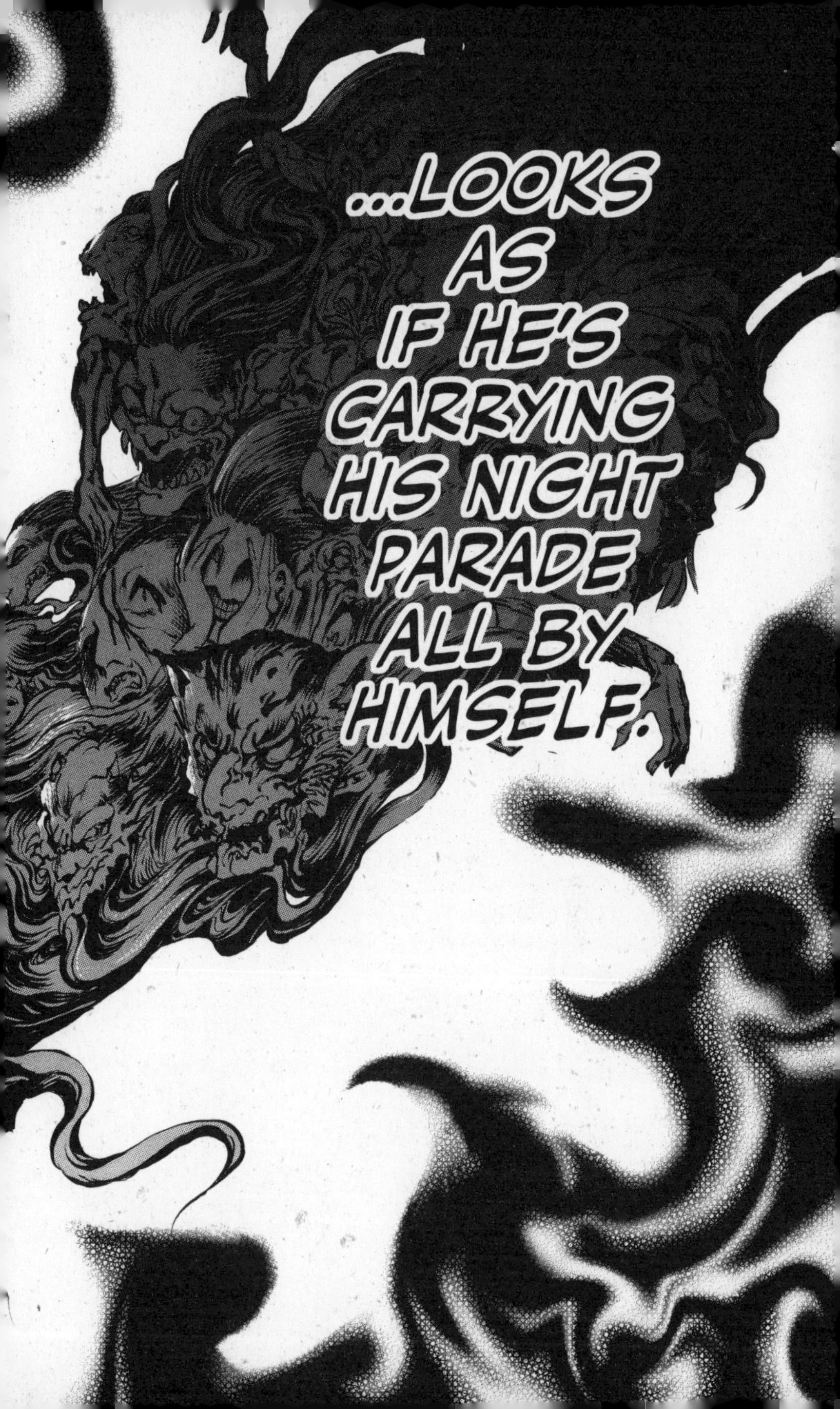
...LOOKS AS IF HE'S CARRYING HIS NIGHT PARADE ALL BY HIMSELF.

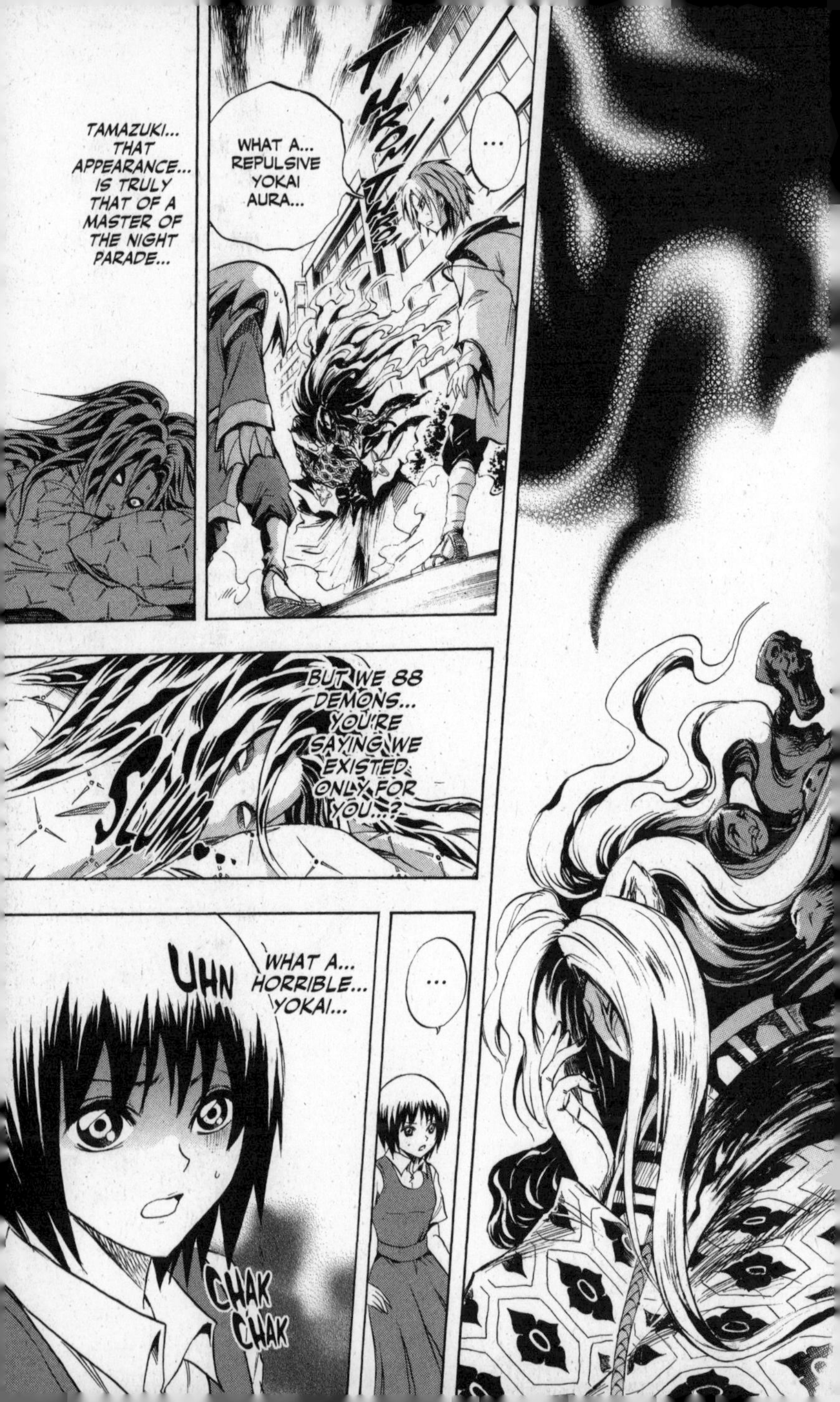
...
WHAT A... REPULSIVE YOKAI AURA...
TAMAZUKI... THAT APPEARANCE... IS TRULY THAT OF A MASTER OF THE NIGHT PARADE...
BUT WE 88 DEMONS... YOU'RE SAYING WE EXISTED ONLY FOR YOU...?
SLUMP
...
WHAT A... HORRIBLE... YOKAI...
UHN
CHAK CHAK

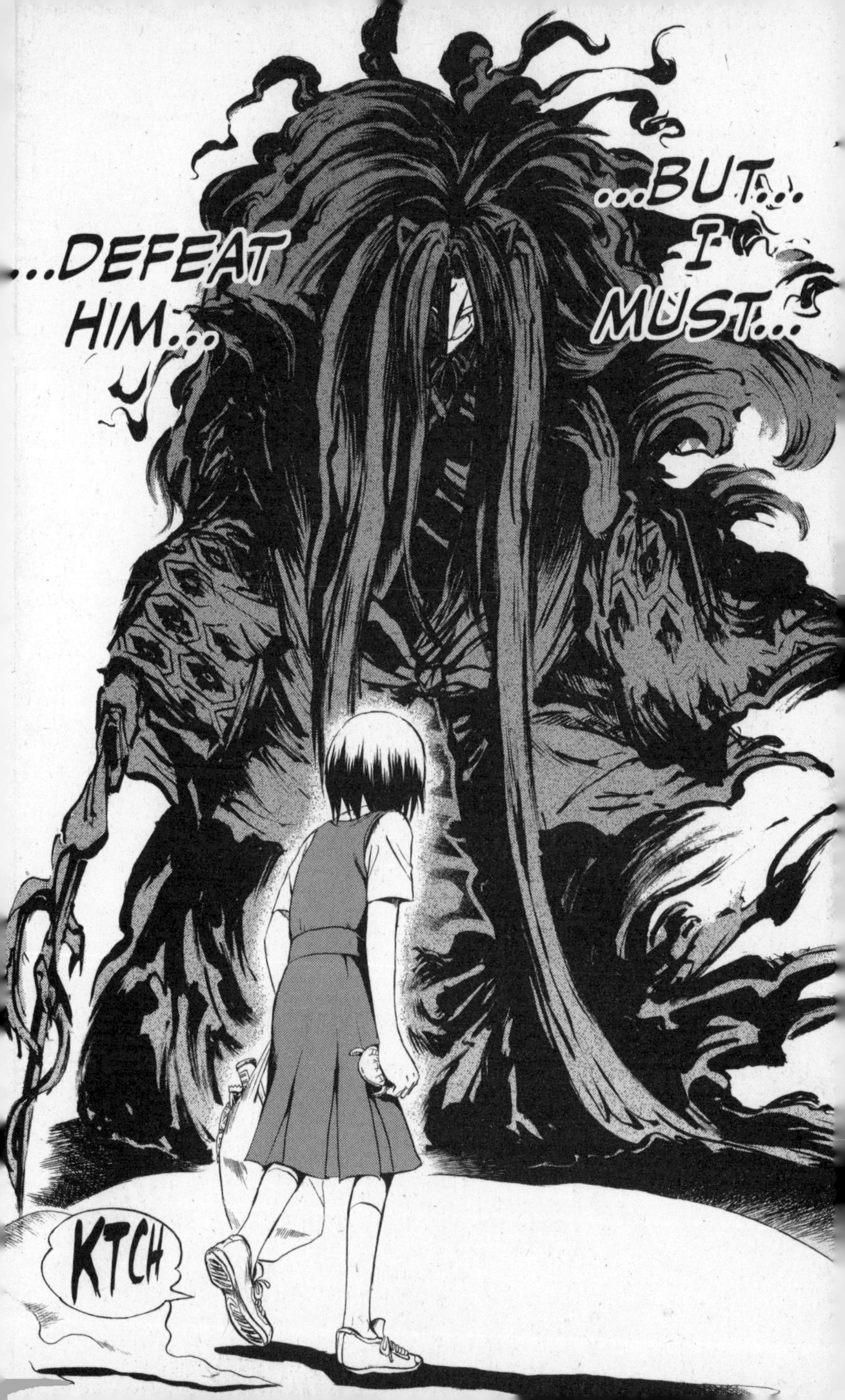
...BUT... I MUST...
...DEFEAT HIM...
KTCH

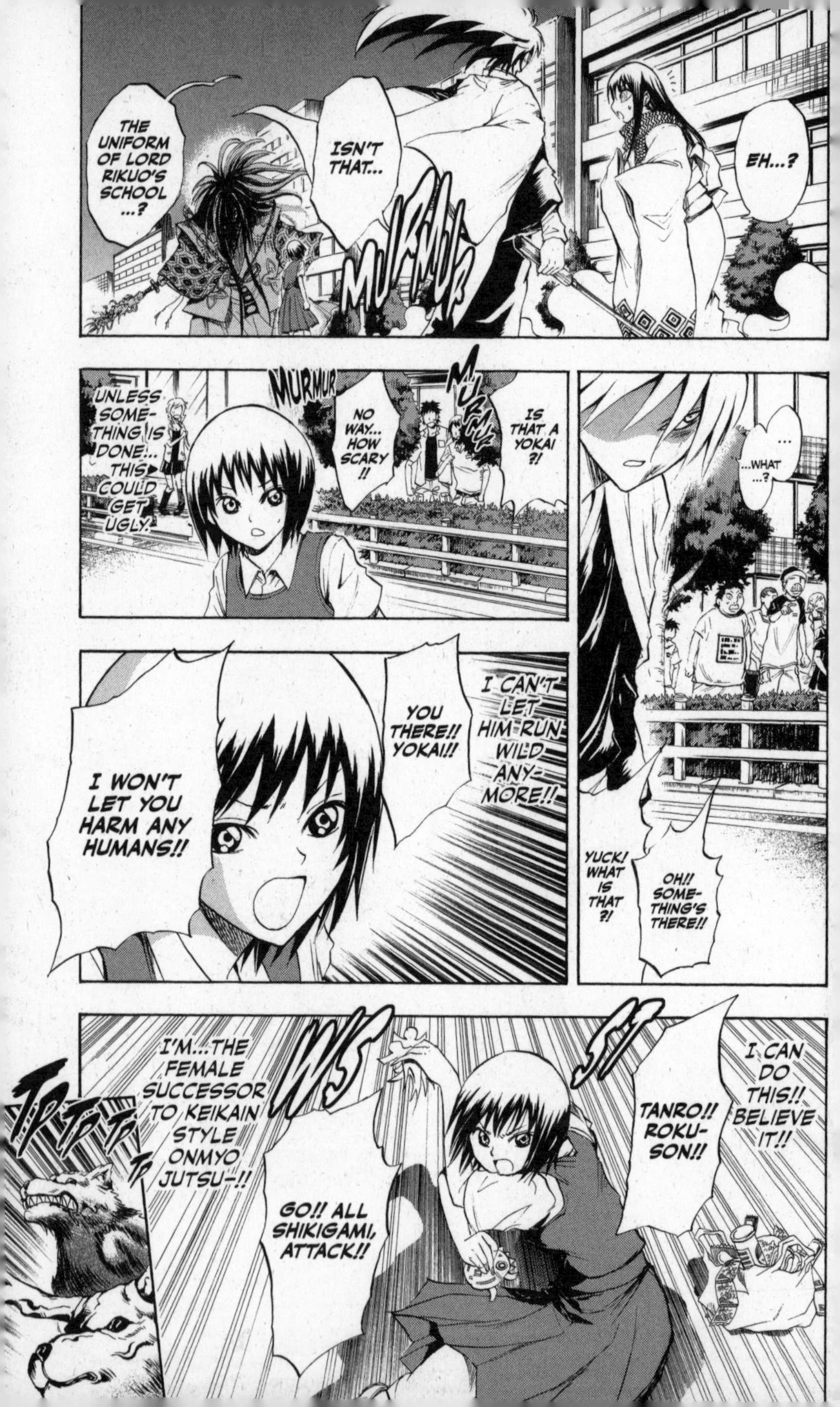
EH...?
ISN'T THAT...
THE UNIFORM OF LORD RIKUO'S SCHOOL ...?
... ...WHAT ...?
OH!! SOME-THING'S THERE!!
YUCK! WHAT IS THAT ?!
IS THAT A YOKAI ?!
MURMUR
NO WAY... HOW SCARY !!
MURMUR
UNLESS SOME-THING IS DONE... THIS COULD GET UGLY.
I CAN'T LET HIM RUN WILD ANY-MORE!!
YOU THERE!! YOKAI!!
I WON'T LET YOU HARM ANY HUMANS!!
I CAN DO THIS!! BELIEVE IT!!
TANRO!! ROKU-SON!!
I'M... THE FEMALE SUCCESSOR TO KEIKAIN STYLE ONMYO JUTSU-!!
GO!! ALL SHIKIGAMI, ATTACK!!

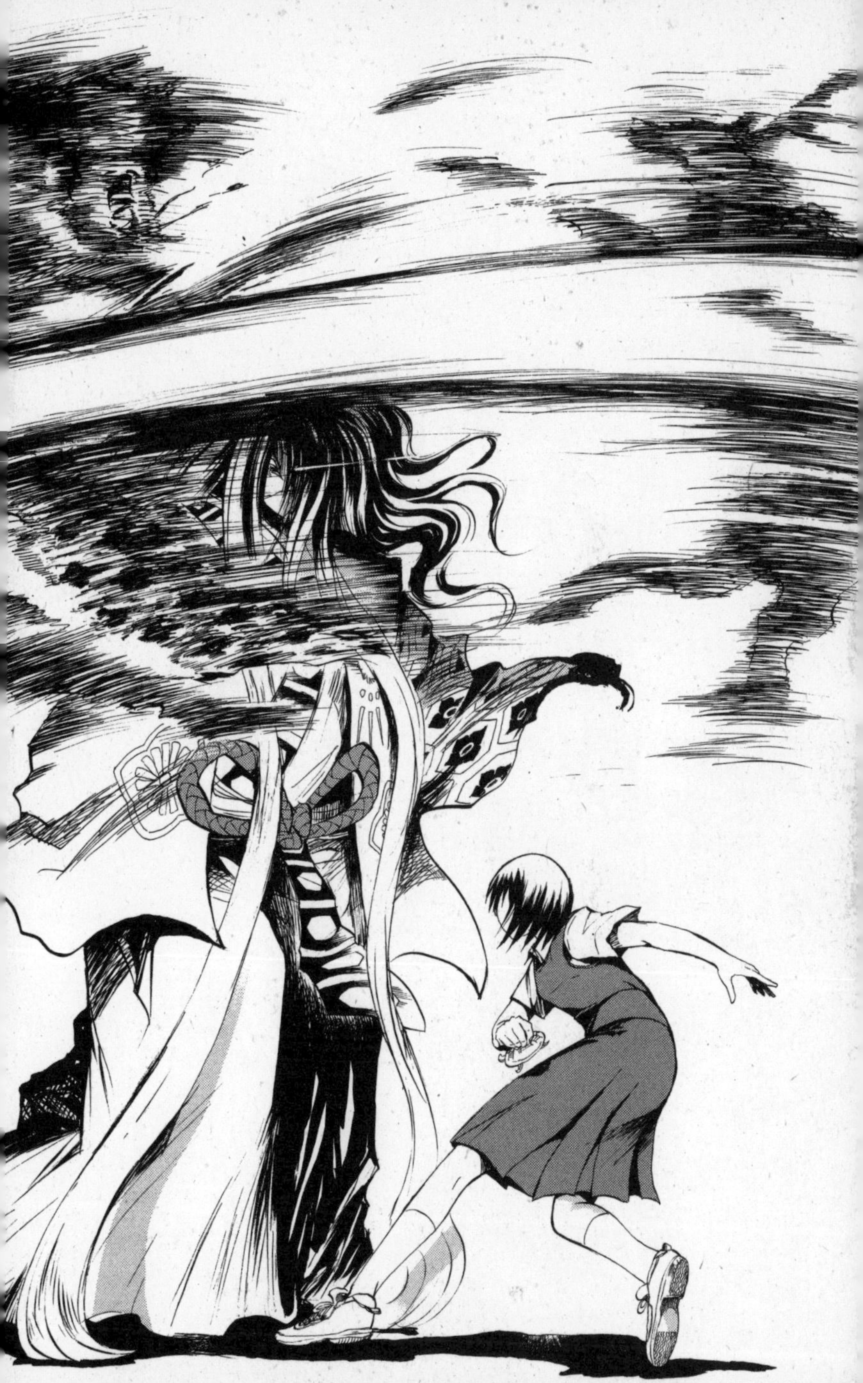

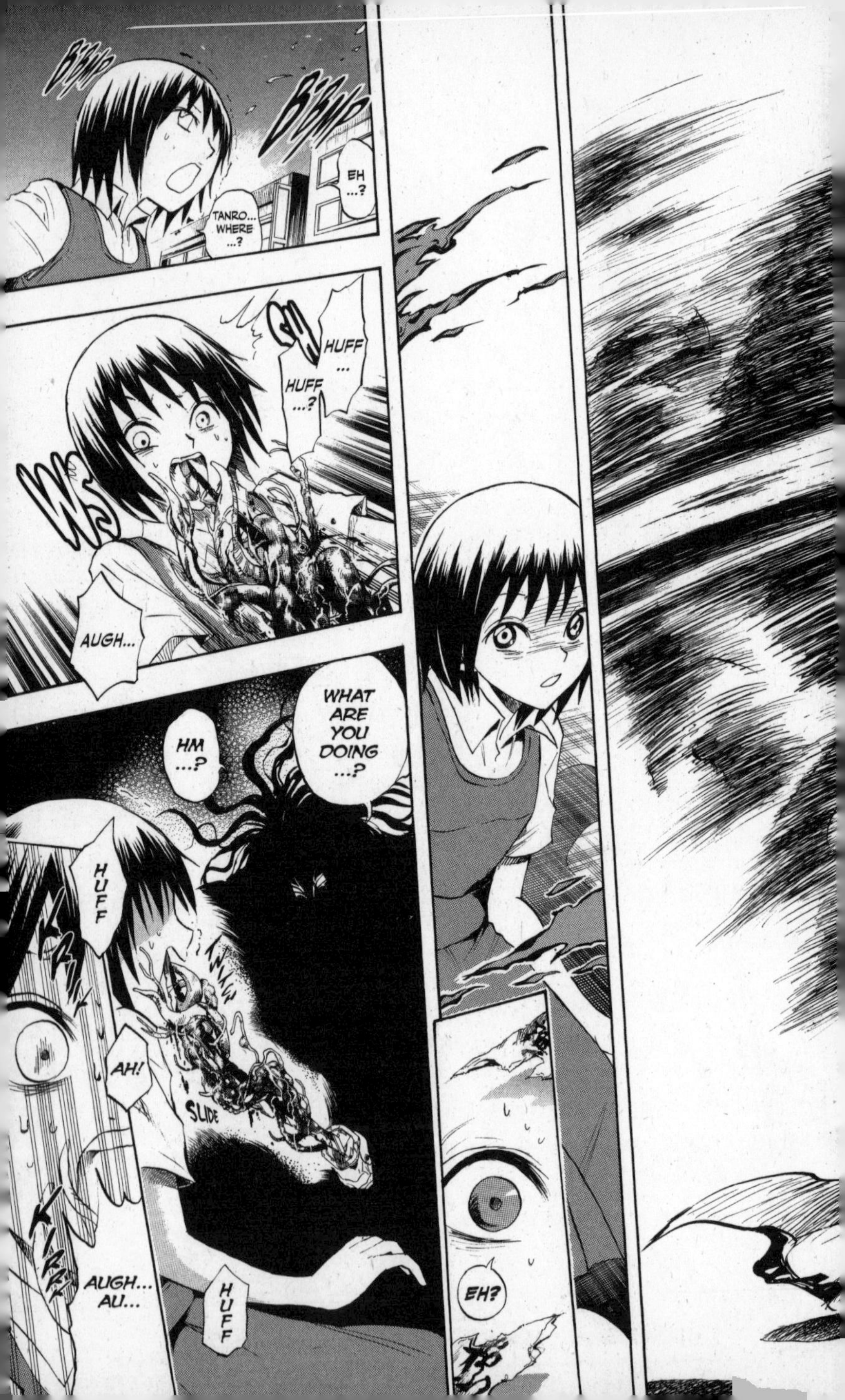
EH?
EH ...?
TANRO... WHERE ...?
HUFF ...
HUFF ...?
AUGH...
WHAT ARE YOU DOING ...?
HM ...?
HUFF
AH!
SLIDE
HUFF
AUGH... AU...

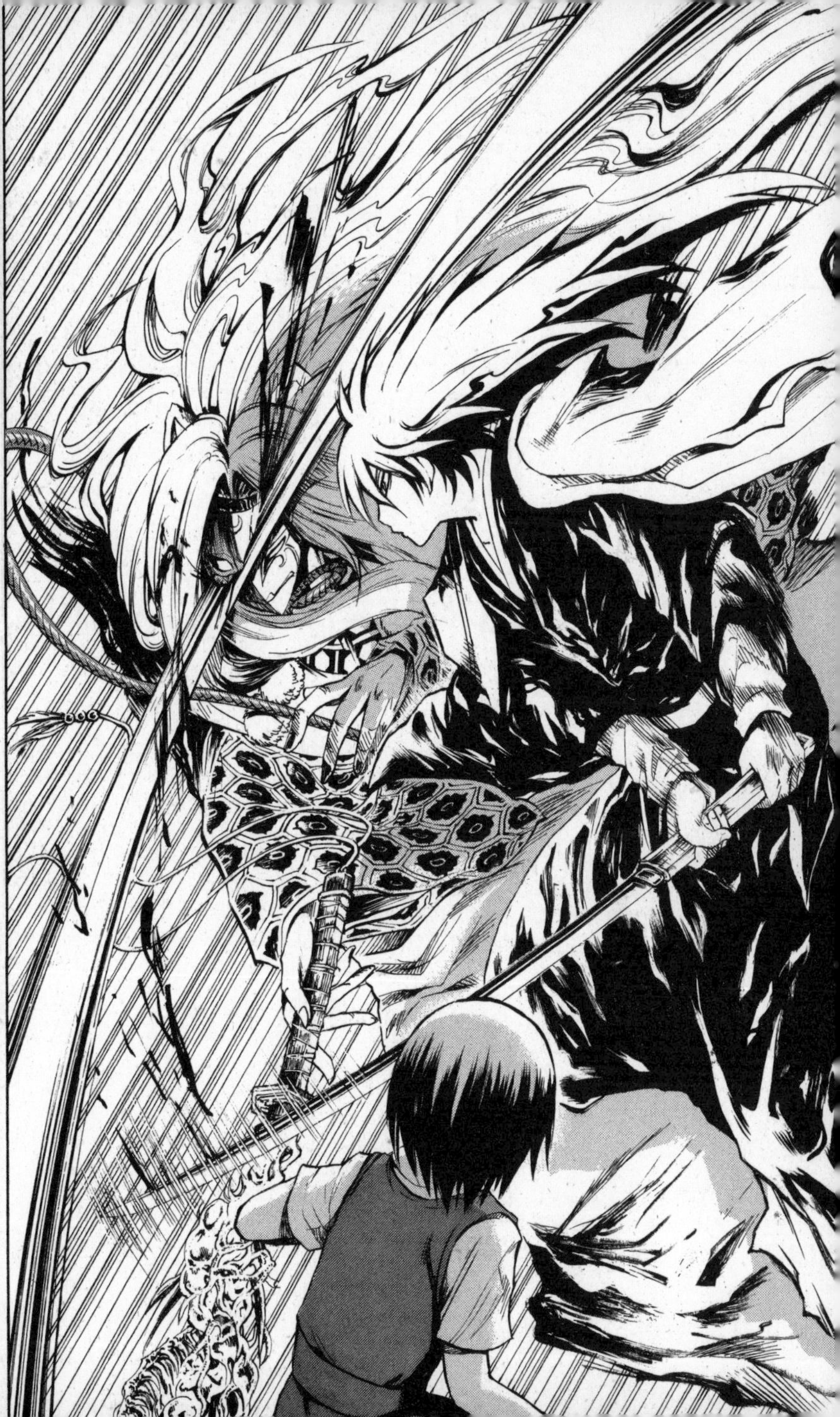

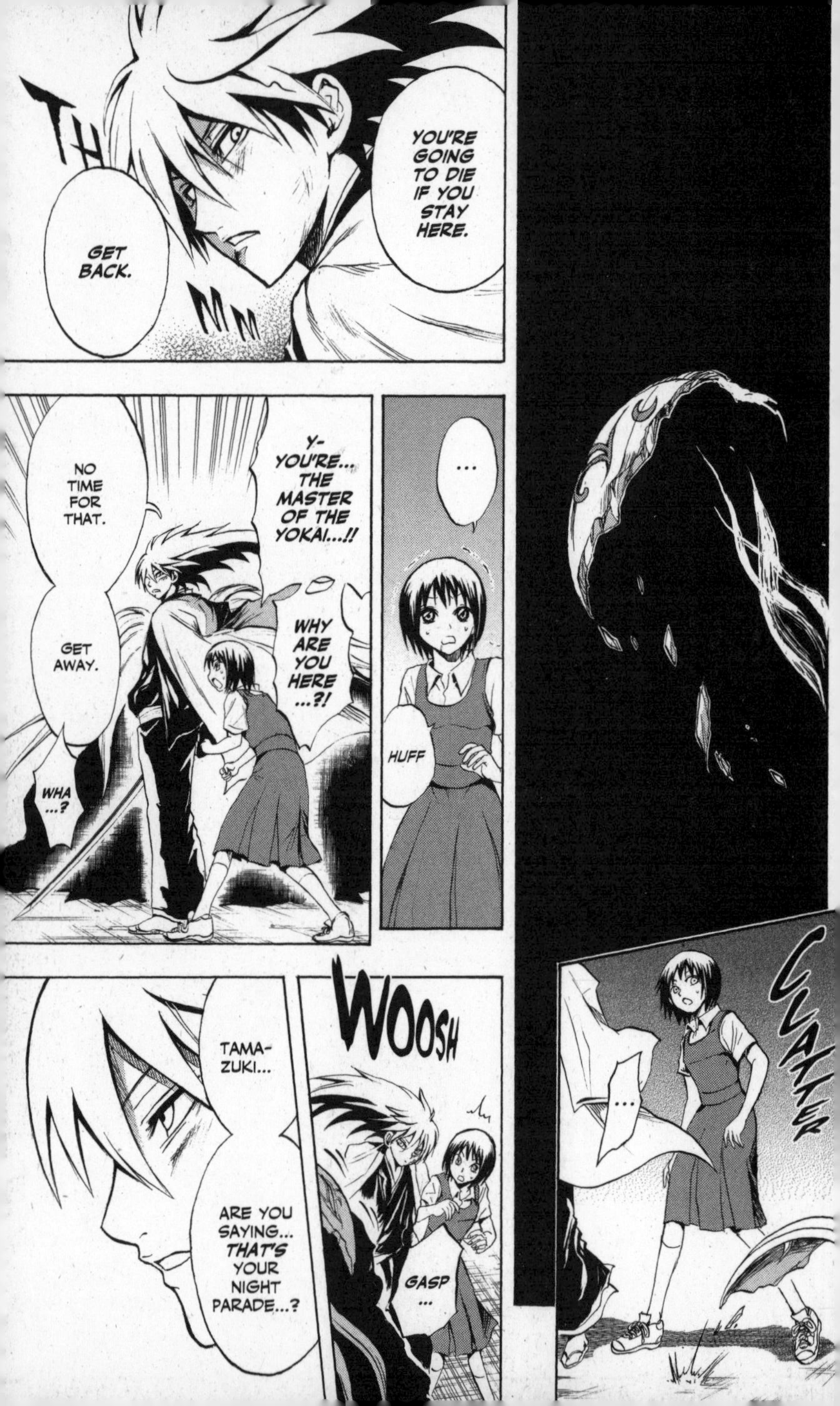

...
CLATTER
YOU'RE GOING TO DIE IF YOU STAY HERE.
TH
MM
GET BACK.
...
HUFF
Y- YOU'RE... THE MASTER OF THE YOKAI...!!
WHY ARE YOU HERE...?!
NO TIME FOR THAT.
GET AWAY.
WHA...?
WOOSH
GASP...
TAMA-ZUKI...
ARE YOU SAYING... THAT'S YOUR NIGHT PARADE...?

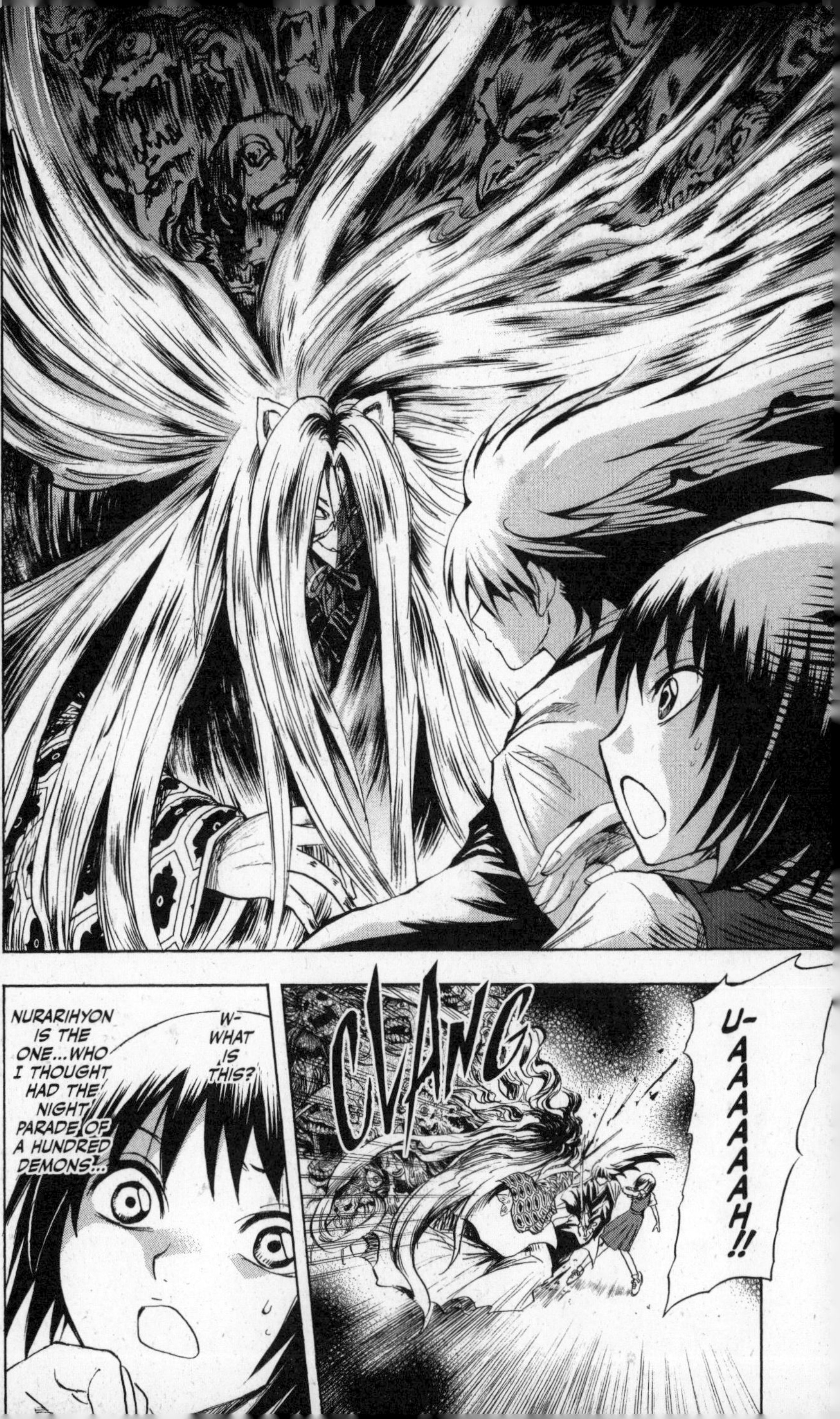
U-AAAAAAAH!!
CLANG
W-WHAT IS THIS?
NURARIHYON IS THE ONE...WHO I THOUGHT HAD THE NIGHT PARADE OF A HUNDRED DEMONS!...

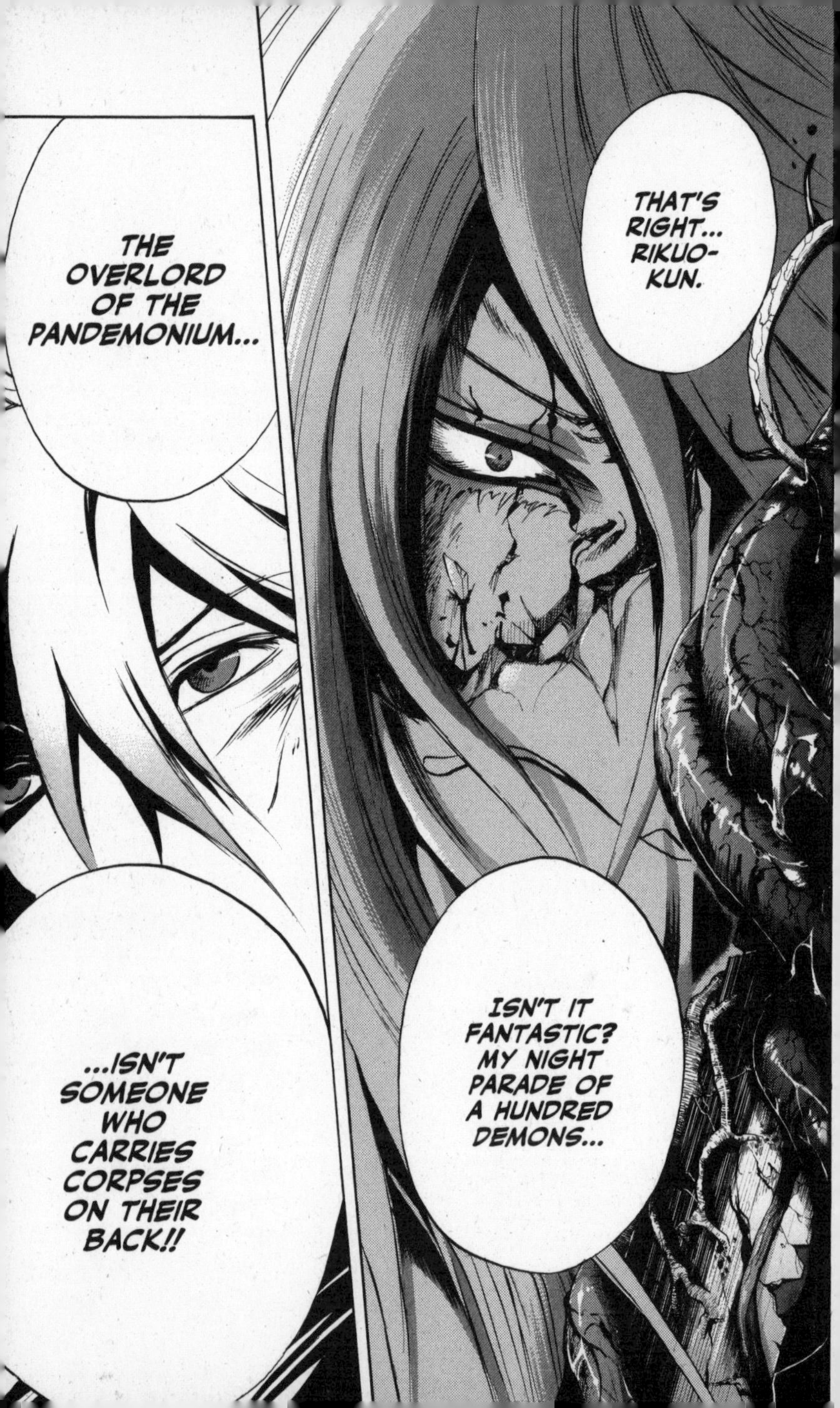
THAT'S RIGHT... RIKUO-KUN.
ISN'T IT FANTASTIC? MY NIGHT PARADE OF A HUNDRED DEMONS...
THE OVERLORD OF THE PANDEMONIUM...
...ISN'T SOMEONE WHO CARRIES CORPSES ON THEIR BACK!!

A Recollection

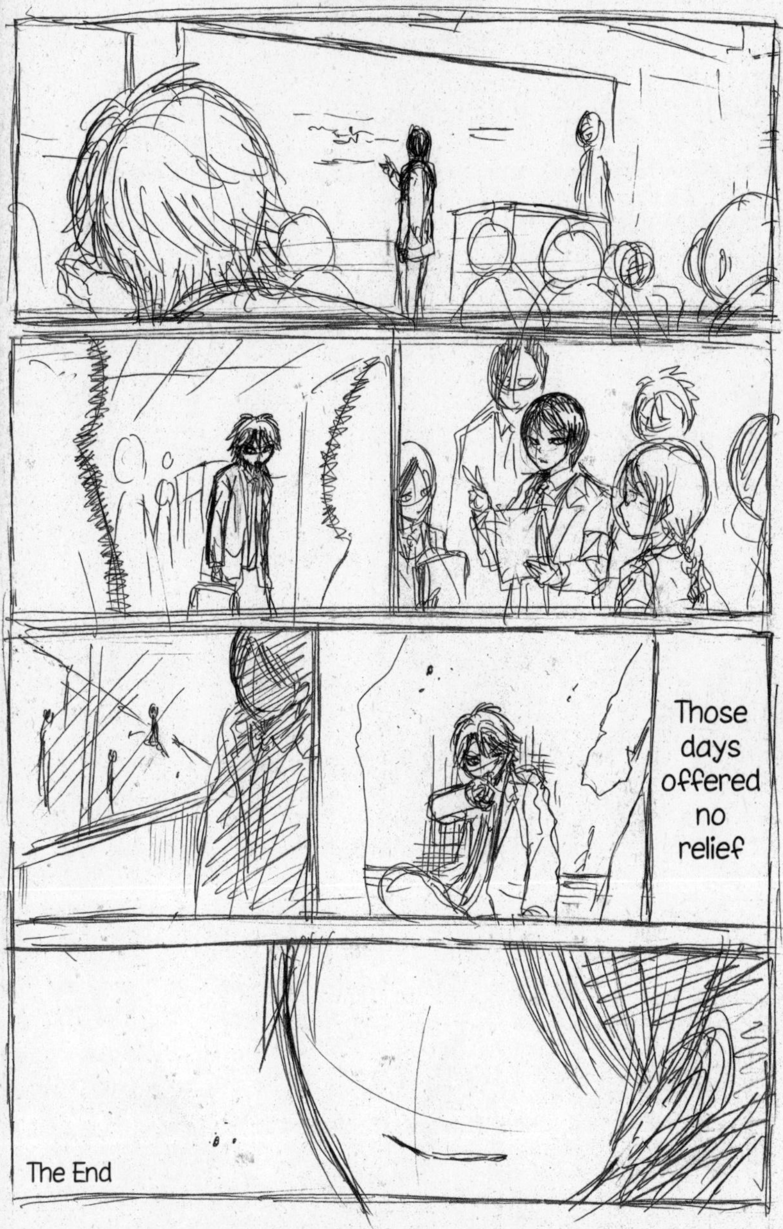
Those days offered no relief
The End

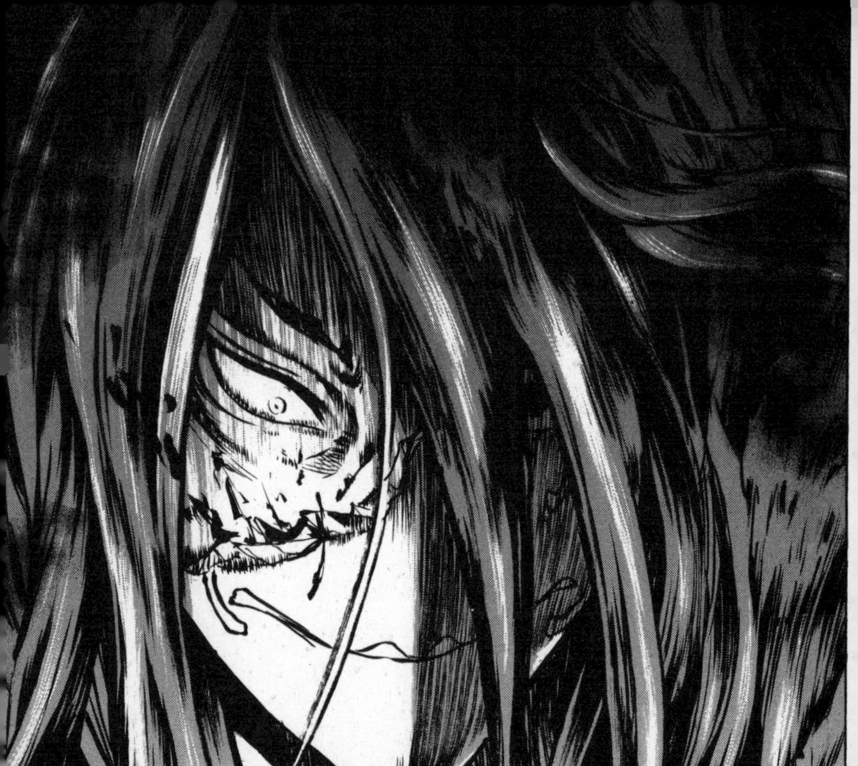
Act 46: Inugamigyobu-Tanuki Tamazuki

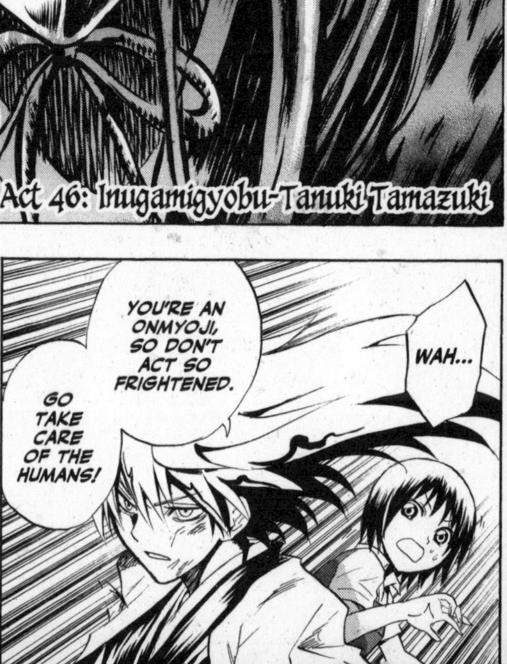
WAH...
YOU'RE AN ONMYOJI, SO DON'T ACT SO FRIGHTENED.
GO TAKE CARE OF THE HUMANS!

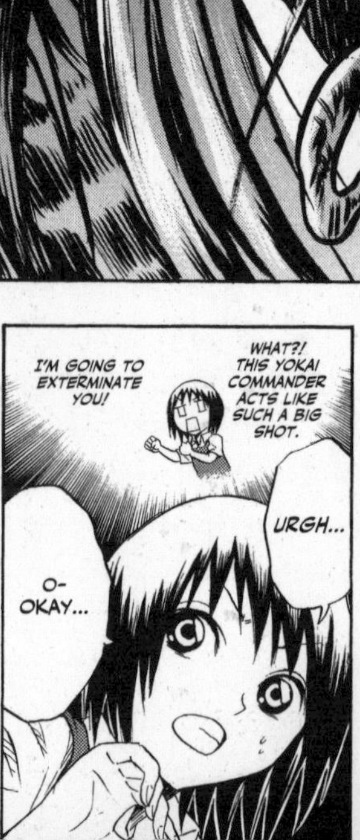
WHAT?! THIS YOKAI COMMANDER ACTS LIKE SUCH A BIG SHOT.
I'M GOING TO EXTERMINATE YOU!
URGH...
O-OKAY...

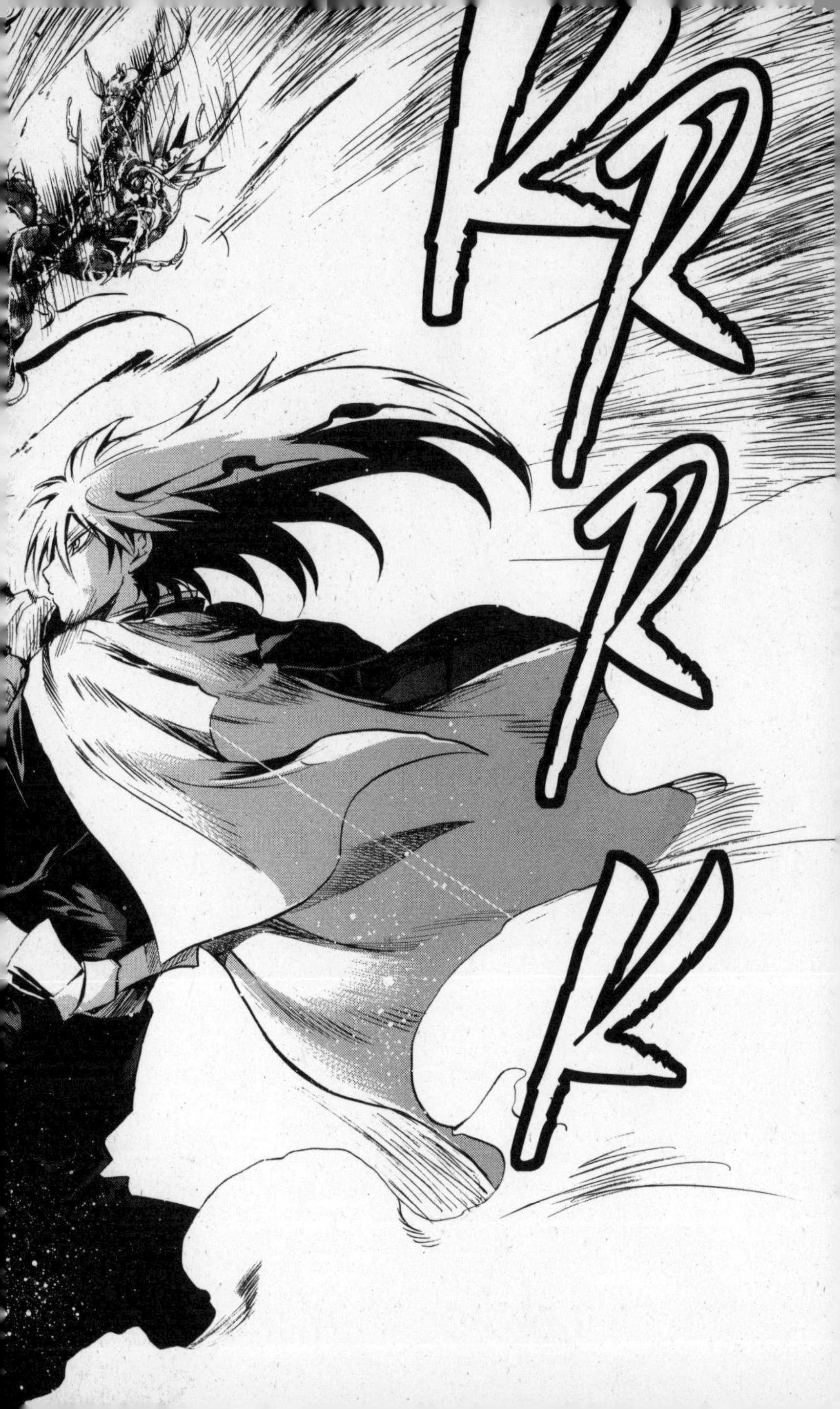
KRRK

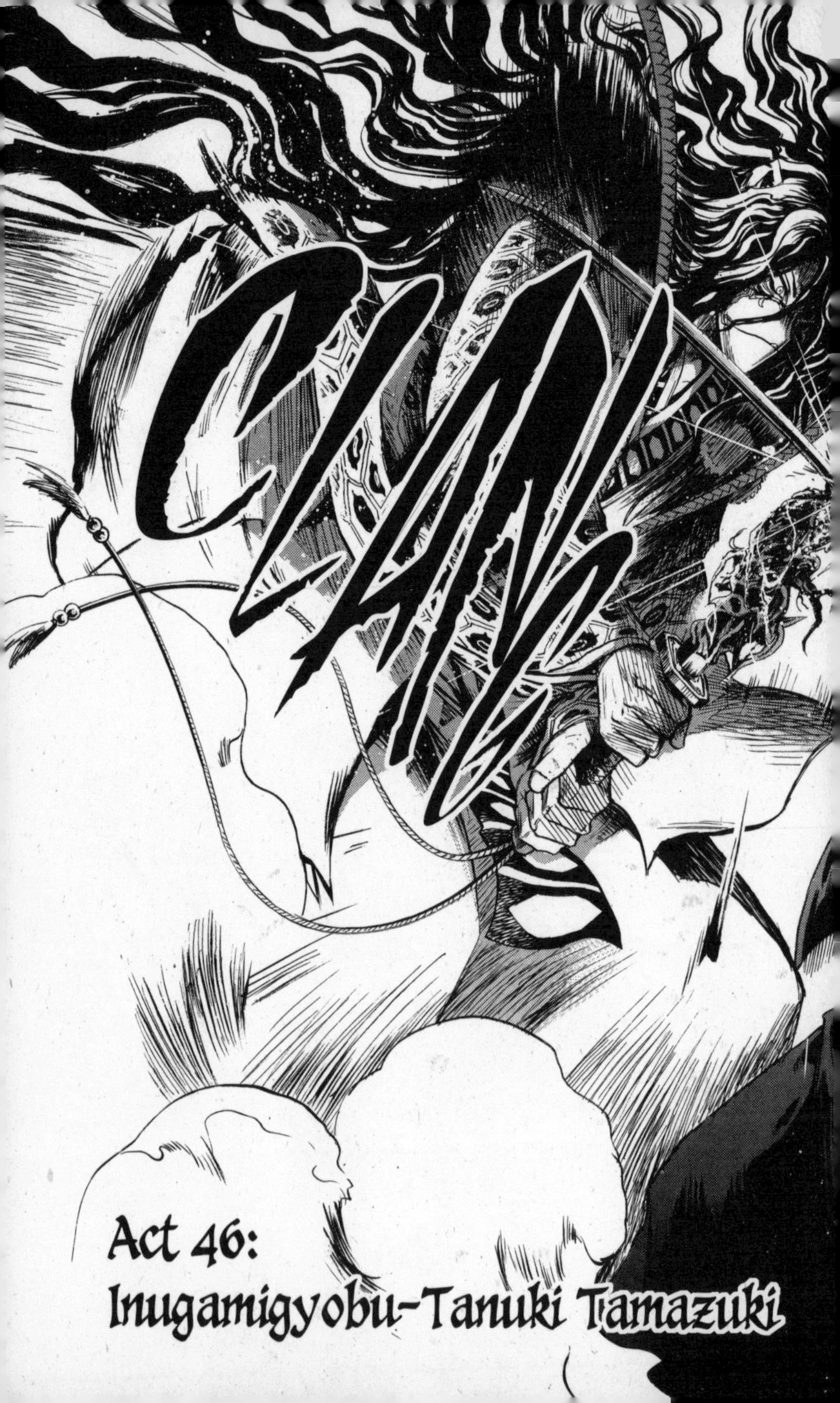

Act 46: Inugamigyobu-Tanuki Tamazuki

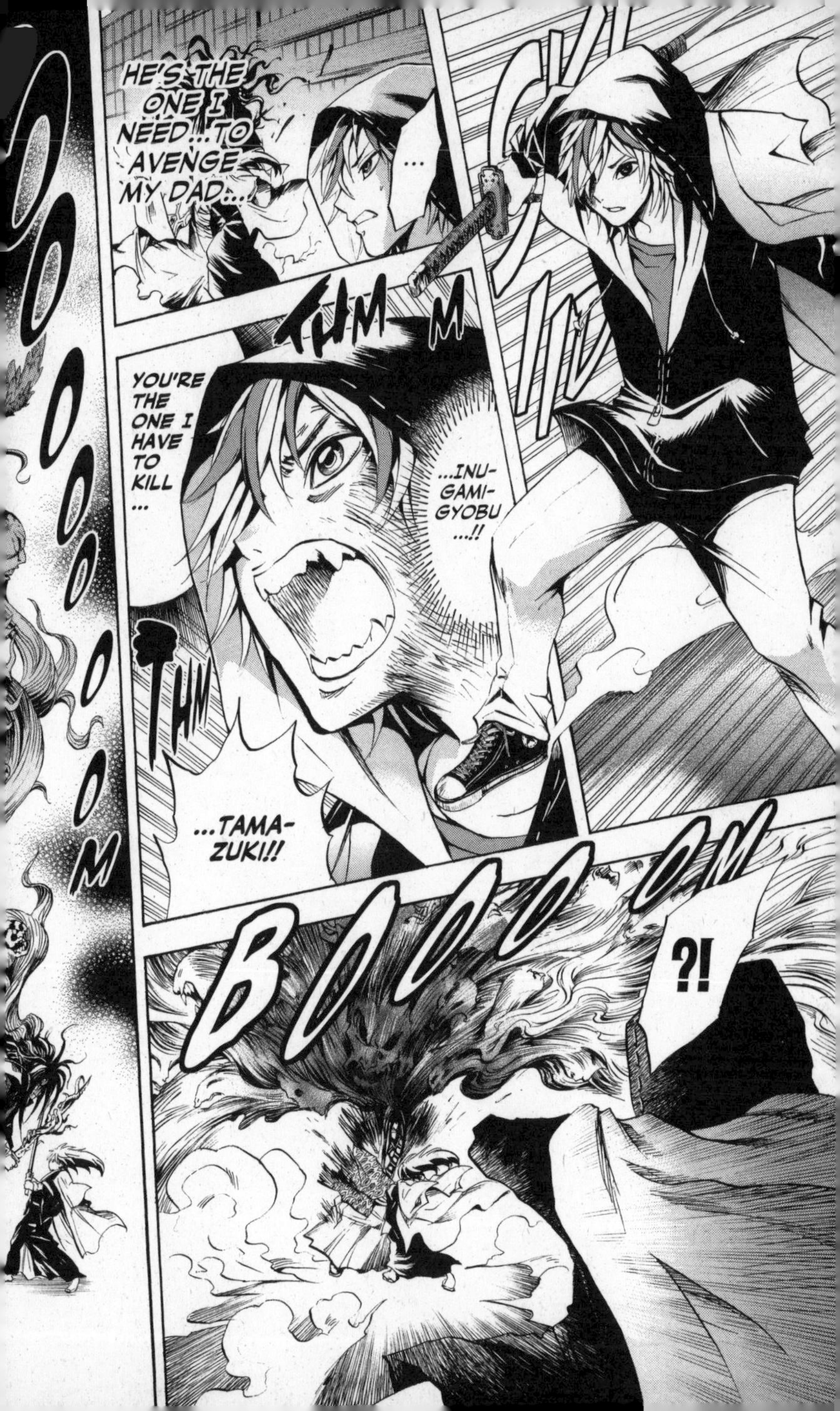
...
HE'S THE ONE I NEED...TO AVENGE MY DAD...
...INUGAMI-GYOBU...!!
THMM
YOU'RE THE ONE I HAVE TO KILL...
...TAMA-ZUKI!!
THM
GOOOOOOOOM
?!
BOOOOOM

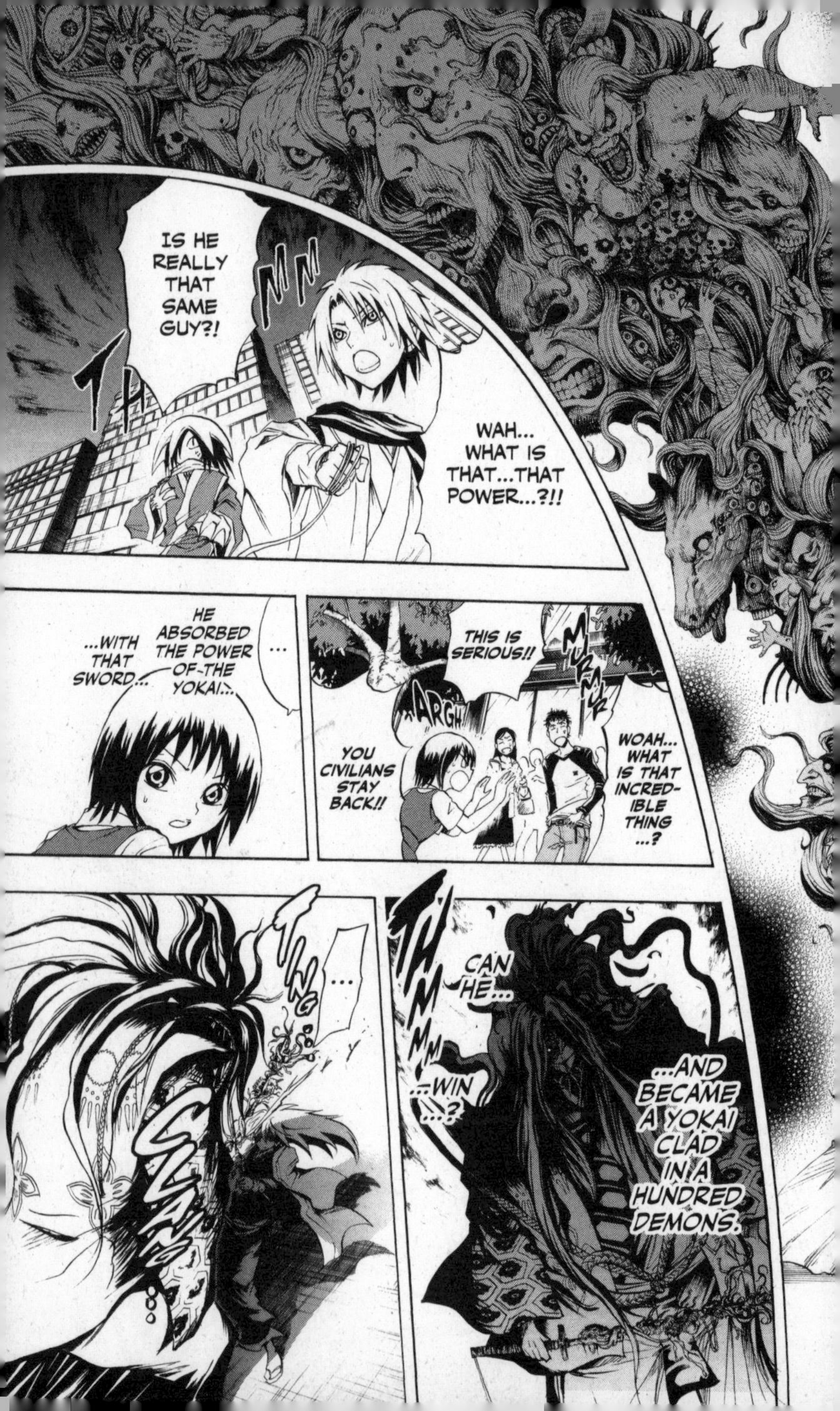
WAH... WHAT IS THAT...THAT POWER...?!!
IS HE REALLY THAT SAME GUY?!
THIS IS SERIOUS!!
MURMUR
ARGH
WOAH... WHAT IS THAT INCREDIBLE THING ...?
YOU CIVILIANS STAY BACK!!
...
HE ABSORBED THE POWER OF THE YOKAI...
...WITH THAT SWORD...
...AND BECAME A YOKAI CLAD IN A HUNDRED DEMONS.
CAN HE...
...WIN ...?
...

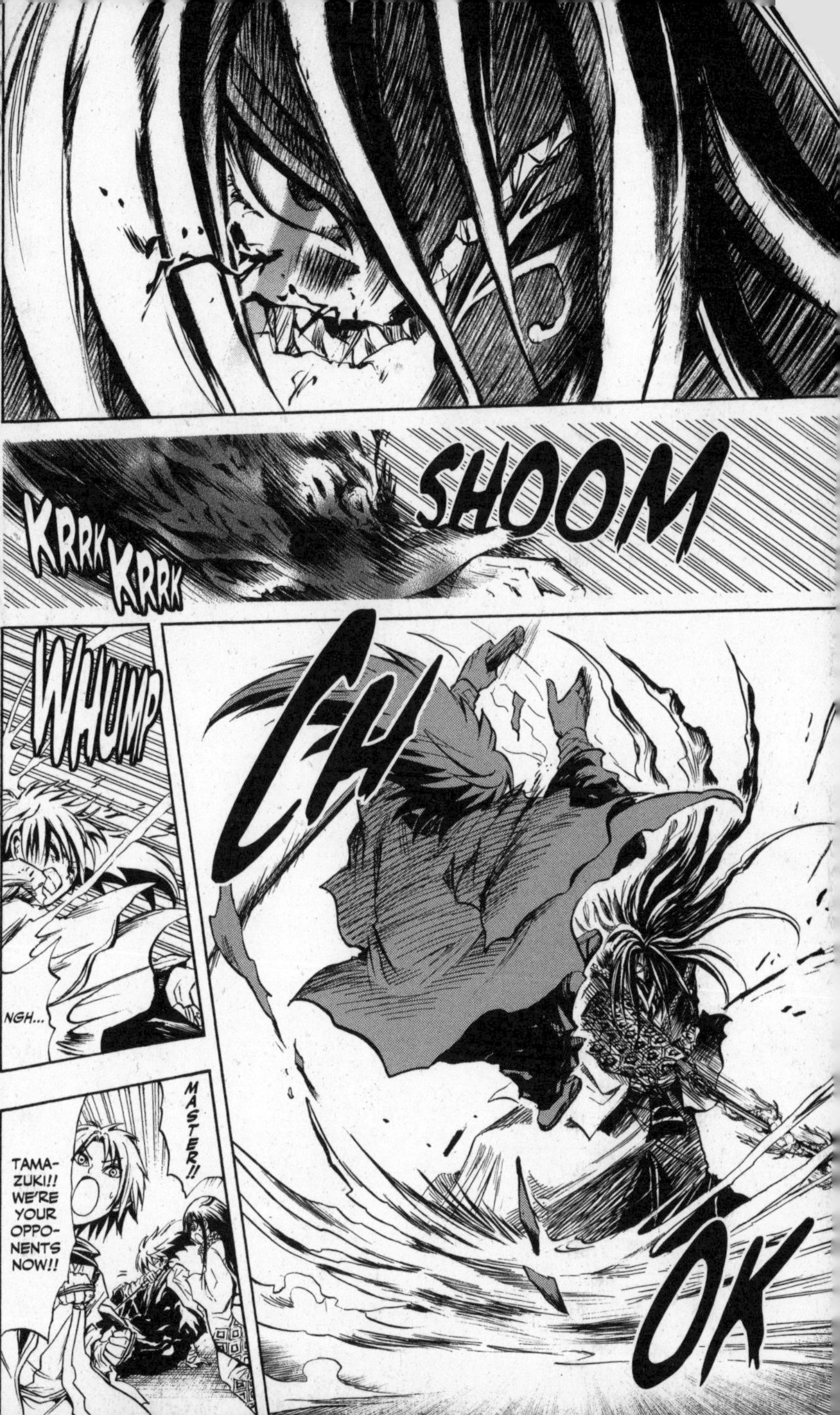
SHOOM
KRRK KRRK
CH
O-K
WHUMP
NGH...
MASTER!!
TAMA-ZUKI!! WE'RE YOUR OPPO-NENTS NOW!!

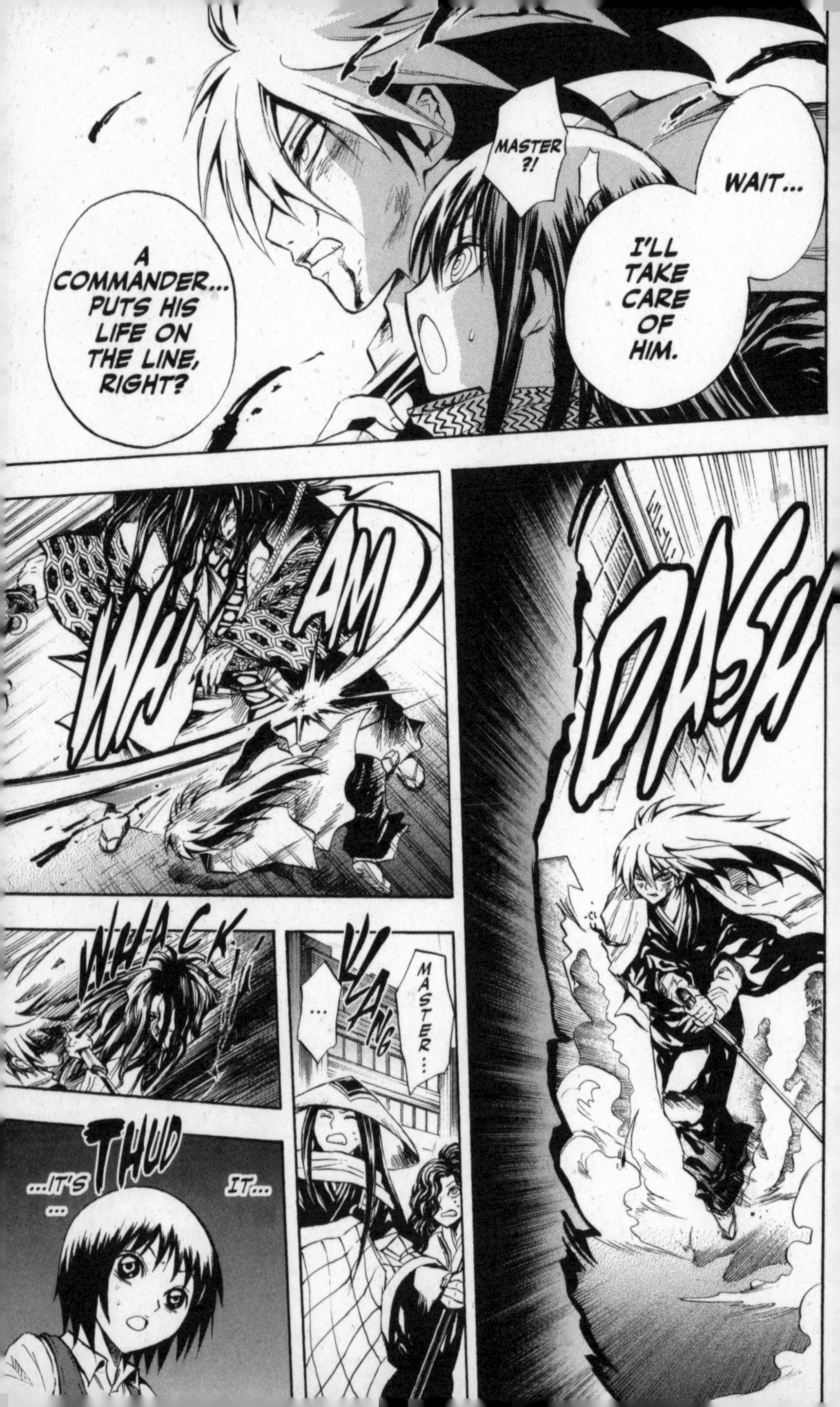
WAIT...
I'LL TAKE CARE OF HIM.
MASTER?!
A COMMANDER... PUTS HIS LIFE ON THE LINE, RIGHT?
DASH
WHAM
KLANG
MASTER...
...
WHACK
THUD
IT...
...IT'S ...

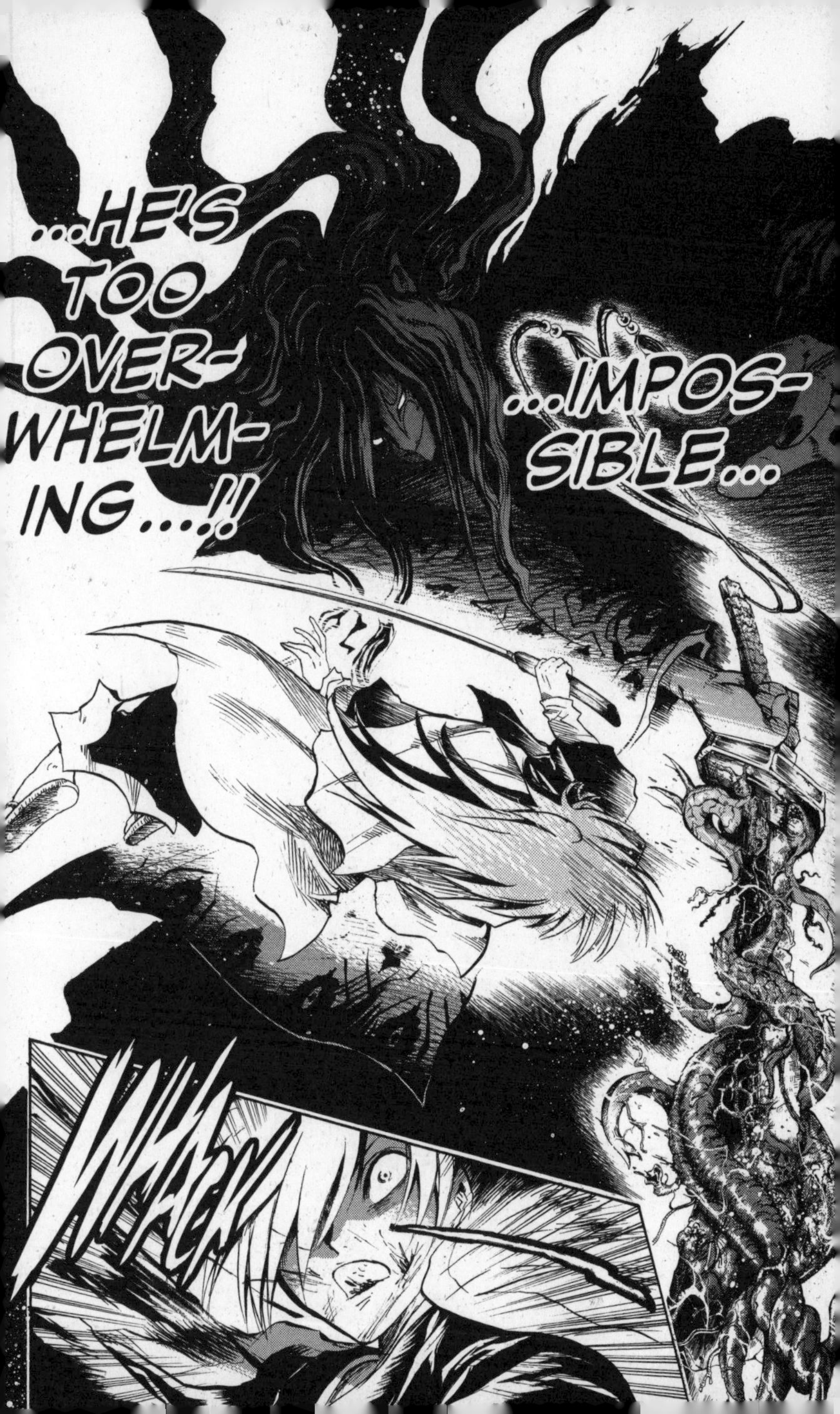
...IMPOS-
SIBLE...
...HE'S
TOO
OVER-
WHELM-
ING...!!
WHACK

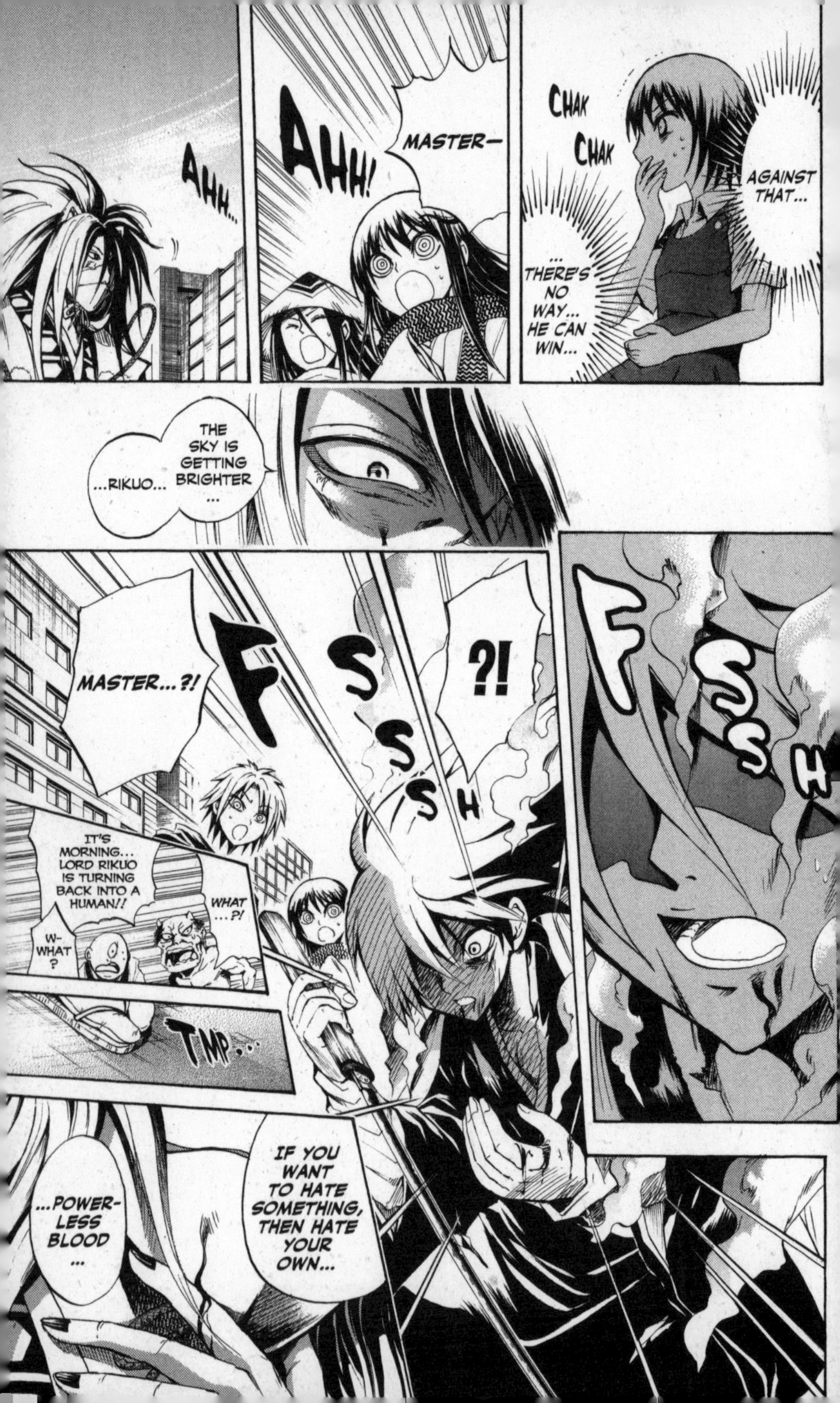
AGAINST THAT...
CHAK
CHAK
...THERE'S NO WAY... HE CAN WIN...
MASTER—
AHHH!
AHH...
THE SKY IS GETTING BRIGHTER...
...RIKUO...
FSSSH
?!
FSSSH
MASTER...?!
IT'S MORNING... LORD RIKUO IS TURNING BACK INTO A HUMAN!!
WHAT...?!
W-WHAT?
TMP...
IF YOU WANT TO HATE SOMETHING, THEN HATE YOUR OWN...
...POWER-LESS BLOOD...

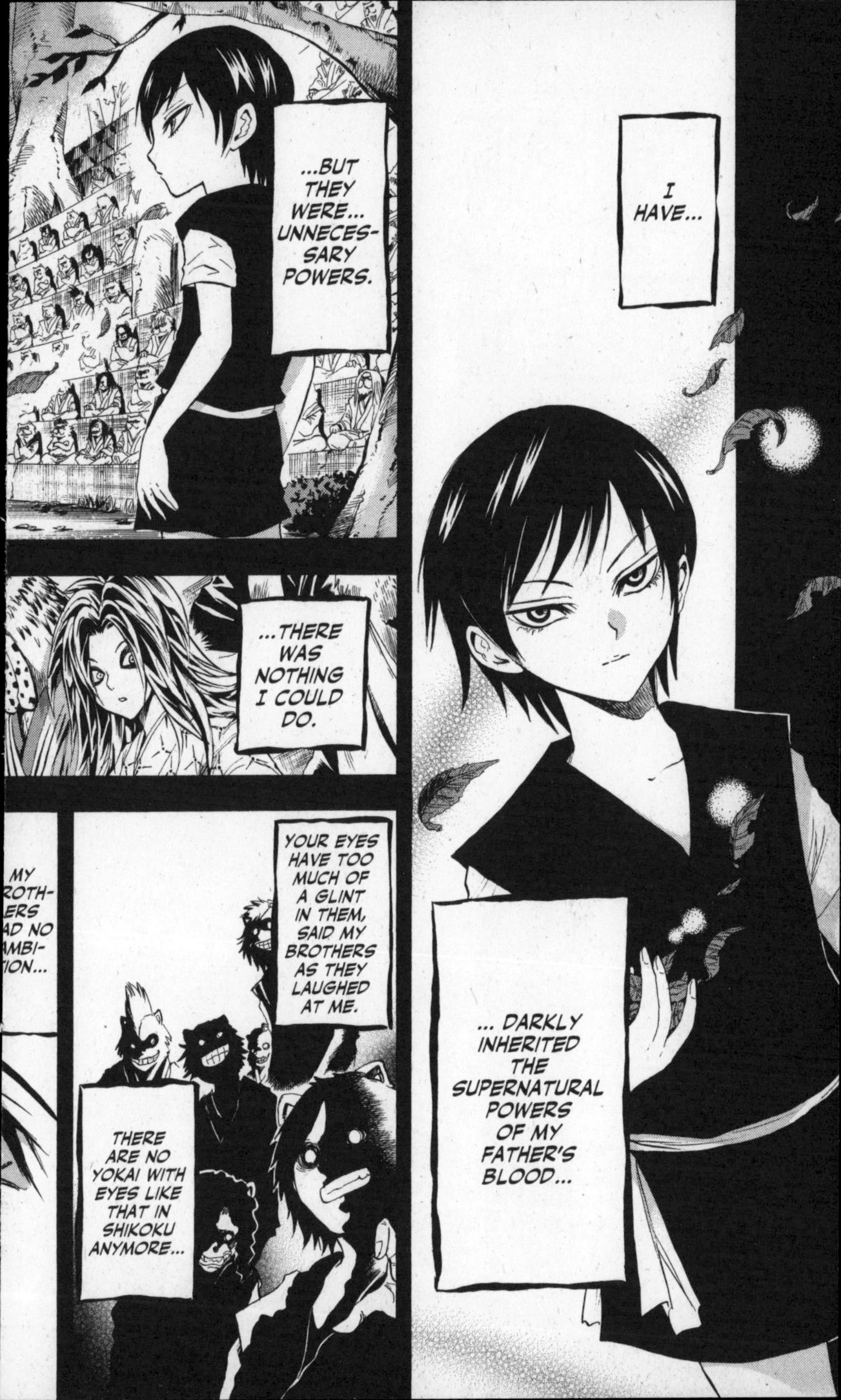
I HAVE...
... DARKLY INHERITED THE SUPERNATURAL POWERS OF MY FATHER'S BLOOD...
...BUT THEY WERE... UNNECES-SARY POWERS.
...THERE WAS NOTHING I COULD DO.
YOUR EYES HAVE TOO MUCH OF A GLINT IN THEM, SAID MY BROTHERS AS THEY LAUGHED AT ME.
THERE ARE NO YOKAI WITH EYES LIKE THAT IN SHIKOKU ANYMORE...
MY ROTH-ERS AD NO AMBI-ION...

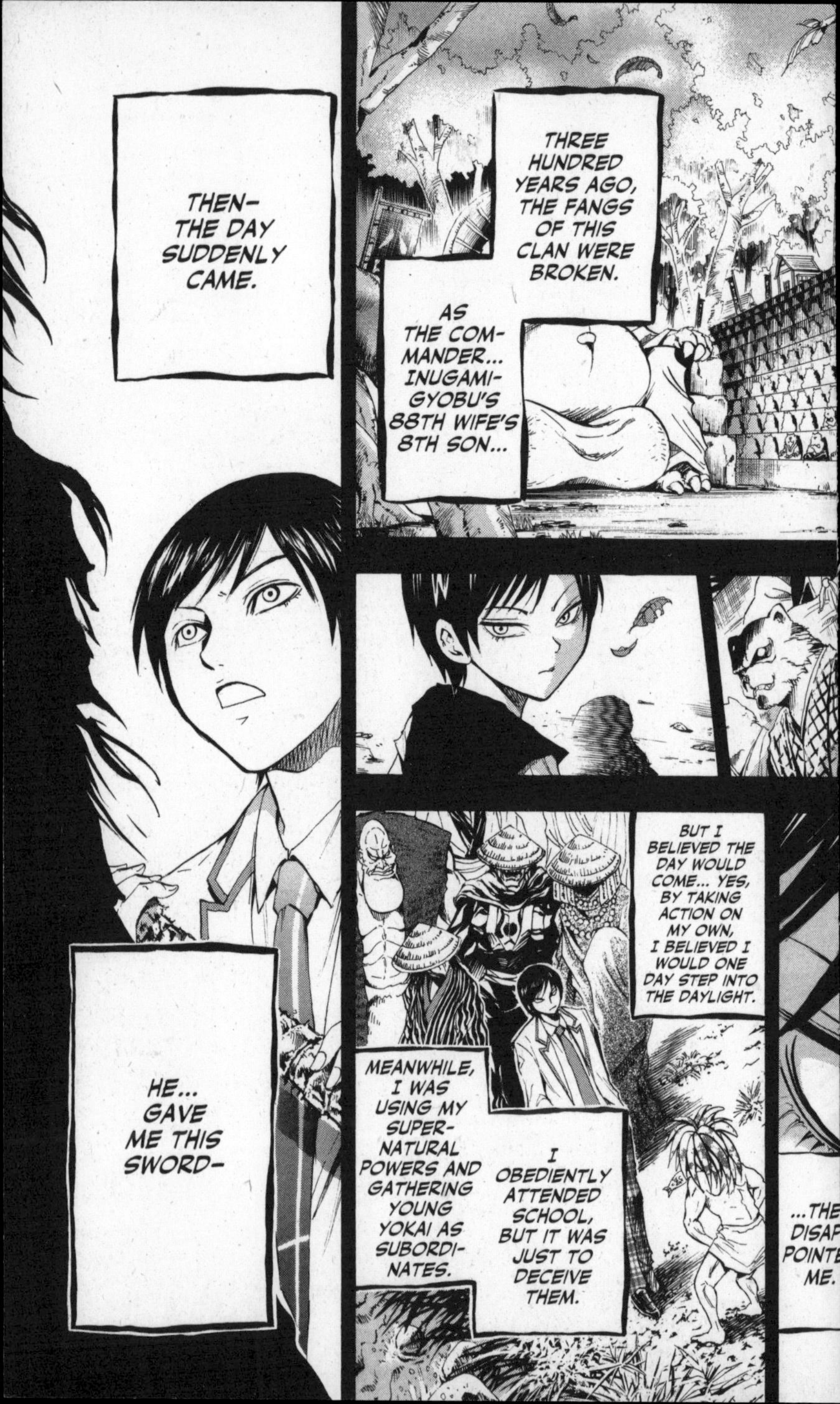
THREE HUNDRED YEARS AGO, THE FANGS OF THIS CLAN WERE BROKEN.
AS THE COMMANDER... INUGAMI-GYOBU'S 88TH WIFE'S 8TH SON...
...THE DISAP POINTE ME.
BUT I BELIEVED THE DAY WOULD COME... YES, BY TAKING ACTION ON MY OWN, I BELIEVED I WOULD ONE DAY STEP INTO THE DAYLIGHT.
I OBEDIENTLY ATTENDED SCHOOL, BUT IT WAS JUST TO DECEIVE THEM.
MEANWHILE, I WAS USING MY SUPERNATURAL POWERS AND GATHERING YOUNG YOKAI AS SUBORDINATES.
THEN- THE DAY SUDDENLY CAME.
HE... GAVE ME THIS SWORD-

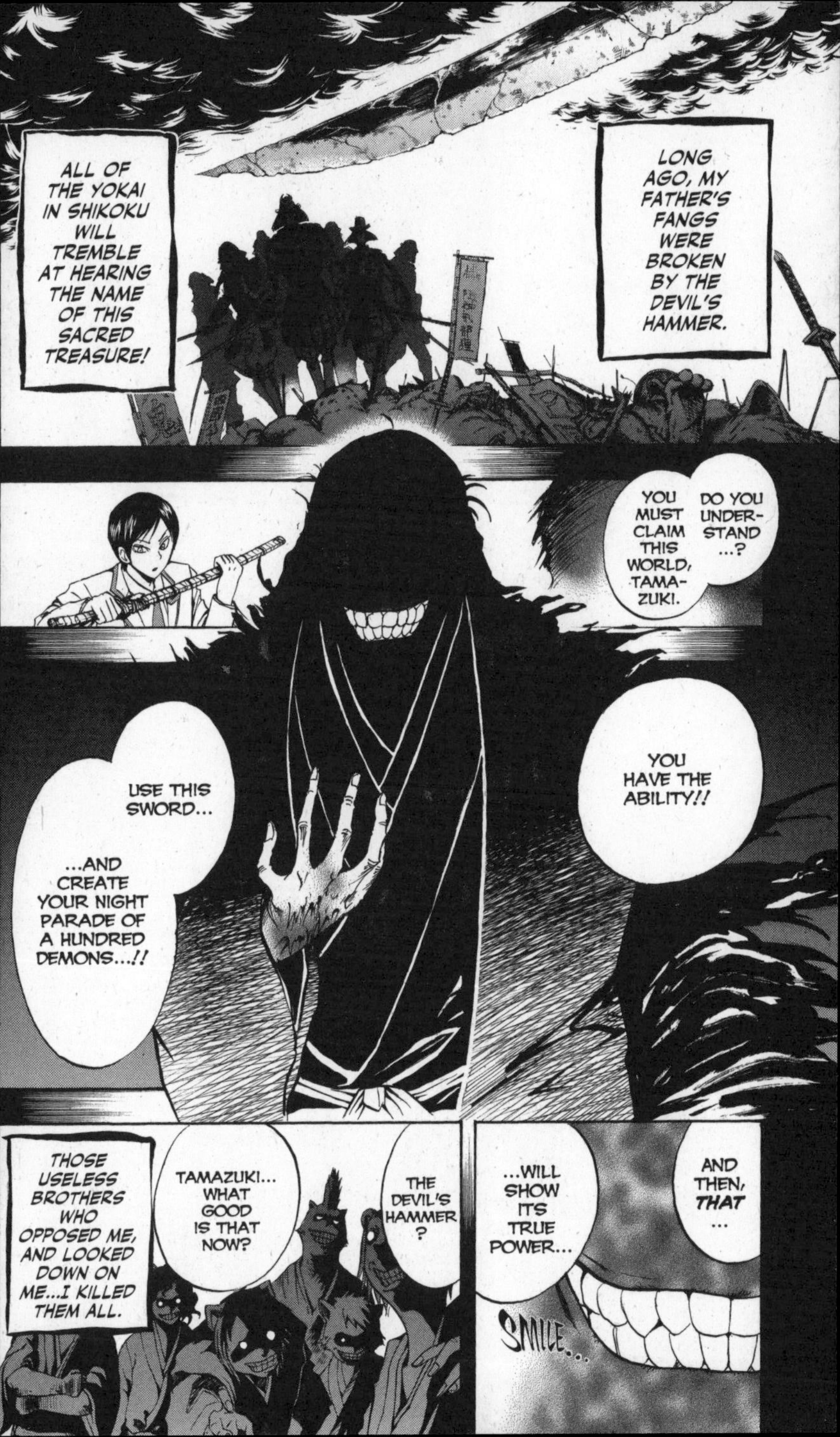
LONG AGO, MY FATHER'S FANGS WERE BROKEN BY THE DEVIL'S HAMMER.
ALL OF THE YOKAI IN SHIKOKU WILL TREMBLE AT HEARING THE NAME OF THIS SACRED TREASURE!
DO YOU UNDERSTAND ...?
YOU MUST CLAIM THIS WORLD, TAMAZUKI.
YOU HAVE THE ABILITY!!
USE THIS SWORD...
...AND CREATE YOUR NIGHT PARADE OF A HUNDRED DEMONS...!!
AND THEN, *THAT* ...
...WILL SHOW ITS TRUE POWER...
SMILE...
THE DEVIL'S HAMMER?
TAMAZUKI... WHAT GOOD IS THAT NOW?
THOSE USELESS BROTHERS WHO OPPOSED ME, AND LOOKED DOWN ON ME...I KILLED THEM ALL.

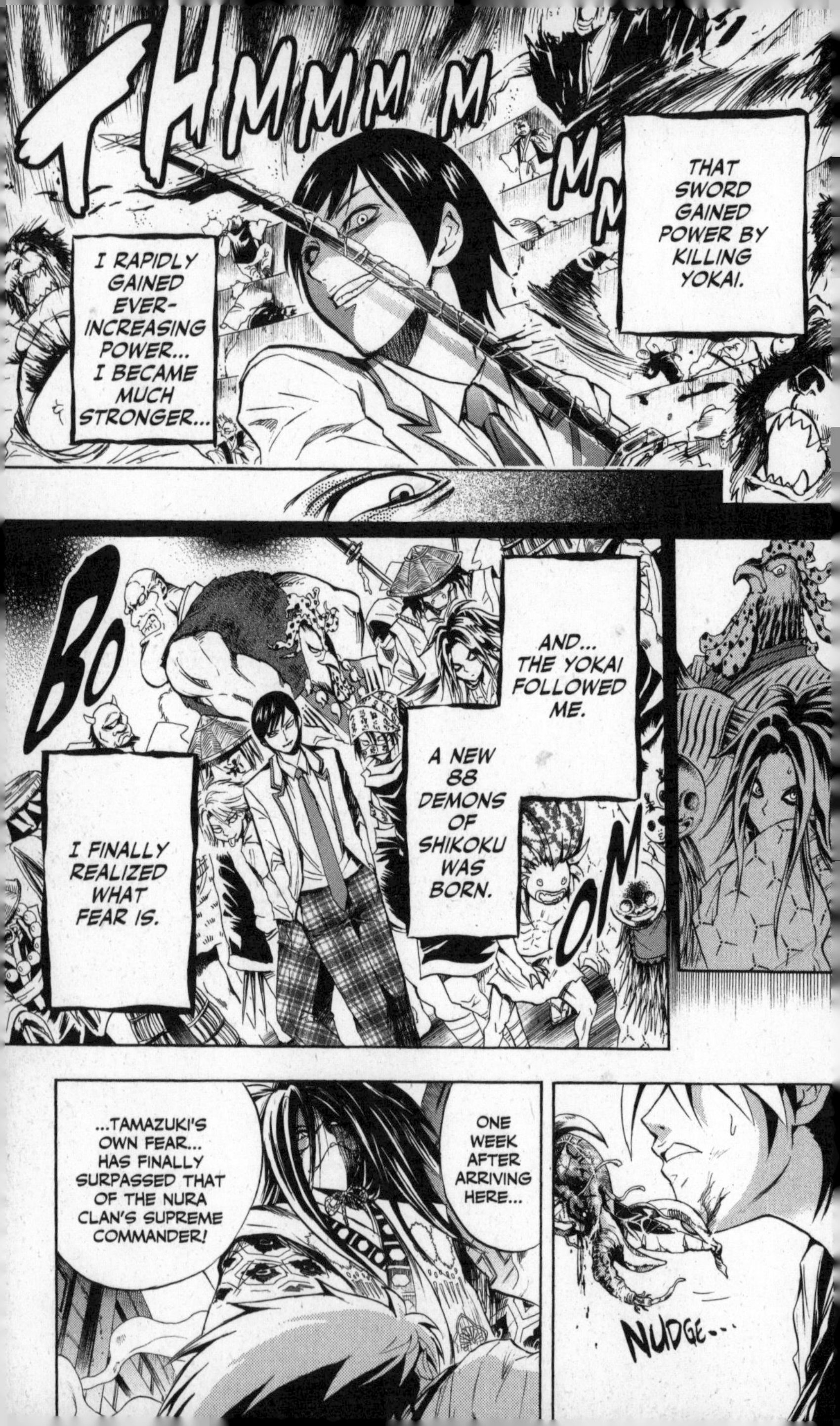

THMMMM MMM
THAT SWORD GAINED POWER BY KILLING YOKAI.
I RAPIDLY GAINED EVER-INCREASING POWER... I BECAME MUCH STRONGER...
AND... THE YOKAI FOLLOWED ME.
A NEW 88 DEMONS OF SHIKOKU WAS BORN.
BOOM
I FINALLY REALIZED WHAT FEAR IS.
NUDGE...
ONE WEEK AFTER ARRIVING HERE...
...TAMAZUKI'S OWN FEAR... HAS FINALLY SURPASSED THAT OF THE NURA CLAN'S SUPREME COMMANDER!

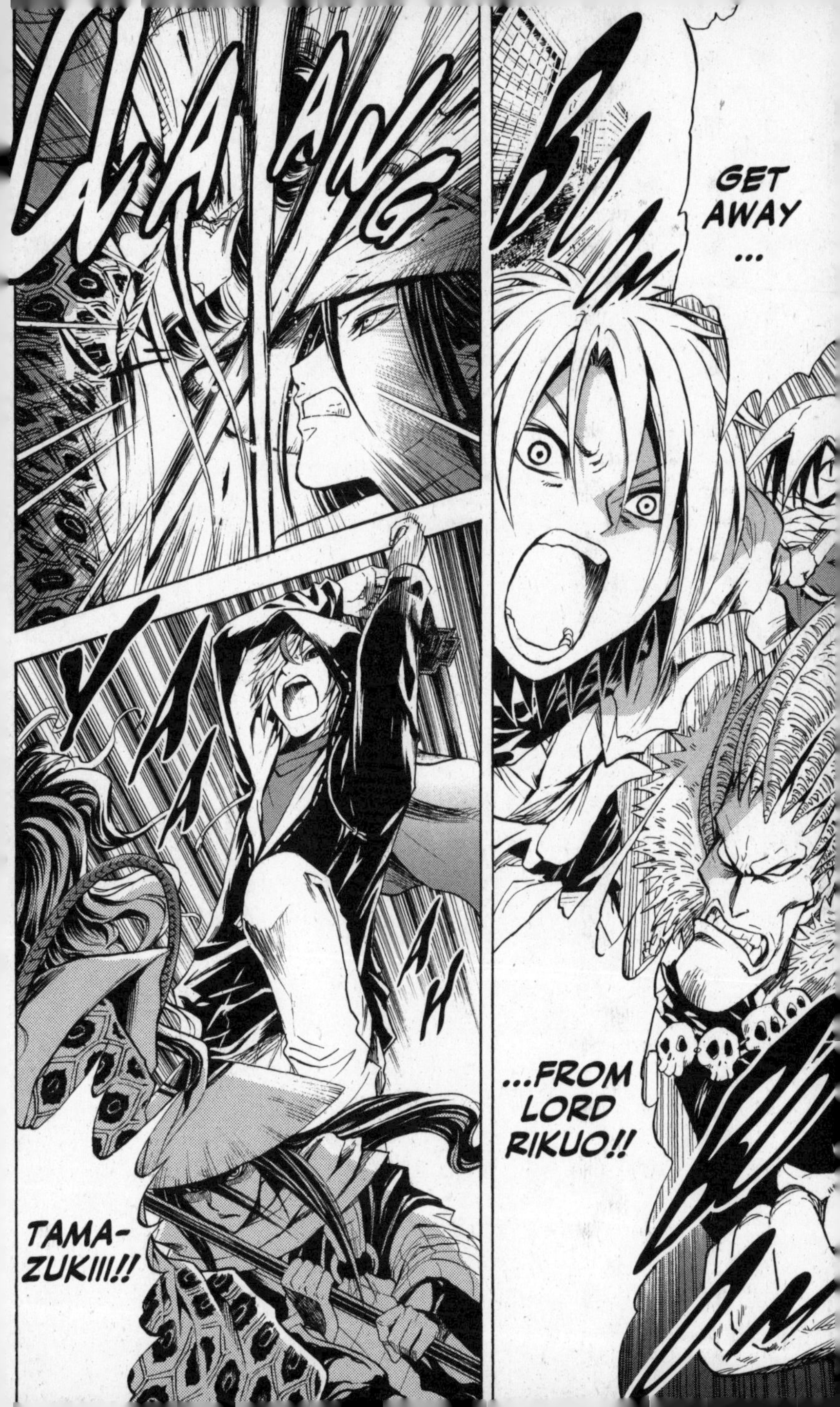
GET AWAY ...
...FROM LORD RIKUO!!
TAMA-ZUKIIII!!

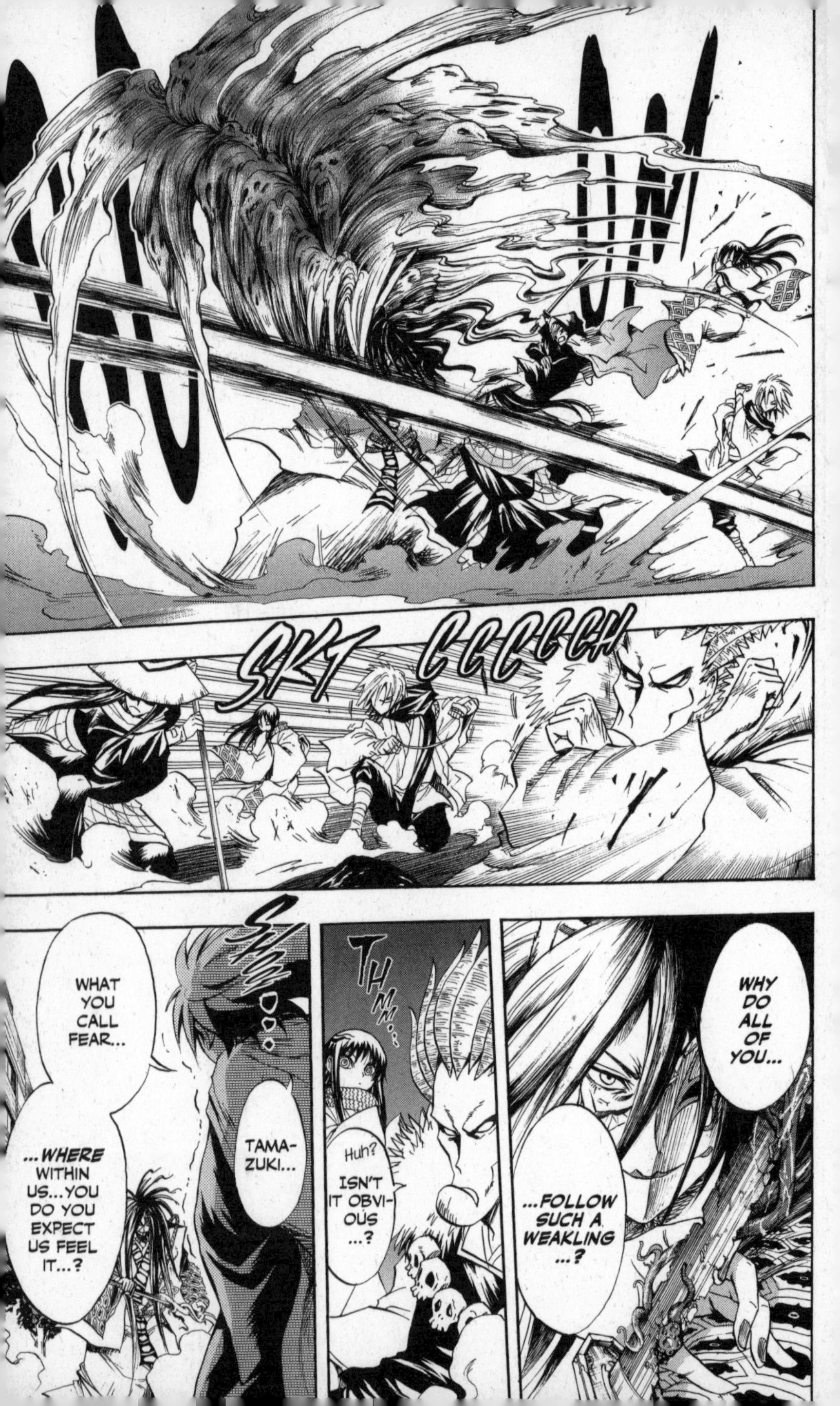

WHY DO ALL OF YOU...
...FOLLOW SUCH A WEAKLING ...?
THMM...
TAMA-ZUKI...
Huh? ISN'T IT OBVIOUS ...?
WHAT YOU CALL FEAR...
...WHERE WITHIN US...YOU DO YOU EXPECT US FEEL IT...?

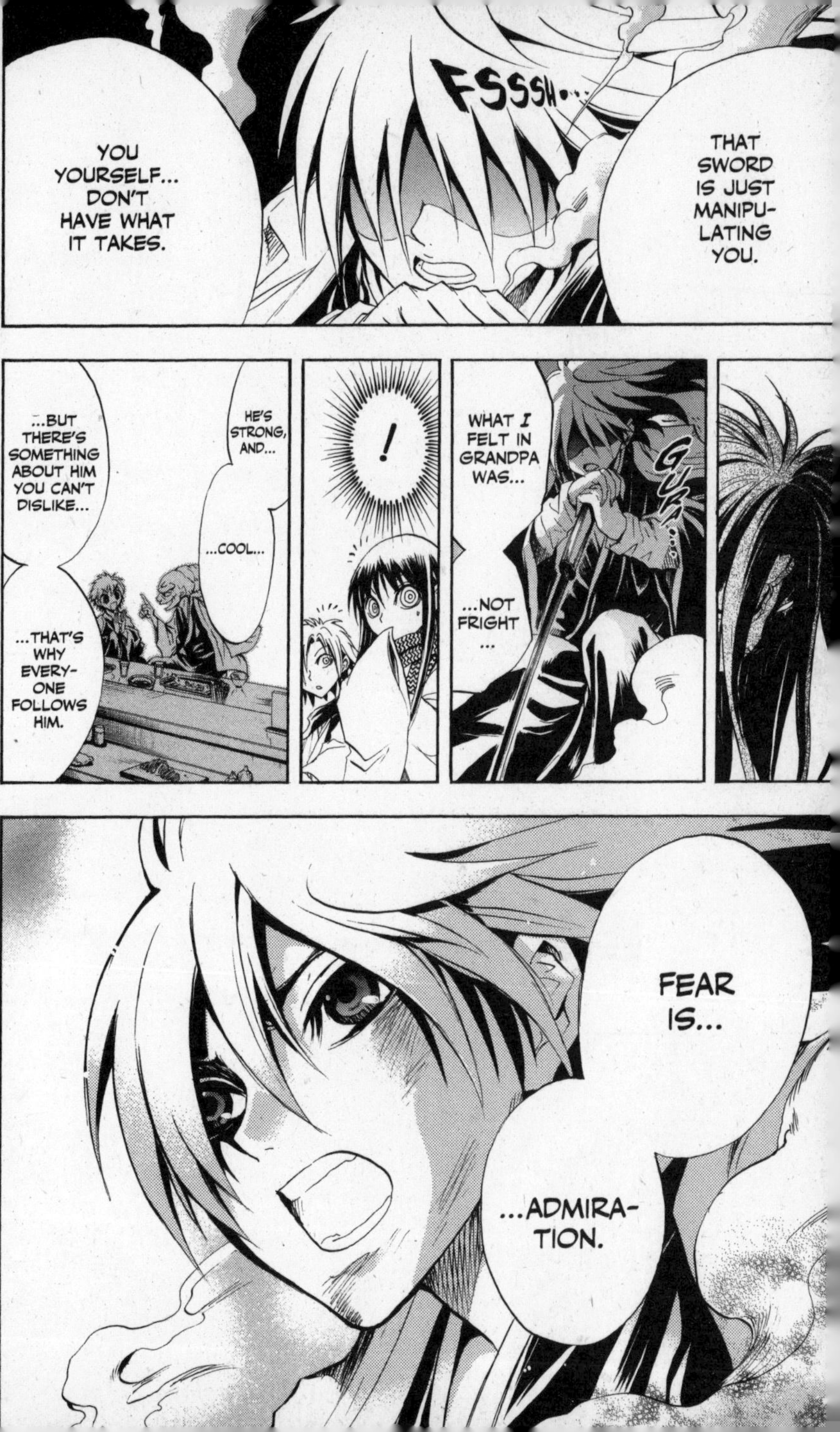
FSSSH...
THAT SWORD IS JUST MANIPU-LATING YOU.
YOU YOURSELF... DON'T HAVE WHAT IT TAKES.
WHAT I FELT IN GRANDPA WAS...
...NOT FRIGHT ...
!
HE'S STRONG, AND...
...COOL...
...BUT THERE'S SOMETHING ABOUT HIM YOU CAN'T DISLIKE...
...THAT'S WHY EVERY-ONE FOLLOWS HIM.
FEAR IS...
...ADMIRA-TION.

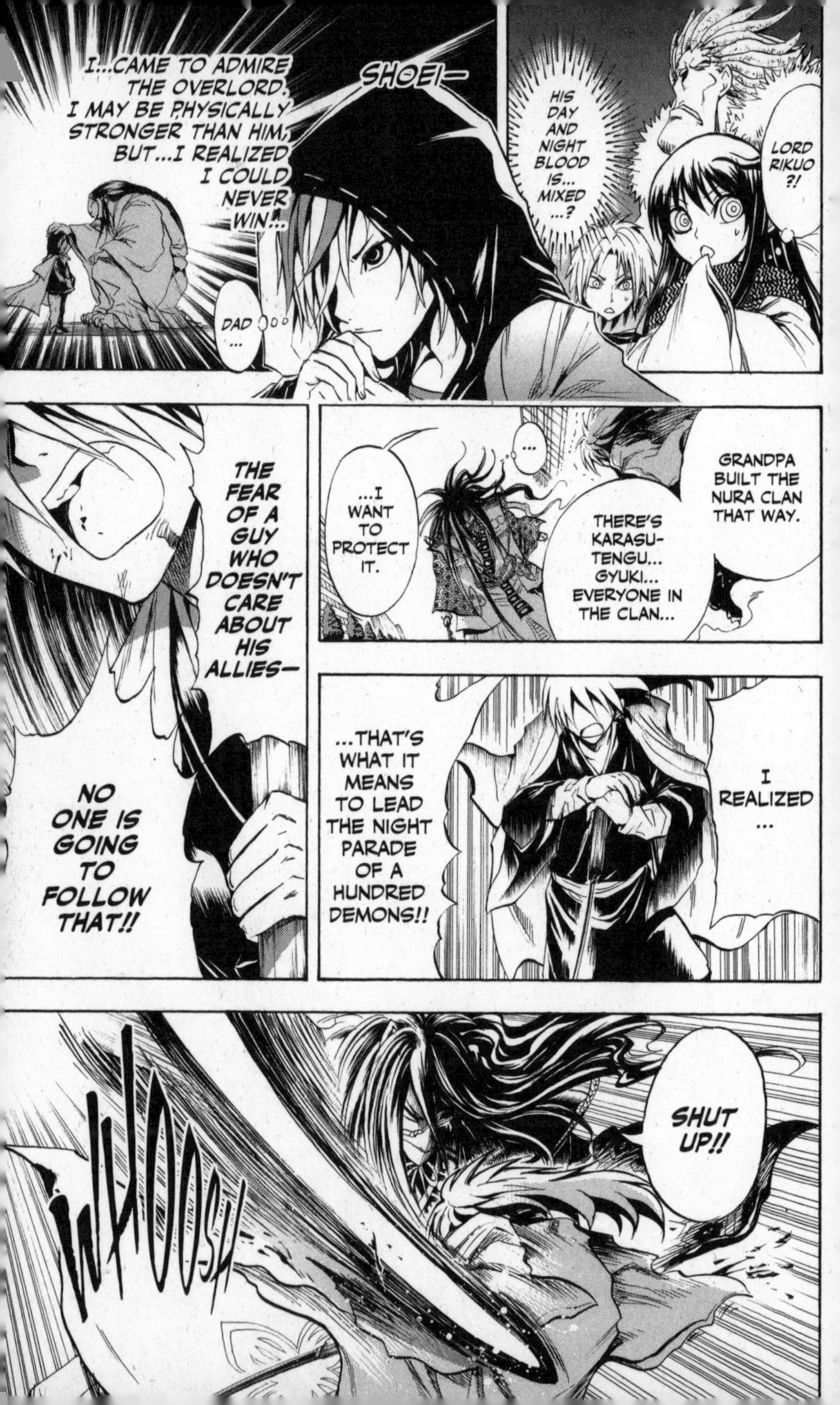
LORD RIKUO?!
HIS DAY AND NIGHT BLOOD IS... MIXED...?
SHOEI—
I...CAME TO ADMIRE THE OVERLORD. I MAY BE PHYSICALLY STRONGER THAN HIM, BUT...I REALIZED I COULD NEVER WIN...
DAD...
GRANDPA BUILT THE NURA CLAN THAT WAY.
THERE'S KARASU-TENGU... GYUKI... EVERYONE IN THE CLAN...
...
...I WANT TO PROTECT IT.
I REALIZED...
...THAT'S WHAT IT MEANS TO LEAD THE NIGHT PARADE OF A HUNDRED DEMONS!!
THE FEAR OF A GUY WHO DOESN'T CARE ABOUT HIS ALLIES—
NO ONE IS GOING TO FOLLOW THAT!!
SHUT UP!!
WHOOSH

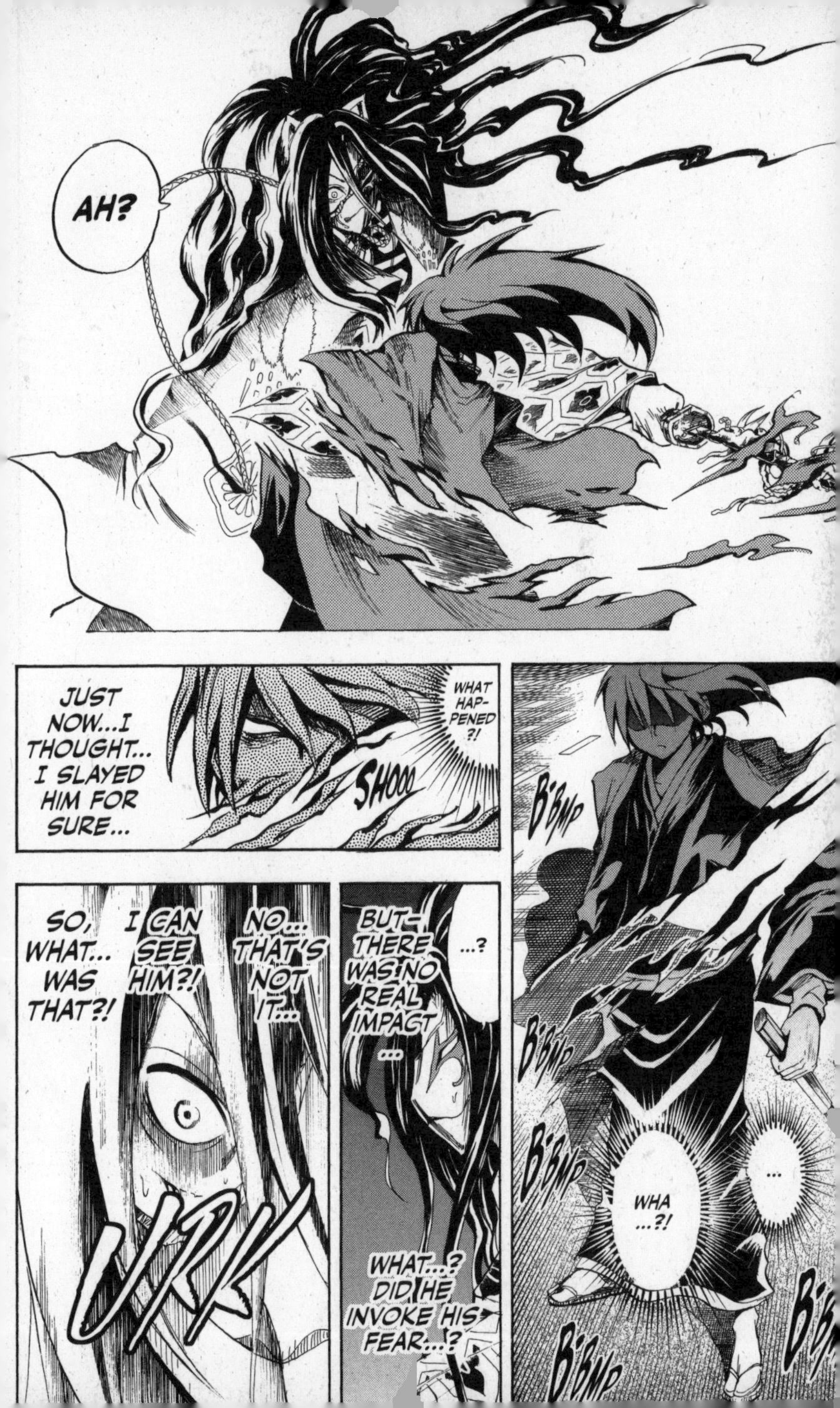

AH?
B'BMP
B'BMP
B'BMP
...
WHA ...?!
B'BMP
B'BMP
WHAT HAP-PENED ?!
JUST NOW...I THOUGHT... I SLAYED HIM FOR SURE...
SHOOO
...?
BUT-THERE WAS NO REAL IMPACT ...
WHAT...? DID HE INVOKE HIS FEAR...?
NO... THAT'S NOT IT...
I CAN SEE HIM?!
SO, WHAT... WAS THAT?!

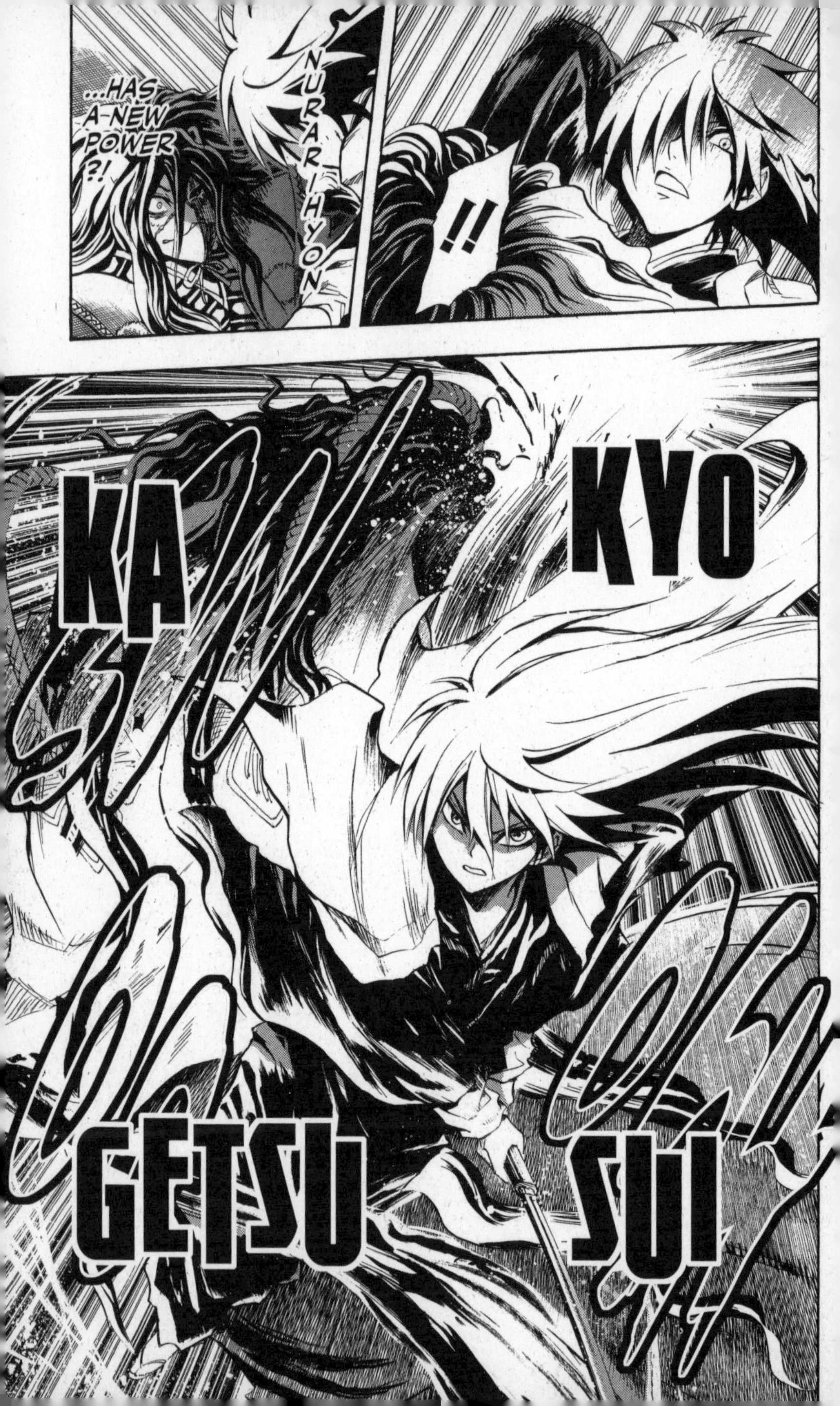
!!
NURARIHYON
...HAS A NEW POWER?!
KYO
KA
SUI
GETSU

NURA: RISE OF THE YOKAI CLAN

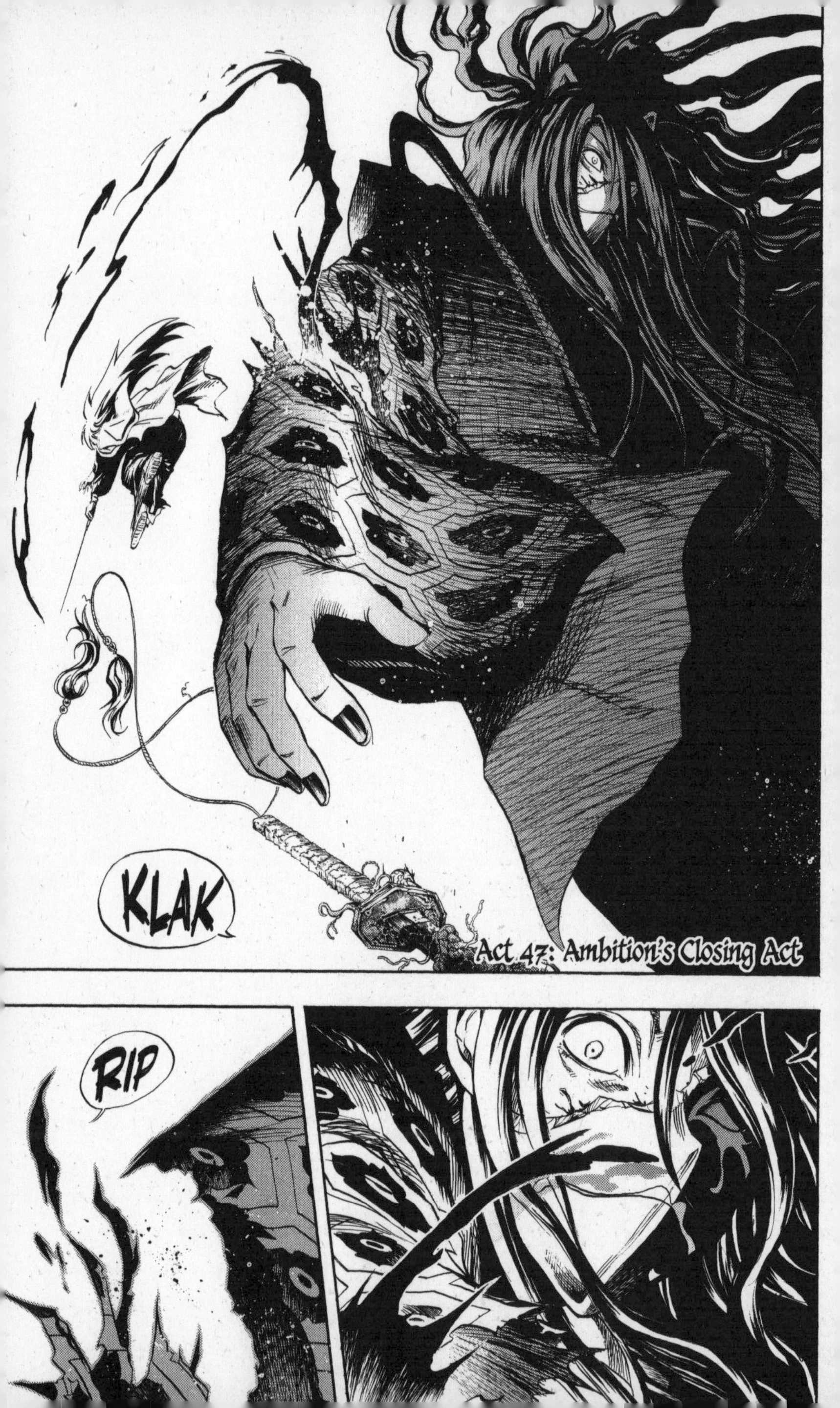
Act 47: Ambition's Closing Act
KLAK
RIP

Act 47: Ambition's Closing Act

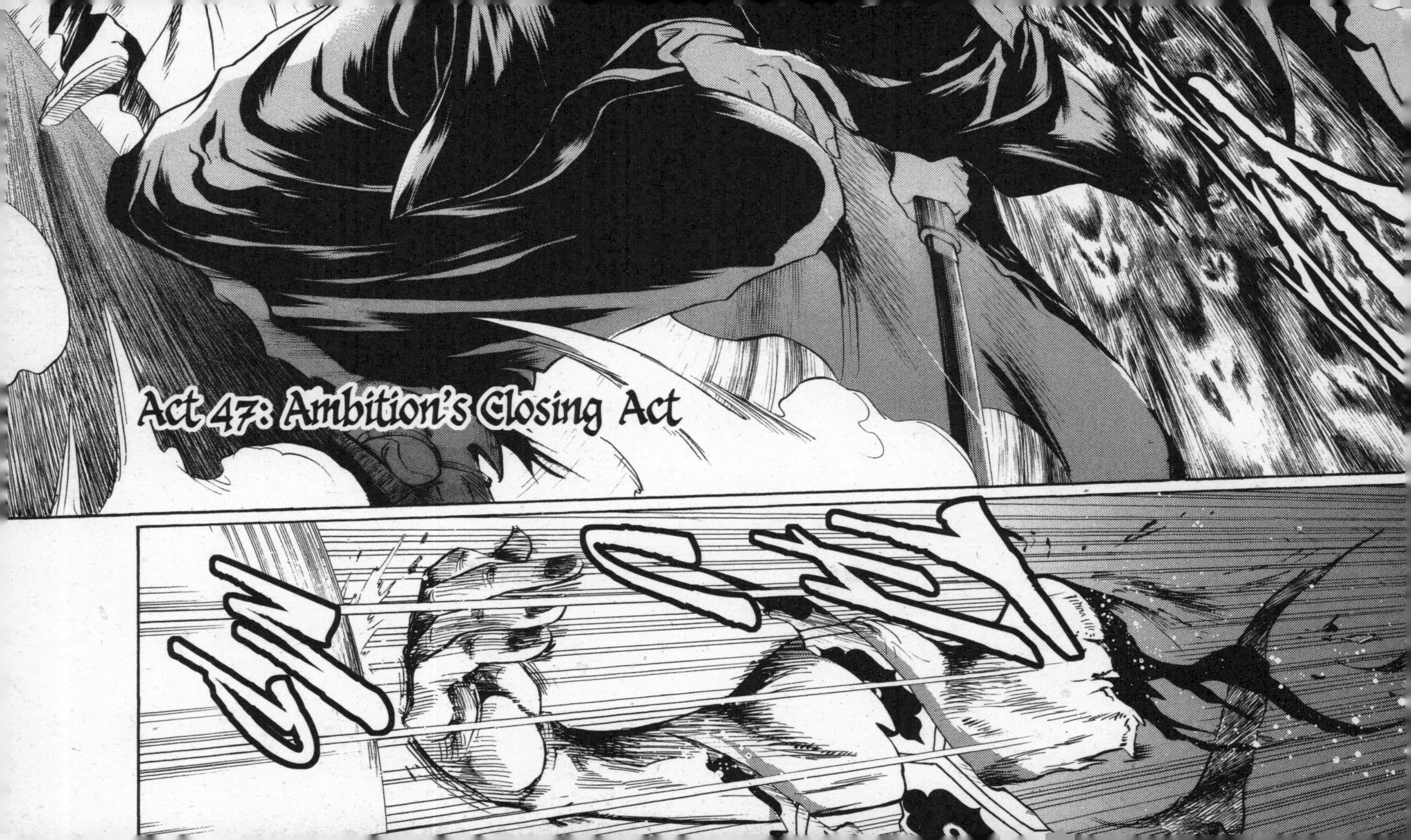

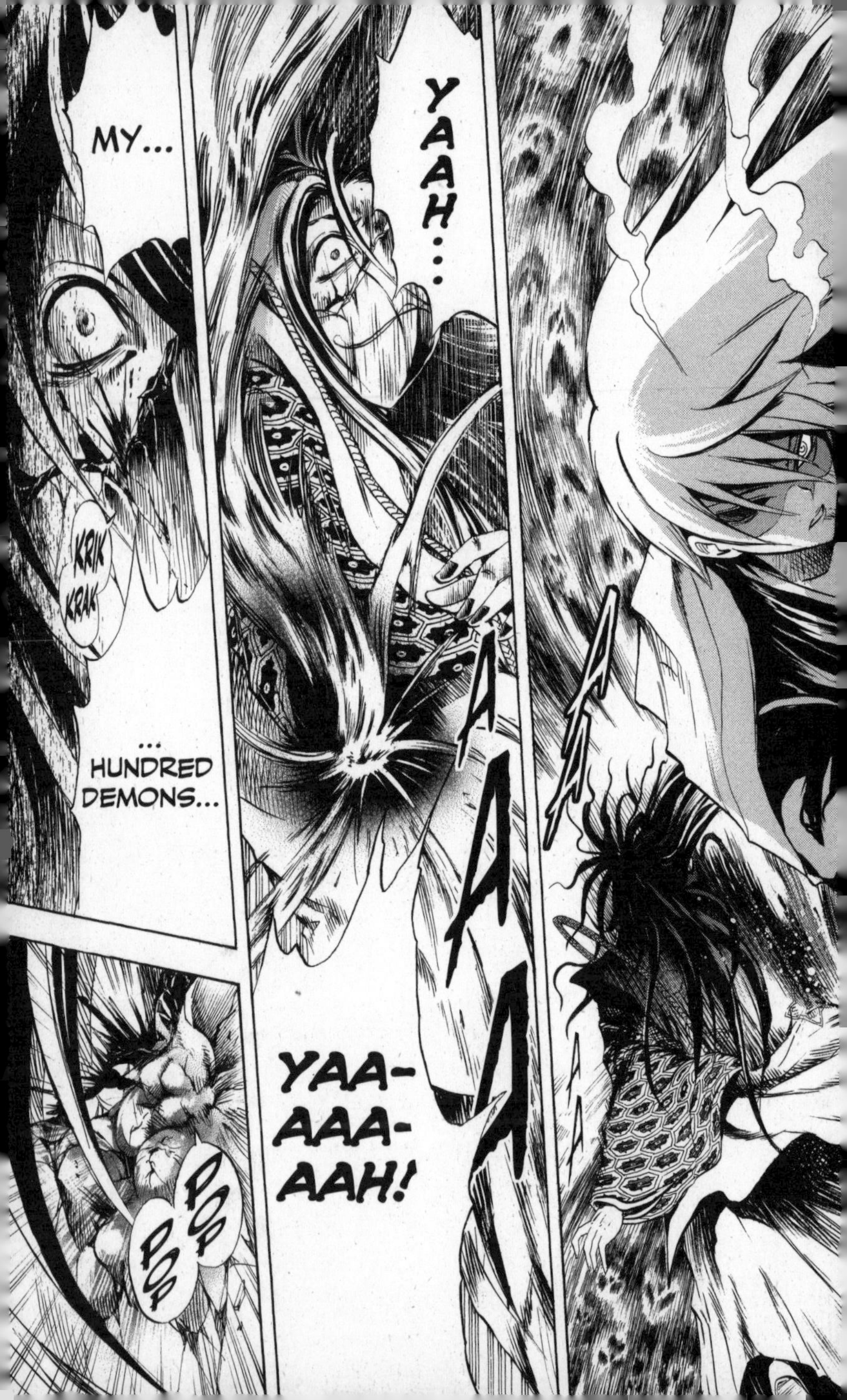
YAAH...
YAA-AAA-AAH!
MY...
KRIK KRAK
...HUNDRED DEMONS...
POP POP

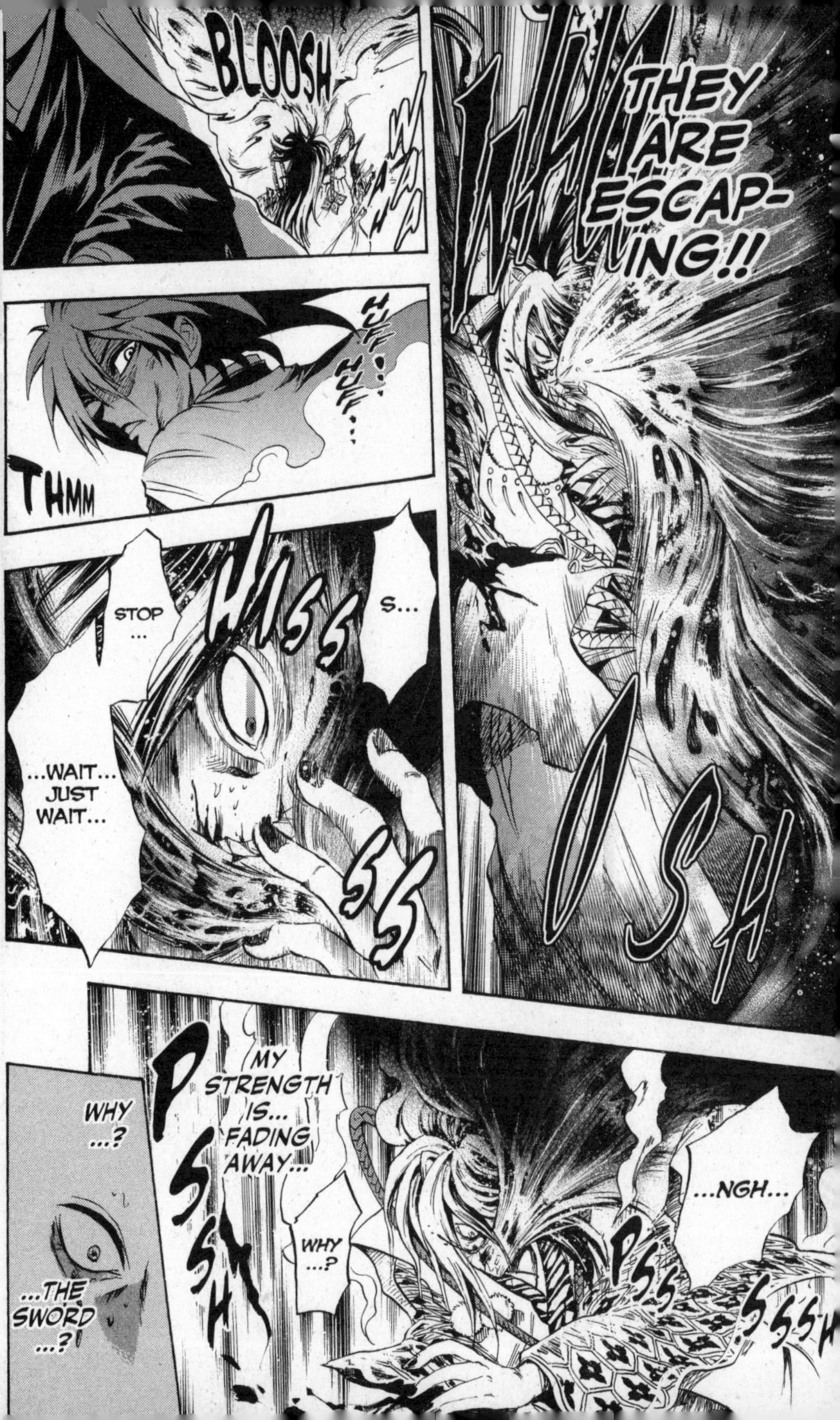
THEY ARE ESCAPING!!
BLOOSH
HUFF HUFF...
THMM
S...
HISSS
STOP...
...WAIT... JUST WAIT...
...NGH...
PSSSSSH
WHY...?
MY STRENGTH IS... FADING AWAY...
PSSH
WHY...?
...THE SWORD...?

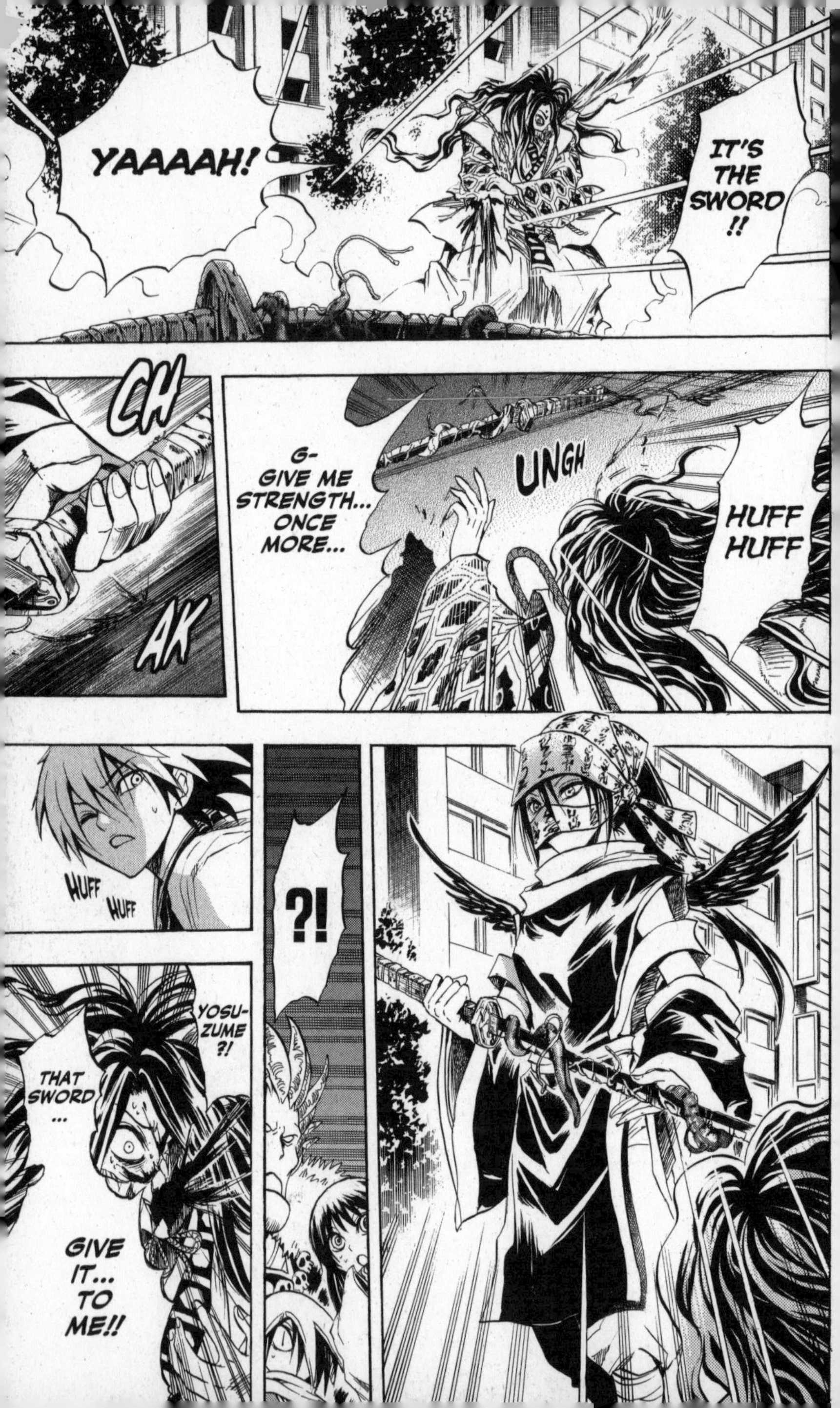
IT'S THE SWORD!!
YAAAAH!
HUFF HUFF
UNGH
G- GIVE ME STRENGTH... ONCE MORE...
CH
AK
?!
HUFF HUFF
YOSU-ZUME?!
THAT SWORD...
GIVE IT... TO ME!!

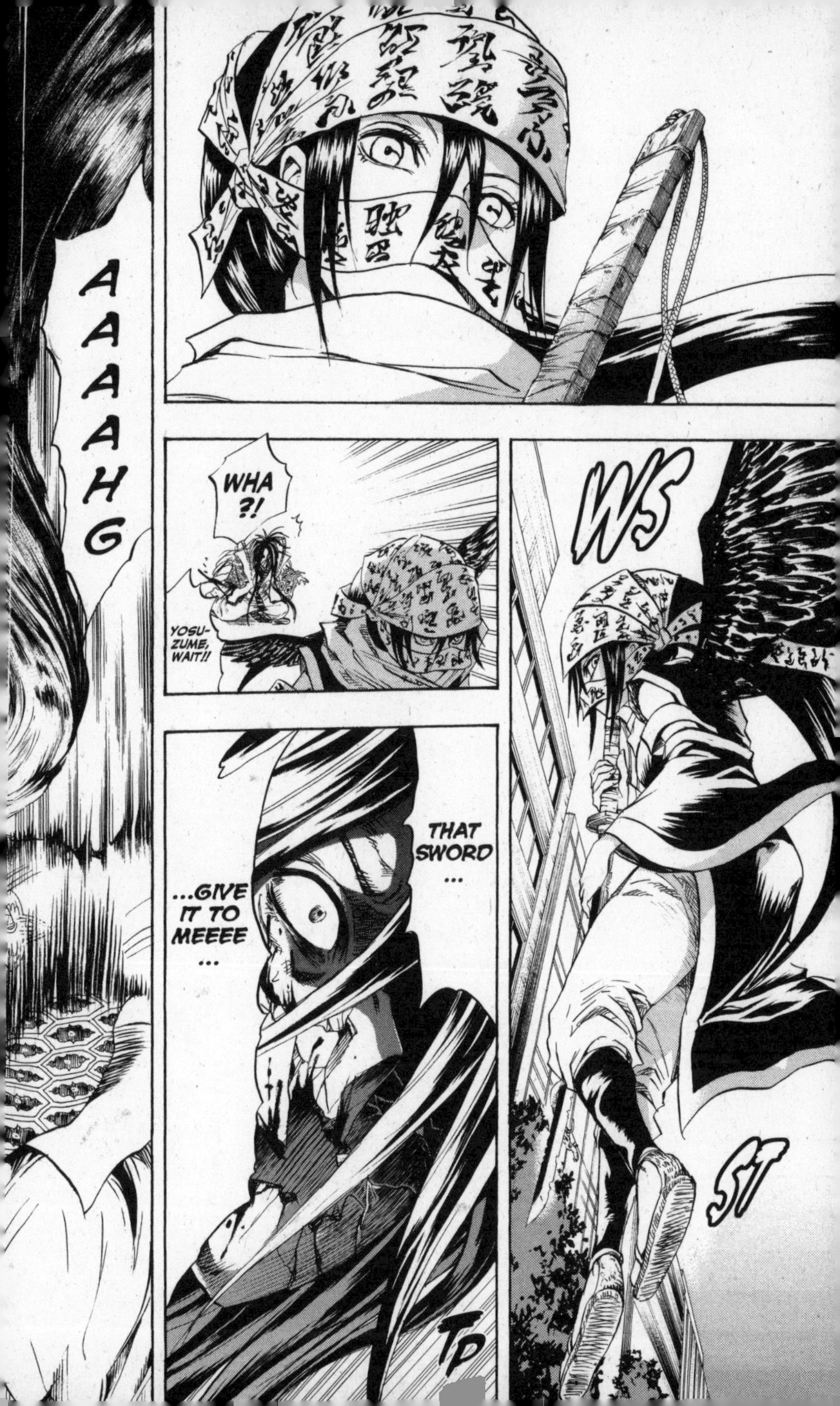

WS
ST
WHA ?!
YOSU-ZUME, WAIT!!
THAT SWORD ...
...GIVE IT TO MEEEE ...
TP
AAAAAHG

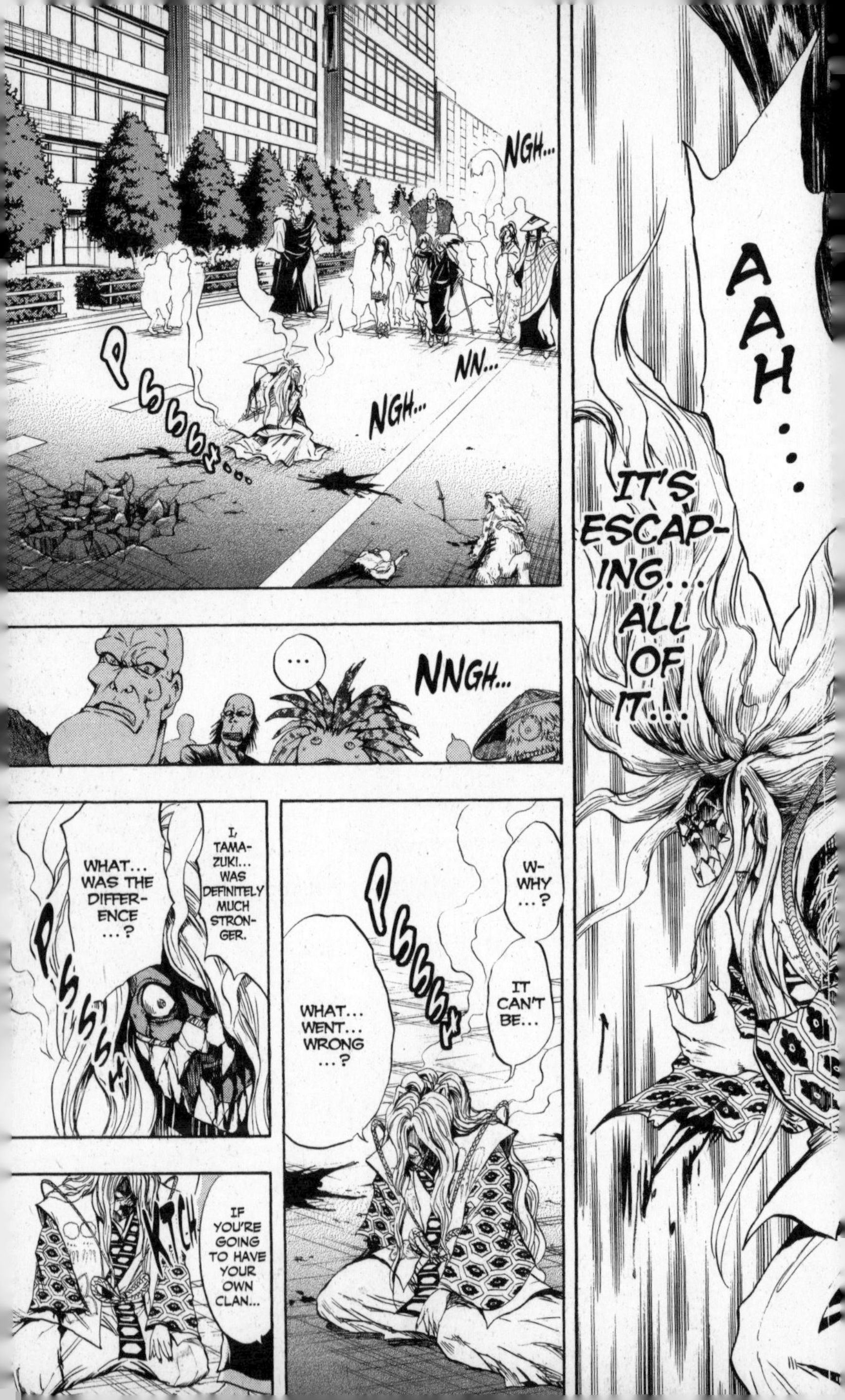
AAH...
IT'S ESCAPING... ALL OF IT...
NGH...
NN...
NGH...
NNGH...
...
W-WHY...?
IT CAN'T BE...
WHAT... WENT... WRONG...?
I, TAMAZUKI... WAS DEFINITELY MUCH STRONGER.
WHAT... WAS THE DIFFERENCE...?
K'TCH
IF YOU'RE GOING TO HAVE YOUR OWN CLAN...

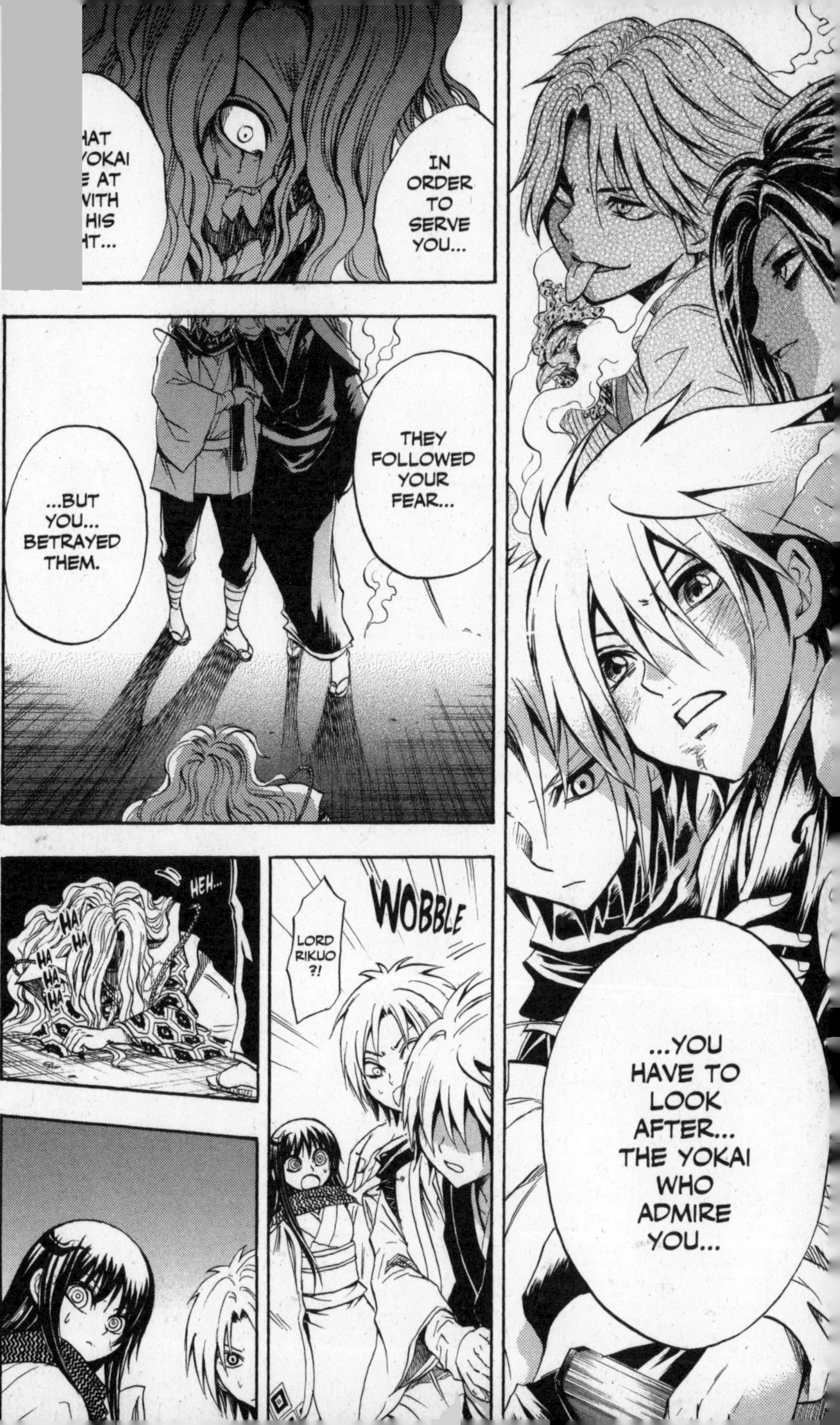
...YOU HAVE TO LOOK AFTER... THE YOKAI WHO ADMIRE YOU...
IN ORDER TO SERVE YOU...
HAT YOKAI E AT WITH HIS HT...
THEY FOLLOWED YOUR FEAR...
...BUT YOU... BETRAYED THEM.
WOBBLE
LORD RIKUO ?!
HEH...
HA HA
HA HA HA

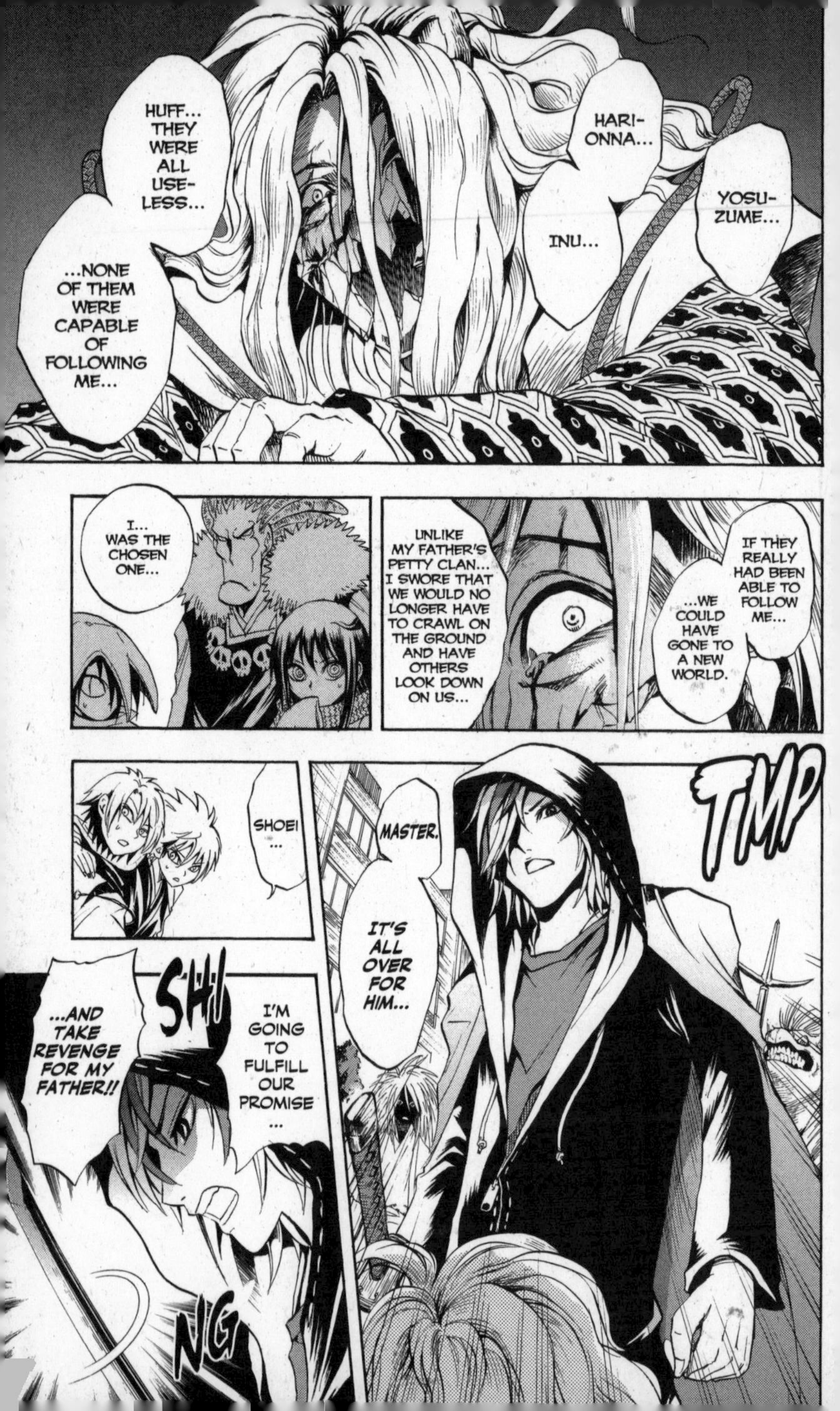
HARI-ONNA...
YOSU-ZUME...
INU...
HUFF... THEY WERE ALL USE-LESS...
...NONE OF THEM WERE CAPABLE OF FOLLOWING ME...
IF THEY REALLY HAD BEEN ABLE TO FOLLOW ME...
...WE COULD HAVE GONE TO A NEW WORLD.
UNLIKE MY FATHER'S PETTY CLAN... I SWORE THAT WE WOULD NO LONGER HAVE TO CRAWL ON THE GROUND AND HAVE OTHERS LOOK DOWN ON US...
I... WAS THE CHOSEN ONE...
TMP
MASTER.
IT'S ALL OVER FOR HIM...
SHOEI...
I'M GOING TO FULFILL OUR PROMISE...
SHI
NG
...AND TAKE REVENGE FOR MY FATHER!!

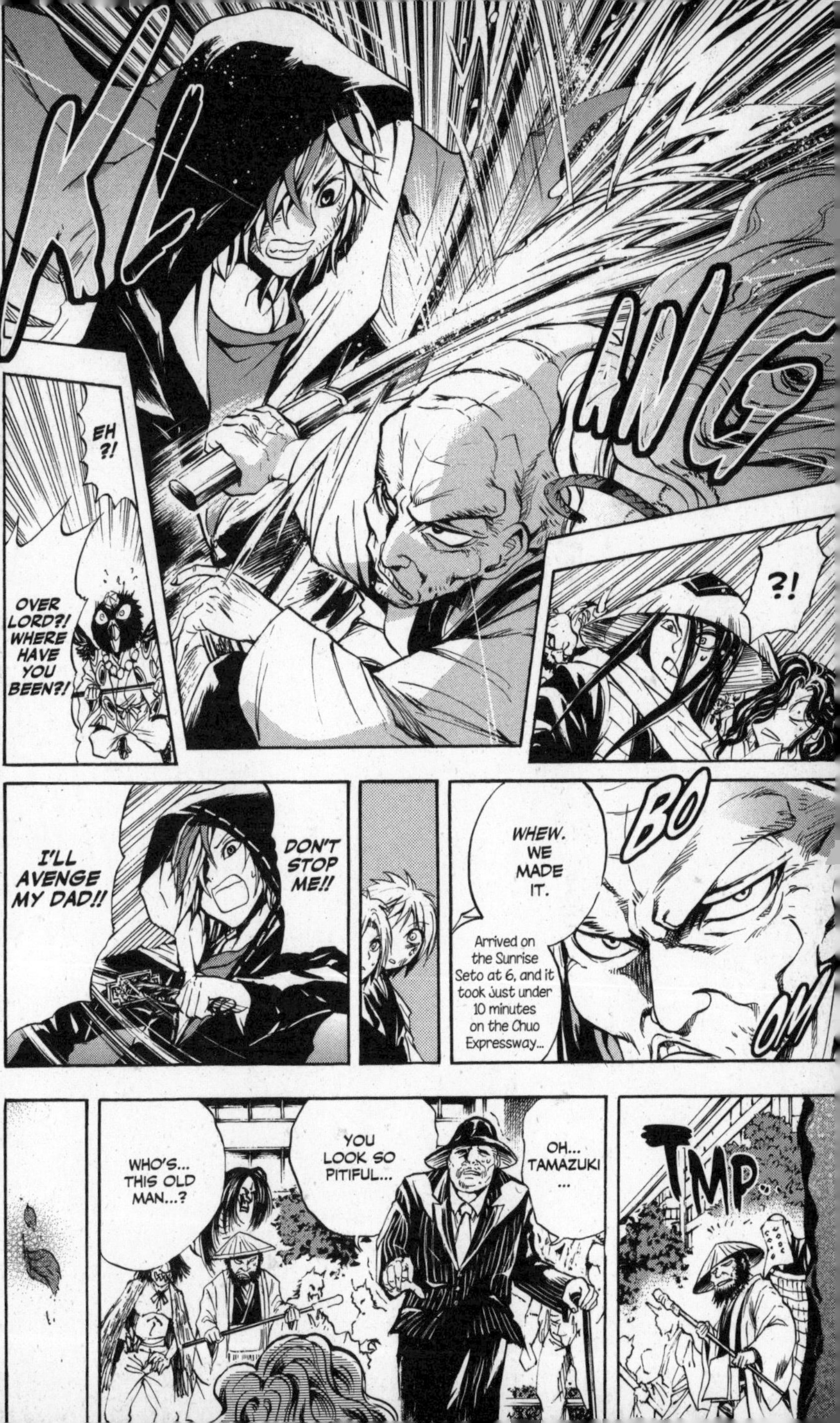
KLANG
?!
EH ?!
OVER LORD?! WHERE HAVE YOU BEEN?!
BOOM
WHEW. WE MADE IT.
Arrived on the Sunrise Seto at 6, and it took just under 10 minutes on the Chuo Expressway...
DON'T STOP ME!!
I'LL AVENGE MY DAD!!
TMP
OH... TAMAZUKI ...
YOU LOOK SO PITIFUL...
WHO'S... THIS OLD MAN...?

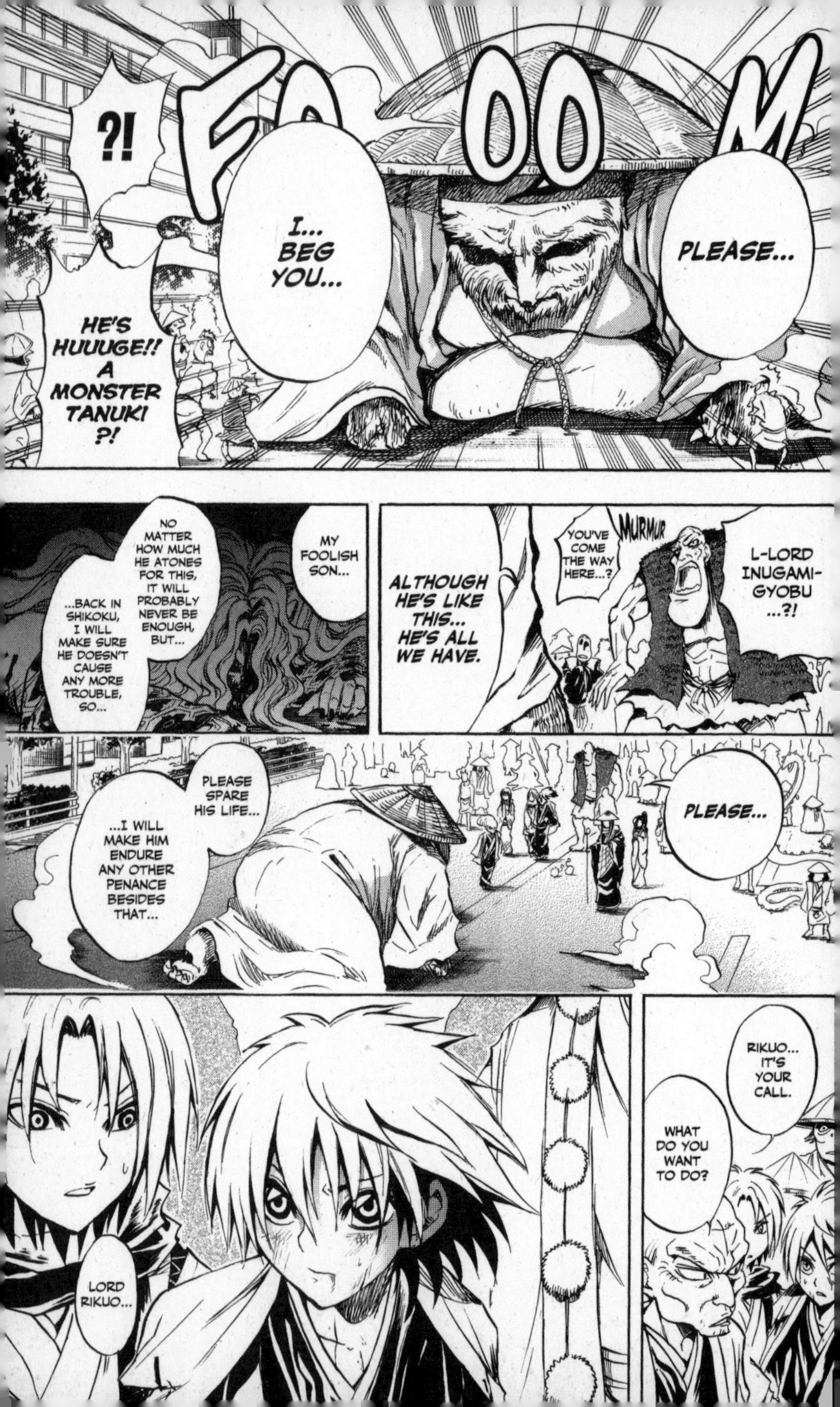

PLEASE...
FOOOM
I... BEG YOU...
?!
HE'S HUUUGE!! A MONSTER TANUKI ?!
L-LORD INUGAMI-GYOBU ...?!
MURMUR
YOU'VE COME THE WAY HERE...?
ALTHOUGH HE'S LIKE THIS... HE'S ALL WE HAVE.
MY FOOLISH SON...
NO MATTER HOW MUCH HE ATONES FOR THIS, IT WILL PROBABLY NEVER BE ENOUGH, BUT...
...BACK IN SHIKOKU, I WILL MAKE SURE HE DOESN'T CAUSE ANY MORE TROUBLE, SO...
PLEASE...
PLEASE SPARE HIS LIFE...
...I WILL MAKE HIM ENDURE ANY OTHER PENANCE BESIDES THAT...
RIKUO... IT'S YOUR CALL.
WHAT DO YOU WANT TO DO?
LORD RIKUO...

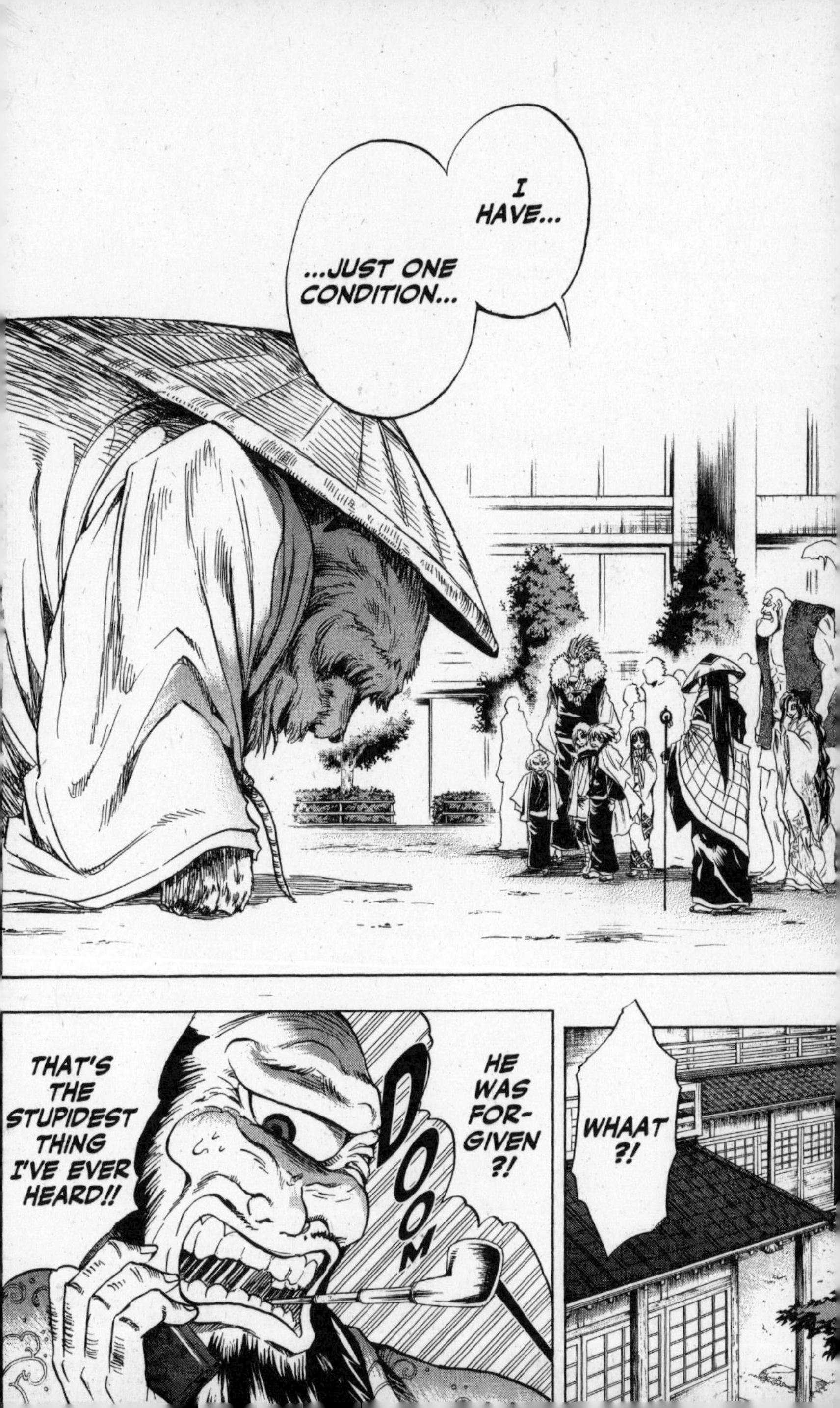
I HAVE...
...JUST ONE CONDITION...
WHAAT?!
HE WAS FOR-GIVEN?!
DOOM
THAT'S THE STUPIDEST THING I'VE EVER HEARD!!

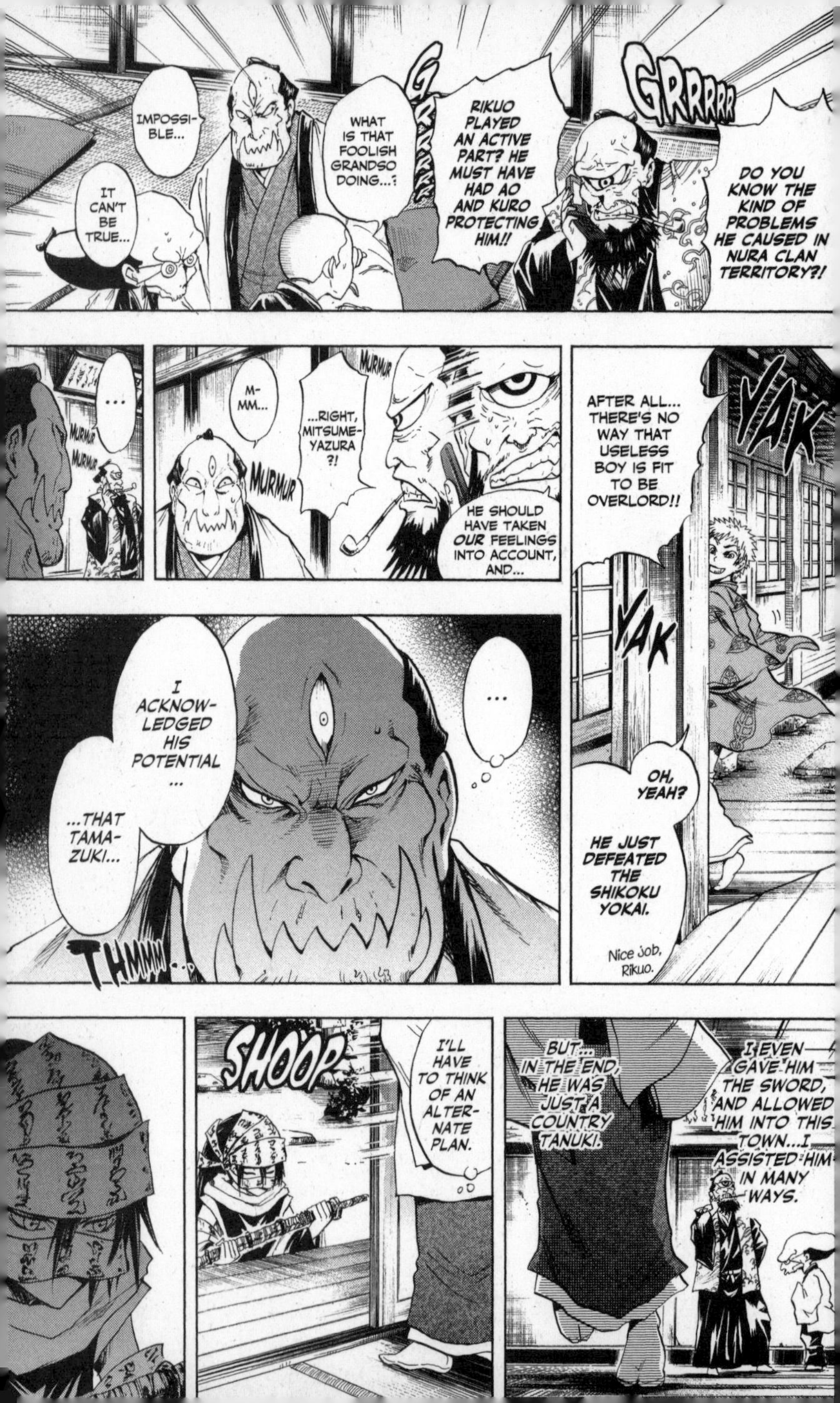
GRRRRR
DO YOU KNOW THE KIND OF PROBLEMS HE CAUSED IN NURA CLAN TERRITORY?!
RIKUO PLAYED AN ACTIVE PART? HE MUST HAVE HAD AO AND KURO PROTECTING HIM!!
GRRRRR
WHAT IS THAT FOOLISH GRANDSO DOING...?
IMPOSSI-BLE...
IT CAN'T BE TRUE...
YAK
AFTER ALL... THERE'S NO WAY THAT USELESS BOY IS FIT TO BE OVERLORD!!
YAK
OH, YEAH?
HE JUST DEFEATED THE SHIKOKU YOKAI.
Nice job, Rikuo.
MURMUR
...RIGHT, MITSUME-YAZURA?!
HE SHOULD HAVE TAKEN OUR FEELINGS INTO ACCOUNT, AND...
M-MM...
MURMUR
...
MURMUR
MURMUR
...
I ACKNOW-LEDGED HIS POTENTIAL...
...THAT TAMA-ZUKI...
THMMM...
I EVEN GAVE HIM THE SWORD, AND ALLOWED HIM INTO THIS TOWN...I ASSISTED HIM IN MANY WAYS.
BUT... IN THE END, HE WAS JUST A COUNTRY TANUKI.
I'LL HAVE TO THINK OF AN ALTERNATE PLAN.
SHOOP

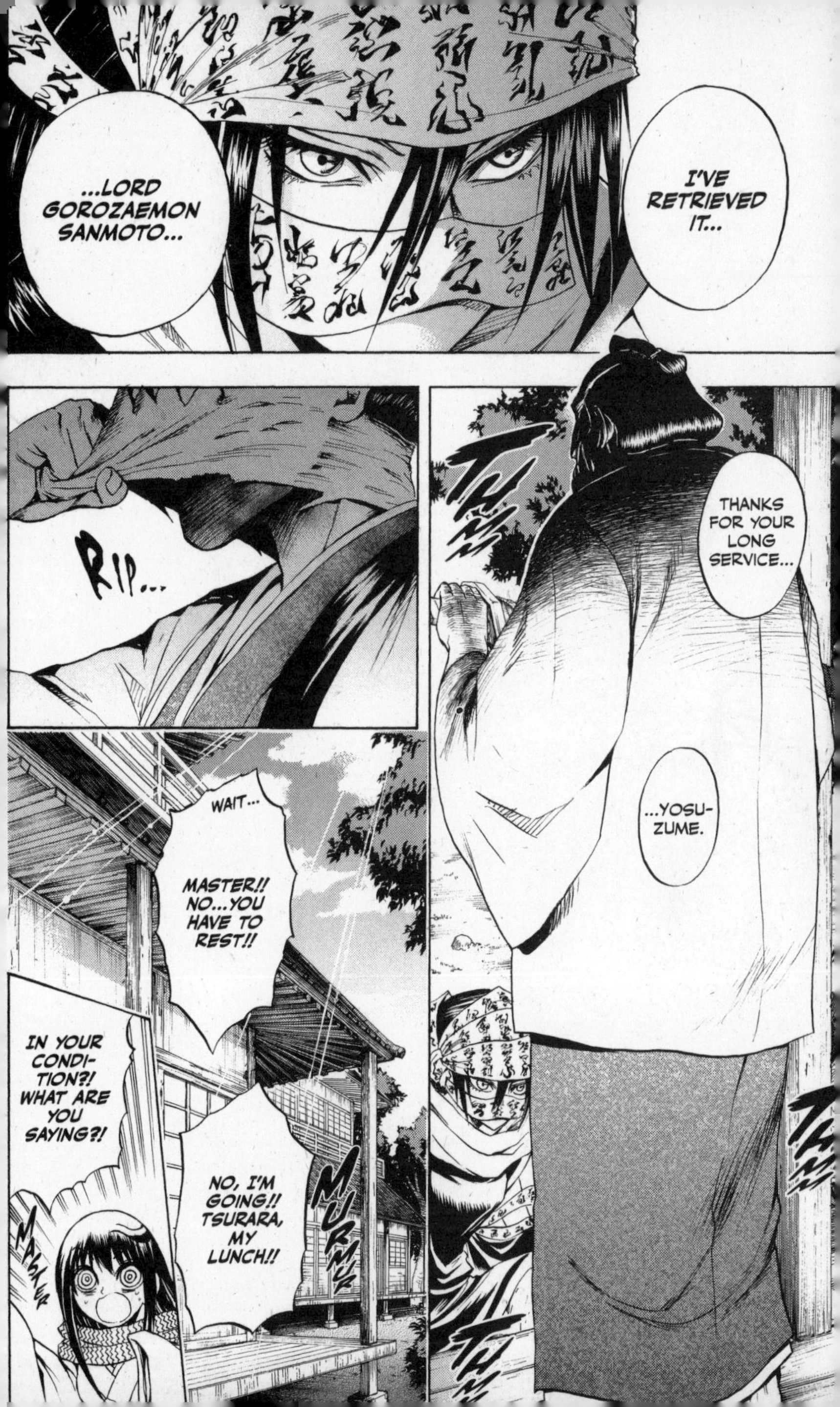

I'VE RETRIEVED IT...
...LORD GOROZAEMON SANMOTO...
THANKS FOR YOUR LONG SERVICE...
...YOSU-ZUME.
RIP...
WAIT...
MASTER!! NO...YOU HAVE TO REST!!
IN YOUR CONDITION?! WHAT ARE YOU SAYING?!
NO, I'M GOING!! TSURARA, MY LUNCH!!

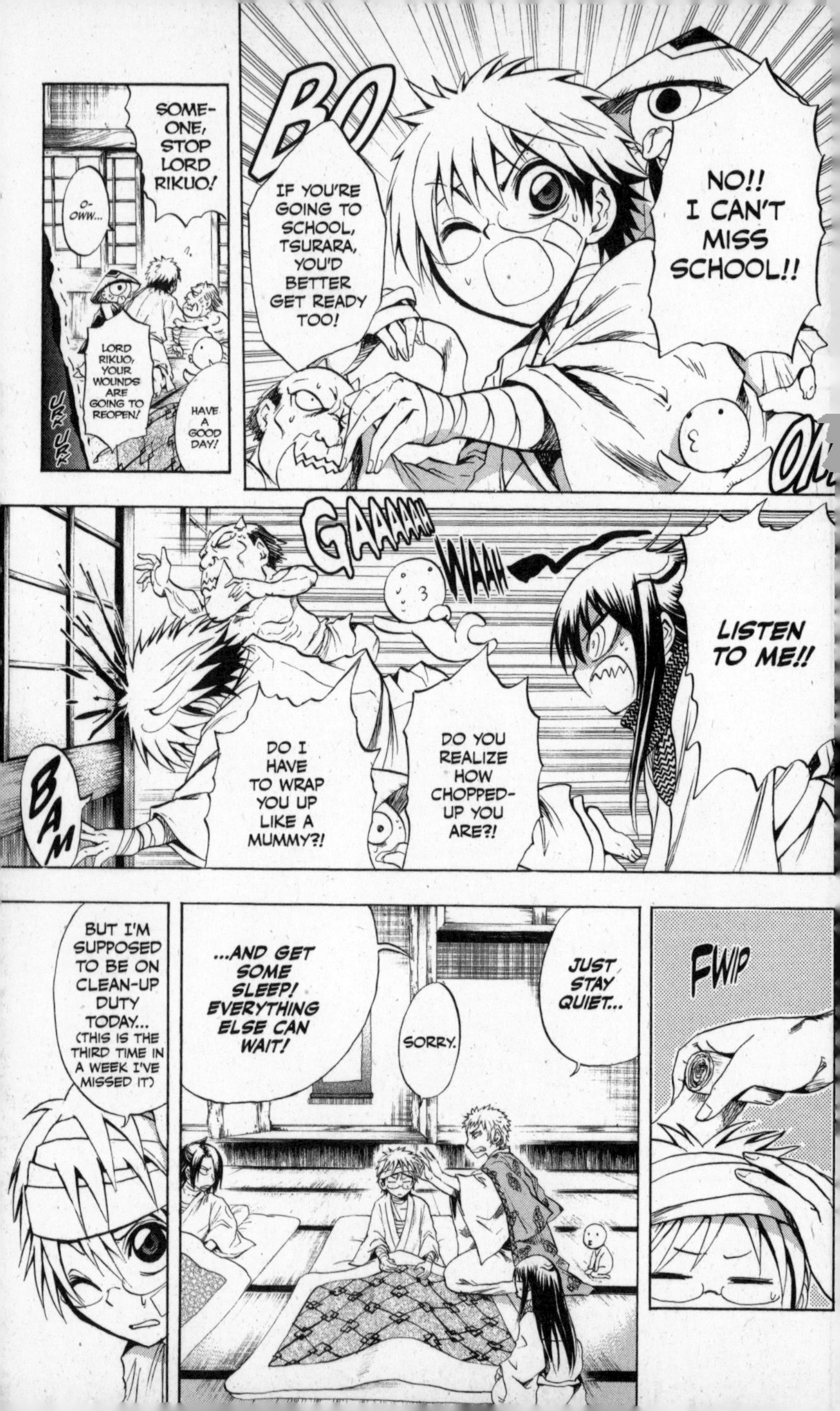
BO
NO!! I CAN'T MISS SCHOOL!!
ON
IF YOU'RE GOING TO SCHOOL, TSURARA, YOU'D BETTER GET READY TOO!
SOME-ONE, STOP LORD RIKUO!
O-OWW...
LORD RIKUO, YOUR WOUNDS ARE GOING TO REOPEN!
HAVE A GOOD DAY!
URK URK
LISTEN TO ME!!
GAAAAH
WAAH
DO YOU REALIZE HOW CHOPPED-UP YOU ARE?!
DO I HAVE TO WRAP YOU UP LIKE A MUMMY?!
BAM
FWIP
JUST STAY QUIET...
SORRY.
...AND GET SOME SLEEP! EVERYTHING ELSE CAN WAIT!
BUT I'M SUPPOSED TO BE ON CLEAN-UP DUTY TODAY... (THIS IS THE THIRD TIME IN A WEEK I'VE MISSED IT)

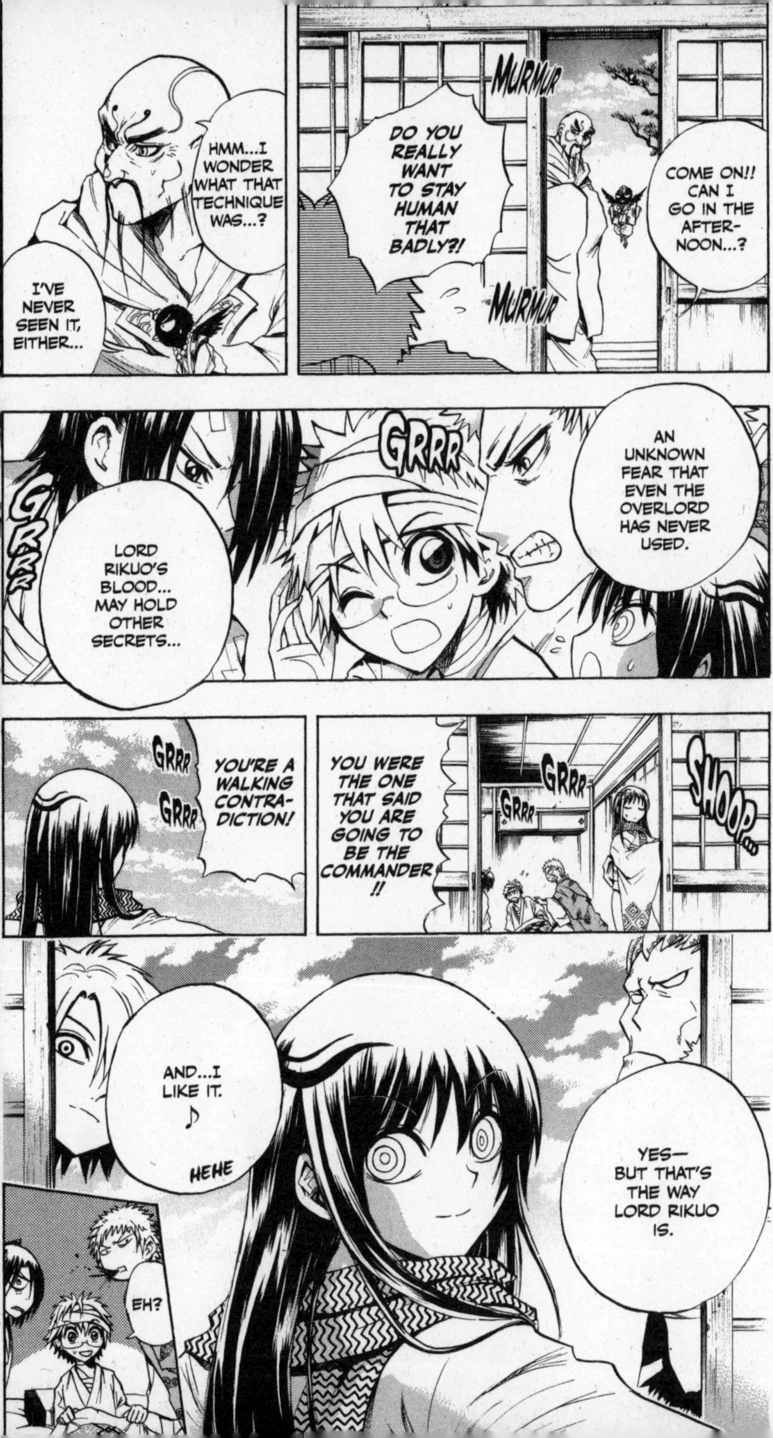
MURMUR
COME ON!! CAN I GO IN THE AFTERNOON...?
DO YOU REALLY WANT TO STAY HUMAN THAT BADLY?!
MURMUR
HMM...I WONDER WHAT THAT TECHNIQUE WAS...?
I'VE NEVER SEEN IT, EITHER...
AN UNKNOWN FEAR THAT EVEN THE OVERLORD HAS NEVER USED.
GRRR
LORD RIKUO'S BLOOD... MAY HOLD OTHER SECRETS...
GRRR
SHOOP...
GRRR
GRRR
YOU WERE THE ONE THAT SAID YOU ARE GOING TO BE THE COMMANDER!!
YOU'RE A WALKING CONTRADICTION!
GRRR
GRRR
YES— BUT THAT'S THE WAY LORD RIKUO IS.
AND...I LIKE IT. ♪
HEHE
EH?

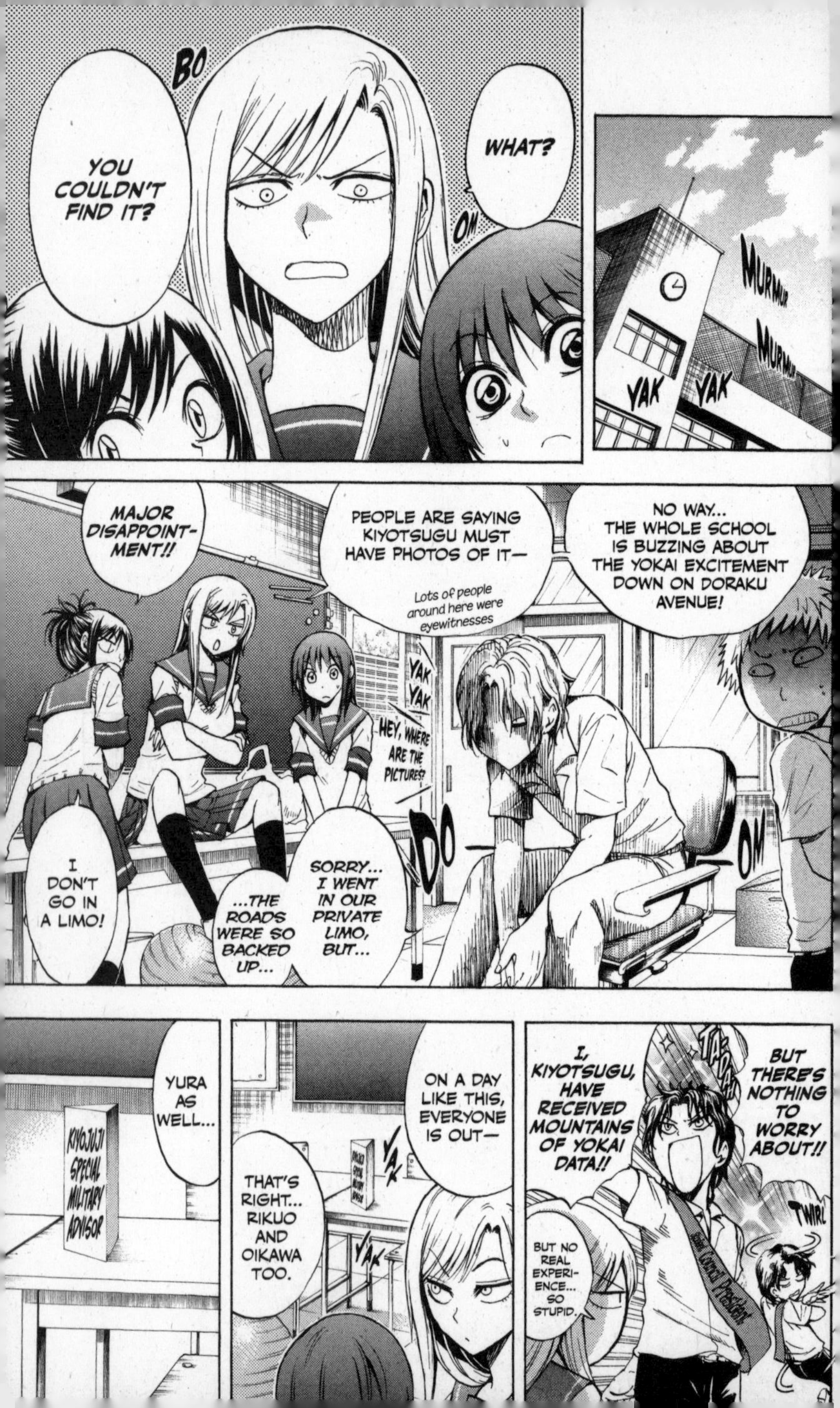

MURMUR
MURMUR
YAK YAK
WHAT?
BO
OM
YOU COULDN'T FIND IT?
NO WAY... THE WHOLE SCHOOL IS BUZZING ABOUT THE YOKAI EXCITEMENT DOWN ON DORAKU AVENUE!
PEOPLE ARE SAYING KIYOTSUGU MUST HAVE PHOTOS OF IT—
Lots of people around here were eyewitnesses
MAJOR DISAPPOINT-MENT!!
YAK YAK
HEY, WHERE ARE THE PICTURES?
OM
DO
SORRY... I WENT IN OUR PRIVATE LIMO, BUT...
...THE ROADS WERE SO BACKED UP...
I DON'T GO IN A LIMO!
BUT THERE'S NOTHING TO WORRY ABOUT!!
I, KIYOTSUGU, HAVE RECEIVED MOUNTAINS OF YOKAI DATA!!
TWIRL
BUT NO REAL EXPERI-ENCE... SO STUPID.
ON A DAY LIKE THIS, EVERYONE IS OUT—
YAK
YAK
THAT'S RIGHT... RIKUO AND OIKAWA TOO.
YURA AS WELL...
KIYOJUJI SPECIAL MILITARY ADVISOR

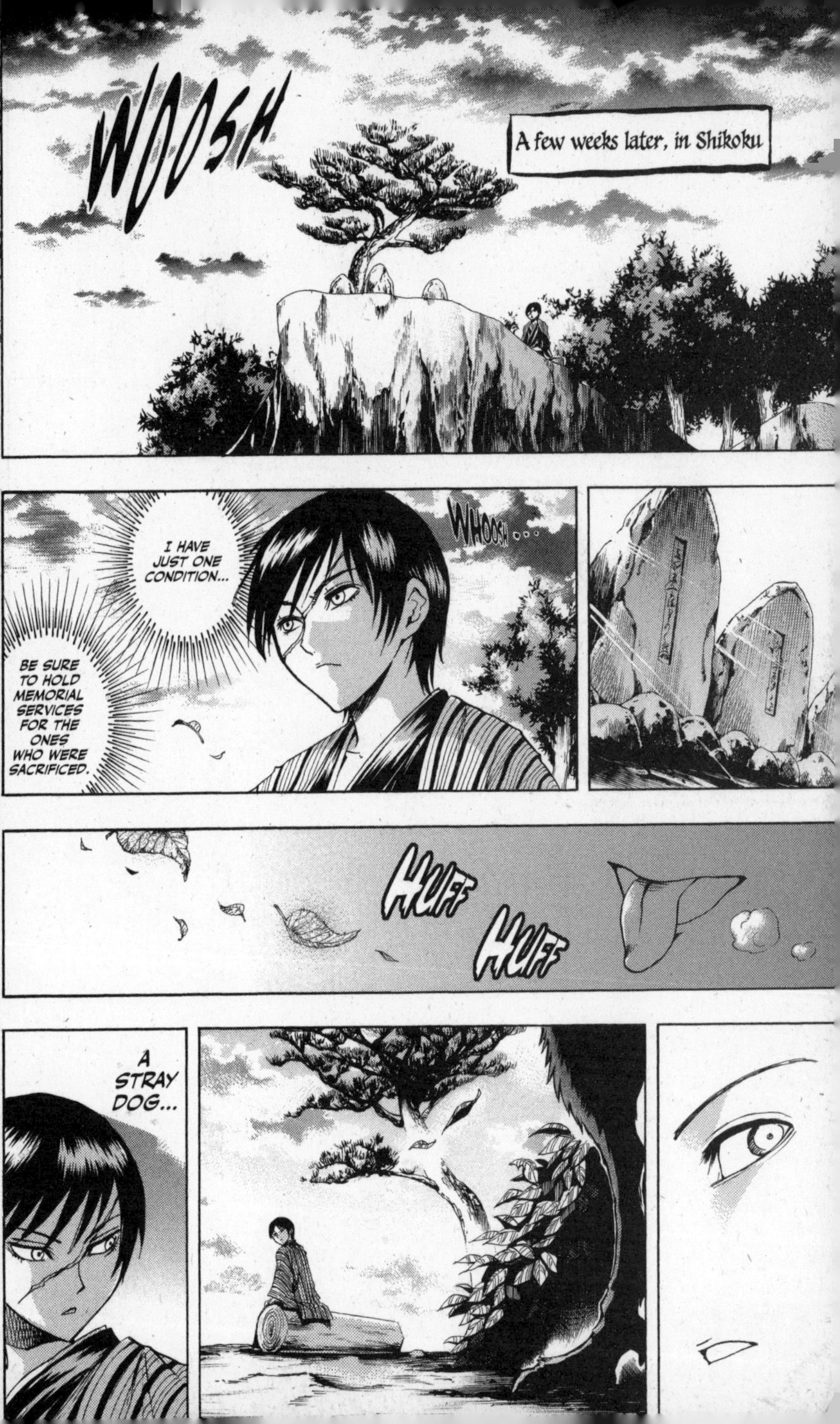

A few weeks later, in Shikoku
WOOSH
WHOOSH...
I HAVE JUST ONE CONDITION...
BE SURE TO HOLD MEMORIAL SERVICES FOR THE ONES WHO WERE SACRIFICED.
HUFF HUFF
A STRAY DOG...

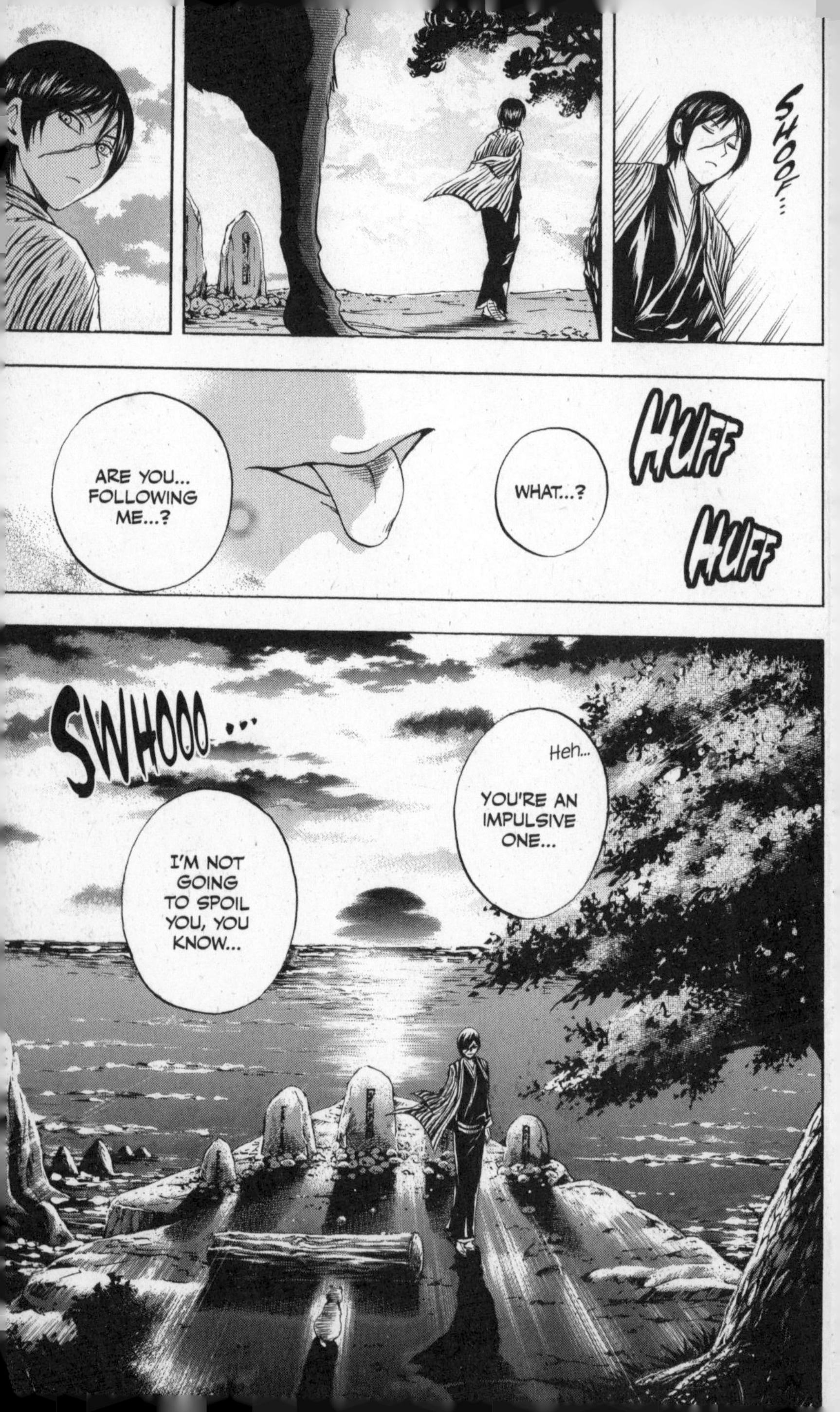
SHOOK...
HUFF
HUFF
WHAT...?
ARE YOU... FOLLOWING ME...?
Heh...
YOU'RE AN IMPULSIVE ONE...
SWHOOO...
I'M NOT GOING TO SPOIL YOU, YOU KNOW...

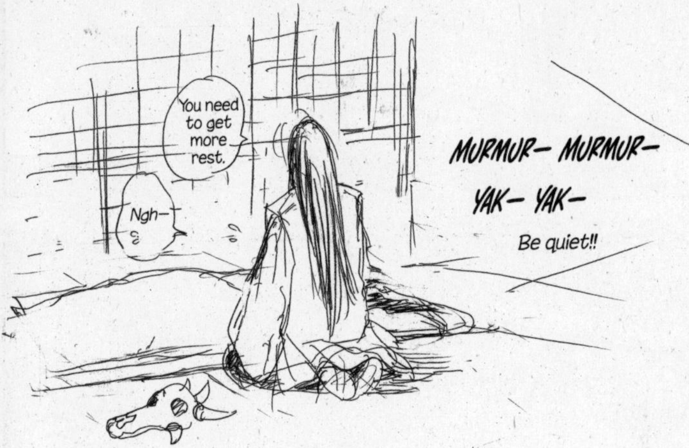
MURMUR- MURMUR-
YAK- YAK-
Be quiet!!
You need to get more rest.
Ngh-

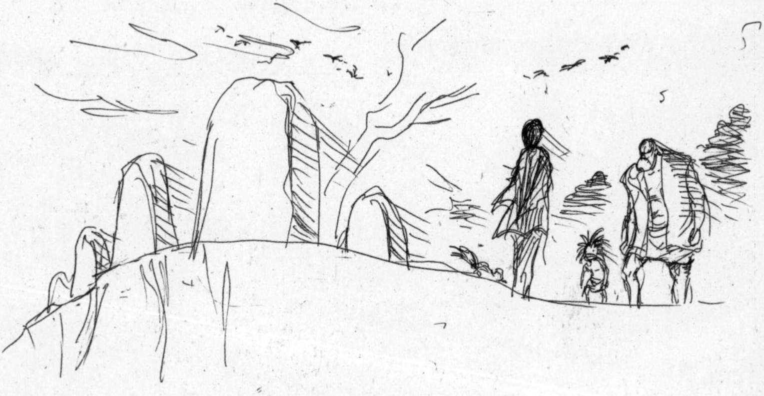

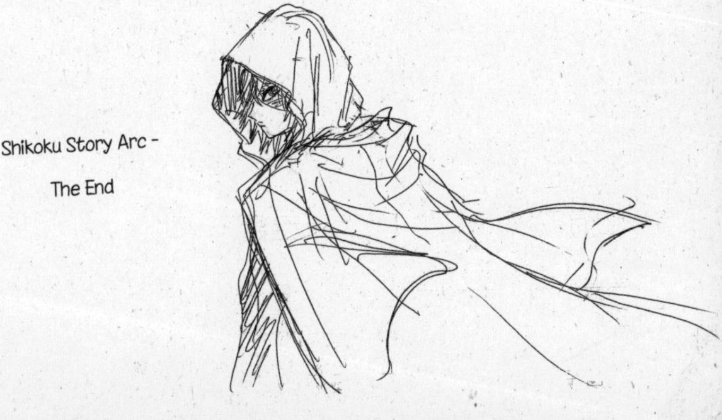
Shikoku Story Arc -
The End

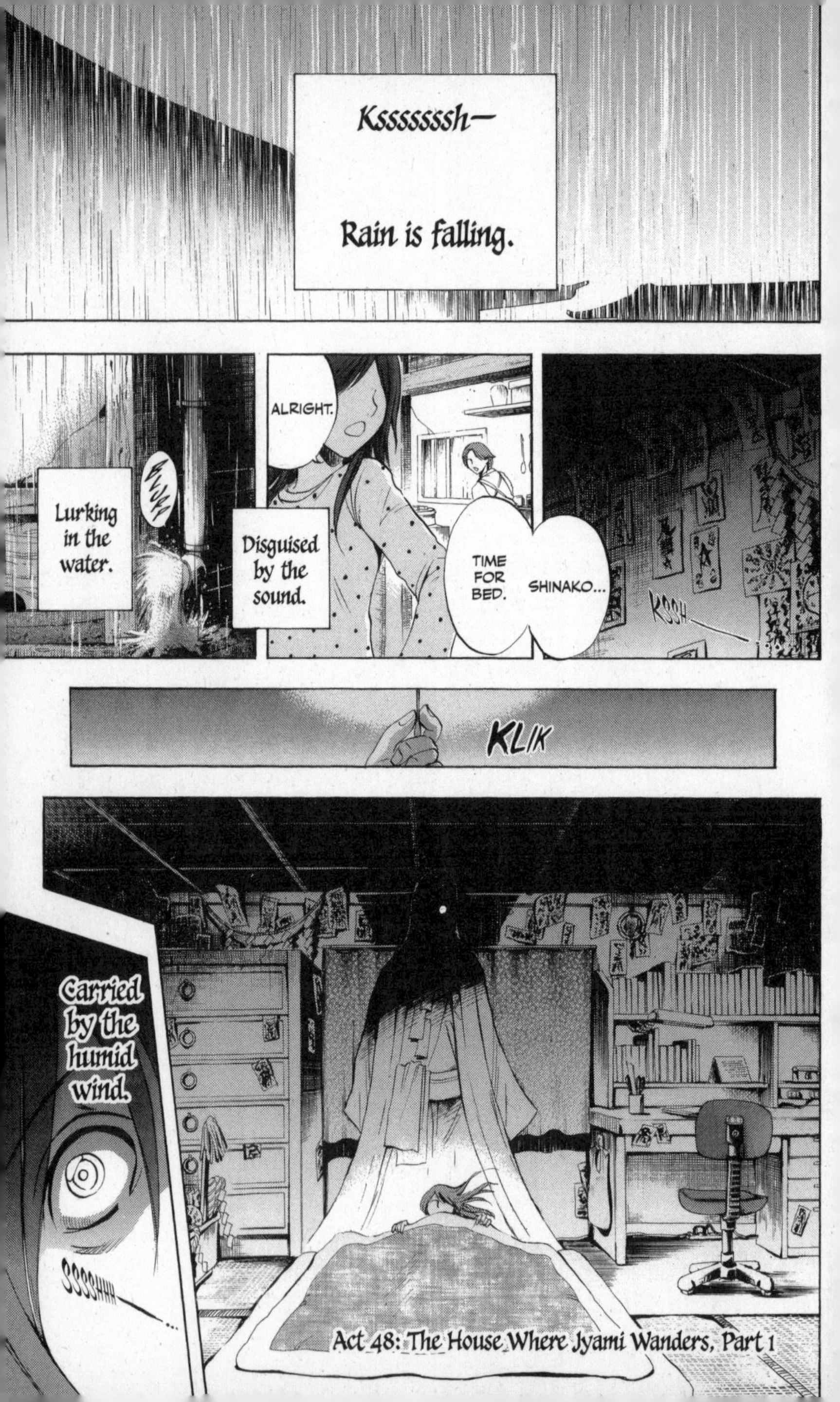
Ksssssssh—
Rain is falling.
KSSH—
SHINAKO...
TIME FOR BED.
ALRIGHT.
Disguised by the sound.
Lurking in the water.
KLIK
Carried by the humid wind.
SSSSHHH—...
Act 48: The House Where Jyami Wanders, Part 1

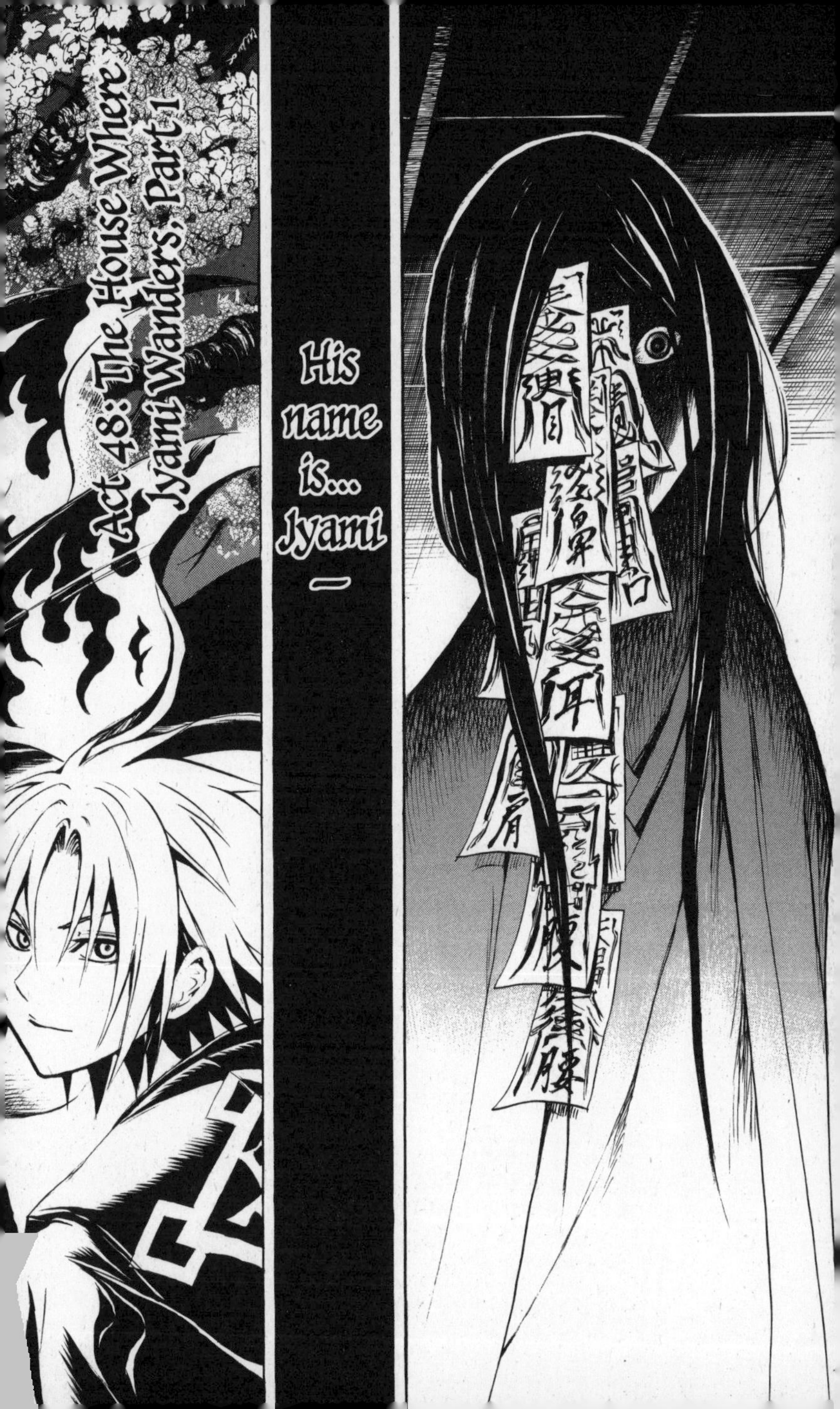
His name is... Jyami —
Act 48: The House Where Jyami Wanders, Part 1

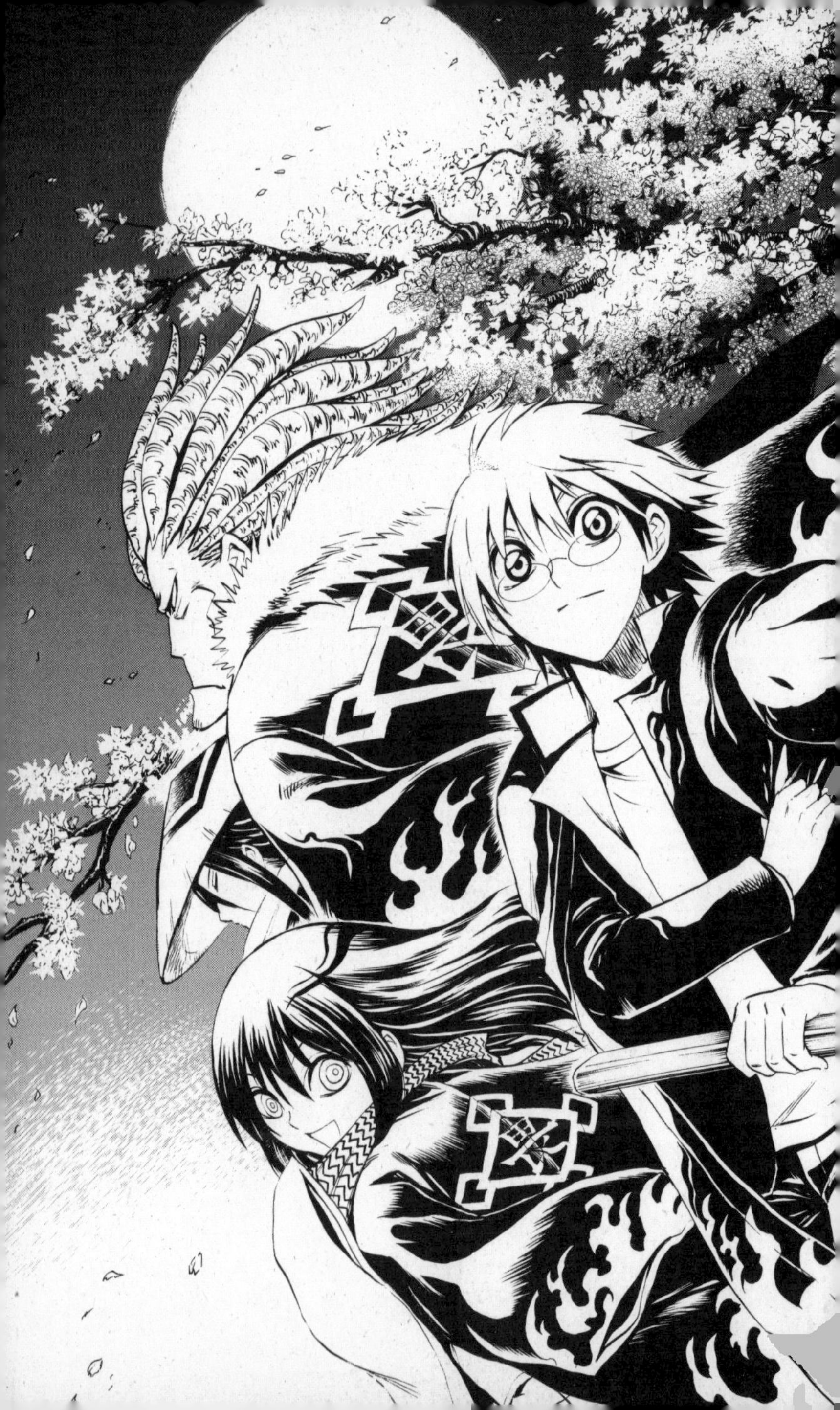

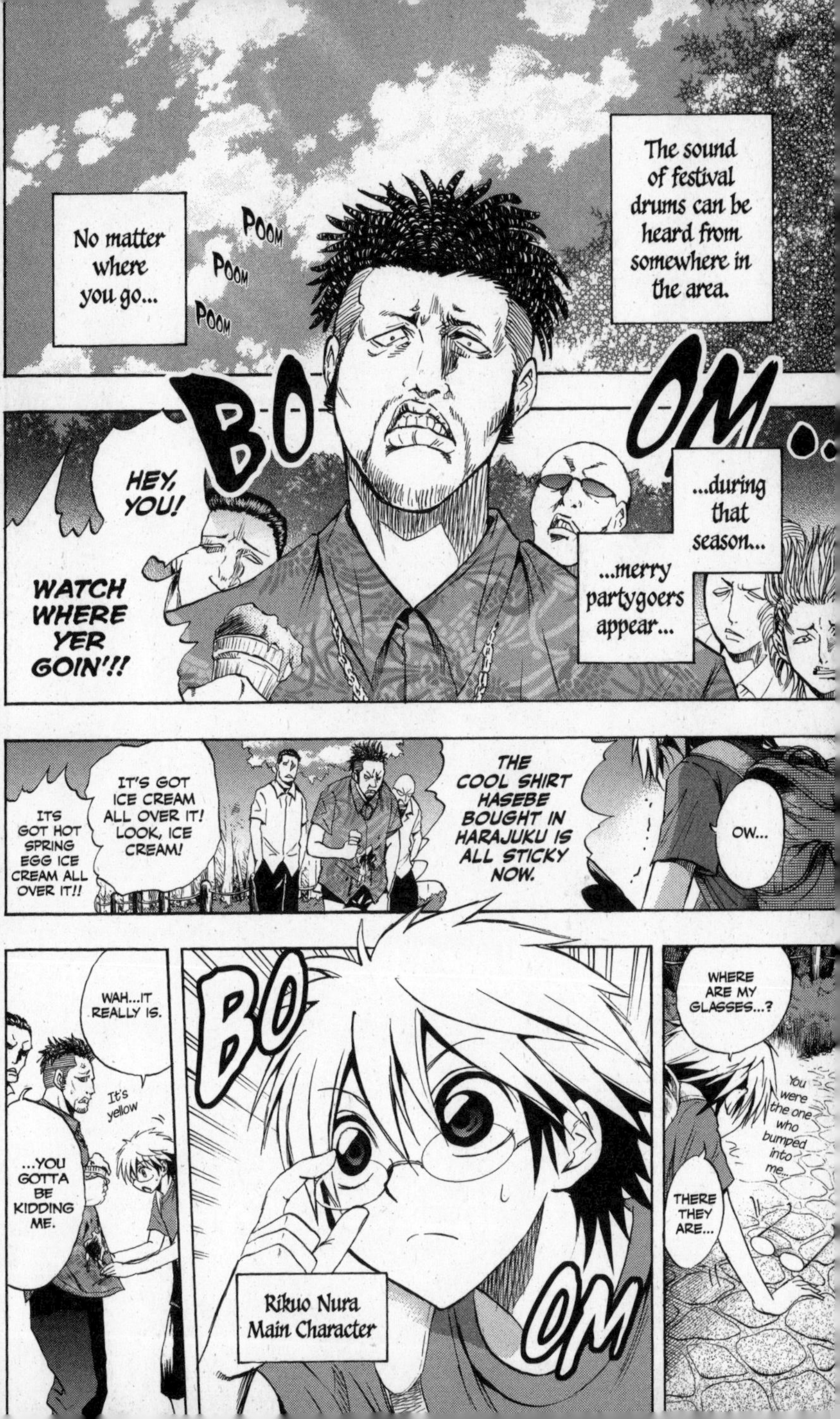
The sound of festival drums can be heard from somewhere in the area.
POOM
POOM
POOM
No matter where you go...
BO-OM..
...during that season...
...merry partygoers appear...
HEY, YOU!
WATCH WHERE YER GOIN'!!
OW...
THE COOL SHIRT HASEBE BOUGHT IN HARAJUKU IS ALL STICKY NOW.
IT'S GOT ICE CREAM ALL OVER IT! LOOK, ICE CREAM!
ITS GOT HOT SPRING EGG ICE CREAM ALL OVER IT!!
WHERE ARE MY GLASSES...?
You were the one who bumped into me...
THERE THEY ARE...
BO
OM
Rikuo Nura
Main Character
WAH...IT REALLY IS.
It's yellow
...YOU GOTTA BE KIDDING ME.

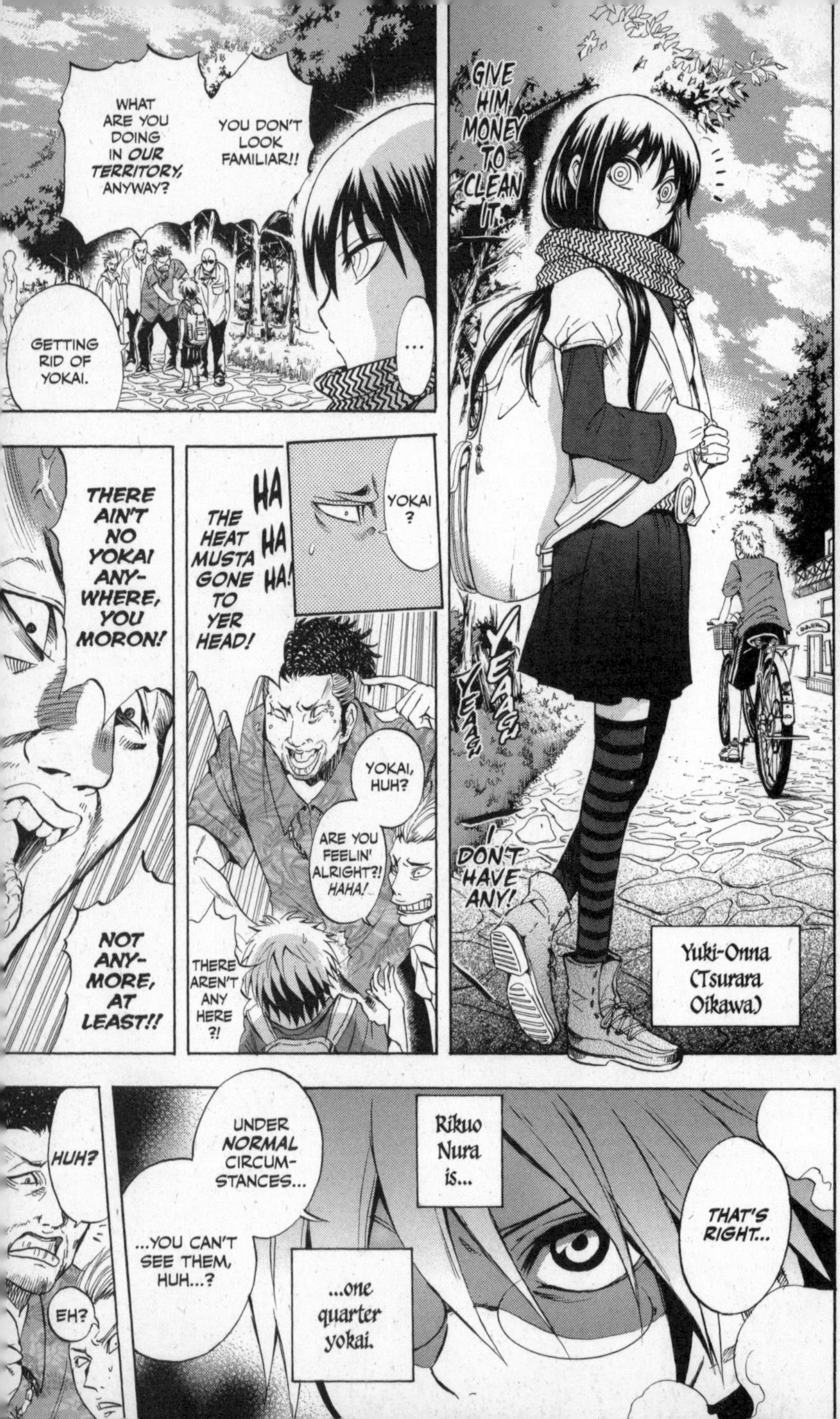
GIVE HIM MONEY TO CLEAN IT.
YEAGH YEAGH YEAGH
I DON'T HAVE ANY!
Yuki-Onna (Tsurara Oikawa)
...
YOU DON'T LOOK FAMILIAR!!
WHAT ARE YOU DOING IN *OUR TERRITORY,* ANYWAY?
GETTING RID OF YOKAI.
YOKAI?
HA HA HA!
THE HEAT MUSTA GONE TO YER HEAD!
YOKAI, HUH?
ARE YOU FEELIN' ALRIGHT?! *HAHA!*
THERE AREN'T ANY HERE ?!
THERE AIN'T NO YOKAI ANYWHERE, YOU MORON!
NOT ANYMORE, AT LEAST!!
THAT'S RIGHT...
Rikuo Nura is...
UNDER *NORMAL* CIRCUMSTANCES...
...YOU CAN'T SEE THEM, HUH...?
...one quarter yokai.
HUH?
EH?

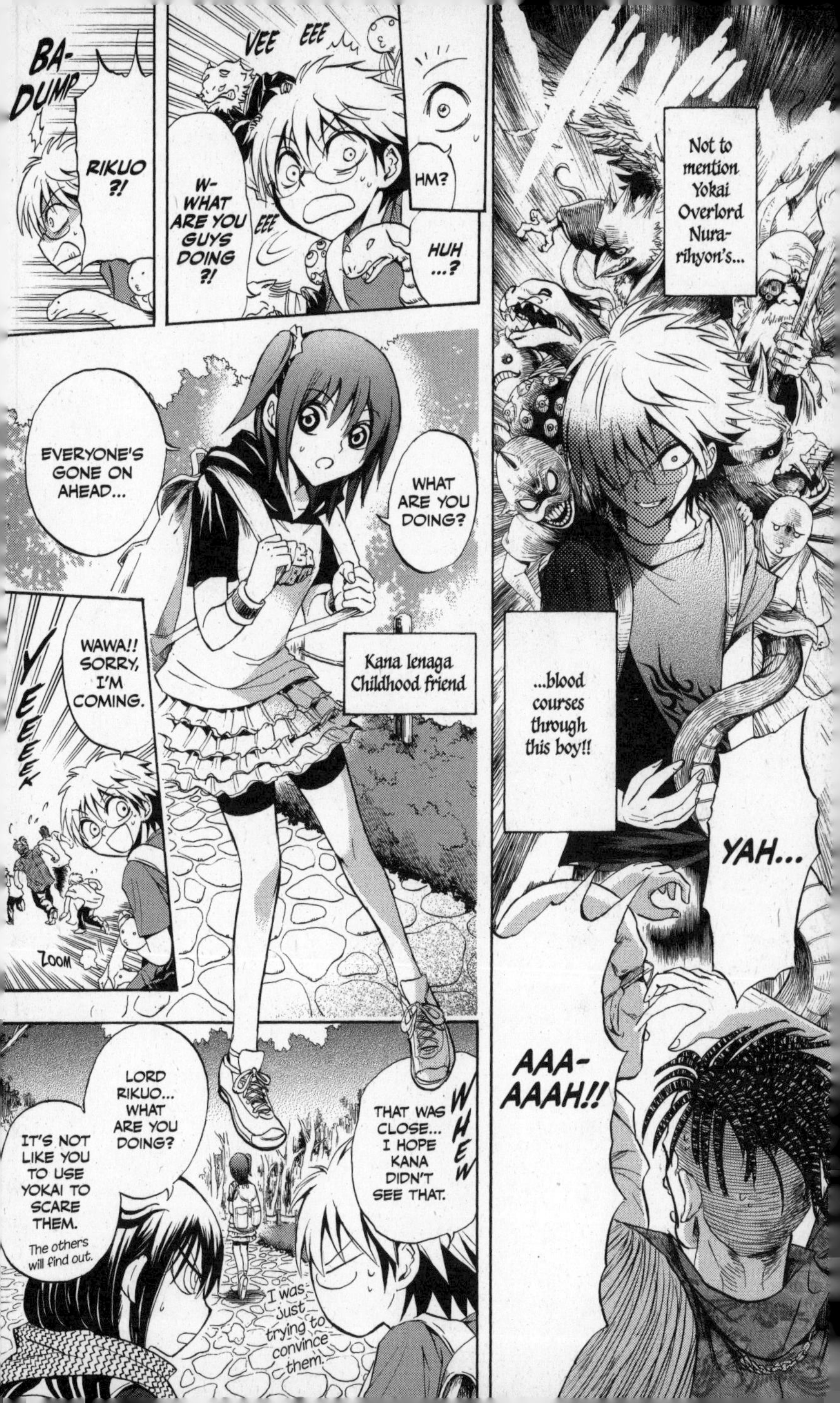
Not to mention Yokai Overlord Nura-rihyon's...
...blood courses through this boy!!
YAH...
AAA-AAAH!!
VEE
EEE
HM?
HUH ...?
W- WHAT ARE YOU GUYS DOING ?!
EEE
BA-DUMP
RIKUO ?!
WHAT ARE YOU DOING?
EVERYONE'S GONE ON AHEAD...
Kana Ienaga Childhood friend
YEEEEK
WAWA!! SORRY, I'M COMING.
ZOOM
WHEW
THAT WAS CLOSE... I HOPE KANA DIDN'T SEE THAT.
LORD RIKUO... WHAT ARE YOU DOING?
IT'S NOT LIKE YOU TO USE YOKAI TO SCARE THEM.
The others will find out.
I was just trying to convince them.

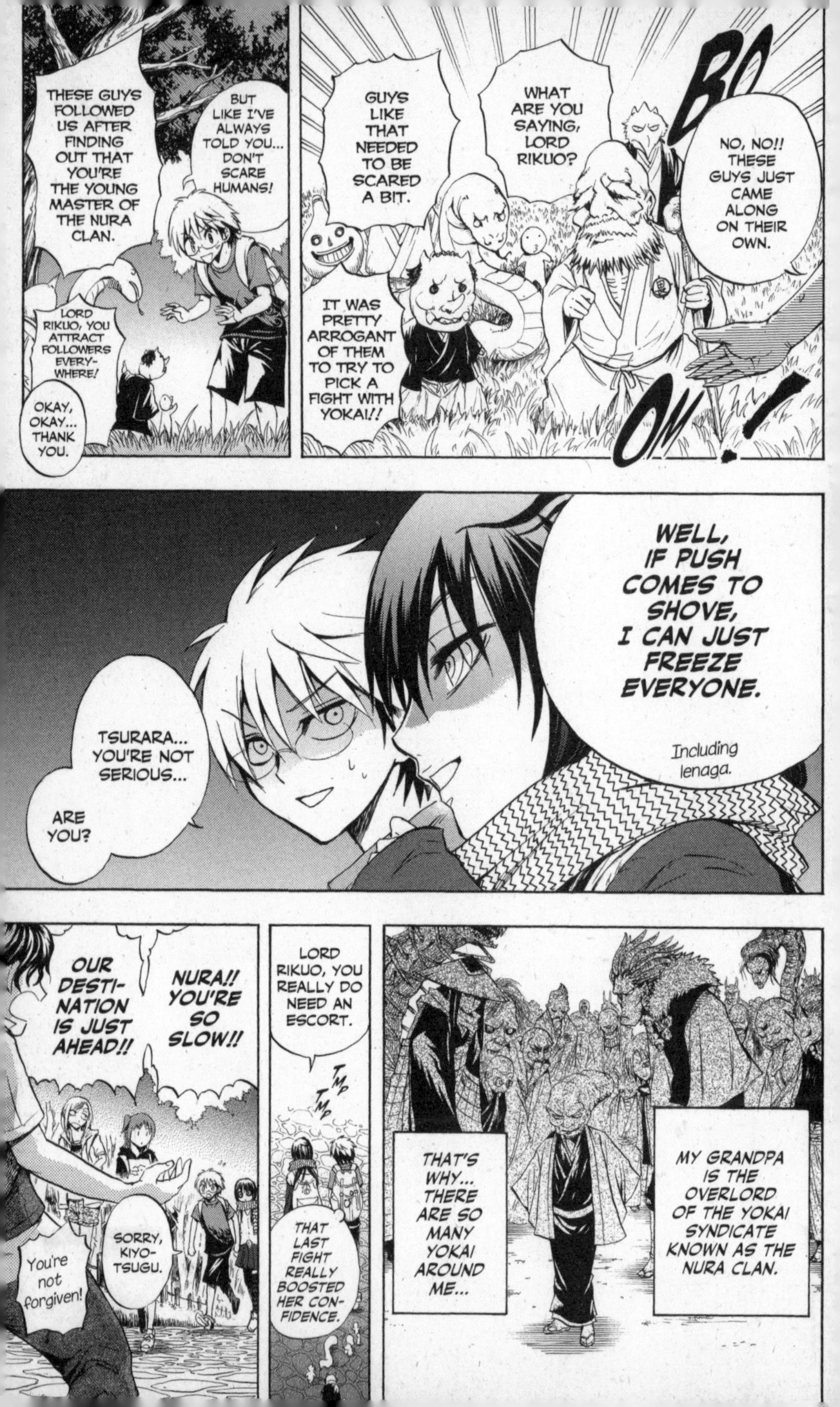

BO
NO, NO!! THESE GUYS JUST CAME ALONG ON THEIR OWN.
WHAT ARE YOU SAYING, LORD RIKUO?
GUYS LIKE THAT NEEDED TO BE SCARED A BIT.
IT WAS PRETTY ARROGANT OF THEM TO TRY TO PICK A FIGHT WITH YOKAI!!
OM!
BUT LIKE I'VE ALWAYS TOLD YOU... DON'T SCARE HUMANS!
THESE GUYS FOLLOWED US AFTER FINDING OUT THAT YOU'RE THE YOUNG MASTER OF THE NURA CLAN.
LORD RIKUO, YOU ATTRACT FOLLOWERS EVERY-WHERE!
OKAY, OKAY... THANK YOU.
WELL, IF PUSH COMES TO SHOVE, I CAN JUST FREEZE EVERYONE.
Including Ienaga.
TSURARA... YOU'RE NOT SERIOUS...
ARE YOU?
MY GRANDPA IS THE OVERLORD OF THE YOKAI SYNDICATE KNOWN AS THE NURA CLAN.
THAT'S WHY... THERE ARE SO MANY YOKAI AROUND ME...
LORD RIKUO, YOU REALLY DO NEED AN ESCORT.
TMP TMP
THAT LAST FIGHT REALLY BOOSTED HER CON-FIDENCE.
NURA!! YOU'RE SO SLOW!!
OUR DESTI-NATION IS JUST AHEAD!!
SORRY, KIYO-TSUGU.
You're not forgiven!

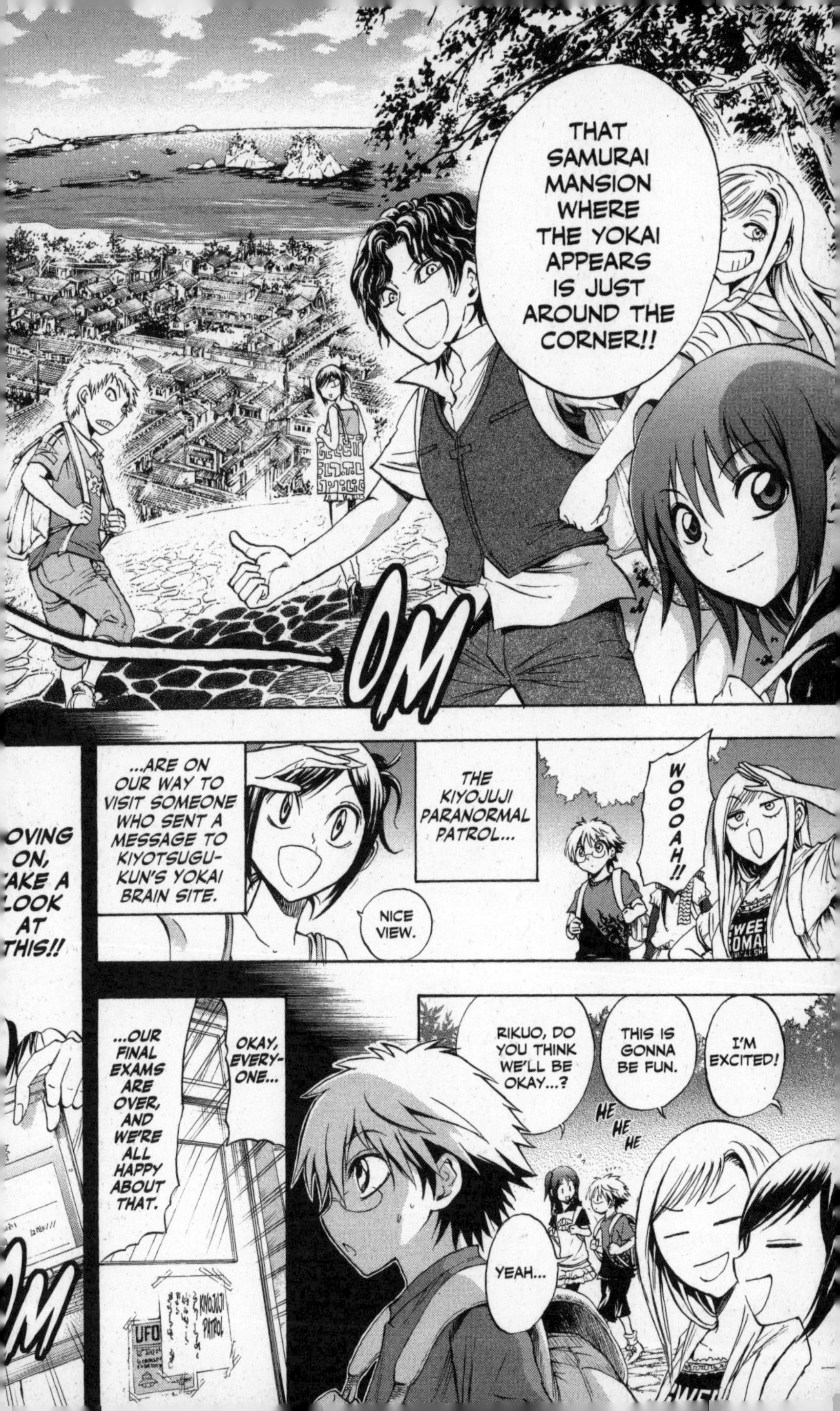
THAT SAMURAI MANSION WHERE THE YOKAI APPEARS IS JUST AROUND THE CORNER!!
OM
WOOOOAH!!
THE KIYOJUJI PARANORMAL PATROL...
...ARE ON OUR WAY TO VISIT SOMEONE WHO SENT A MESSAGE TO KIYOTSUGU-KUN'S YOKAI BRAIN SITE.
NICE VIEW.
OVING ON, AKE A OOK AT THIS!!
I'M EXCITED!
THIS IS GONNA BE FUN.
HE HE HE
RIKUO, DO YOU THINK WE'LL BE OKAY...?
YEAH...
OKAY, EVERYONE...
...OUR FINAL EXAMS ARE OVER, AND WE'RE ALL HAPPY ABOUT THAT.
KIYOJUJI PATROL
UFO
OM

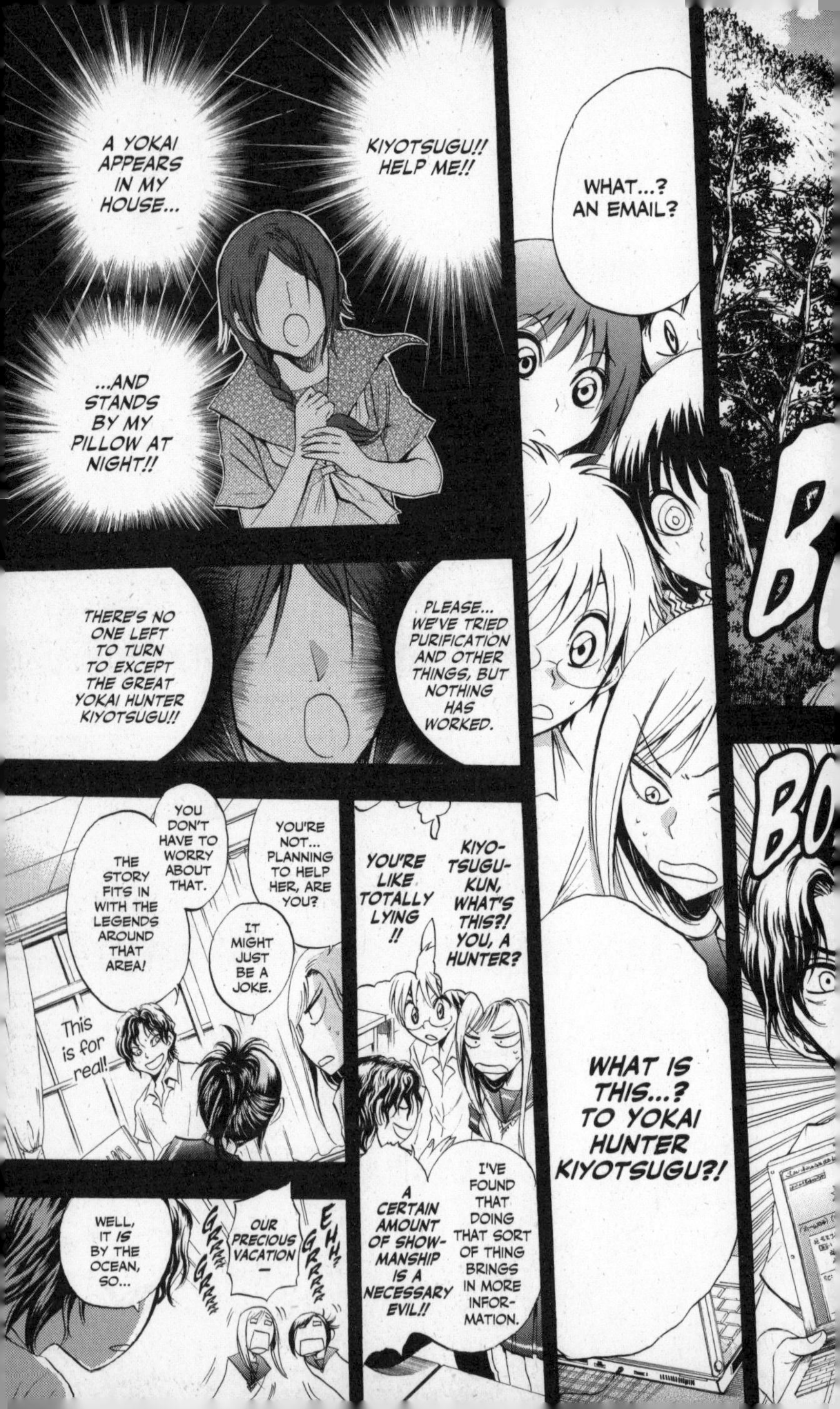
B
BO
WHAT...? AN EMAIL?
WHAT IS THIS...? TO YOKAI HUNTER KIYOTSUGU?!
KIYOTSUGU!! HELP ME!!
A YOKAI APPEARS IN MY HOUSE...
...AND STANDS BY MY PILLOW AT NIGHT!!
PLEASE... WE'VE TRIED PURIFICATION AND OTHER THINGS, BUT NOTHING HAS WORKED.
THERE'S NO ONE LEFT TO TURN TO EXCEPT THE GREAT YOKAI HUNTER KIYOTSUGU!!
KIYO-TSUGU-KUN, WHAT'S THIS?! YOU, A HUNTER?
YOU'RE LIKE TOTALLY LYING!!
I'VE FOUND THAT DOING THAT SORT OF THING BRINGS IN MORE INFOR-MATION.
A CERTAIN AMOUNT OF SHOW-MANSHIP IS A NECESSARY EVIL!!
YOU'RE NOT... PLANNING TO HELP HER, ARE YOU?
YOU DON'T HAVE TO WORRY ABOUT THAT.
IT MIGHT JUST BE A JOKE.
THE STORY FITS IN WITH THE LEGENDS AROUND THAT AREA!
This is for real!
EHH?
GRRRR
OUR PRECIOUS VACATION—
GRRRR
WELL, IT IS BY THE OCEAN, SO...

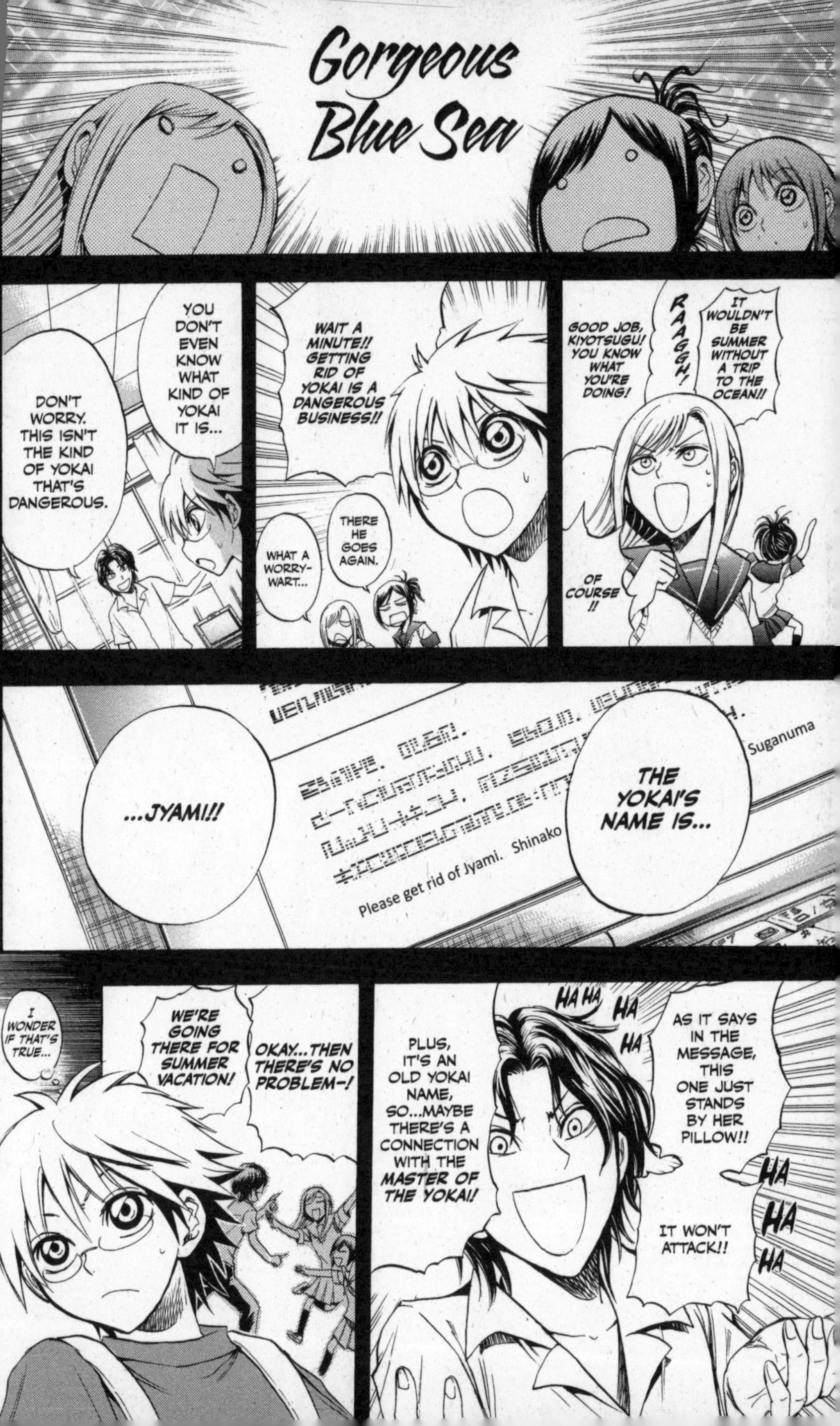
Gorgeous Blue Sea
IT WOULDN'T BE SUMMER WITHOUT A TRIP TO THE OCEAN!!
RAAGGH!
GOOD JOB, KIYOTSUGU! YOU KNOW WHAT YOU'RE DOING!
OF COURSE!!
WAIT A MINUTE!! GETTING RID OF YOKAI IS A DANGEROUS BUSINESS!!
THERE HE GOES AGAIN.
WHAT A WORRY-WART...
YOU DON'T EVEN KNOW WHAT KIND OF YOKAI IT IS...
DON'T WORRY. THIS ISN'T THE KIND OF YOKAI THAT'S DANGEROUS.
THE YOKAI'S NAME IS...
Suganuma
Please get rid of Jyami. Shinako
...JYAMI!!
AS IT SAYS IN THE MESSAGE, THIS ONE JUST STANDS BY HER PILLOW!!
HA HA HA HA
IT WON'T ATTACK!!
HA HA HA
PLUS, IT'S AN OLD YOKAI NAME, SO...MAYBE THERE'S A CONNECTION WITH THE MASTER OF THE YOKAI!
OKAY...THEN THERE'S NO PROBLEM-!
WE'RE GOING THERE FOR SUMMER VACATION!
I WONDER IF THAT'S TRUE...

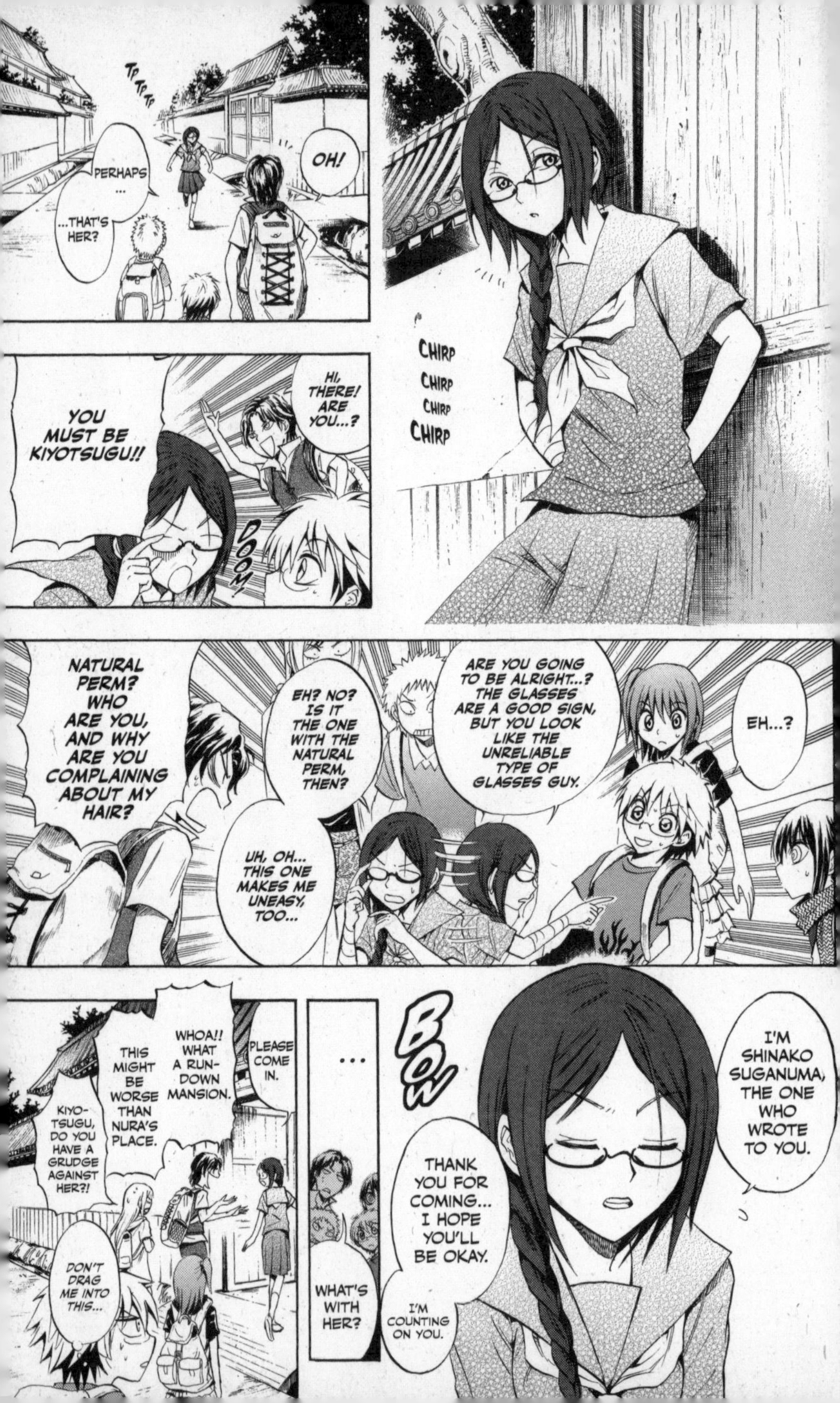
CHIRP
CHIRP
CHIRP
CHIRP
TP TP TP
OH!
PERHAPS...
...THAT'S HER?
HI, THERE! ARE YOU...?
YOU MUST BE KIYOTSUGU!!
DOOOM!
EH...?
ARE YOU GOING TO BE ALRIGHT...? THE GLASSES ARE A GOOD SIGN, BUT YOU LOOK LIKE THE UNRELIABLE TYPE OF GLASSES GUY.
EH? NO? IS IT THE ONE WITH THE NATURAL PERM, THEN?
UH, OH... THIS ONE MAKES ME UNEASY, TOO...
NATURAL PERM? WHO ARE YOU, AND WHY ARE YOU COMPLAINING ABOUT MY HAIR?
BOW
I'M SHINAKO SUGANUMA, THE ONE WHO WROTE TO YOU.
THANK YOU FOR COMING... I HOPE YOU'LL BE OKAY.
I'M COUNTING ON YOU.
...
WHAT'S WITH HER?
PLEASE COME IN.
WHOA!! WHAT A RUN-DOWN MANSION.
THIS MIGHT BE WORSE THAN NURA'S PLACE.
KIYOTSUGU, DO YOU HAVE A GRUDGE AGAINST HER?!
DON'T DRAG ME INTO THIS...

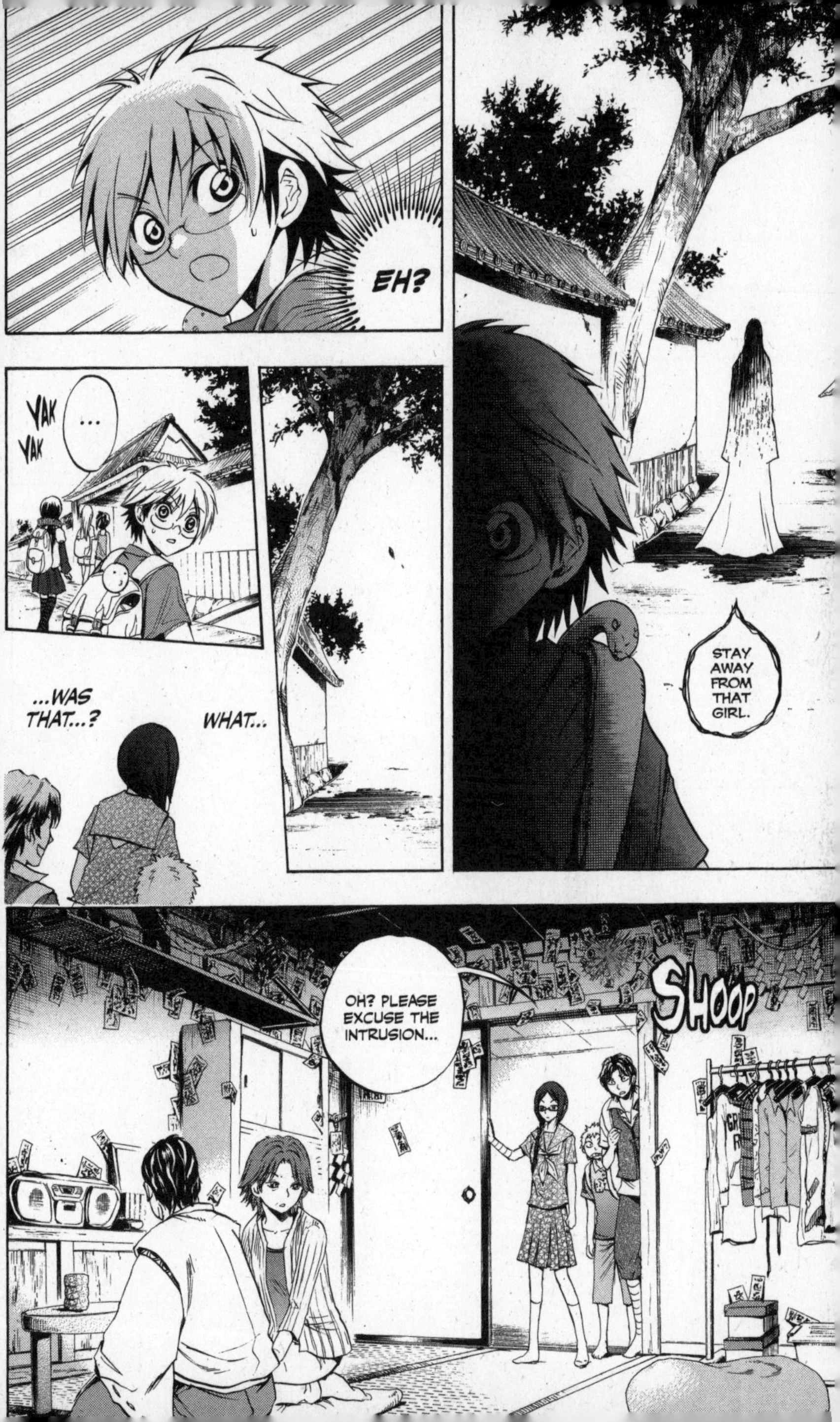
STAY AWAY FROM THAT GIRL.
EH?
...
YAK YAK
WHAT...
...WAS THAT...?
SHOOP
OH? PLEASE EXCUSE THE INTRUSION...

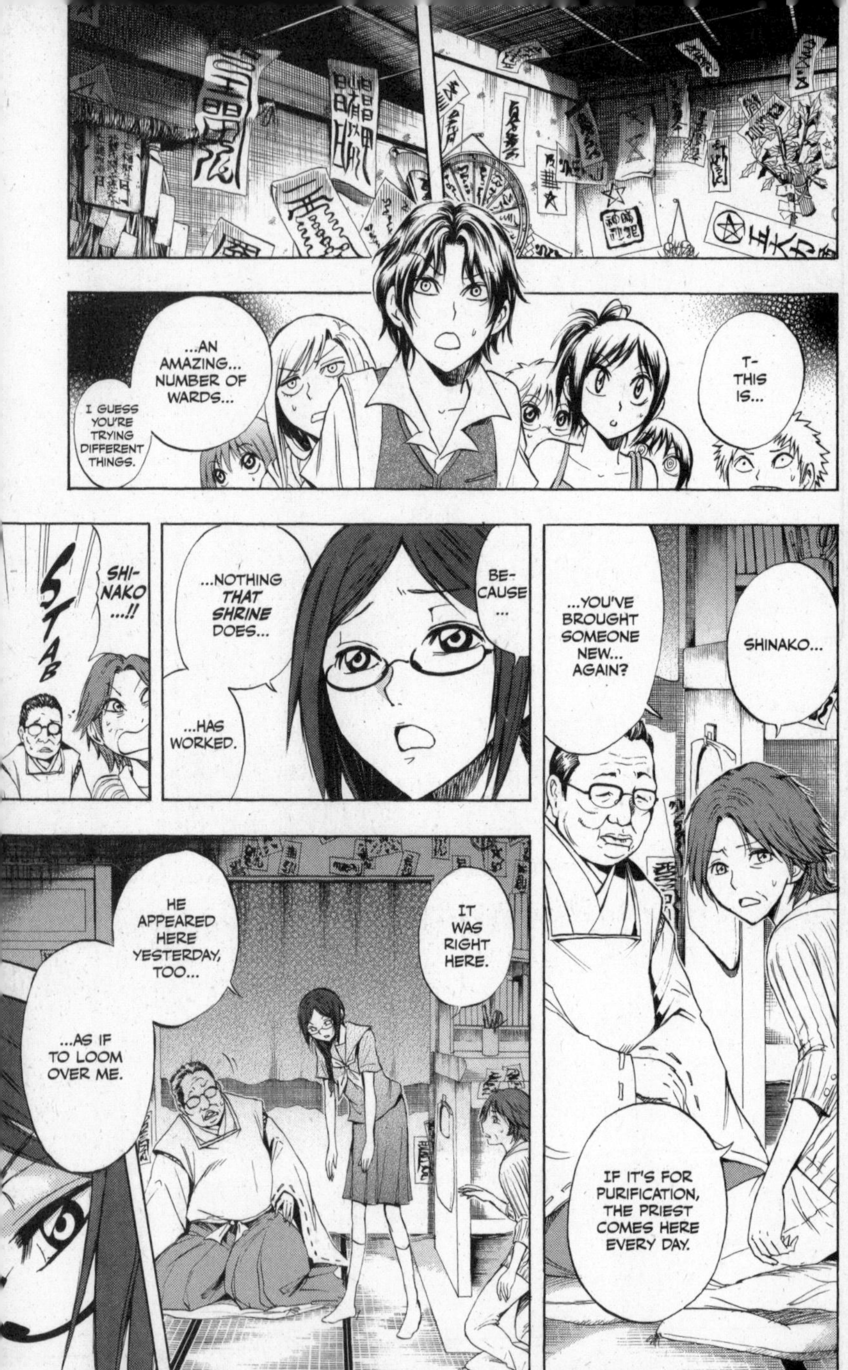
T- THIS IS...
...AN AMAZING... NUMBER OF WARDS...
I GUESS YOU'RE TRYING DIFFERENT THINGS.
SHINAKO...
...YOU'VE BROUGHT SOMEONE NEW... AGAIN?
IF IT'S FOR PURIFICATION, THE PRIEST COMES HERE EVERY DAY.
BE-CAUSE...
...NOTHING THAT SHRINE DOES...
...HAS WORKED.
STAB
SHI-NAKO...!!
IT WAS RIGHT HERE.
HE APPEARED HERE YESTERDAY, TOO...
...AS IF TO LOOM OVER ME.

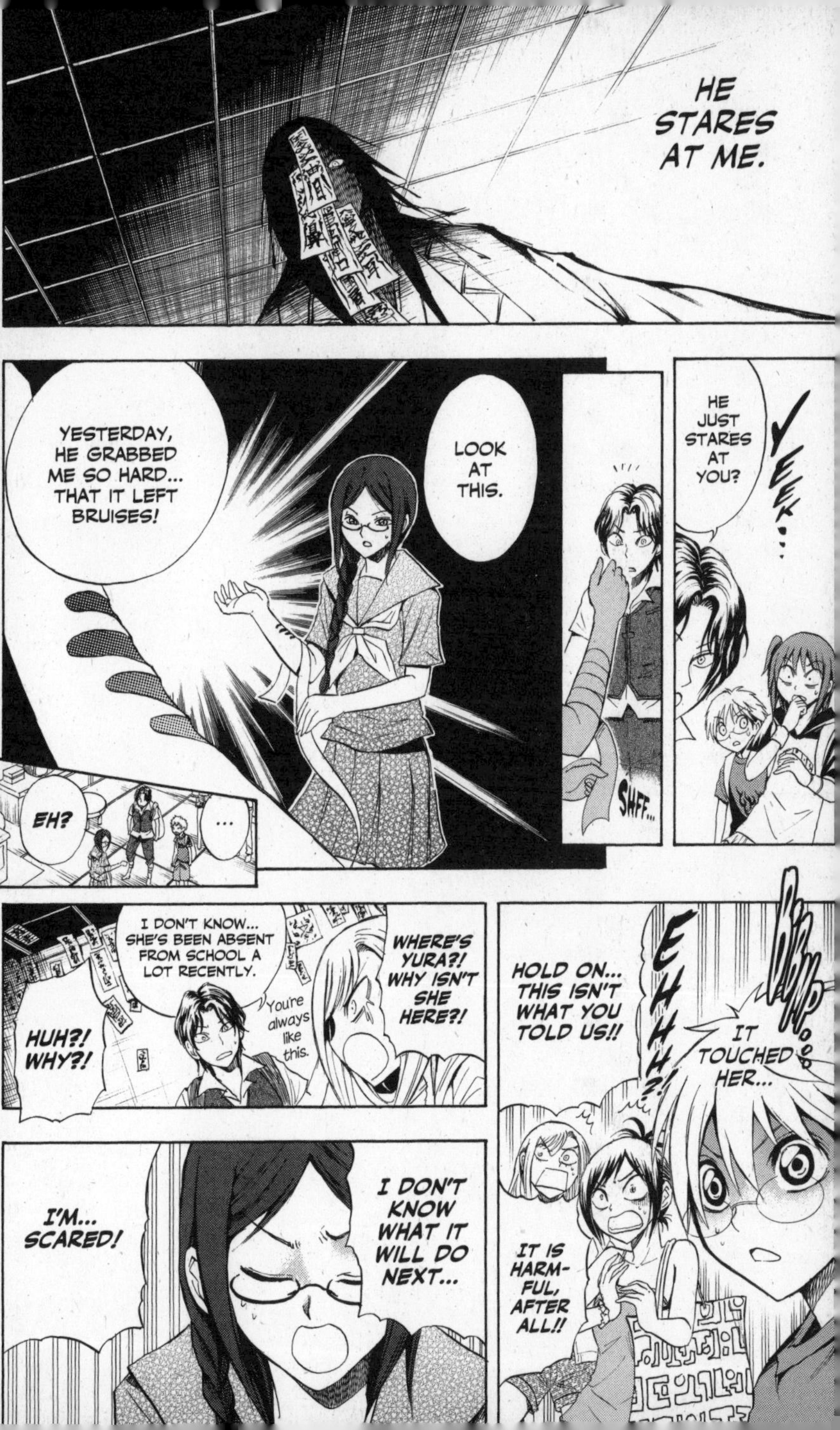
HE STARES AT ME.
HE JUST STARES AT YOU?
YEEK...
SHFF...
LOOK AT THIS.
YESTERDAY, HE GRABBED ME SO HARD... THAT IT LEFT BRUISES!
...
EH?
EHHHH?
IT TOUCHED HER...
HOLD ON... THIS ISN'T WHAT YOU TOLD US!!
IT IS HARMFUL, AFTER ALL!!
WHERE'S YURA?! WHY ISN'T SHE HERE?!
I DON'T KNOW... SHE'S BEEN ABSENT FROM SCHOOL A LOT RECENTLY.
You're always like this.
HUH?! WHY?!
I DON'T KNOW WHAT IT WILL DO NEXT...
I'M... SCARED!

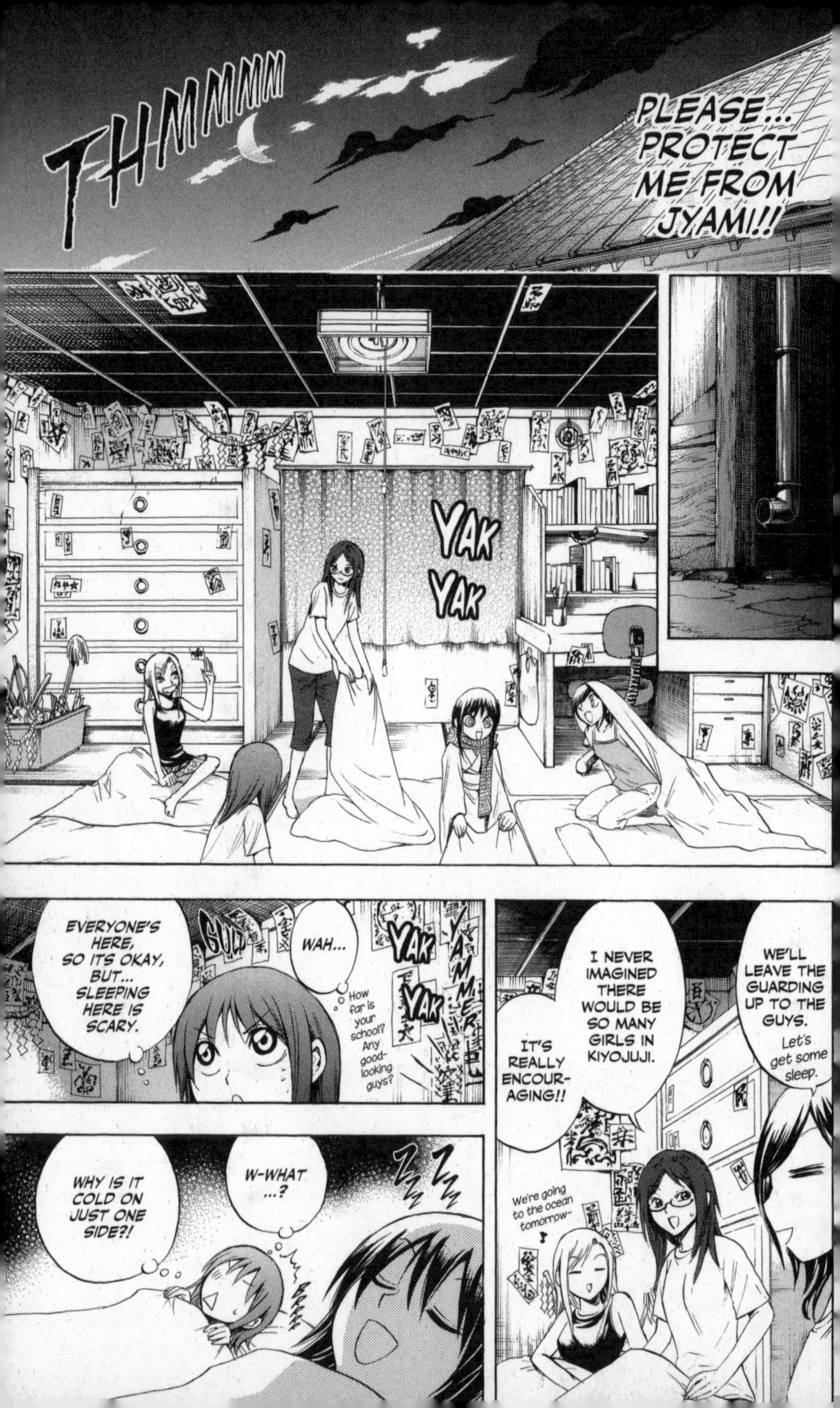
PLEASE... PROTECT ME FROM JYAMI!!
THMMMM
YAK YAK
WE'LL LEAVE THE GUARDING UP TO THE GUYS.
Let's get some sleep.
I NEVER IMAGINED THERE WOULD BE SO MANY GIRLS IN KIYOJUJI.
IT'S REALLY ENCOURAGING!!
We're going to the ocean tomorrow~♪
YAMMER
YAK YAK
How far is your school? Any good-looking guys?
WAH...
GULP
EVERYONE'S HERE, SO ITS OKAY, BUT... SLEEPING HERE IS SCARY.
Z Z
W-WHAT ...?
WHY IS IT COLD ON JUST ONE SIDE?!

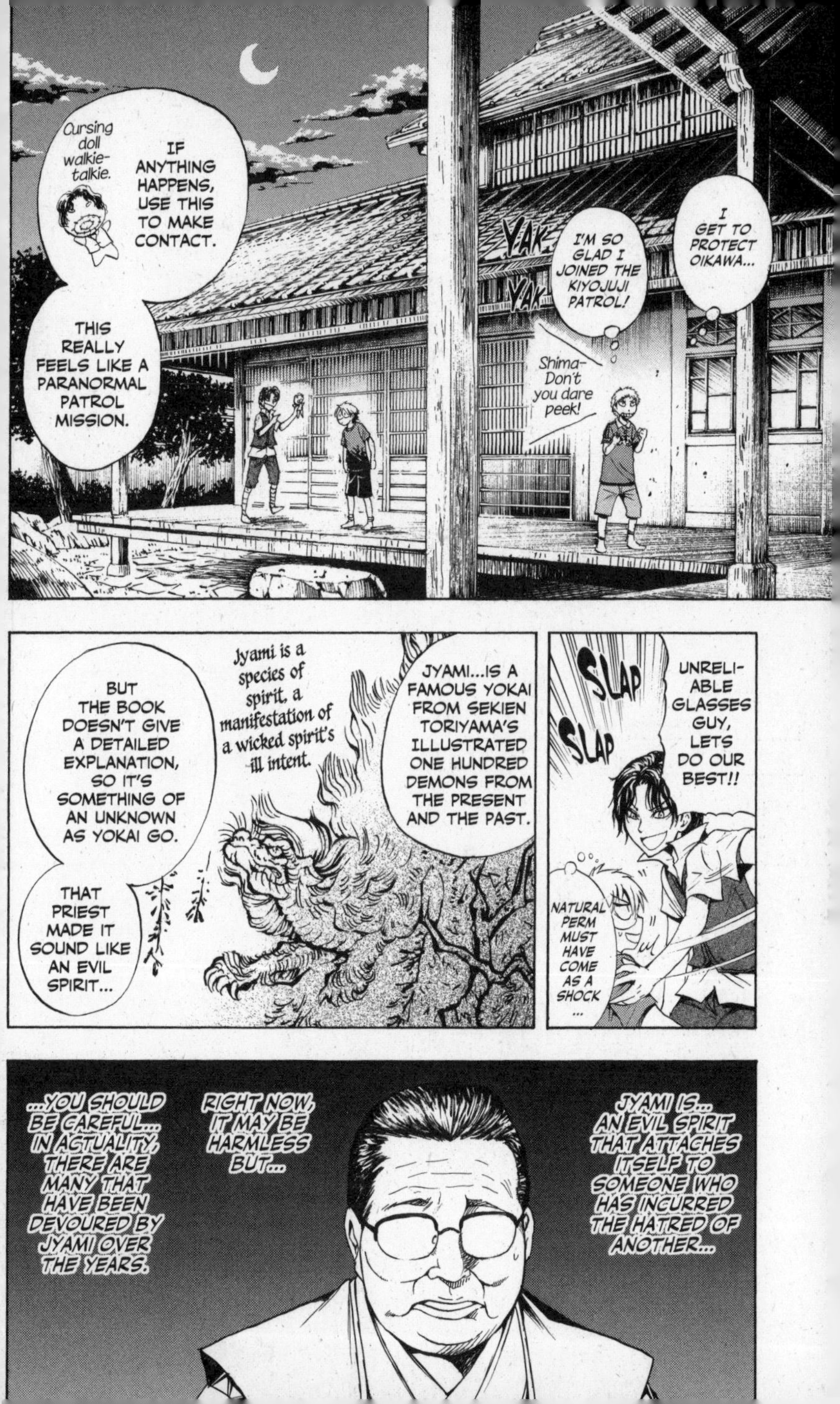
I GET TO PROTECT OIKAWA...
I'M SO GLAD I JOINED THE KIYOJUJI PATROL!
YAK
YAK
Shima- Don't you dare peek!
Cursing doll walkie-talkie.
IF ANYTHING HAPPENS, USE THIS TO MAKE CONTACT.
THIS REALLY FEELS LIKE A PARANORMAL PATROL MISSION.
SLAP
SLAP
UNRELI-ABLE GLASSES GUY, LETS DO OUR BEST!!
NATURAL PERM MUST HAVE COME AS A SHOCK ...
JYAMI...IS A FAMOUS YOKAI FROM SEKIEN TORIYAMA'S ILLUSTRATED ONE HUNDRED DEMONS FROM THE PRESENT AND THE PAST.
Jyami is a species of spirit, a manifestation of a wicked spirit's ill intent.
BUT THE BOOK DOESN'T GIVE A DETAILED EXPLANATION, SO IT'S SOMETHING OF AN UNKNOWN AS YOKAI GO.
THAT PRIEST MADE IT SOUND LIKE AN EVIL SPIRIT...
JYAMI IS... AN EVIL SPIRIT THAT ATTACHES ITSELF TO SOMEONE WHO HAS INCURRED THE HATRED OF ANOTHER...
RIGHT NOW, IT MAY BE HARMLESS BUT...
...YOU SHOULD BE CAREFUL... IN ACTUALITY, THERE ARE MANY THAT HAVE BEEN DEVOURED BY JYAMI OVER THE YEARS.

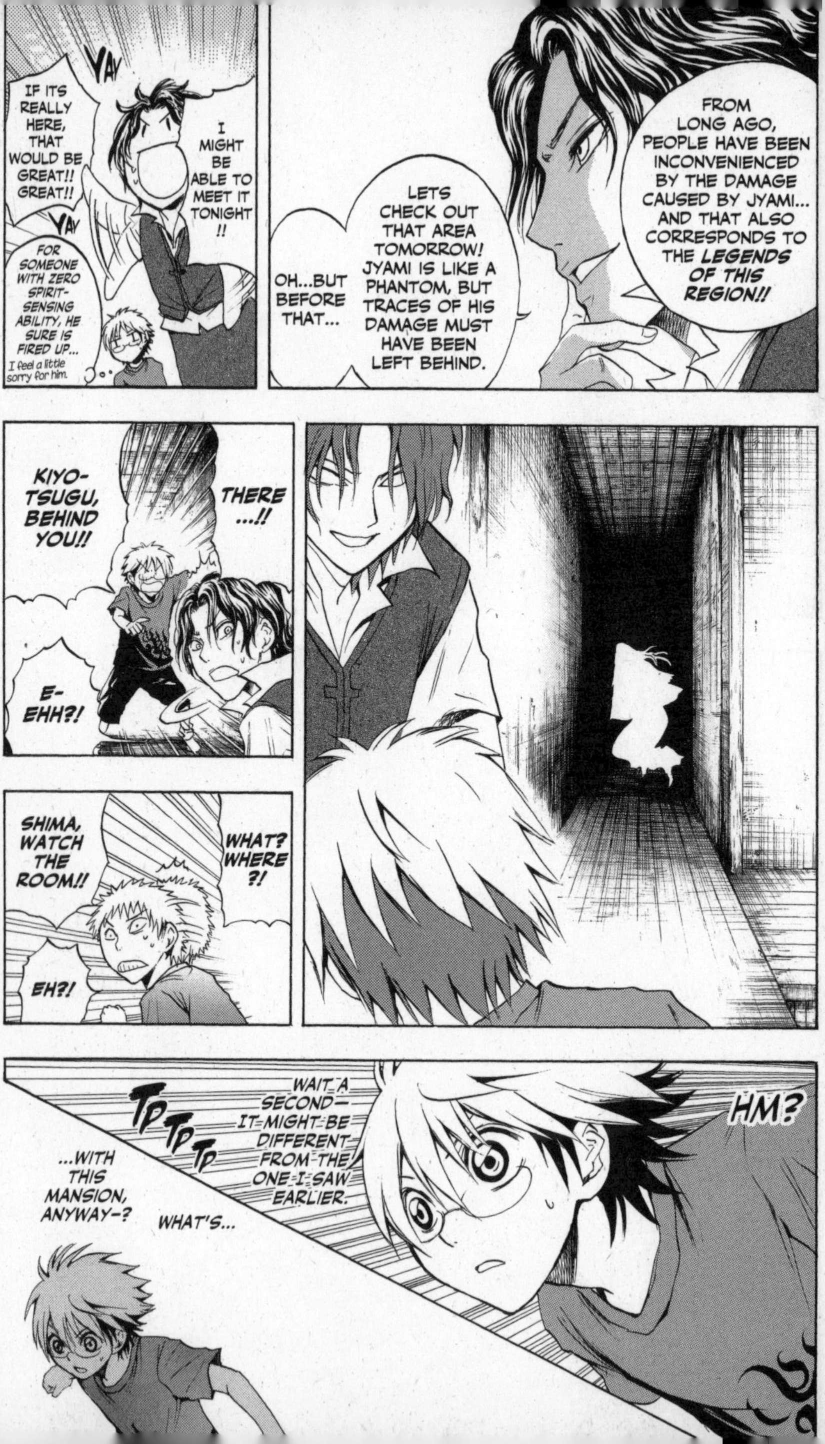
FROM LONG AGO, PEOPLE HAVE BEEN INCONVENIENCED BY THE DAMAGE CAUSED BY JYAMI... AND THAT ALSO CORRESPONDS TO THE *LEGENDS OF THIS REGION!!*
LETS CHECK OUT THAT AREA TOMORROW! JYAMI IS LIKE A PHANTOM, BUT TRACES OF HIS DAMAGE MUST HAVE BEEN LEFT BEHIND.
OH...BUT BEFORE THAT...
I MIGHT BE ABLE TO MEET IT TONIGHT !!
YAY
IF ITS REALLY HERE, THAT WOULD BE GREAT!! GREAT!!
YAY
FOR SOMEONE WITH ZERO SPIRIT-SENSING ABILITY, HE SURE IS FIRED UP...
I feel a little sorry for him.
THERE ...!!
KIYO-TSUGU, BEHIND YOU!!
E-EHH?!
WHAT? WHERE ?!
SHIMA, WATCH THE ROOM!!
EH?!
HM?
WAIT A SECOND— IT MIGHT BE DIFFERENT FROM THE ONE I SAW EARLIER.
TP TP TP
WHAT'S...
...WITH THIS MANSION, ANYWAY-?

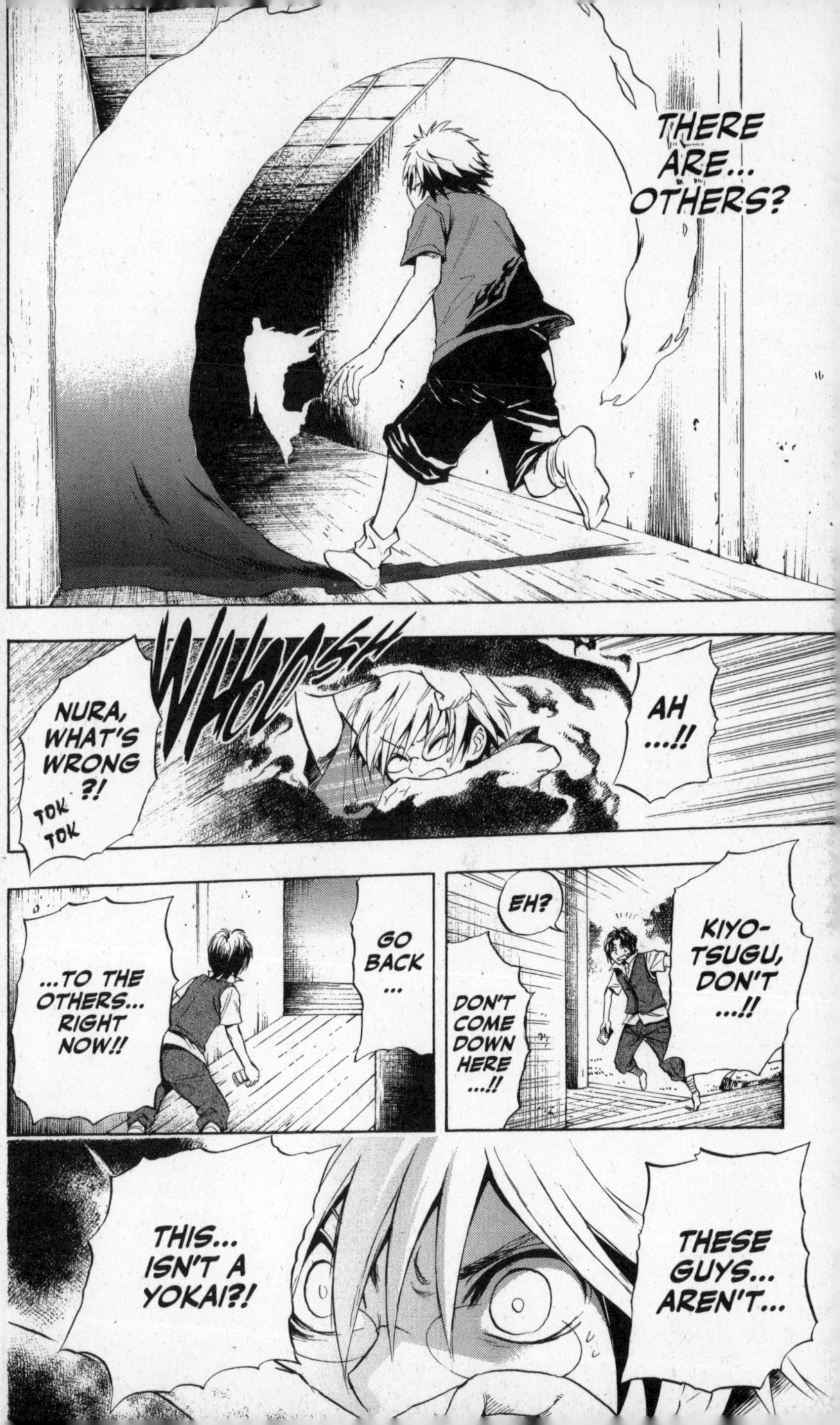
THERE ARE... OTHERS?
AH ...!!
WHOOSH
NURA, WHAT'S WRONG ?!
TOK TOK
KIYO-TSUGU, DON'T ...!!
EH?
DON'T COME DOWN HERE ...!!
GO BACK ...
...TO THE OTHERS... RIGHT NOW!!
THESE GUYS... AREN'T...
THIS... ISN'T A YOKAI?!

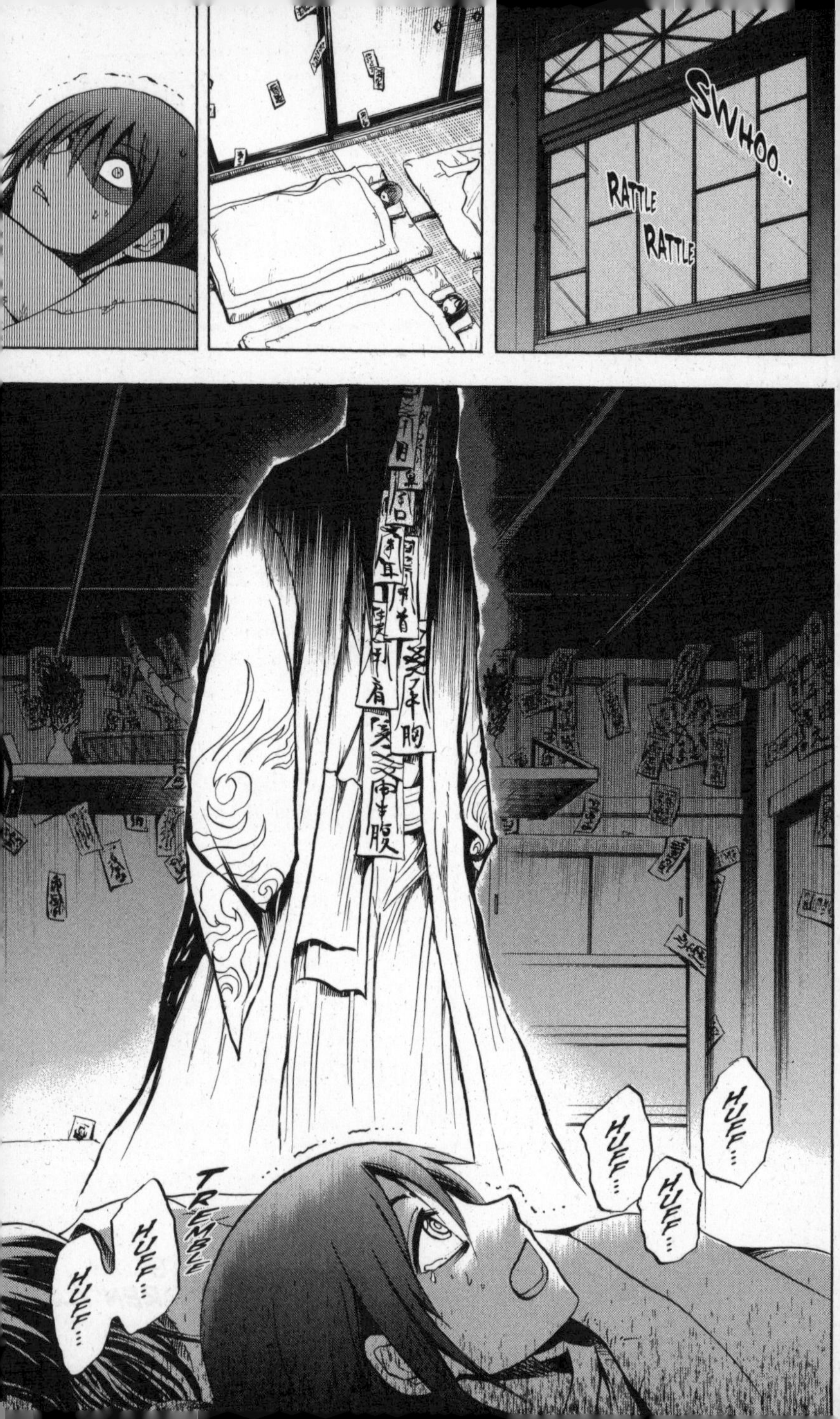
SWHOO...
RATTLE
RATTLE
HUFF...
HUFF...
HUFF...
TREMBLE
HUFF...
HUFF...

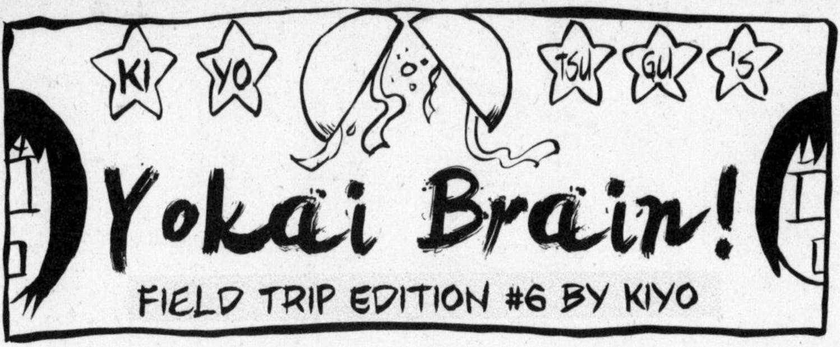
KI YO TSU GU 'S
Yokai Brain!
FIELD TRIP EDITION #6 BY KIYO

Karasu-Tengu: Well, the Shikoku Yokai's assault has finally come to an end. Lord Rikuo played a huge part in that.

The scene is the Nura clan main house. In the living room, the yokai who have finished dinner are relaxing and having tea together.

Karasu-Tengu: Lord Rikuo, how is school? Are you enjoying it? *Slurp*...(drinking tea)

Rikuo: Never mind that, Karasu-Tengu...what are you doing with that cell phone...? Oh, I see!!

Karasu-Tengu: You're accessing Yokai Brain to check up on us again!!

Karasu-Tengu: *Gulp!* A-absolutely not...
Crack! [tea cup dropping] Wah, my tea!!

Rikuo: No matter how you look at it, these are Karasu-Tengu's words!! See, right here!!

Rikuo sets a laptop computer down.

Question: The Nura family's meals are made by Yuki-Onna? What about the mother?
No. 38, Miyagi Prefecture

Answer: Hmmm. That's a good question. The Nura family has a large number of yokai, but only certain yokai are allowed into the living room to enjoy their meal. Still, there are about a hundred of them. To make meals for that many is very difficult!! So, Yuki-Onna and many other yokai help prepare the meals!! Lord Rikuo's mother, Lady Wakana, also helps out in the kitchen. It's hard work.

Other Yokai: Oh, this must be that Internet thing that Karasu-Tengu always talks about...

Rikuo: See, I knew it!!

Karasu-Tengu: N-no!! It's just because I want to know more about Lord Rikuo's situation at school. I'm not accessing that site!!

Question: Karasu-Tengu, who are you married to?
Take, Tokyo

Answer: Hmmm. We Karasu-Tengu have many allies in this nation. I wonder how many years ago it's been since the day I was to leave on a trip around the country with the Overlord? It was on that day that she gave me a gift. She told me that she'd always had feelings for me.., so I told her, "If I return alive. let's get married..." I traveled all over the nation and met many Karasu-Tengu, but none was as beautiful as she. I returned safely and was married thereafter...

Rikuo: No matter how you look at it, this answer clearly came from you, Karasu-Tengu!!

Karasu-Tengu: B-but Lord Rikuo!! Yokai Brain has a lot of questions regarding the Nura clan yokai!! Over ten people wanted to know the names of my sons!! So, from now on, please don't limit it to just the Kiyojuji members! It's better if we can all reply.

Rikuo: Y-yeah...I guess so. I know Kiyotsugu was having trouble keeping up.

Karasu-Tengu: So, in regard to my sons, I wrote their names on the inner cover!! Thank you to everyone who asked! That's it for now. Bye-bye.

Rikuo: Karasu-Tengu, who are you waving to...?

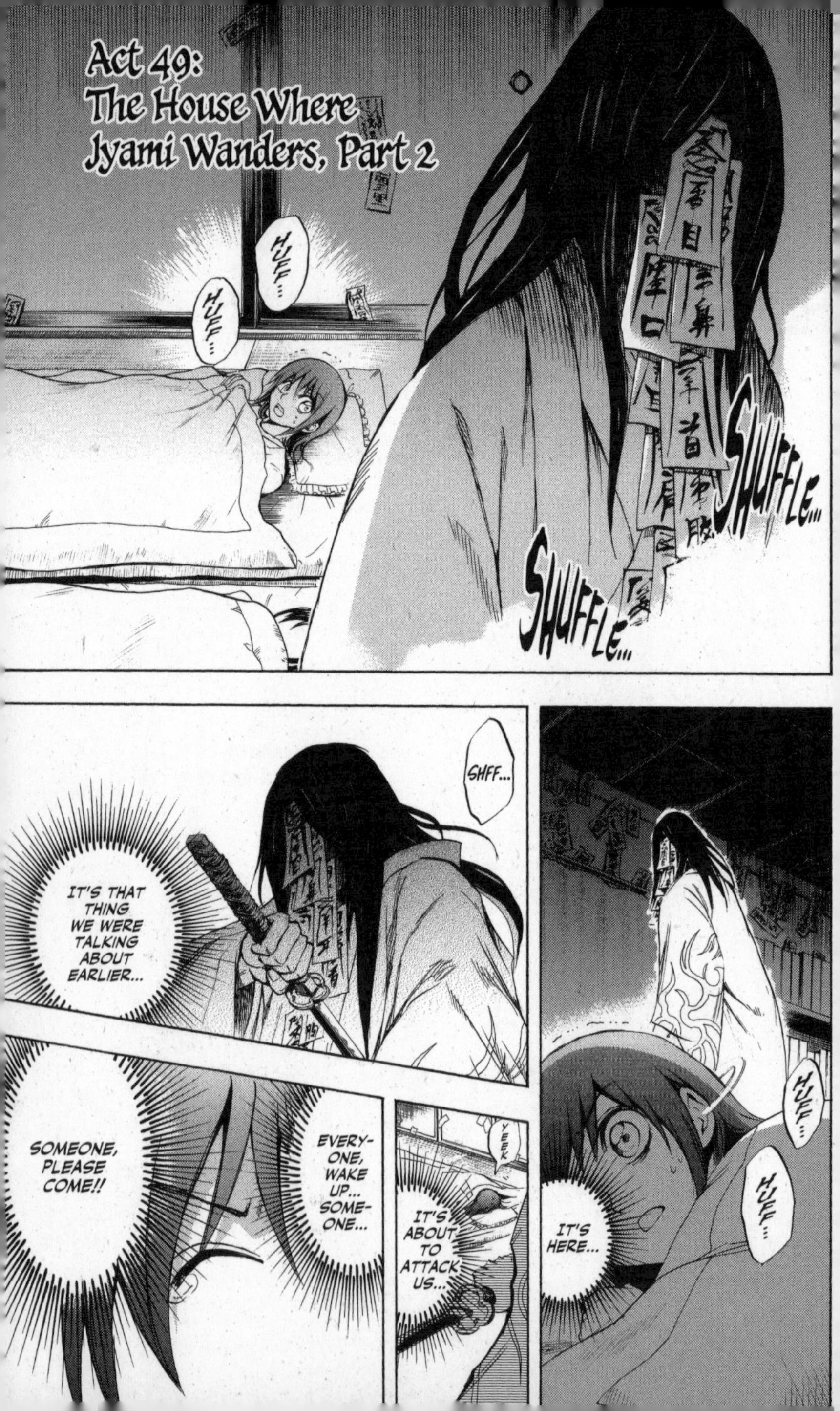
Act 49:
The House Where Jyami Wanders, Part 2
SHUFFLE...
SHUFFLE...
HUFF...
HUFF...
HUFF...
HUFF...
IT'S HERE...
SHFF...
IT'S THAT THING WE WERE TALKING ABOUT EARLIER...
YEEK
IT'S ABOUT TO ATTACK US...
EVERY-ONE, WAKE UP... SOME-ONE...
SOMEONE, PLEASE COME!!

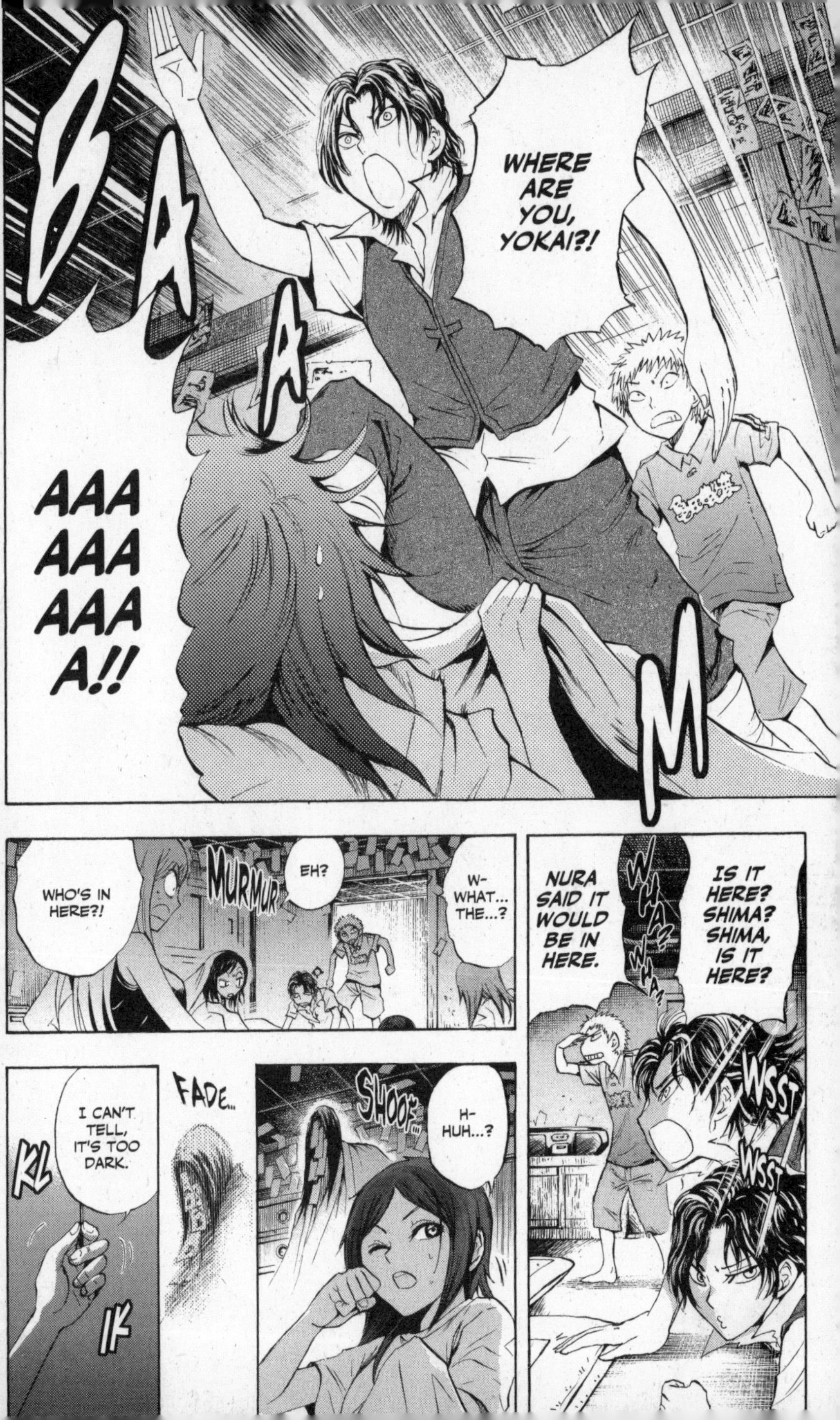
WHERE ARE YOU, YOKAI?!
ZAAAM
AAAAAAAAAA!!
IS IT HERE? SHIMA? SHIMA, IS IT HERE?
NURA SAID IT WOULD BE IN HERE.
WHAM WHAM WHAM
WSST
WSST
W-WHAT... THE...?
EH?
MURMUR
WHO'S IN HERE?!
H-HUH...?
SHOOF...
FADE...
I CAN'T TELL, IT'S TOO DARK.
KLIK

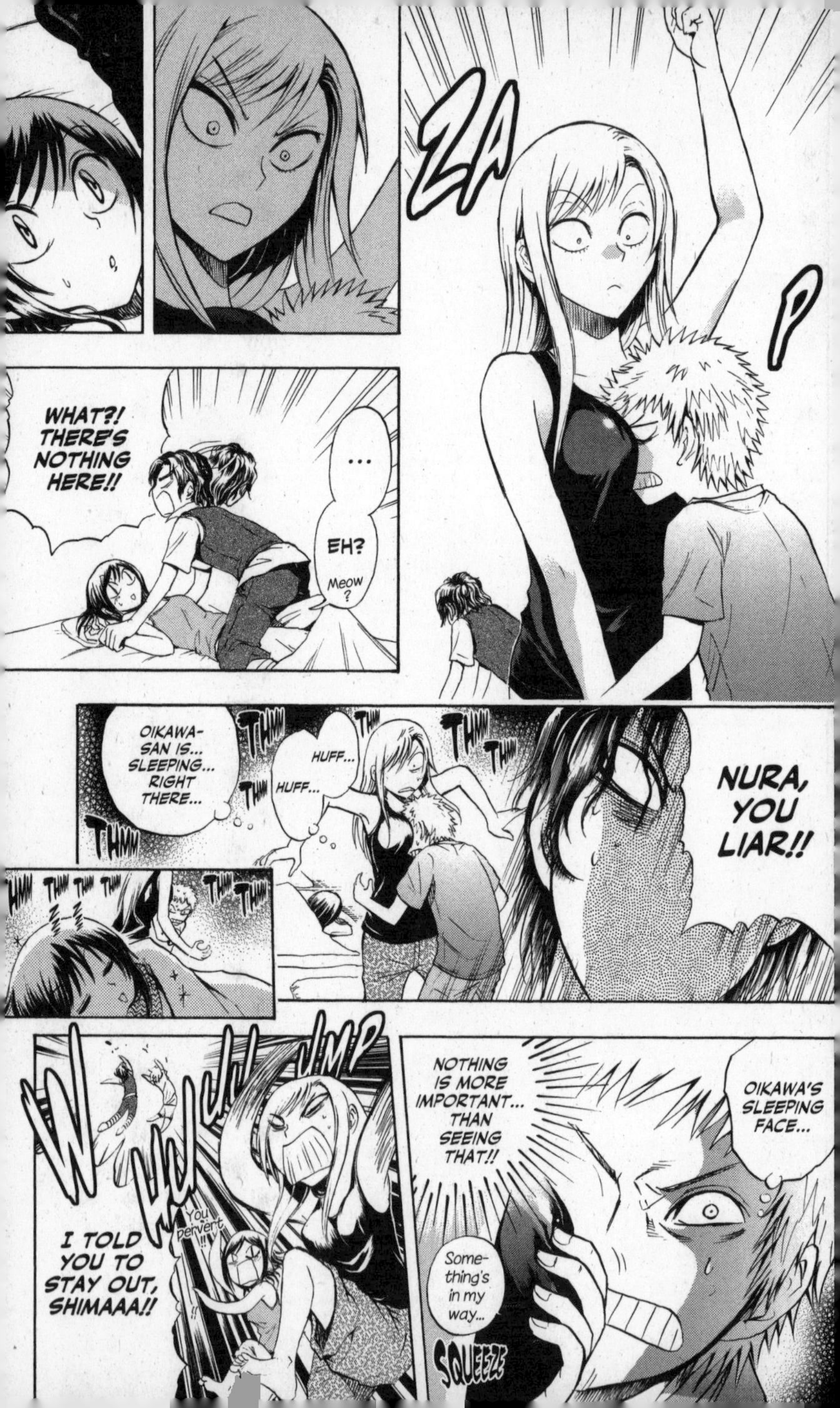
ZA
P
...
WHAT?! THERE'S NOTHING HERE!!
EH?
Meow ?
NURA, YOU LIAR!!
THM THM
HUFF...
HUFF...
OIKAWA-SAN IS... SLEEPING... RIGHT THERE...
THM THM
THM THM THM THM
OIKAWA'S SLEEPING FACE...
NOTHING IS MORE IMPORTANT... THAN SEEING THAT!!
Some-thing's in my way...
SQUEEZE
JMP
WHUD
You pervert!!
I TOLD YOU TO STAY OUT, SHIMAAA!!

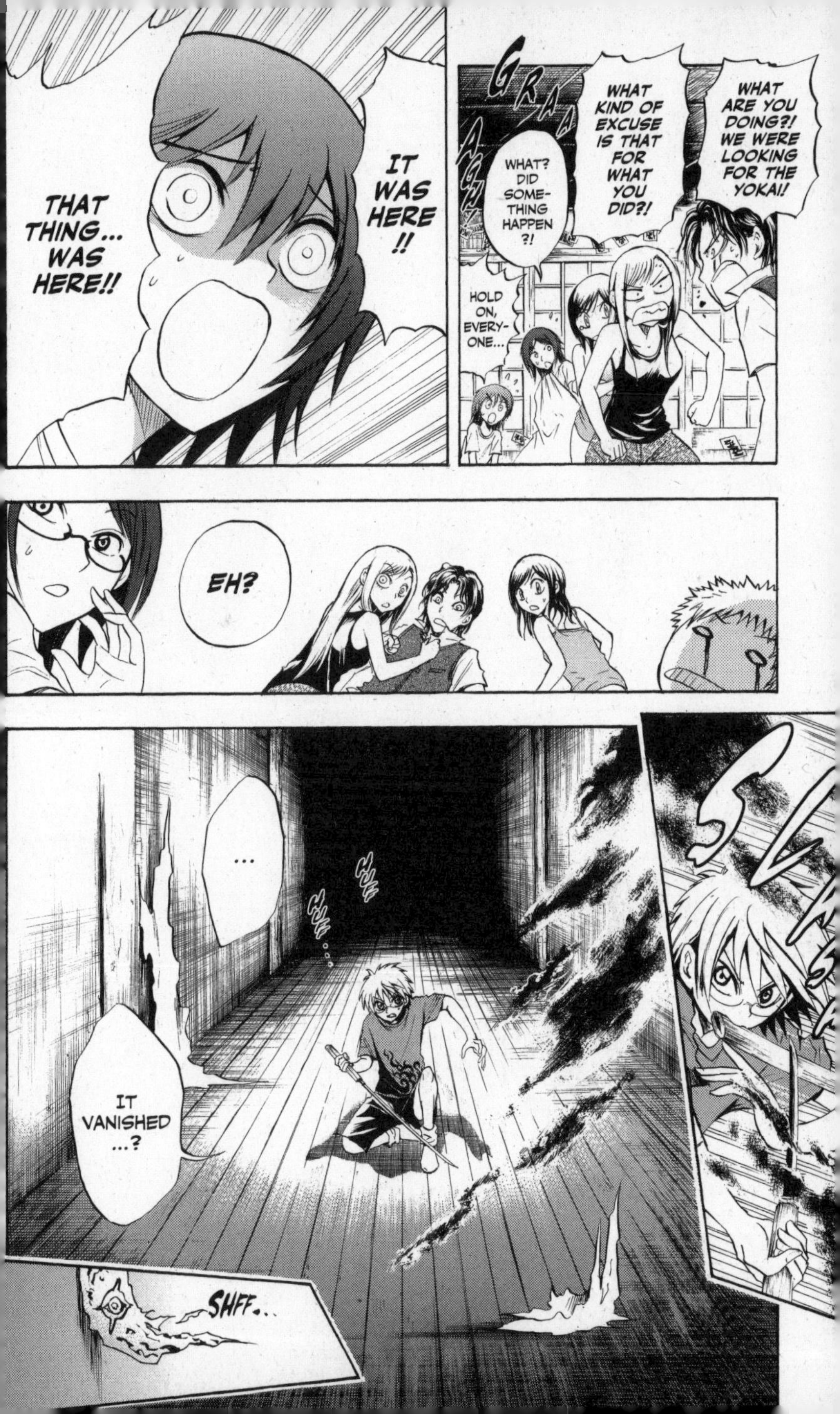
WHAT ARE YOU DOING?! WE WERE LOOKING FOR THE YOKAI!
WHAT KIND OF EXCUSE IS THAT FOR WHAT YOU DID?!
WHAT? DID SOME-THING HAPPEN?!
HOLD ON, EVERY-ONE...
IT WAS HERE!!
THAT THING... WAS HERE!!
EH?
...
IT VANISHED...?
SHFF...

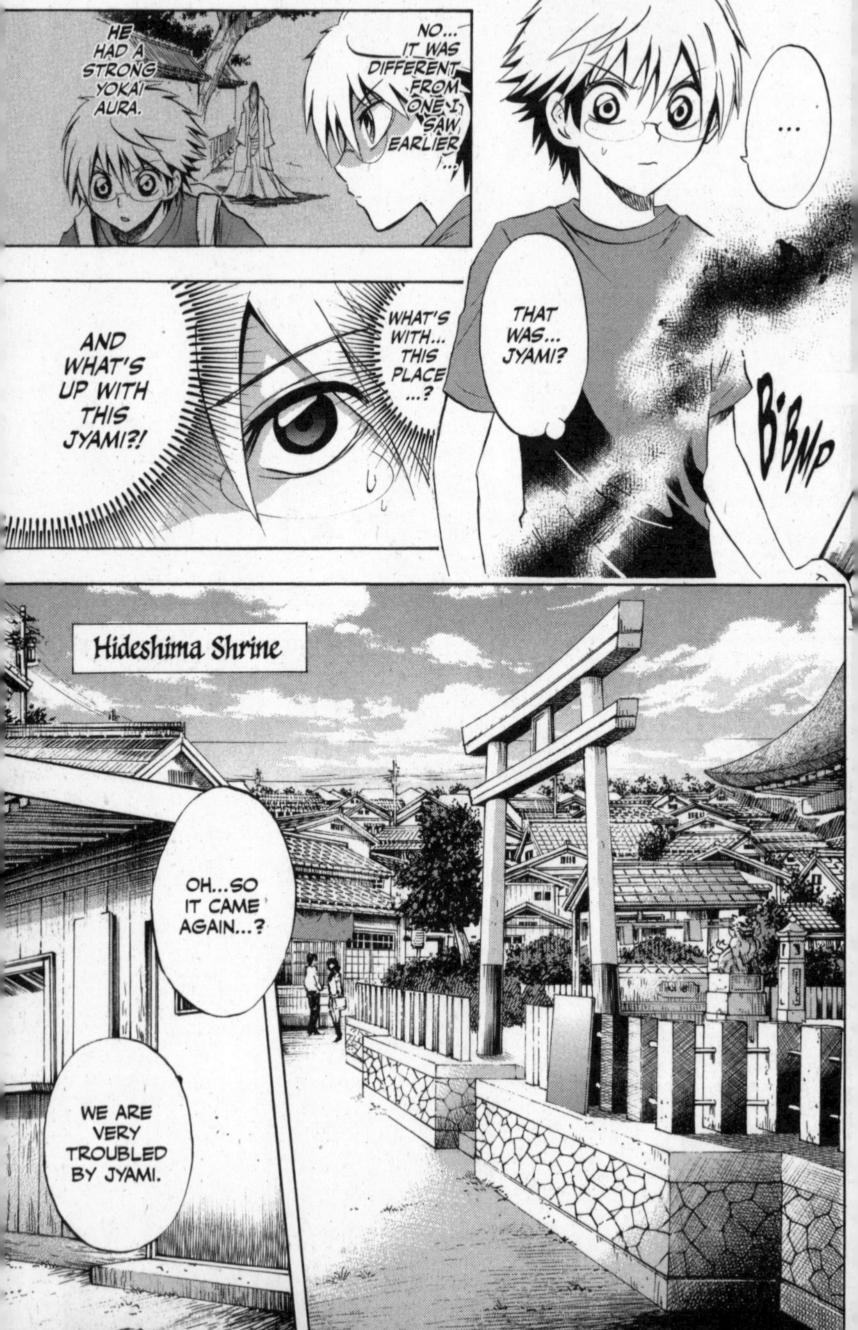
...
THAT WAS... JYAMI?
B'BMP
NO... IT WAS DIFFERENT FROM ONE I SAW EARLIER...
HE HAD A STRONG YOKAI AURA.
WHAT'S WITH... THIS PLACE ...?
AND WHAT'S UP WITH THIS JYAMI?!
Hideshima Shrine
OH...SO IT CAME AGAIN...?
WE ARE VERY TROUBLED BY JYAMI.

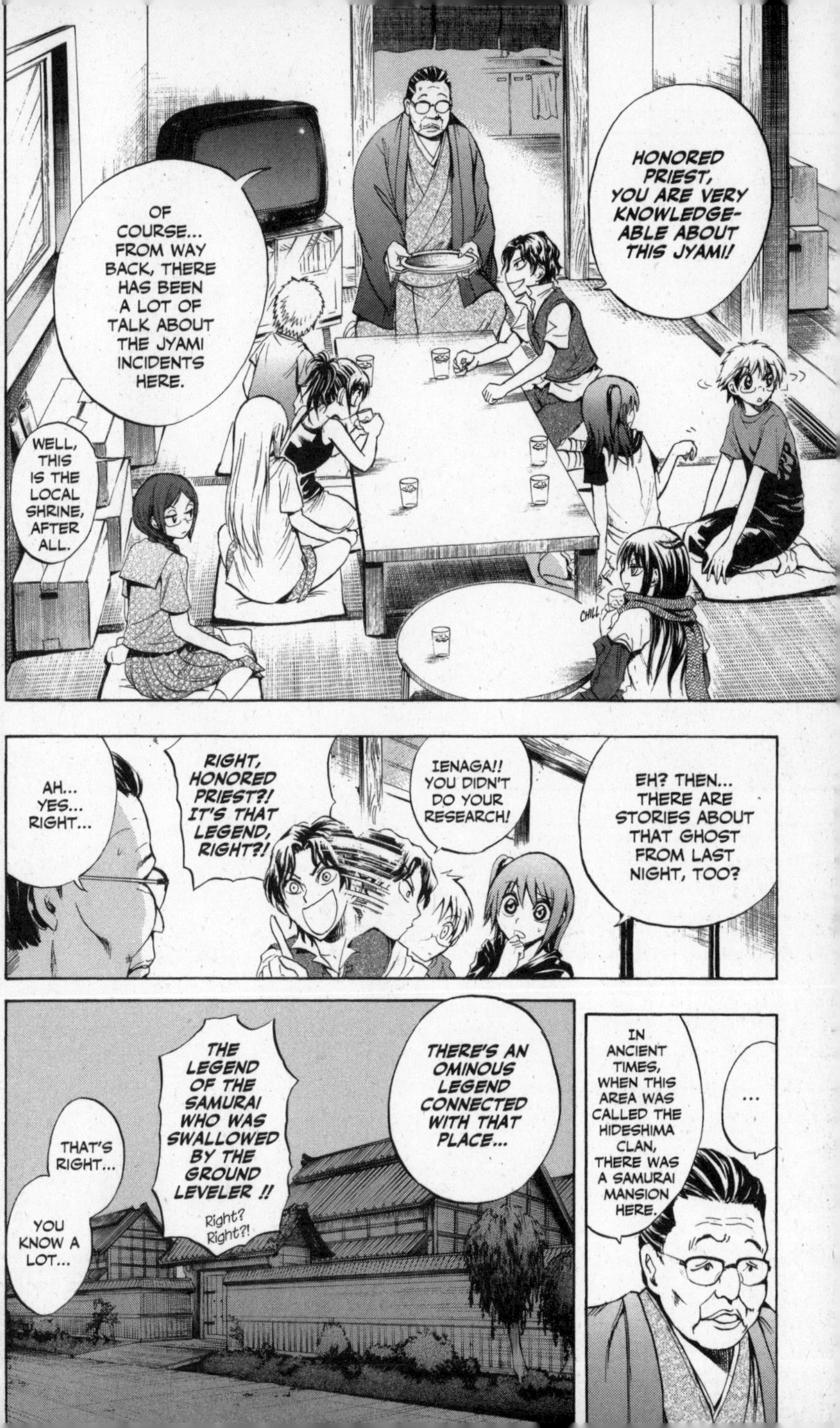
HONORED PRIEST, YOU ARE VERY KNOWLEDGE-ABLE ABOUT THIS JYAMI!
OF COURSE... FROM WAY BACK, THERE HAS BEEN A LOT OF TALK ABOUT THE JYAMI INCIDENTS HERE.
WELL, THIS IS THE LOCAL SHRINE, AFTER ALL.
CHILL
EH? THEN... THERE ARE STORIES ABOUT THAT GHOST FROM LAST NIGHT, TOO?
IENAGA!! YOU DIDN'T DO YOUR RESEARCH!
RIGHT, HONORED PRIEST?! IT'S THAT LEGEND, RIGHT?!
AH... YES... RIGHT...
...
IN ANCIENT TIMES, WHEN THIS AREA WAS CALLED THE HIDESHIMA CLAN, THERE WAS A SAMURAI MANSION HERE.
THERE'S AN OMINOUS LEGEND CONNECTED WITH THAT PLACE...
THE LEGEND OF THE SAMURAI WHO WAS SWALLOWED BY THE GROUND LEVELER !!
Right? Right?!
THAT'S RIGHT...
YOU KNOW A LOT...

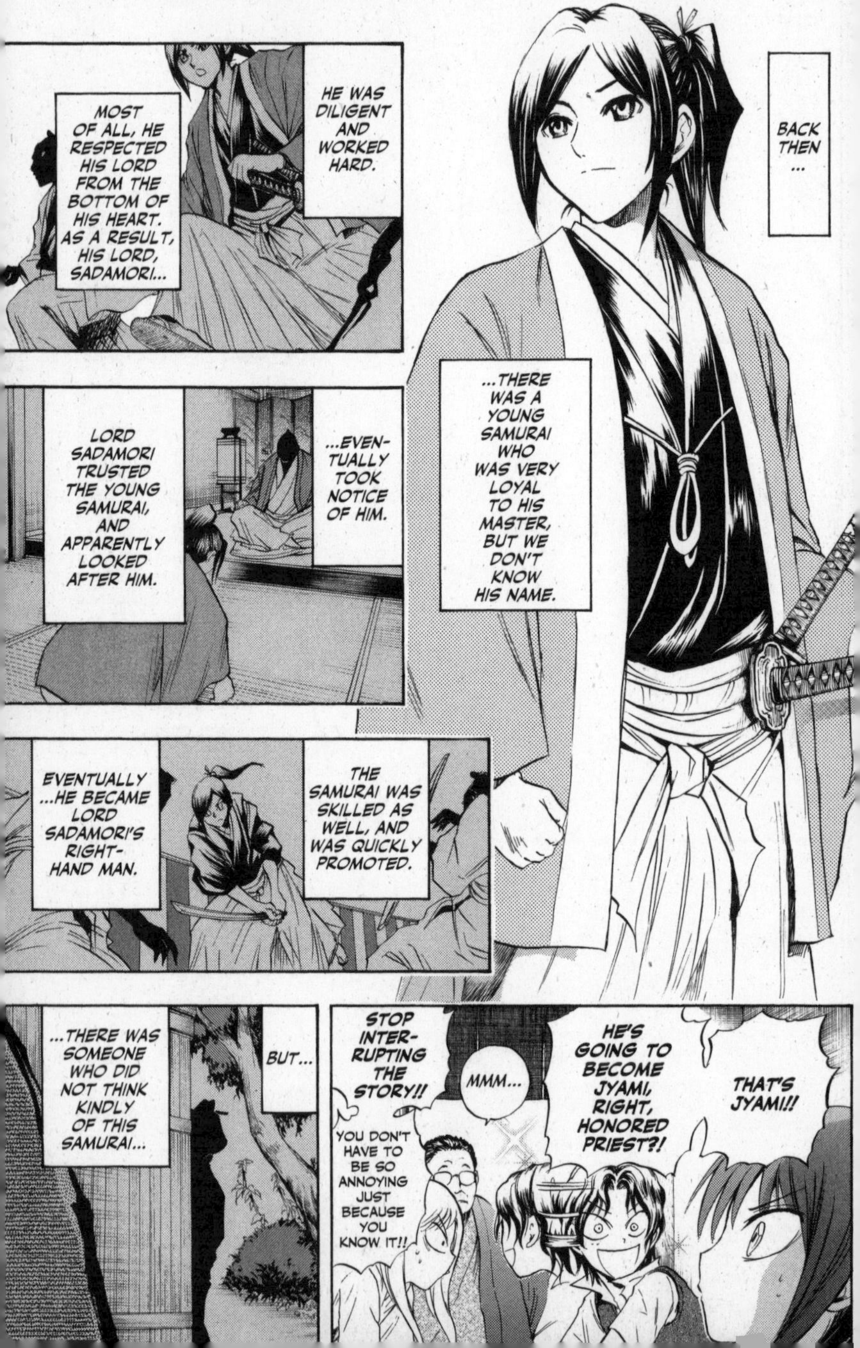
BACK THEN...
...THERE WAS A YOUNG SAMURAI WHO WAS VERY LOYAL TO HIS MASTER, BUT WE DON'T KNOW HIS NAME.
HE WAS DILIGENT AND WORKED HARD.
MOST OF ALL, HE RESPECTED HIS LORD FROM THE BOTTOM OF HIS HEART. AS A RESULT, HIS LORD, SADAMORI...
...EVENTUALLY TOOK NOTICE OF HIM.
LORD SADAMORI TRUSTED THE YOUNG SAMURAI, AND APPARENTLY LOOKED AFTER HIM.
THE SAMURAI WAS SKILLED AS WELL, AND WAS QUICKLY PROMOTED.
EVENTUALLY ...HE BECAME LORD SADAMORI'S RIGHT-HAND MAN.
THAT'S JYAMI!!
HE'S GOING TO BECOME JYAMI, RIGHT, HONORED PRIEST?!
MMM...
STOP INTER-RUPTING THE STORY!!
YOU DON'T HAVE TO BE SO ANNOYING JUST BECAUSE YOU KNOW IT!!
BUT...
...THERE WAS SOMEONE WHO DID NOT THINK KINDLY OF THIS SAMURAI...

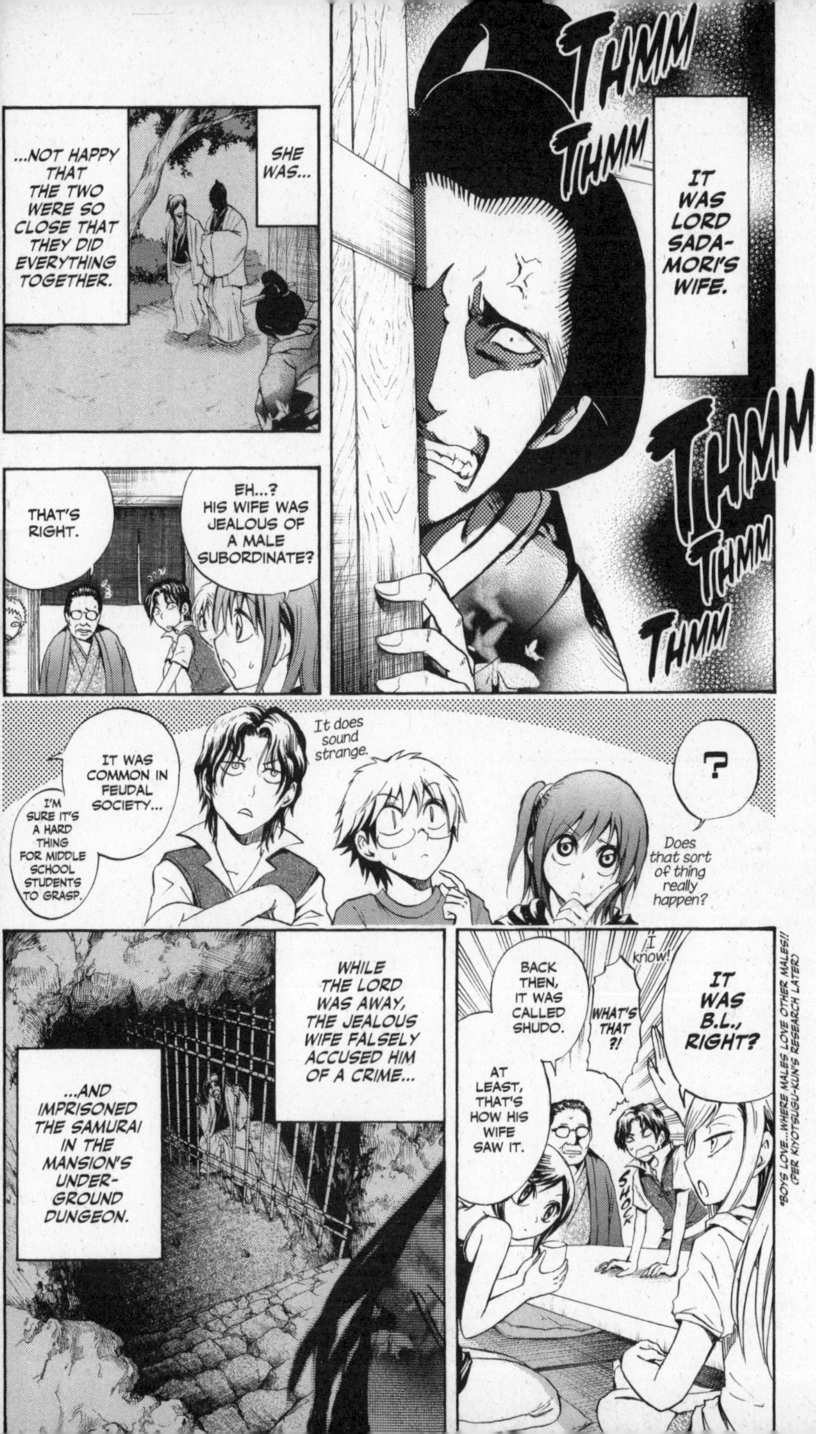
IT WAS LORD SADAMORI'S WIFE.
THMM THMM
THMM THMM THMM
SHE WAS...
...NOT HAPPY THAT THE TWO WERE SO CLOSE THAT THEY DID EVERYTHING TOGETHER.
EH...? HIS WIFE WAS JEALOUS OF A MALE SUBORDINATE?
THAT'S RIGHT.
?
Does that sort of thing really happen?
It does sound strange.
IT WAS COMMON IN FEUDAL SOCIETY...
I'M SURE IT'S A HARD THING FOR MIDDLE SCHOOL STUDENTS TO GRASP.
IT WAS B.L., RIGHT?
I know!
WHAT'S THAT?!
BACK THEN, IT WAS CALLED SHUDO.
AT LEAST, THAT'S HOW HIS WIFE SAW IT.
SHOCK
*BOYS LOVE...WHERE MALES LOVE OTHER MALES!! (PER KIYOTSUGU-KUN'S RESEARCH LATER)
WHILE THE LORD WAS AWAY, THE JEALOUS WIFE FALSELY ACCUSED HIM OF A CRIME...
...AND IMPRISONED THE SAMURAI IN THE MANSION'S UNDERGROUND DUNGEON.

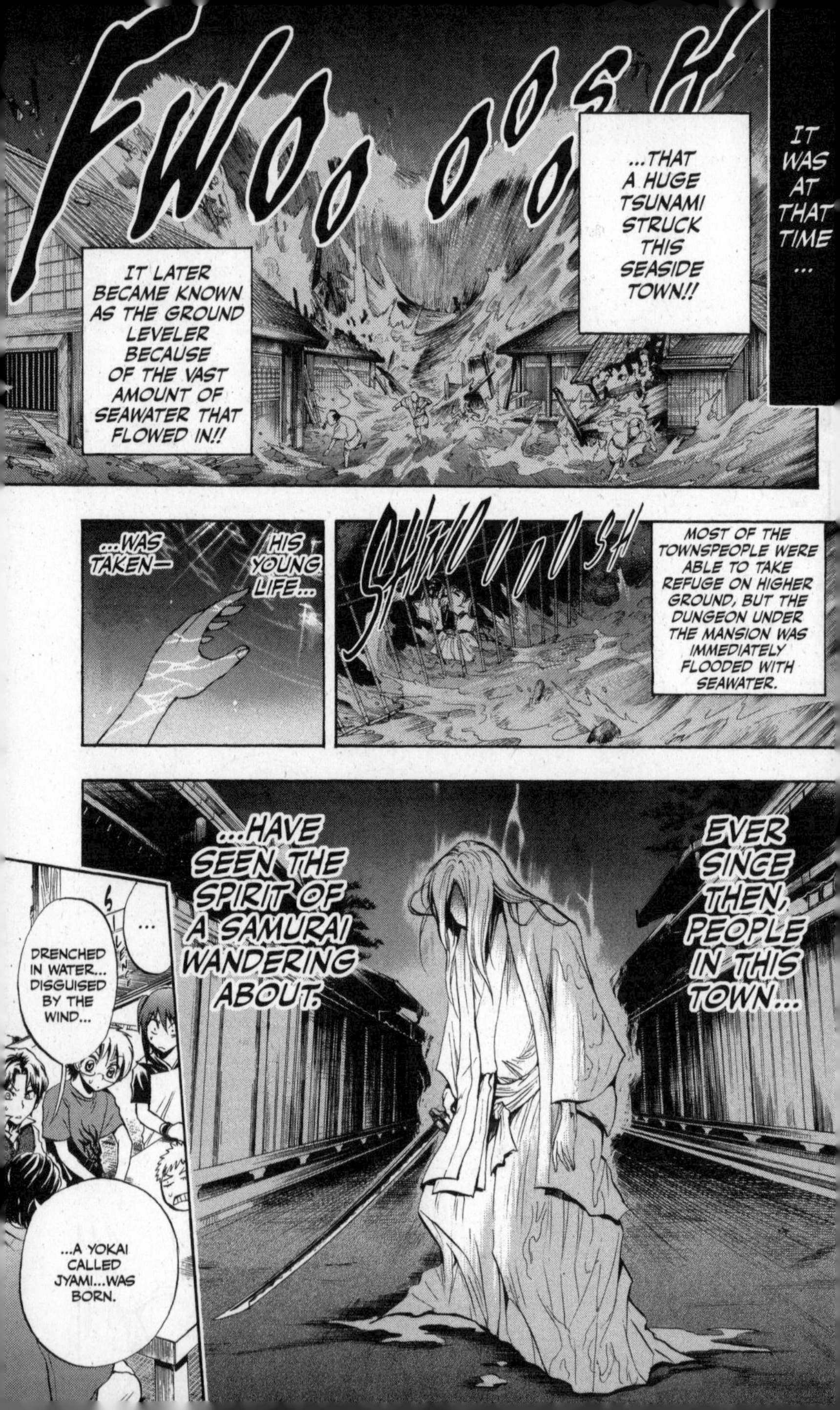
IT WAS AT THAT TIME...
FWOOOOOSH
...THAT A HUGE TSUNAMI STRUCK THIS SEASIDE TOWN!!
IT LATER BECAME KNOWN AS THE GROUND LEVELER BECAUSE OF THE VAST AMOUNT OF SEAWATER THAT FLOWED IN!!
MOST OF THE TOWNSPEOPLE WERE ABLE TO TAKE REFUGE ON HIGHER GROUND, BUT THE DUNGEON UNDER THE MANSION WAS IMMEDIATELY FLOODED WITH SEAWATER.
SHWOOOOSH
HIS YOUNG LIFE...
...WAS TAKEN—
EVER SINCE THEN, PEOPLE IN THIS TOWN...
...HAVE SEEN THE SPIRIT OF A SAMURAI WANDERING ABOUT.
...
DRENCHED IN WATER... DISGUISED BY THE WIND...
...A YOKAI CALLED JYAMI...WAS BORN.

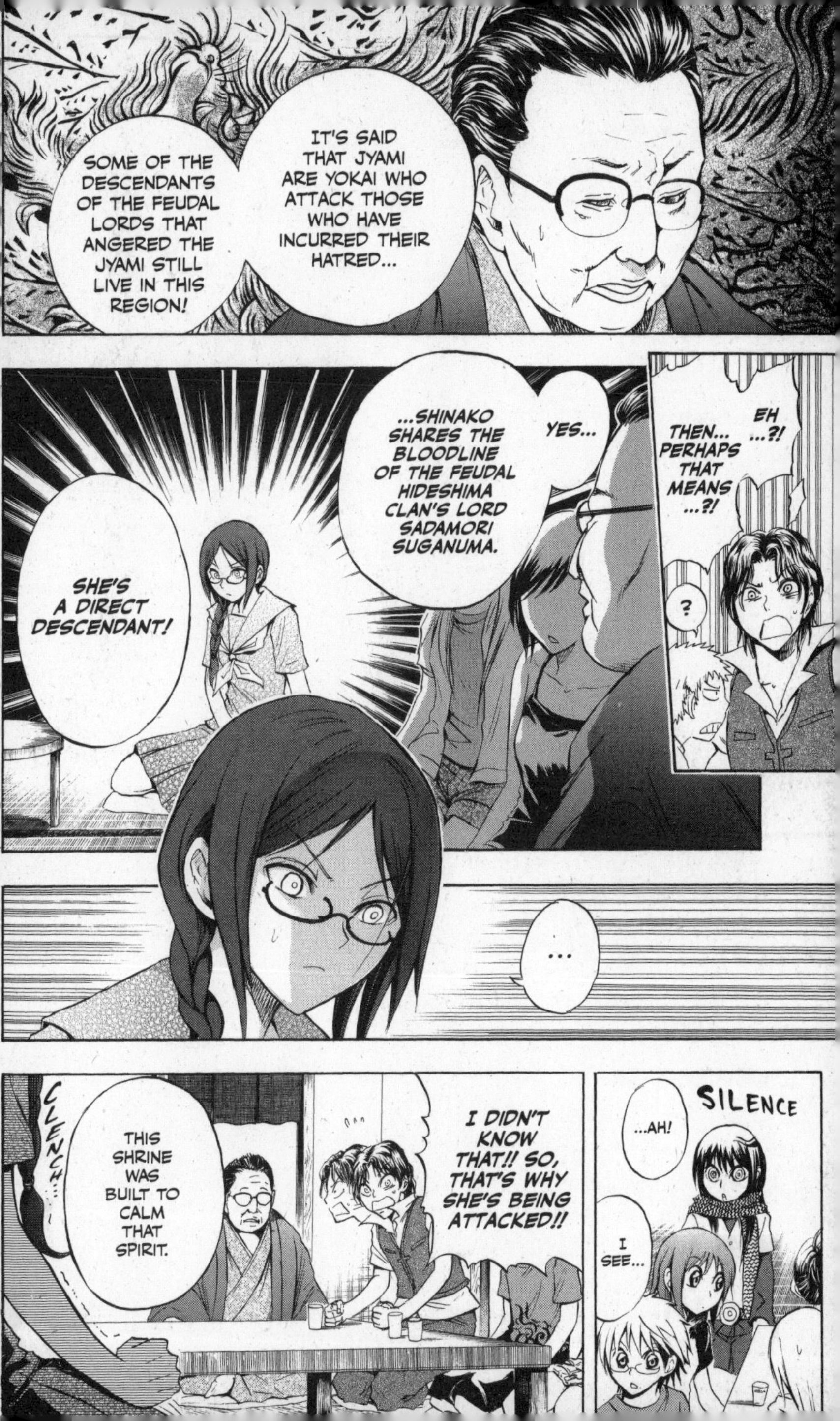
IT'S SAID THAT JYAMI ARE YOKAI WHO ATTACK THOSE WHO HAVE INCURRED THEIR HATRED...
SOME OF THE DESCENDANTS OF THE FEUDAL LORDS THAT ANGERED THE JYAMI STILL LIVE IN THIS REGION!
EH ...?!
THEN... PERHAPS THAT MEANS ...?!
?
YES...
...SHINAKO SHARES THE BLOODLINE OF THE FEUDAL HIDESHIMA CLAN'S LORD SADAMORI SUGANUMA.
SHE'S A DIRECT DESCENDANT!
...
SILENCE
...AH!
I SEE...
I DIDN'T KNOW THAT!! SO, THAT'S WHY SHE'S BEING ATTACKED!!
THIS SHRINE WAS BUILT TO CALM THAT SPIRIT.
CLENCH...

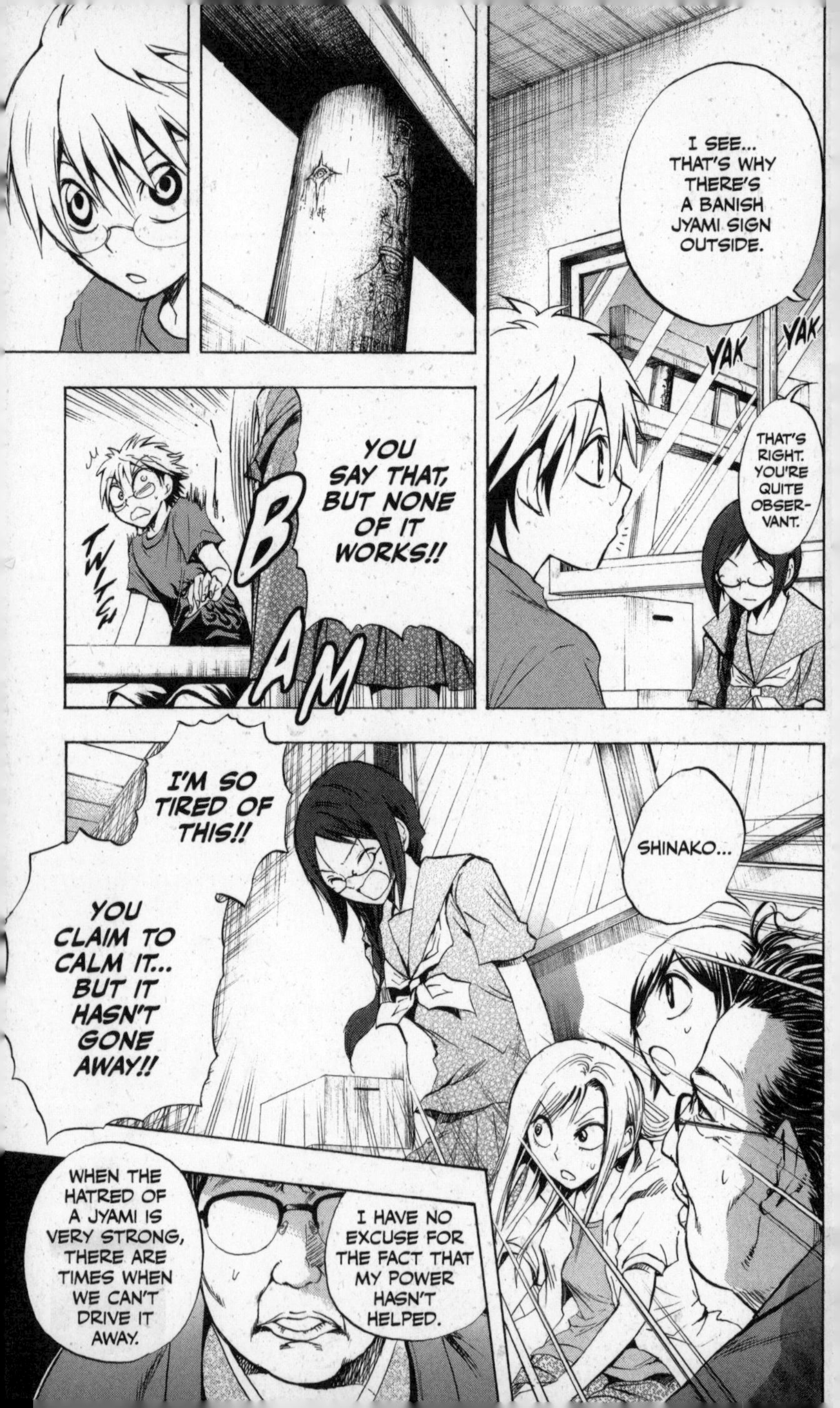
I SEE... THAT'S WHY THERE'S A BANISH JYAMI SIGN OUTSIDE.
YAK YAK
THAT'S RIGHT. YOU'RE QUITE OBSERVANT.
YOU SAY THAT, BUT NONE OF IT WORKS!!
BAM
TWITCH
SHINAKO...
I'M SO TIRED OF THIS!!
YOU CLAIM TO CALM IT... BUT IT HASN'T GONE AWAY!!
I HAVE NO EXCUSE FOR THE FACT THAT MY POWER HASN'T HELPED.
WHEN THE HATRED OF A JYAMI IS VERY STRONG, THERE ARE TIMES WHEN WE CAN'T DRIVE IT AWAY.

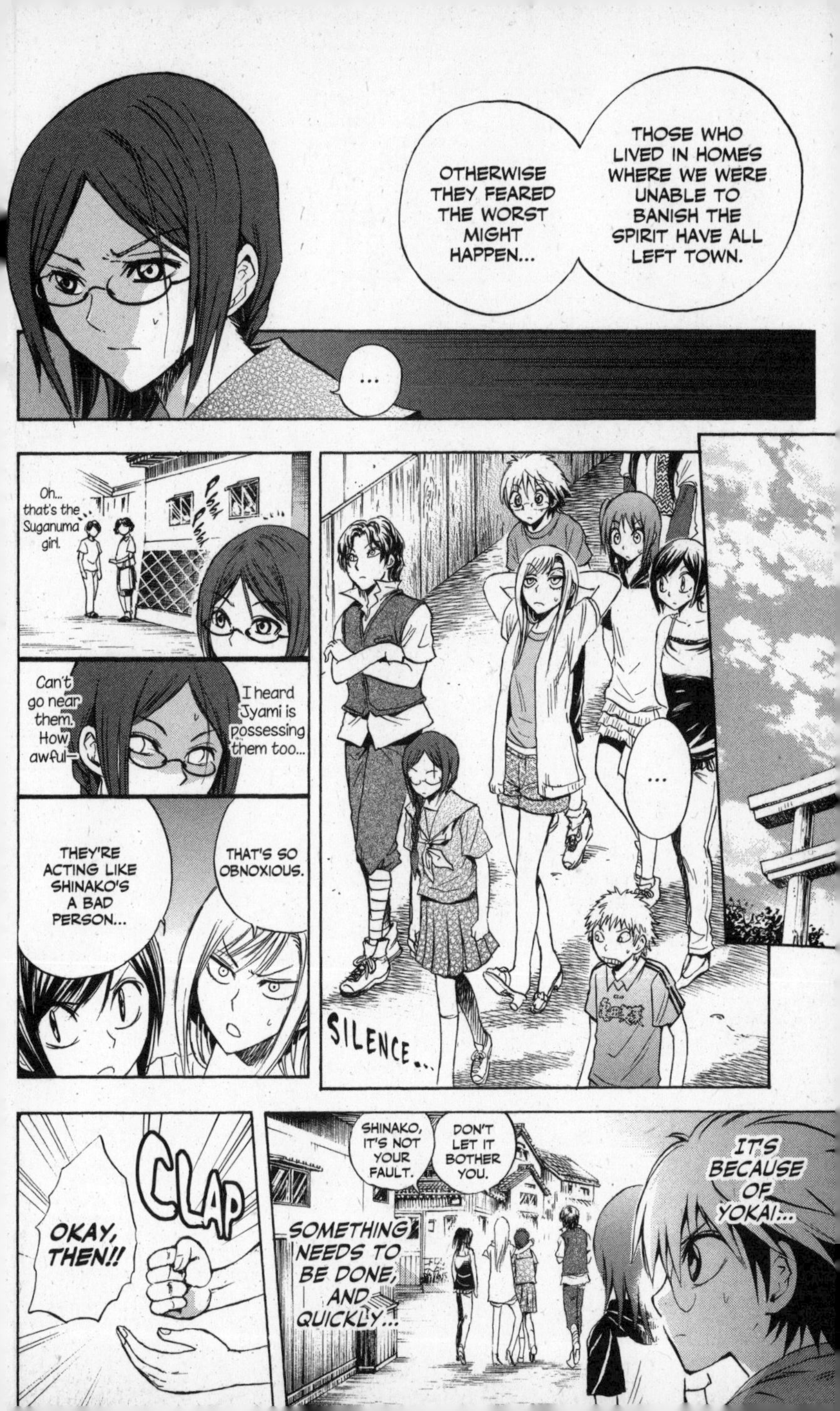
THOSE WHO LIVED IN HOMES WHERE WE WERE UNABLE TO BANISH THE SPIRIT HAVE ALL LEFT TOWN.
OTHERWISE THEY FEARED THE WORST MIGHT HAPPEN...
...
...
SILENCE...
Oh... that's the Suganuma girl.
I heard Jyami is possessing them too...
Can't go near them. How awful—
THAT'S SO OBNOXIOUS.
THEY'RE ACTING LIKE SHINAKO'S A BAD PERSON...
IT'S BECAUSE OF YOKAI...
DON'T LET IT BOTHER YOU.
SHINAKO, IT'S NOT YOUR FAULT.
SOMETHING NEEDS TO BE DONE, AND QUICKLY...
CLAP
OKAY, THEN!!

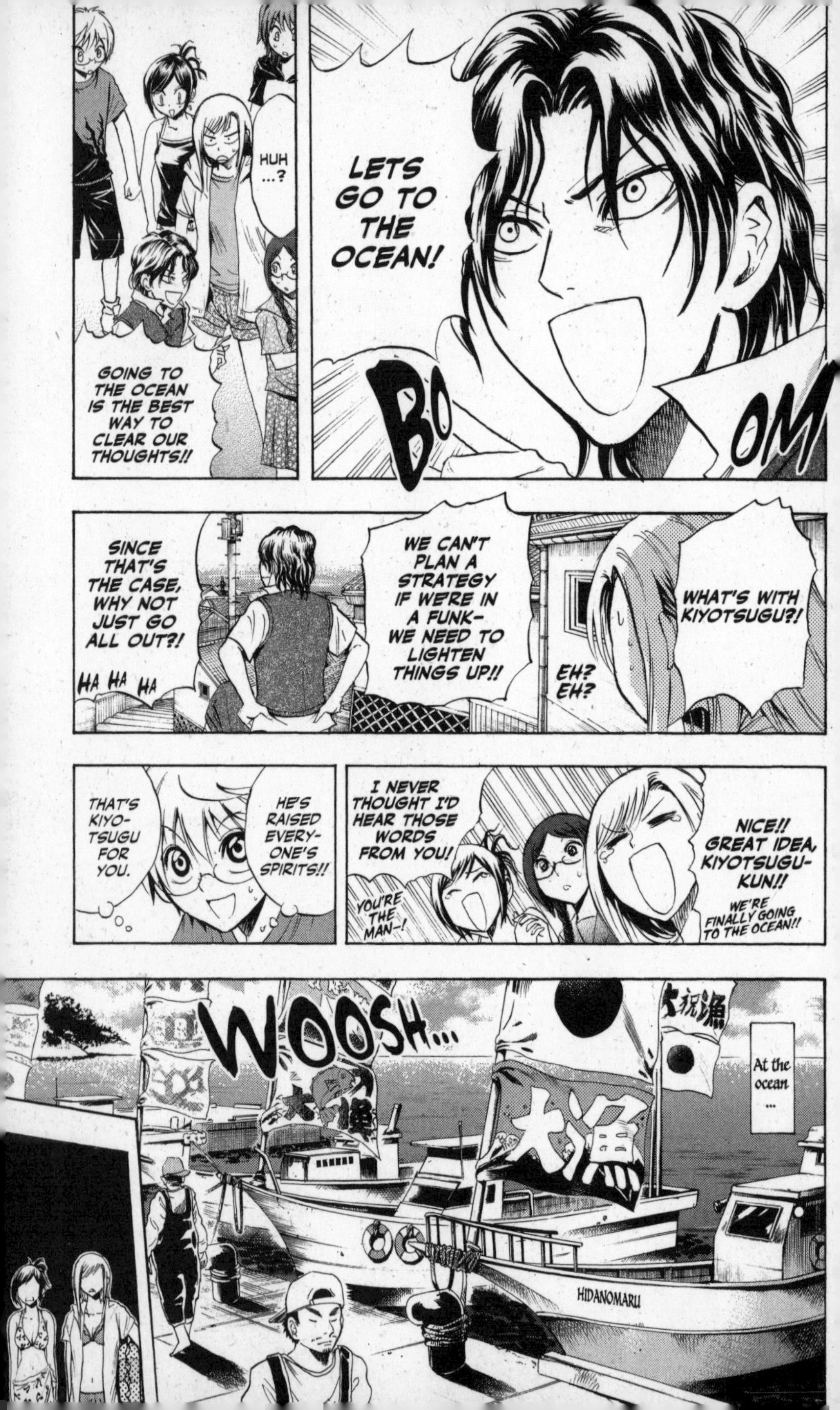
LETS GO TO THE OCEAN!
BOOM
HUH ...?
GOING TO THE OCEAN IS THE BEST WAY TO CLEAR OUR THOUGHTS!!
WHAT'S WITH KIYOTSUGU?!
EH? EH?
WE CAN'T PLAN A STRATEGY IF WE'RE IN A FUNK-WE NEED TO LIGHTEN THINGS UP!!
SINCE THAT'S THE CASE, WHY NOT JUST GO ALL OUT?!
HA HA HA
NICE!! GREAT IDEA, KIYOTSUGU-KUN!!
WE'RE FINALLY GOING TO THE OCEAN!!
I NEVER THOUGHT I'D HEAR THOSE WORDS FROM YOU!
YOU'RE THE MAN-!
HE'S RAISED EVERY-ONE'S SPIRITS!!
THAT'S KIYO-TSUGU FOR YOU.
At the ocean ...
WOOSH...
HIDANOMARU

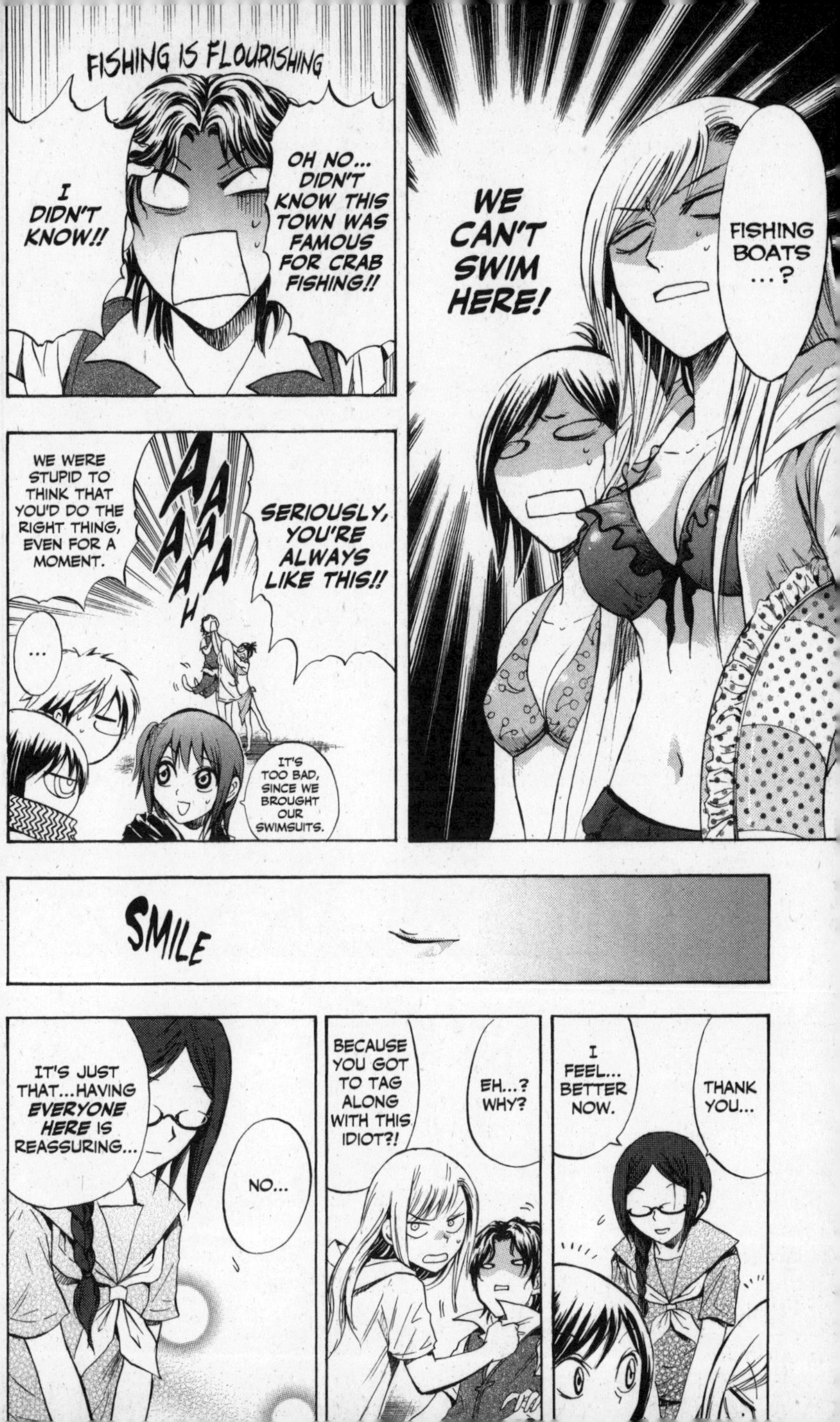
FISHING BOATS ...?
WE CAN'T SWIM HERE!
FISHING IS FLOURISHING
OH NO... DIDN'T KNOW THIS TOWN WAS FAMOUS FOR CRAB FISHING!!
I DIDN'T KNOW!!
SERIOUSLY, YOU'RE ALWAYS LIKE THIS!!
AAAAAAH
WE WERE STUPID TO THINK THAT YOU'D DO THE RIGHT THING, EVEN FOR A MOMENT.
...
IT'S TOO BAD, SINCE WE BROUGHT OUR SWIMSUITS.
SMILE
THANK YOU...
I FEEL... BETTER NOW.
EH...? WHY?
BECAUSE YOU GOT TO TAG ALONG WITH THIS IDIOT?!
NO...
IT'S JUST THAT...HAVING *EVERYONE HERE* IS REASSURING...

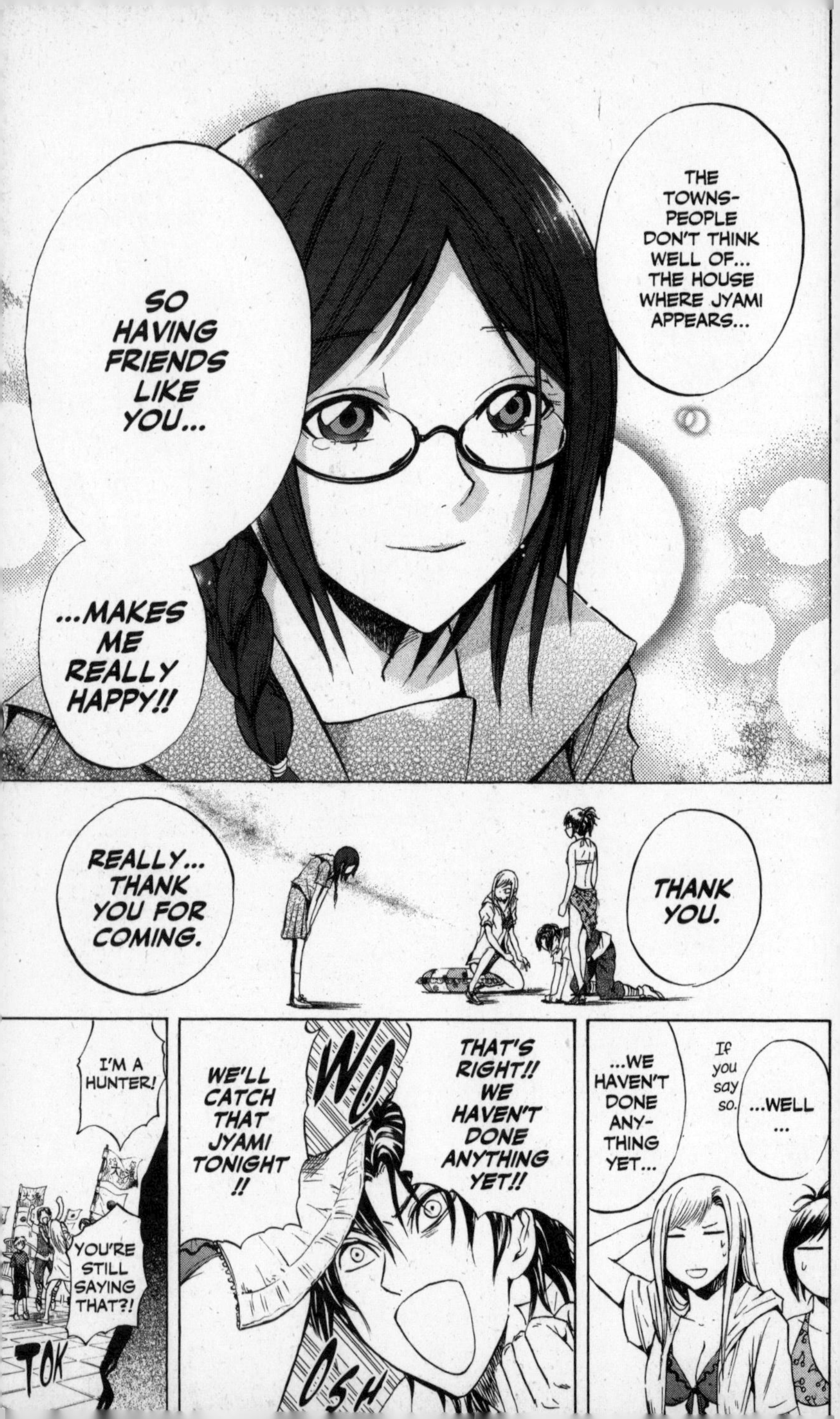
THE TOWNS-PEOPLE DON'T THINK WELL OF... THE HOUSE WHERE JYAMI APPEARS...
SO HAVING FRIENDS LIKE YOU...
...MAKES ME REALLY HAPPY!!
THANK YOU.
REALLY... THANK YOU FOR COMING.
...WELL ...
If you say so.
...WE HAVEN'T DONE ANYTHING YET...
THAT'S RIGHT!! WE HAVEN'T DONE ANYTHING YET!!
WE'LL CATCH THAT JYAMI TONIGHT !!
WO
OSH
I'M A HUNTER!
YOU'RE STILL SAYING THAT?!
TOK

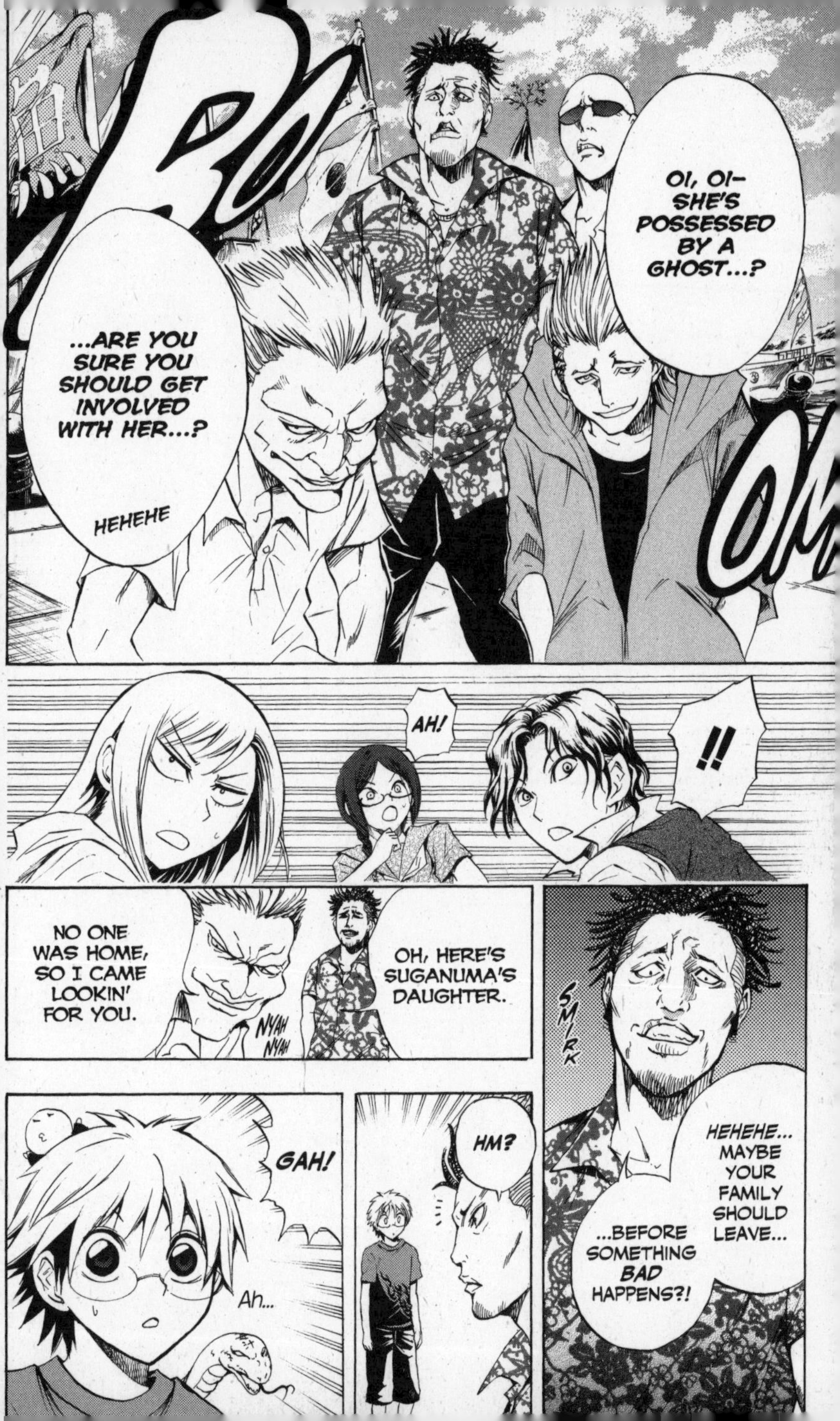
OI, OI—
SHE'S POSSESSED BY A GHOST...?
...ARE YOU SURE YOU SHOULD GET INVOLVED WITH HER...?
HEHEHE
!!
AH!
SMIRK
HEHEHE... MAYBE YOUR FAMILY SHOULD LEAVE...
...BEFORE SOMETHING BAD HAPPENS?!
OH, HERE'S SUGANUMA'S DAUGHTER.
NO ONE WAS HOME, SO I CAME LOOKIN' FOR YOU.
NYAH NYAH
HM?
GAH!
Ah...

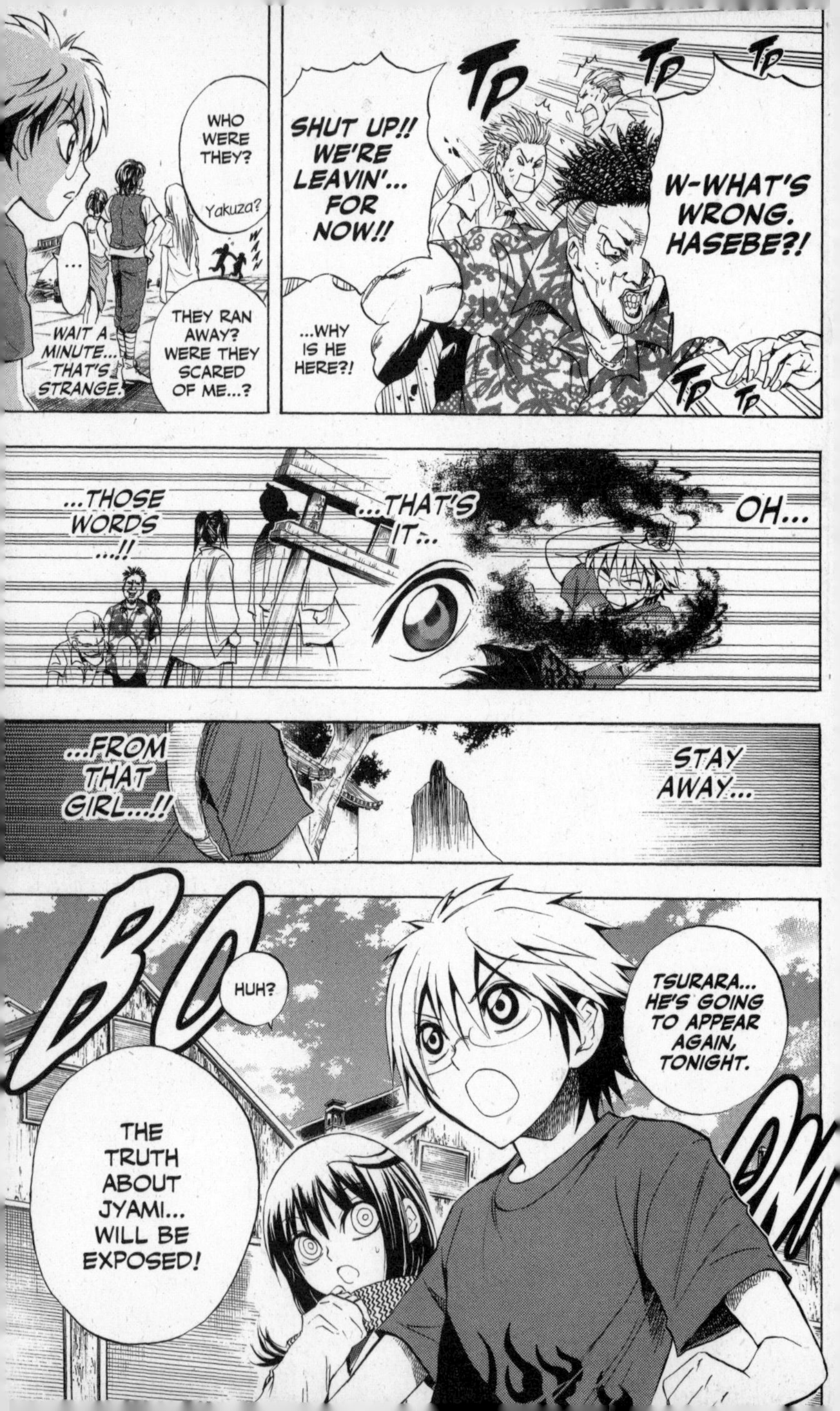
TP
TP
TP
W-WHAT'S WRONG. HASEBE?!
SHUT UP!! WE'RE LEAVIN'... FOR NOW!!
...WHY IS HE HERE?!
TP
TP
WHO WERE THEY?
Yakuza?
THEY RAN AWAY? WERE THEY SCARED OF ME...?
...
WAIT A MINUTE... THAT'S STRANGE.
OH...
...THAT'S IT...
...THOSE WORDS ...!!
STAY AWAY...
...FROM THAT GIRL...!!
TSURARA... HE'S GOING TO APPEAR AGAIN, TONIGHT.
HUH?
BO
OM
THE TRUTH ABOUT JYAMI... WILL BE EXPOSED!

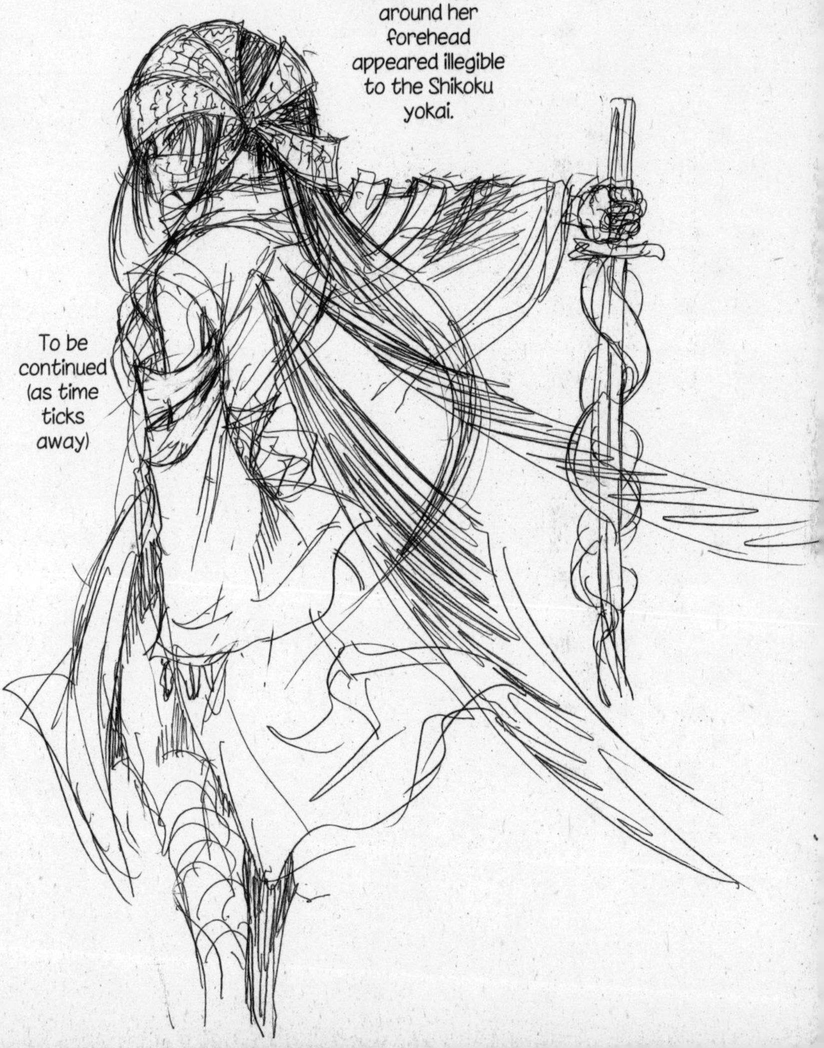
The onmyo characters written on the fabric wrapped around her forehead appeared illegible to the Shikoku yokai.
To be continued (as time ticks away)

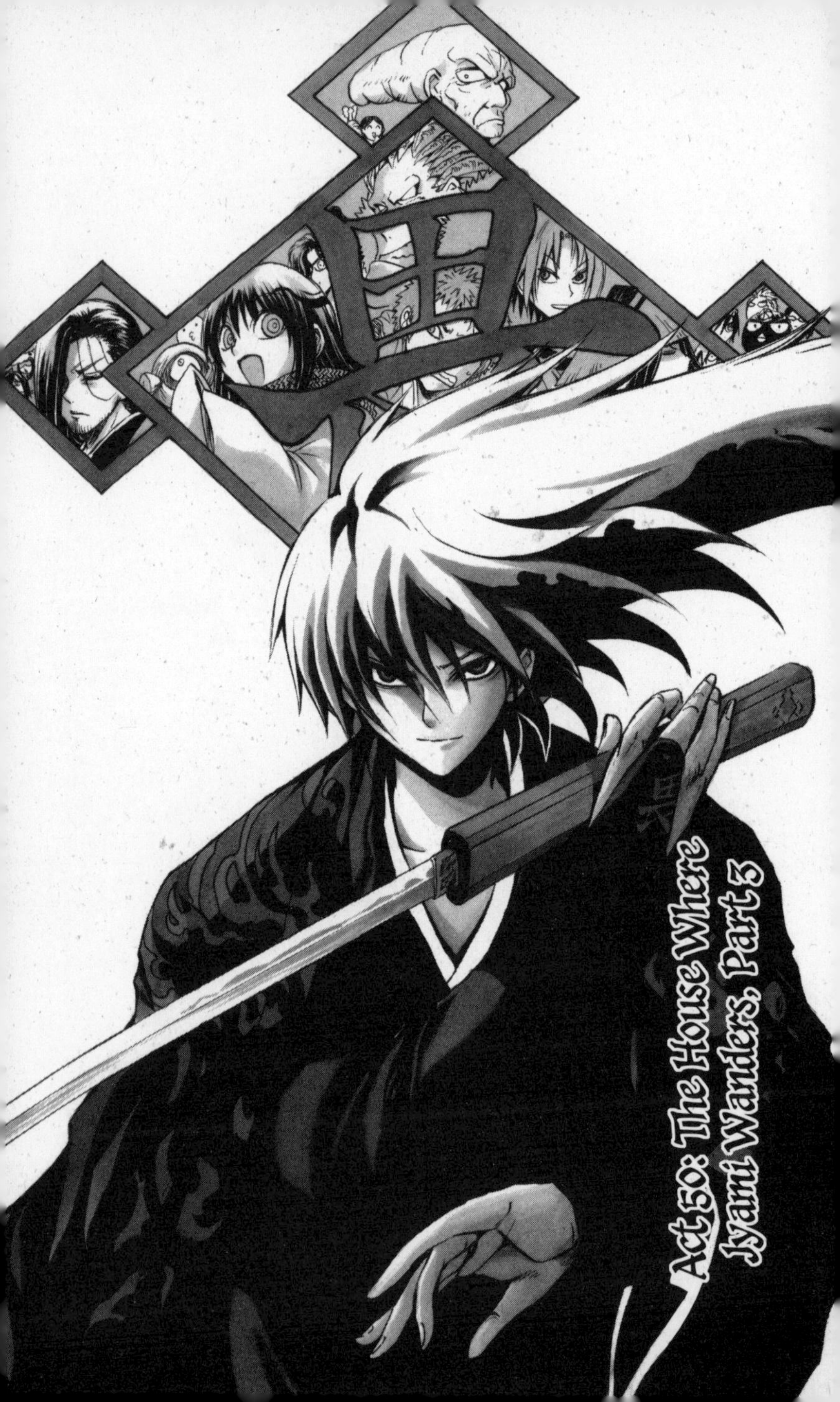
Act 50: The House Where
Jyami Wanders, Part 3

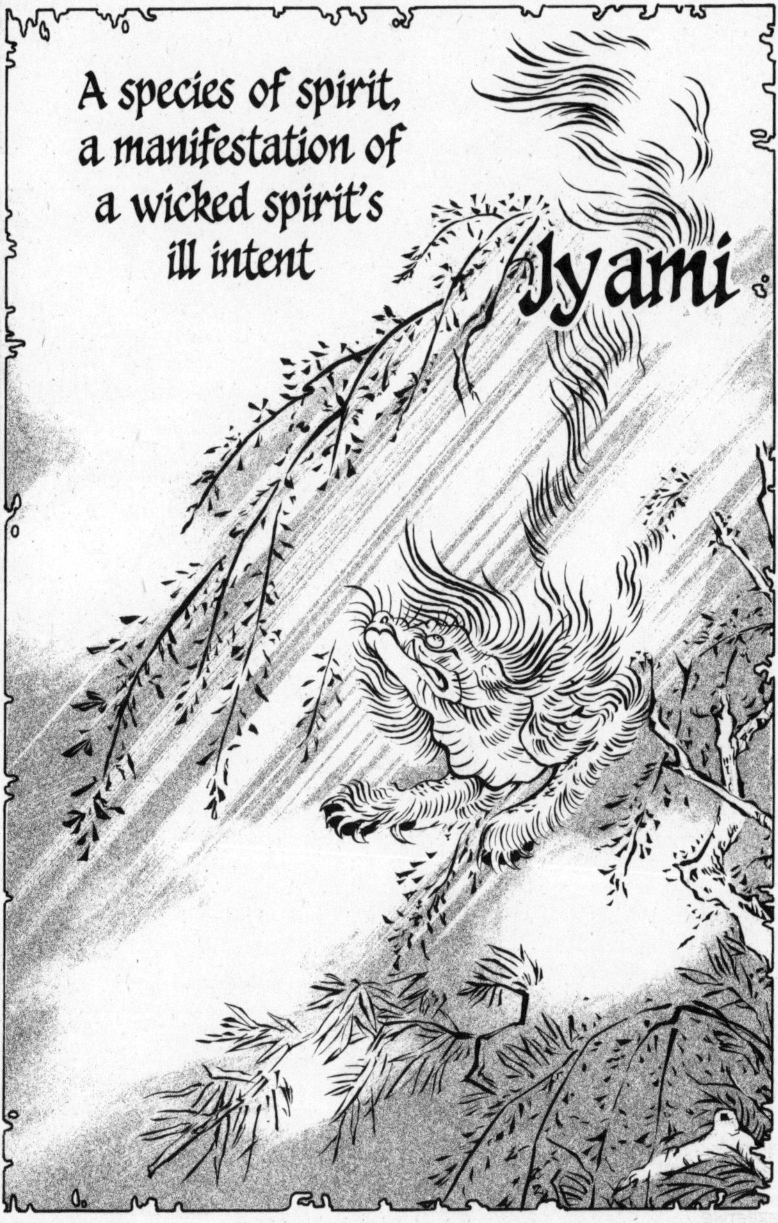
A species of spirit, a manifestation of a wicked spirit's ill intent
Jyami

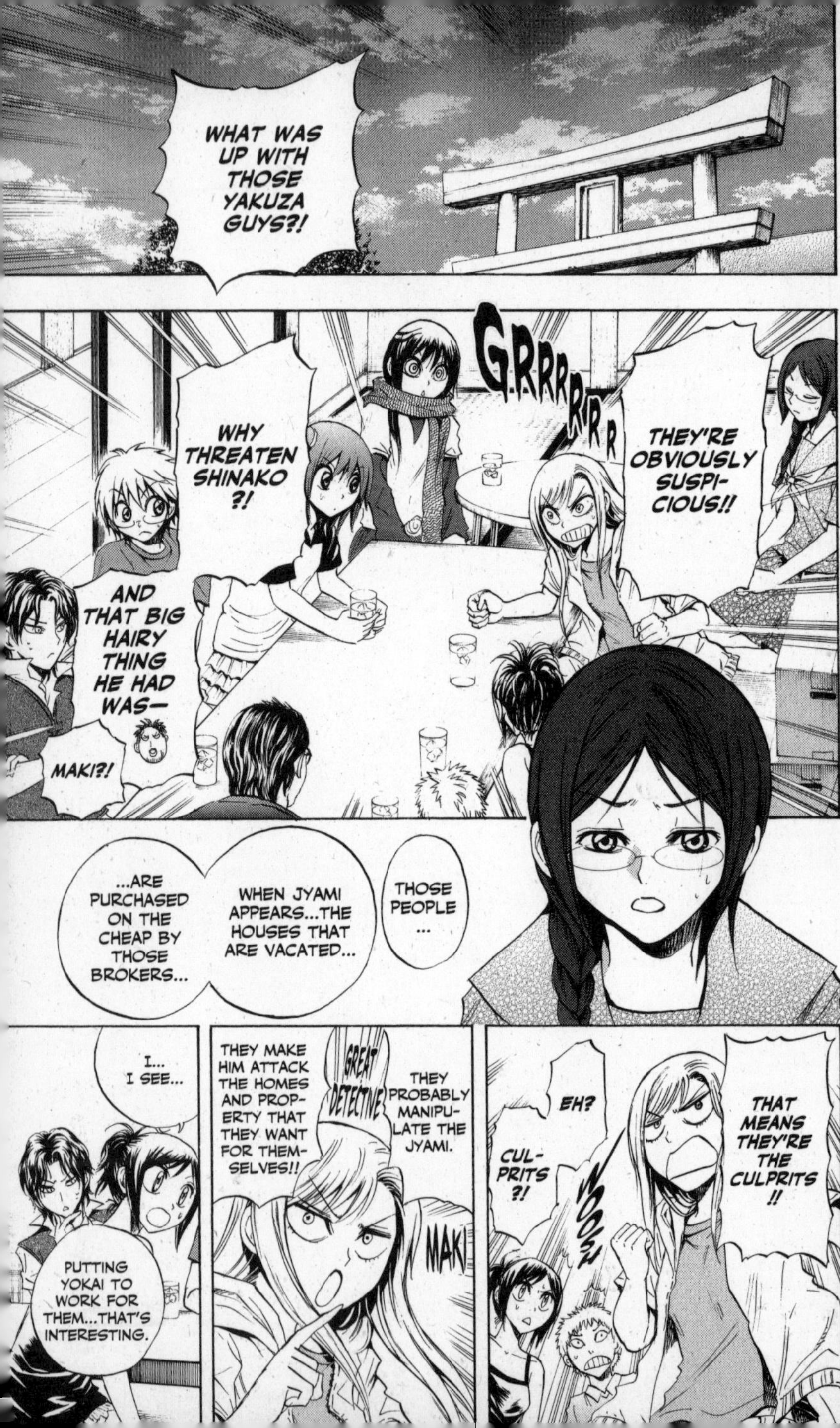
WHAT WAS UP WITH THOSE YAKUZA GUYS?!
THEY'RE OBVIOUSLY SUSPICIOUS!!
GRRRRRRR
WHY THREATEN SHINAKO?!
AND THAT BIG HAIRY THING HE HAD WAS—
MAKI?!
THOSE PEOPLE...
WHEN JYAMI APPEARS...THE HOUSES THAT ARE VACATED...
...ARE PURCHASED ON THE CHEAP BY THOSE BROKERS...
THAT MEANS THEY'RE THE CULPRITS!!
EH?
CULPRITS?!
THEY PROBABLY MANIPULATE THE JYAMI.
GREAT DETECTIVE
THEY MAKE HIM ATTACK THE HOMES AND PROPERTY THAT THEY WANT FOR THEMSELVES!!
MAKI
I... I SEE...
PUTTING YOKAI TO WORK FOR THEM...THAT'S INTERESTING.

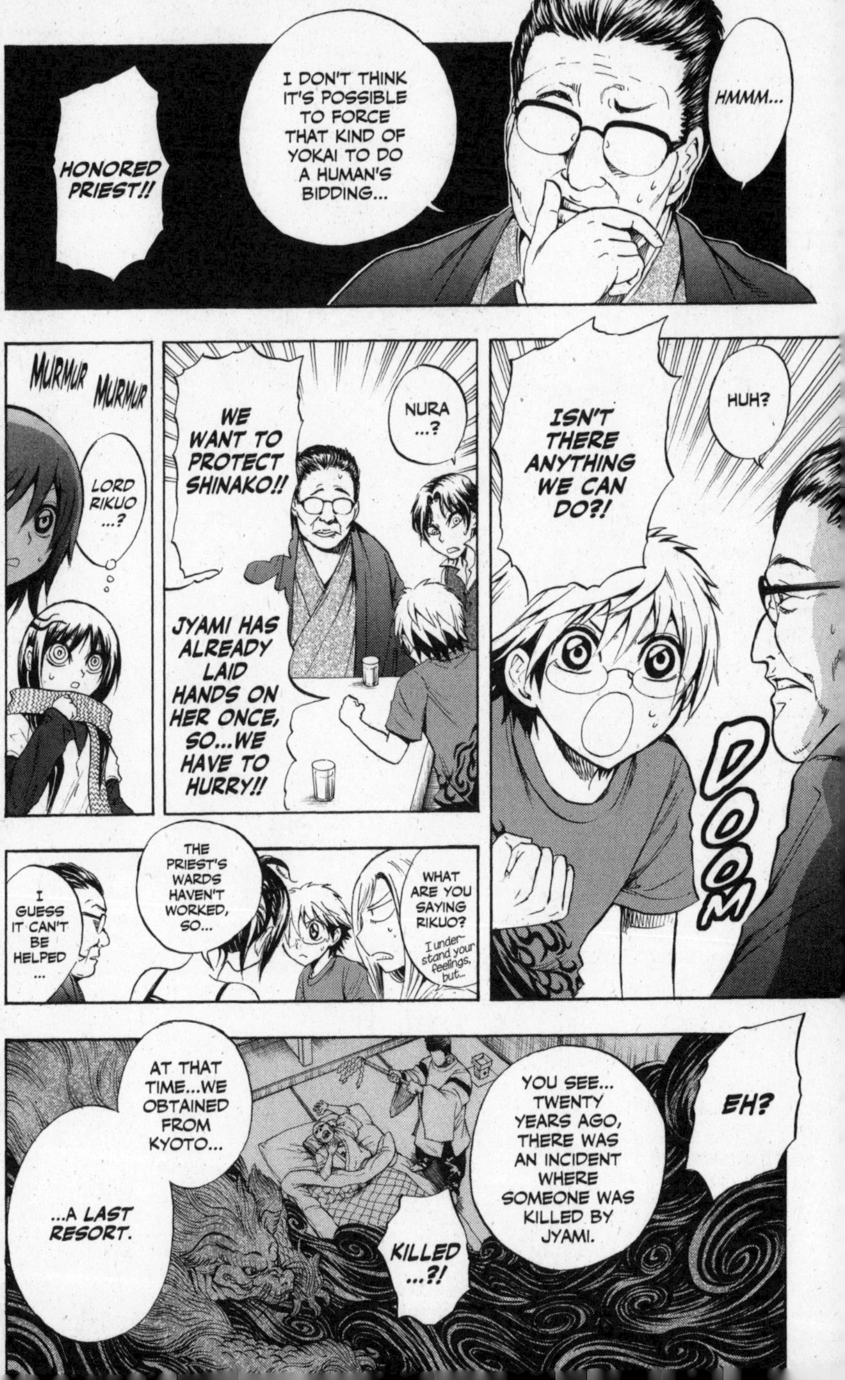
HMMM...
I DON'T THINK IT'S POSSIBLE TO FORCE THAT KIND OF YOKAI TO DO A HUMAN'S BIDDING...
HONORED PRIEST!!
HUH?
ISN'T THERE ANYTHING WE CAN DO?!
DOOM
NURA...?
WE WANT TO PROTECT SHINAKO!!
JYAMI HAS ALREADY LAID HANDS ON HER ONCE, SO...WE HAVE TO HURRY!!
MURMUR MURMUR
LORD RIKUO...?
WHAT ARE YOU SAYING RIKUO?
I understand your feelings, but...
THE PRIEST'S WARDS HAVEN'T WORKED, SO...
I GUESS IT CAN'T BE HELPED...
EH?
YOU SEE... TWENTY YEARS AGO, THERE WAS AN INCIDENT WHERE SOMEONE WAS KILLED BY JYAMI.
KILLED...?!
AT THAT TIME...WE OBTAINED FROM KYOTO...
...A LAST RESORT.

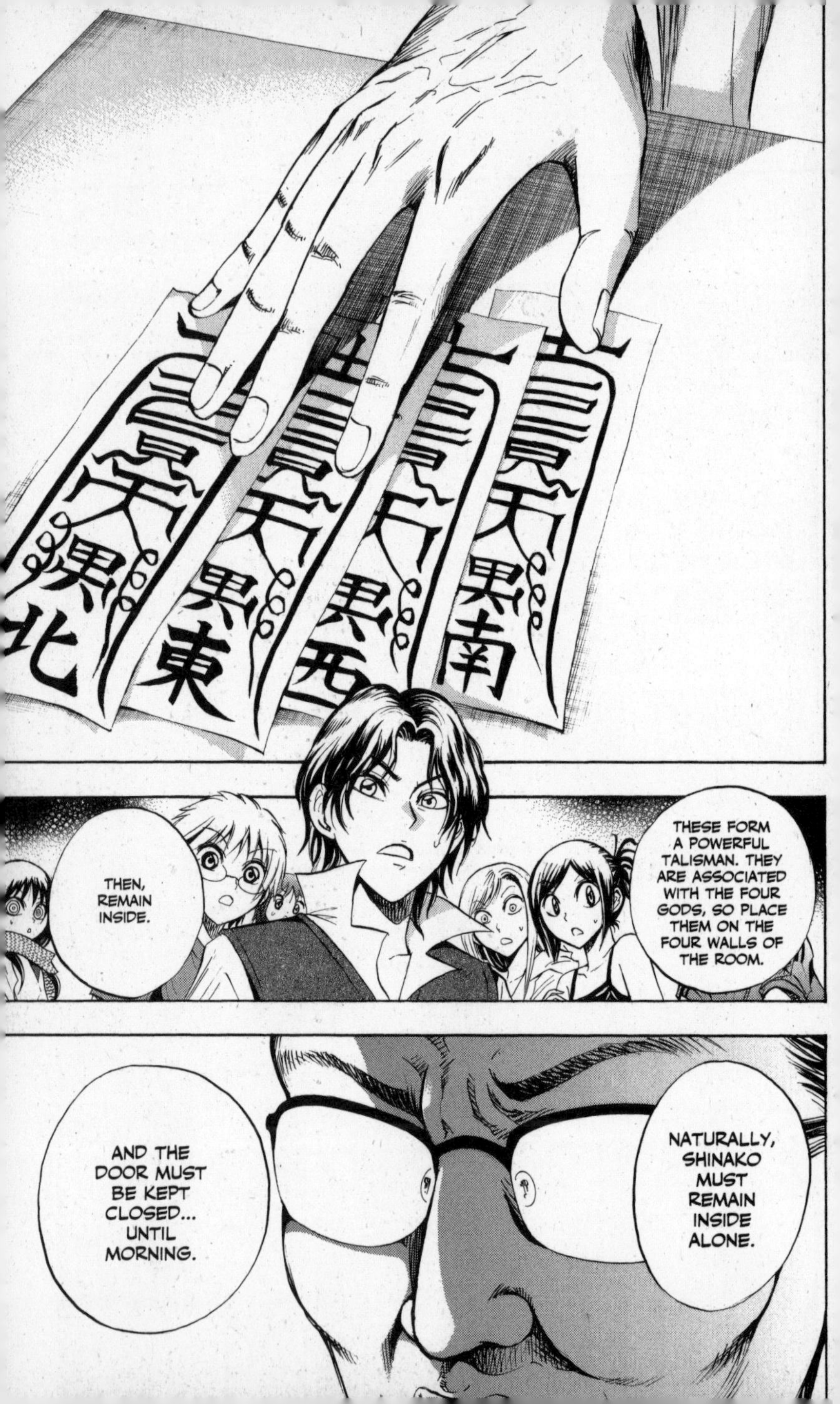
THESE FORM A POWERFUL TALISMAN. THEY ARE ASSOCIATED WITH THE FOUR GODS, SO PLACE THEM ON THE FOUR WALLS OF THE ROOM.
THEN, REMAIN INSIDE.
NATURALLY, SHINAKO MUST REMAIN INSIDE ALONE.
AND THE DOOR MUST BE KEPT CLOSED... UNTIL MORNING.

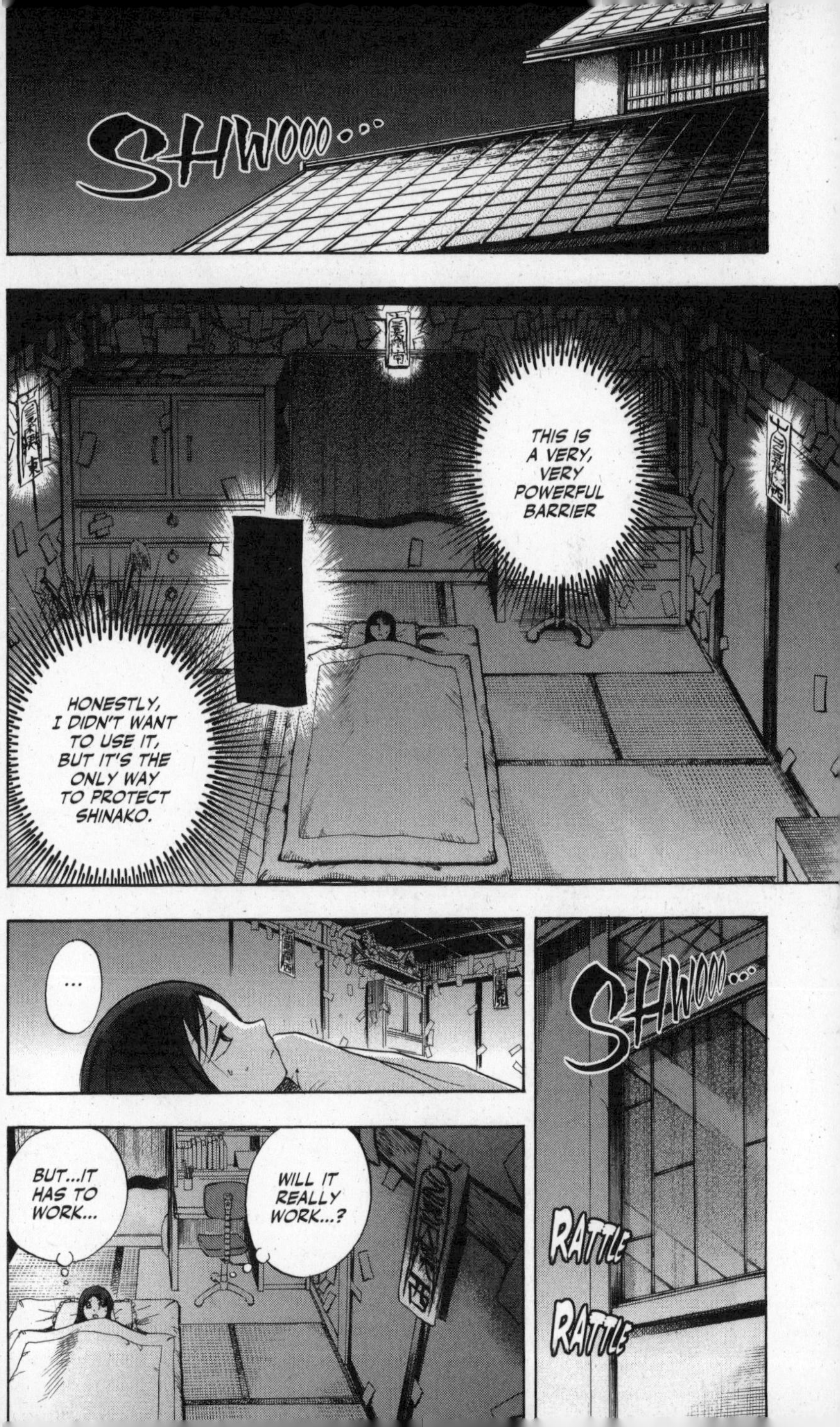
SHWOOO...
THIS IS A VERY, VERY POWERFUL BARRIER
HONESTLY, I DIDN'T WANT TO USE IT, BUT IT'S THE ONLY WAY TO PROTECT SHINAKO.
SHWOOO...
RATTLE
RATTLE
...
WILL IT REALLY WORK...?
BUT...IT HAS TO WORK...

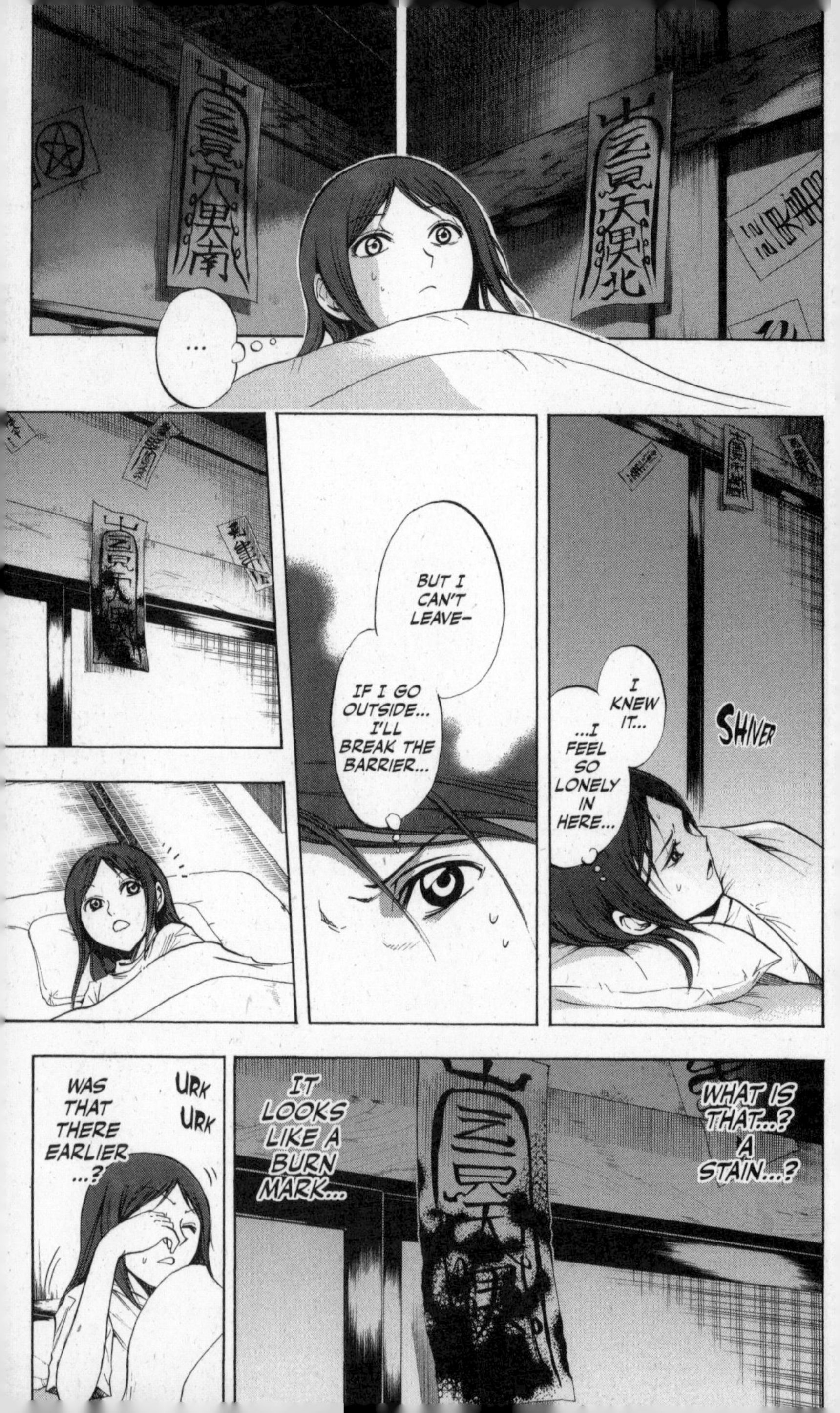
...
SHIVER
I KNEW IT... ...I FEEL SO LONELY IN HERE...
BUT I CAN'T LEAVE–
IF I GO OUTSIDE... I'LL BREAK THE BARRIER...
WHAT IS THAT...? A STAIN...?
IT LOOKS LIKE A BURN MARK...
URK URK
WAS THAT THERE EARLIER...?

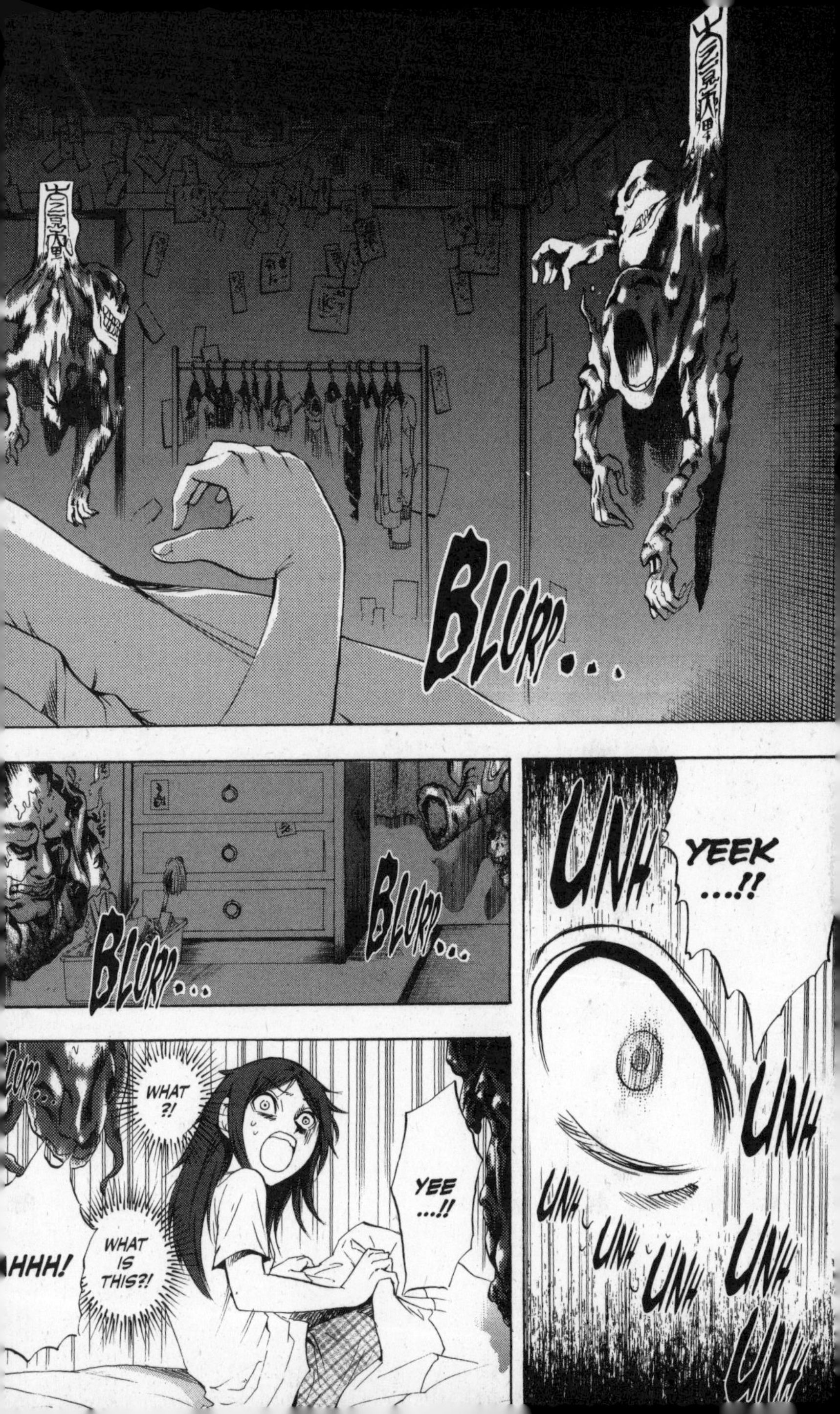
BLURP...
UNH
YEEK ...!!
UNH
UNH
UNH
UNH
UNH
UNH
UNH
BLURP...
BLURP...
WHAT ?!
YEE ...!!
WHAT IS THIS?!
HHH!

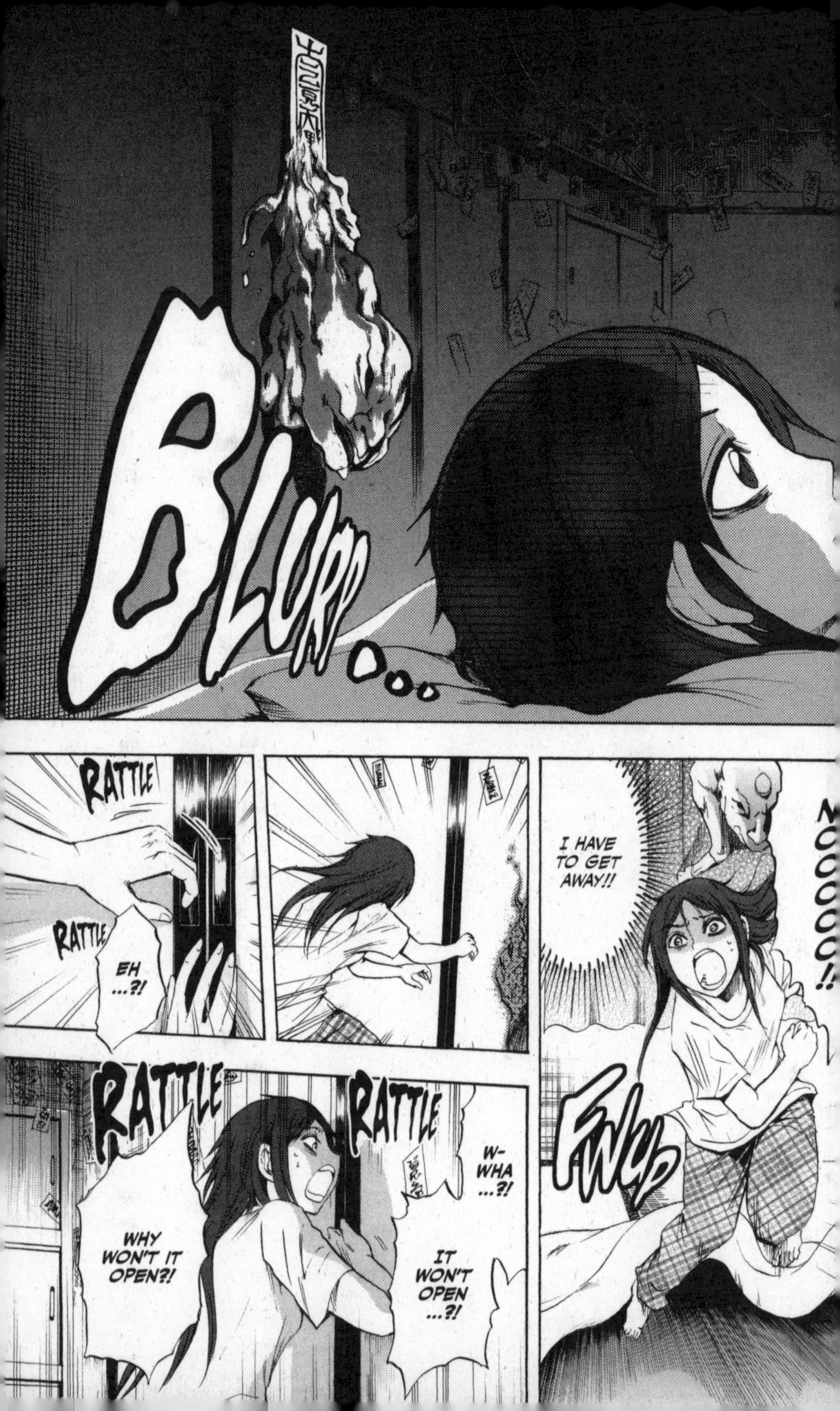
BLURP...
NOOOOOO!!
I HAVE TO GET AWAY!!
FWUP
RATTLE
RATTLE
EH ...?!
RATTLE
RATTLE
W-WHA ...?!
IT WON'T OPEN ...?!
WHY WON'T IT OPEN?!

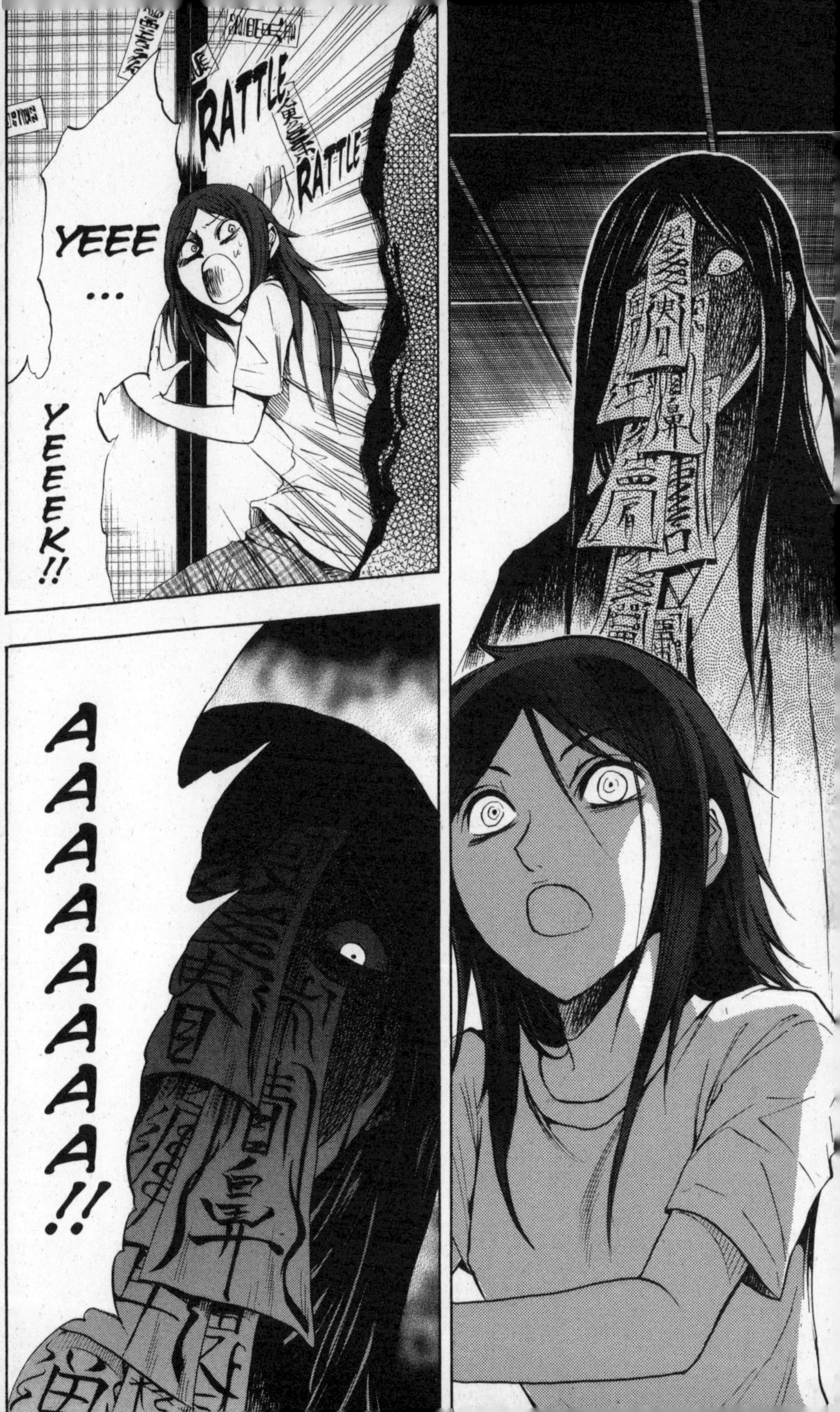
RATTLE
RATTLE
YEEEE...
YEEEEK!!
AAAAAAAA!!

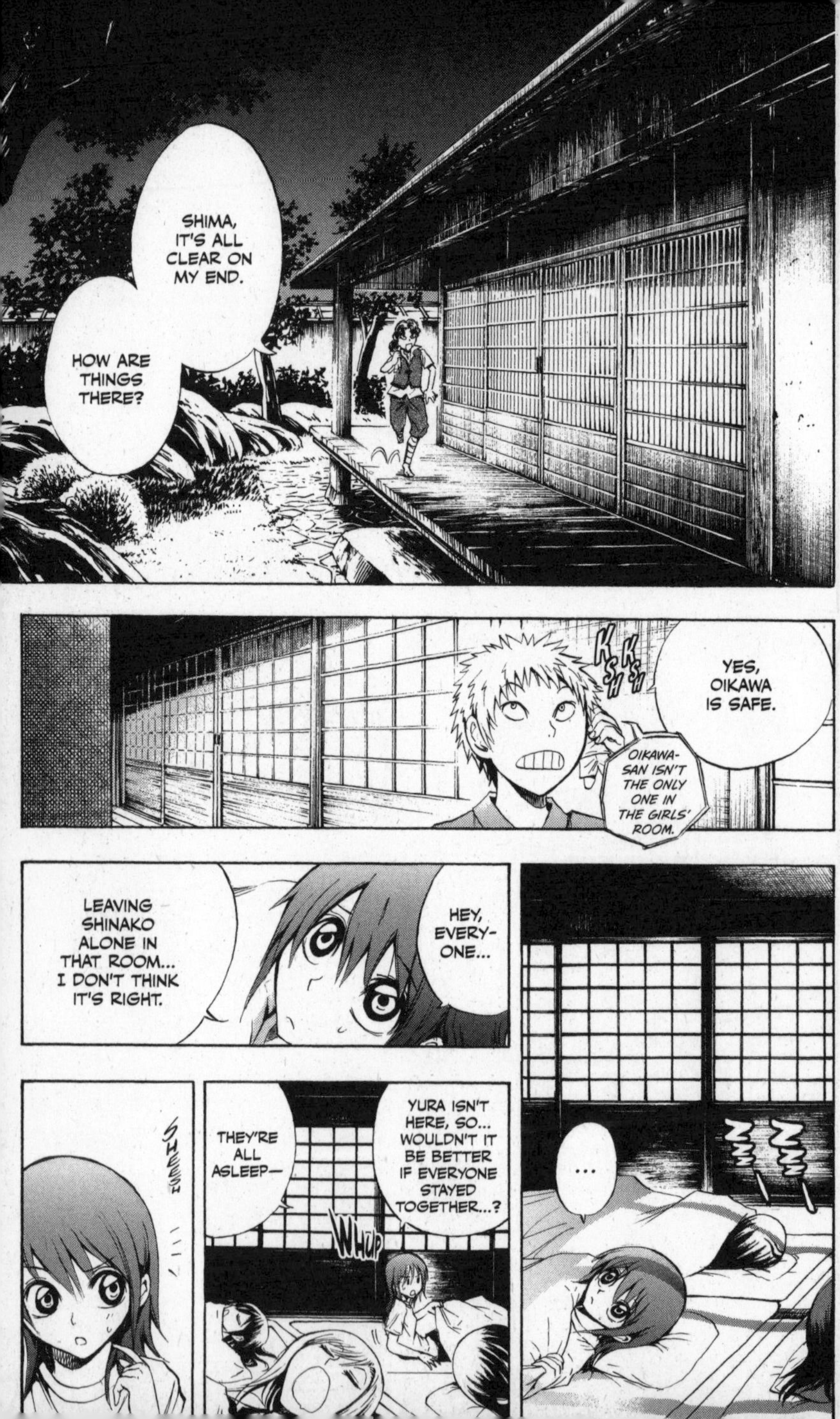
SHIMA, IT'S ALL CLEAR ON MY END.
HOW ARE THINGS THERE?
KSH KSH
YES, OIKAWA IS SAFE.
OIKAWA-SAN ISN'T THE ONLY ONE IN THE GIRLS' ROOM.
ZZZ
ZZZ
...
HEY, EVERY-ONE...
LEAVING SHINAKO ALONE IN THAT ROOM... I DON'T THINK IT'S RIGHT.
YURA ISN'T HERE, SO... WOULDN'T IT BE BETTER IF EVERYONE STAYED TOGETHER...?
THEY'RE ALL ASLEEP—
WHUP
SHEESH

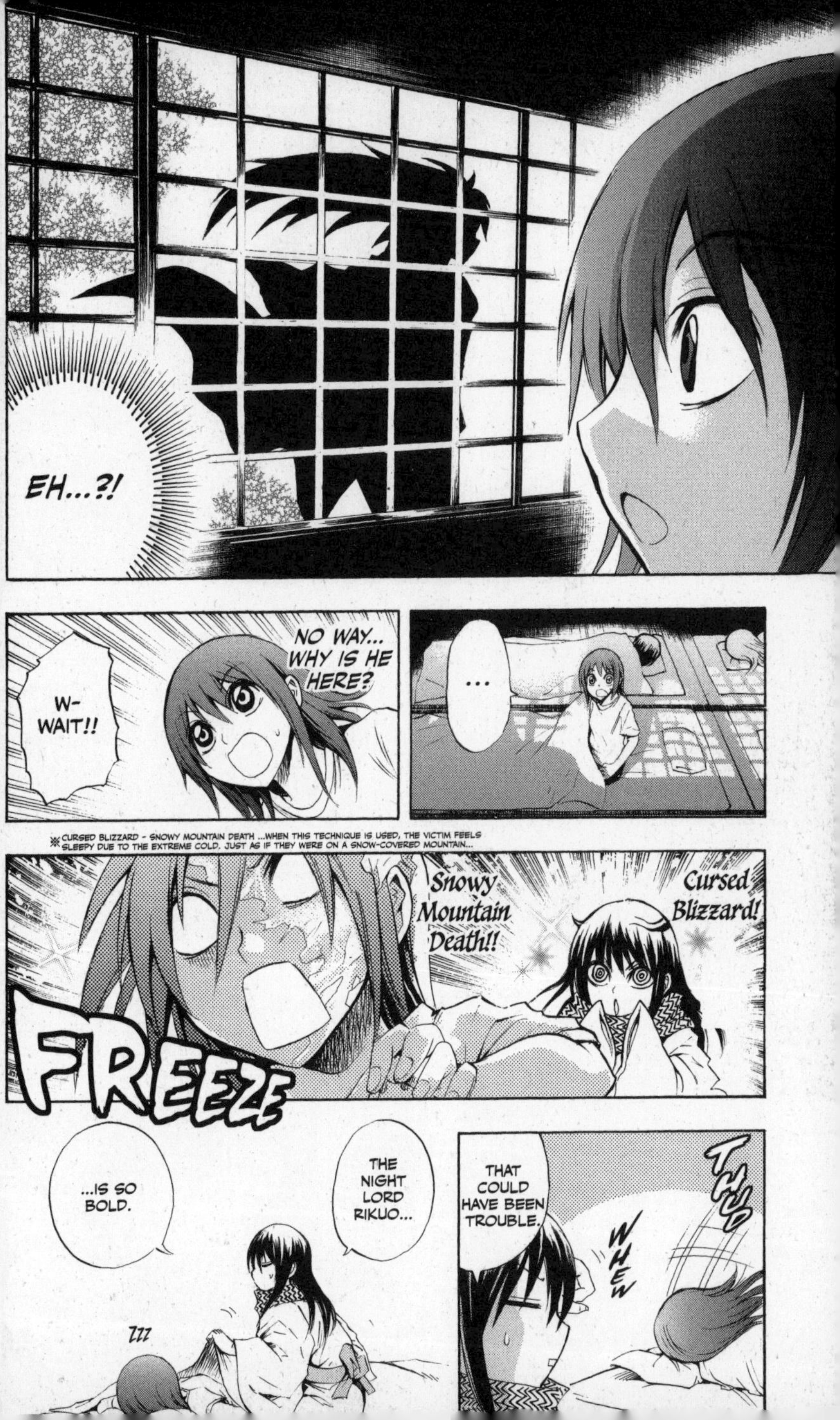
EH...?!
...
NO WAY... WHY IS HE HERE?
W-WAIT!!
Cursed Blizzard!
Snowy Mountain Death!!
FREEZE
THUD
WHEW
THAT COULD HAVE BEEN TROUBLE.
THE NIGHT LORD RIKUO...
...IS SO BOLD.
ZZZ

※CURSED BLIZZARD - SNOWY MOUNTAIN DEATH ...WHEN THIS TECHNIQUE IS USED, THE VICTIM FEELS SLEEPY DUE TO THE EXTREME COLD, JUST AS IF THEY WERE ON A SNOW-COVERED MOUNTAIN...

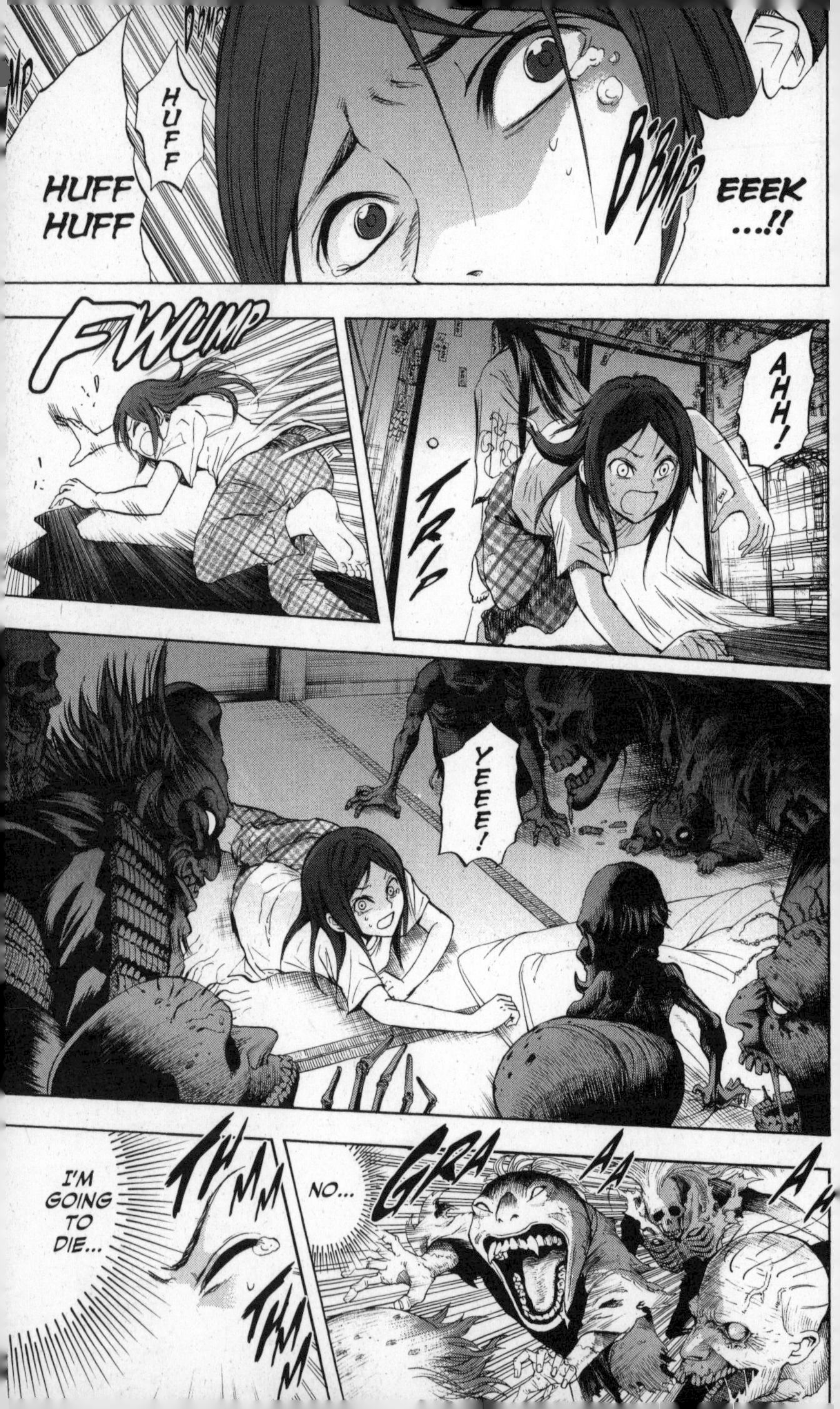
EEEK ...!!
B'BMP
HUFF
HUFF HUFF
HUFF
AHH!
TRIP
FWUMP
YEEE!
AAAAH
GRA
NO...
THMMM
I'M GOING TO DIE...

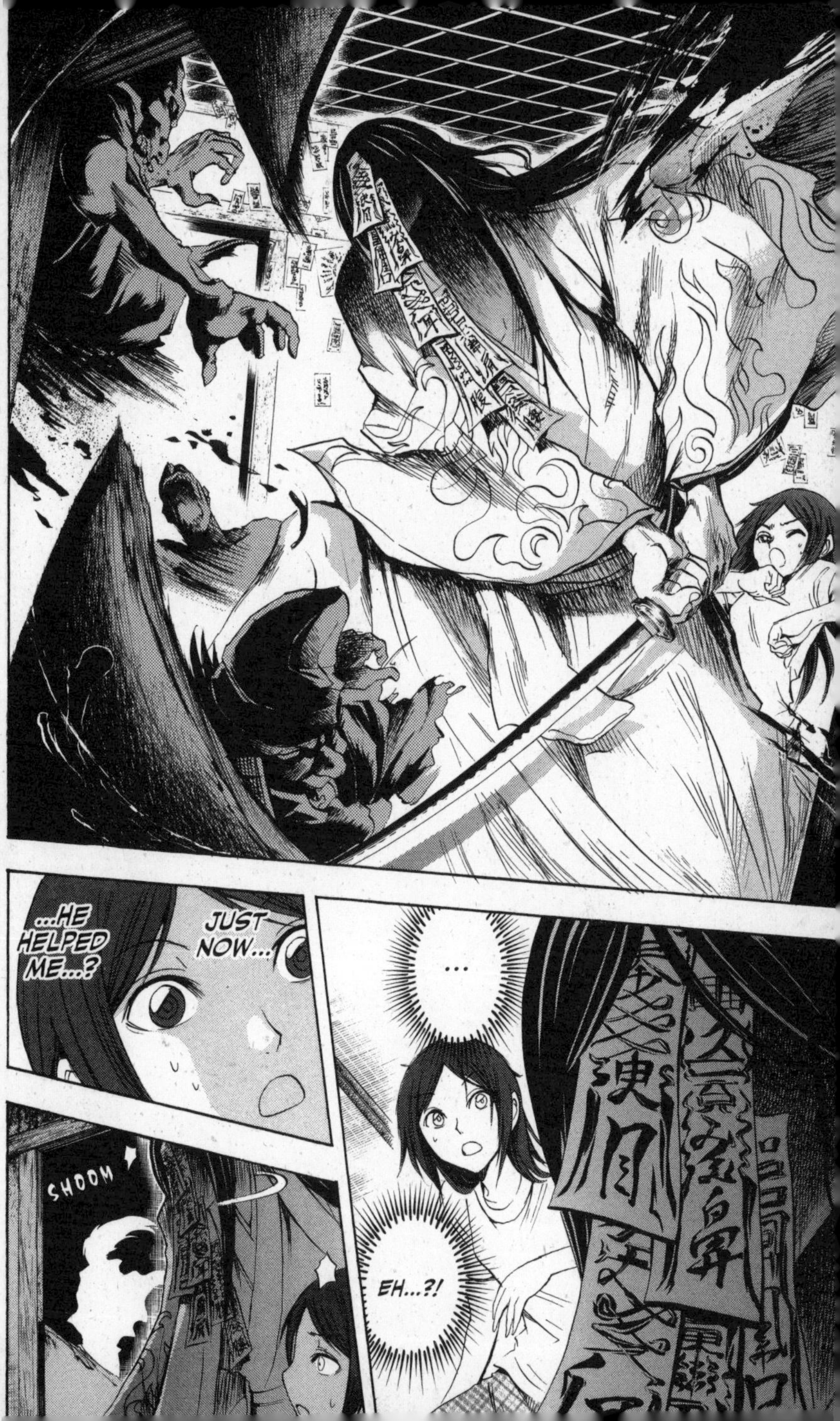
...
EH...?!
JUST NOW...
...HE HELPED ME...?
SHOOM

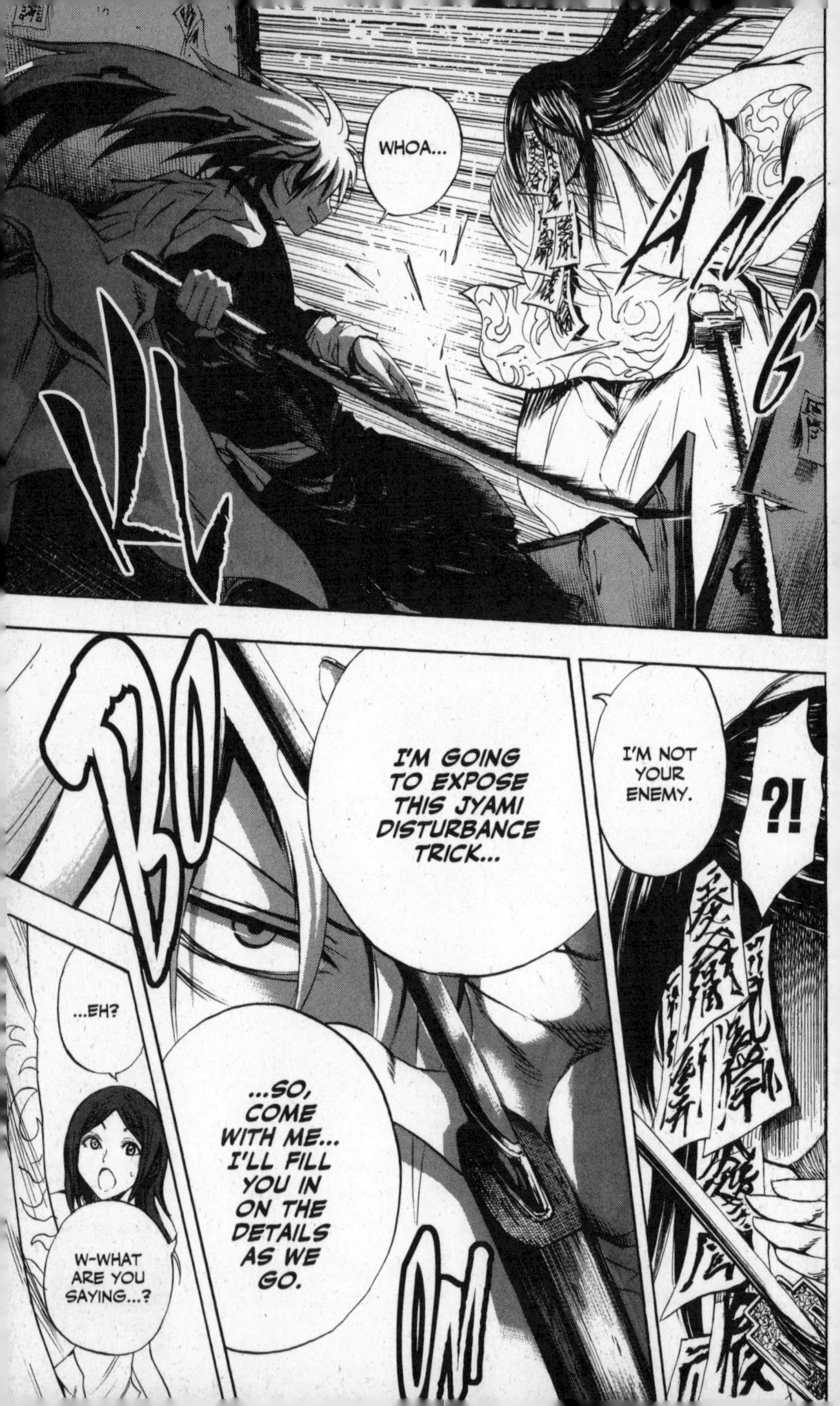
WHOA...
I'M NOT YOUR ENEMY.
?!
I'M GOING TO EXPOSE THIS JYAMI DISTURBANCE TRICK...
...SO, COME WITH ME... I'LL FILL YOU IN ON THE DETAILS AS WE GO.
...EH?
W-WHAT ARE YOU SAYING...?

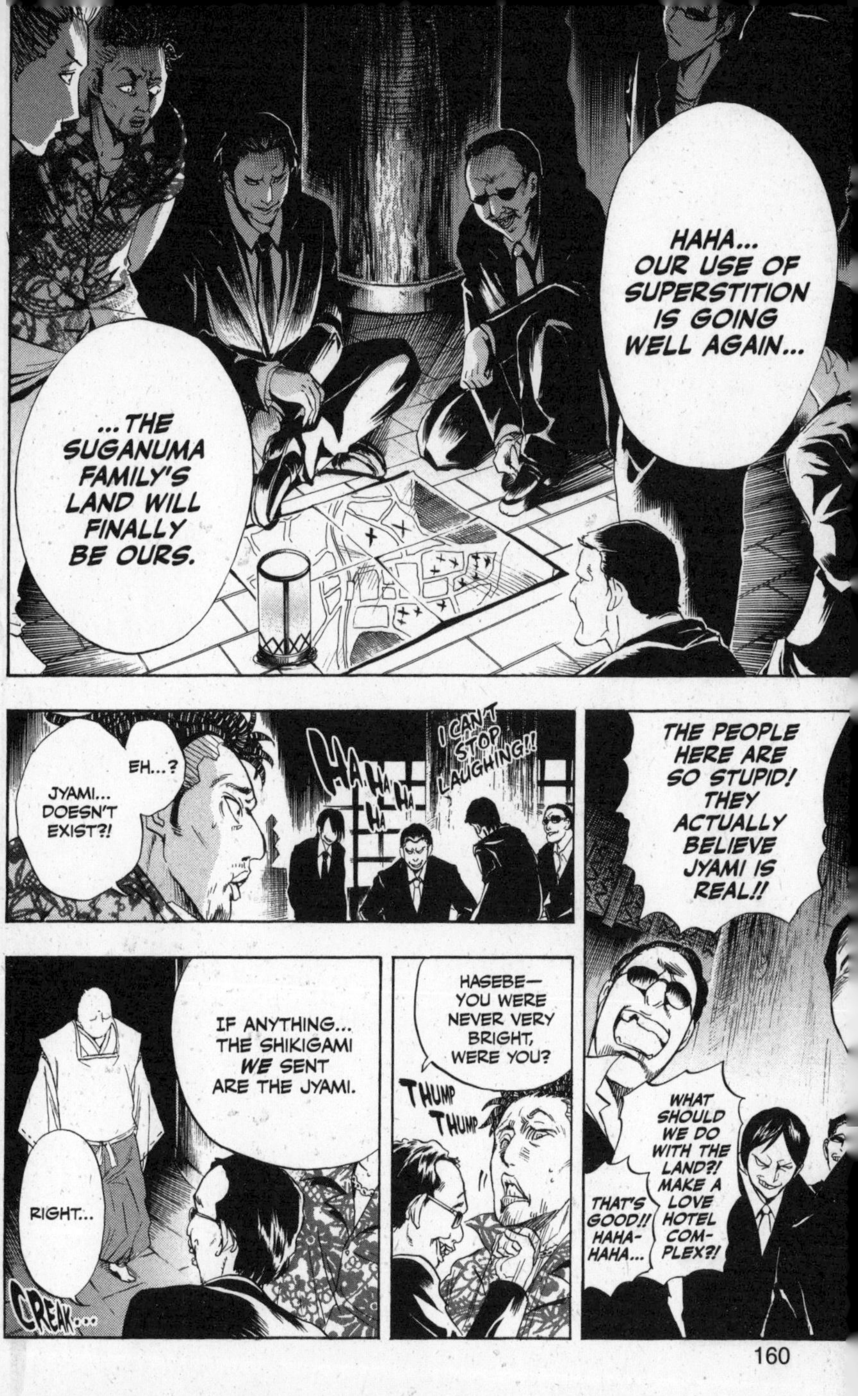
HAHA... OUR USE OF SUPERSTITION IS GOING WELL AGAIN...
...THE SUGANUMA FAMILY'S LAND WILL FINALLY BE OURS.
THE PEOPLE HERE ARE SO STUPID! THEY ACTUALLY BELIEVE JYAMI IS REAL!!
WHAT SHOULD WE DO WITH THE LAND?! MAKE A LOVE HOTEL COMPLEX?!
THAT'S GOOD!! HAHAHAHA...
I CAN'T STOP LAUGHING!!
HA HA HA HA
EH...?
JYAMI... DOESN'T EXIST?!
HASEBE— YOU WERE NEVER VERY BRIGHT, WERE YOU?
THUMP THUMP
IF ANYTHING... THE SHIKIGAMI *WE* SENT ARE THE JYAMI.
RIGHT...
CREAK...

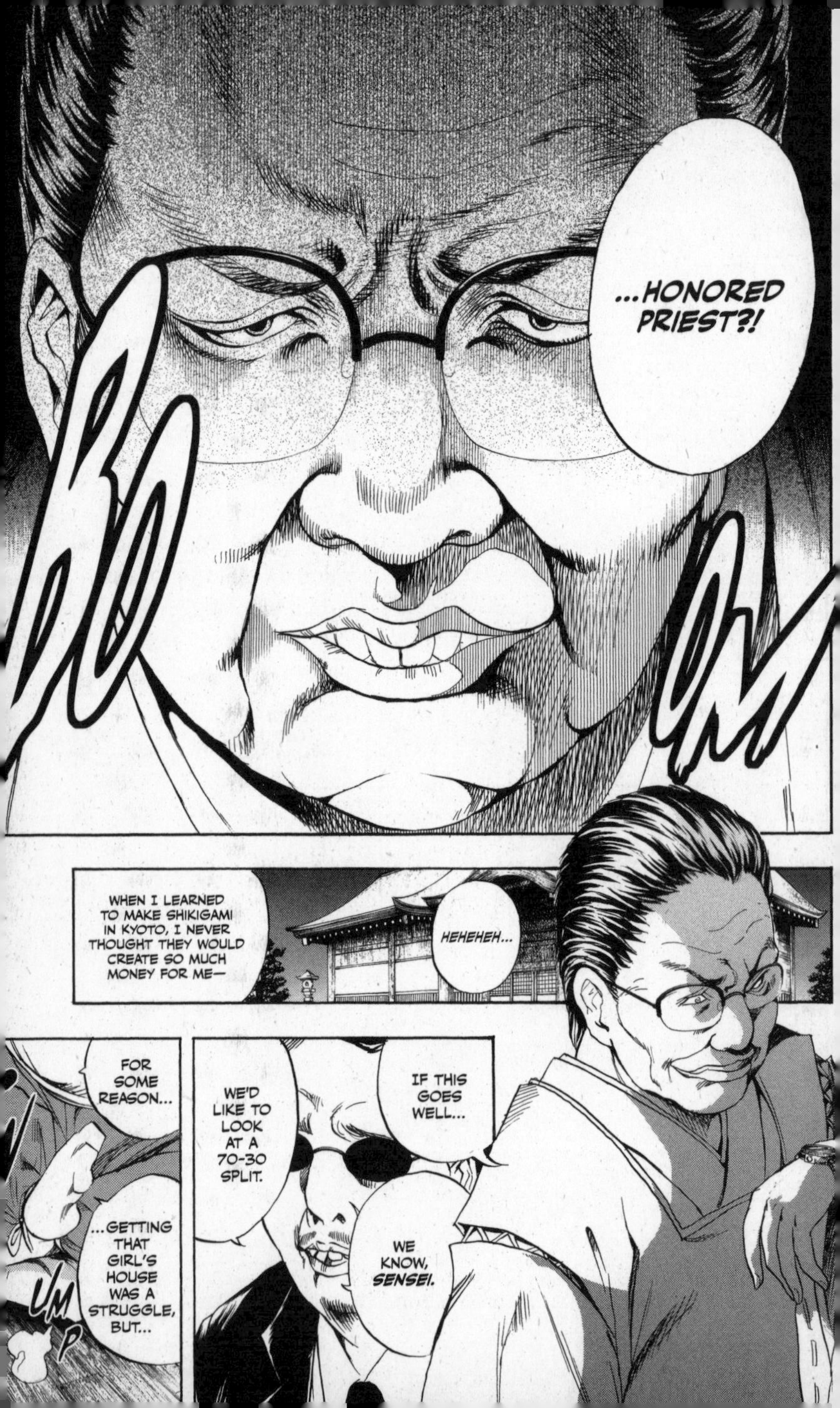
...HONORED PRIEST?!
HEHEHEH...
WHEN I LEARNED TO MAKE SHIKIGAMI IN KYOTO, I NEVER THOUGHT THEY WOULD CREATE SO MUCH MONEY FOR ME—
IF THIS GOES WELL...
WE'D LIKE TO LOOK AT A 70-30 SPLIT.
WE KNOW, *SENSEI.*
FOR SOME REASON...
...GETTING THAT GIRL'S HOUSE WAS A STRUGGLE, BUT...

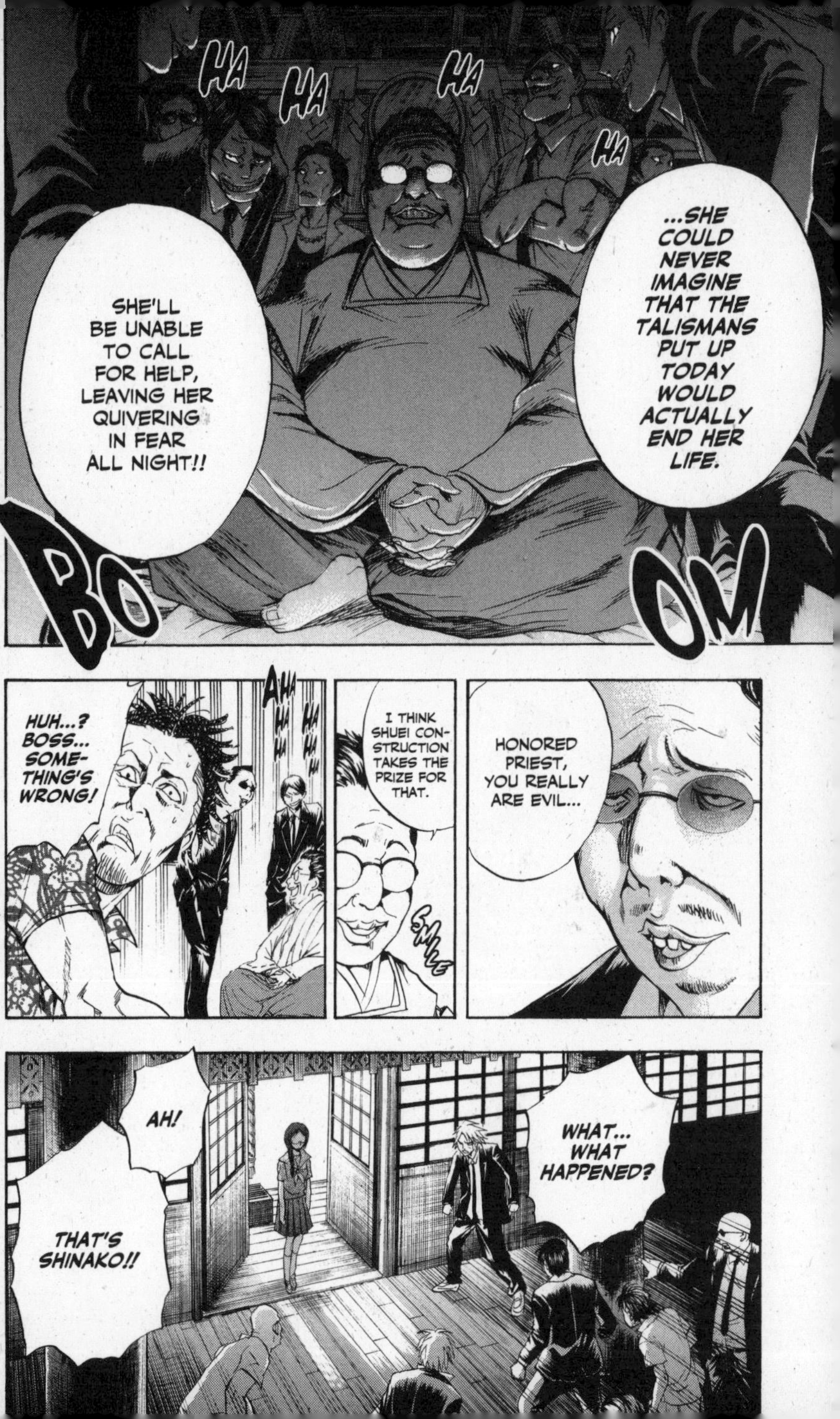
HA
HA
HA
HA
...SHE COULD NEVER IMAGINE THAT THE TALISMANS PUT UP TODAY WOULD ACTUALLY END HER LIFE.
SHE'LL BE UNABLE TO CALL FOR HELP, LEAVING HER QUIVERING IN FEAR ALL NIGHT!!
BOOM
HONORED PRIEST, YOU REALLY ARE EVIL...
I THINK SHUEI CONSTRUCTION TAKES THE PRIZE FOR THAT.
SMILE
AHA HA HA HA HA HA
HUH...? BOSS... SOMETHING'S WRONG!
WHAT... WHAT HAPPENED?
AH!
THAT'S SHINAKO!!

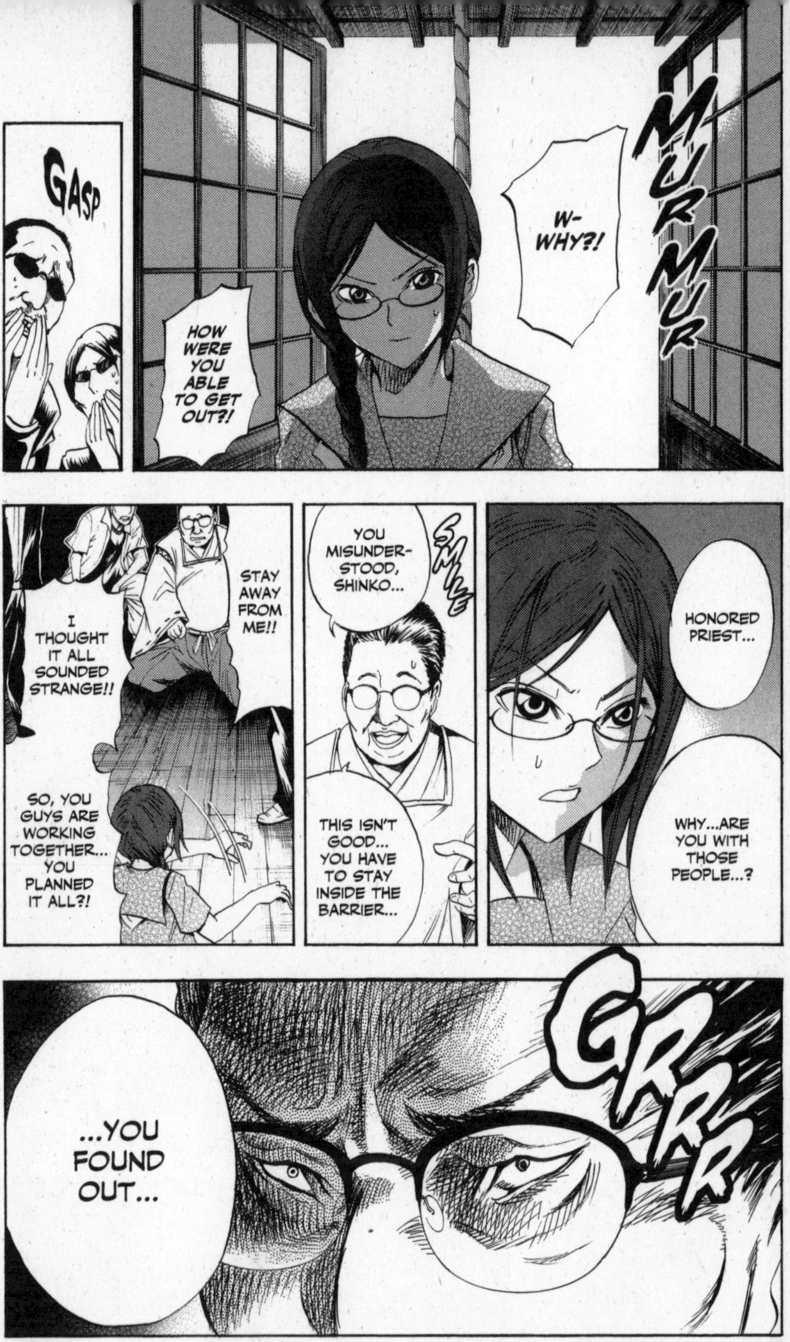
MURMUR
W-WHY?!
HOW WERE YOU ABLE TO GET OUT?!
GASP
HONORED PRIEST...
WHY...ARE YOU WITH THOSE PEOPLE...?
SMILE
YOU MISUNDERSTOOD, SHINKO...
THIS ISN'T GOOD... YOU HAVE TO STAY INSIDE THE BARRIER...
STAY AWAY FROM ME!!
I THOUGHT IT ALL SOUNDED STRANGE!!
SO, YOU GUYS ARE WORKING TOGETHER... YOU PLANNED IT ALL?!
GRRR
...YOU FOUND OUT...

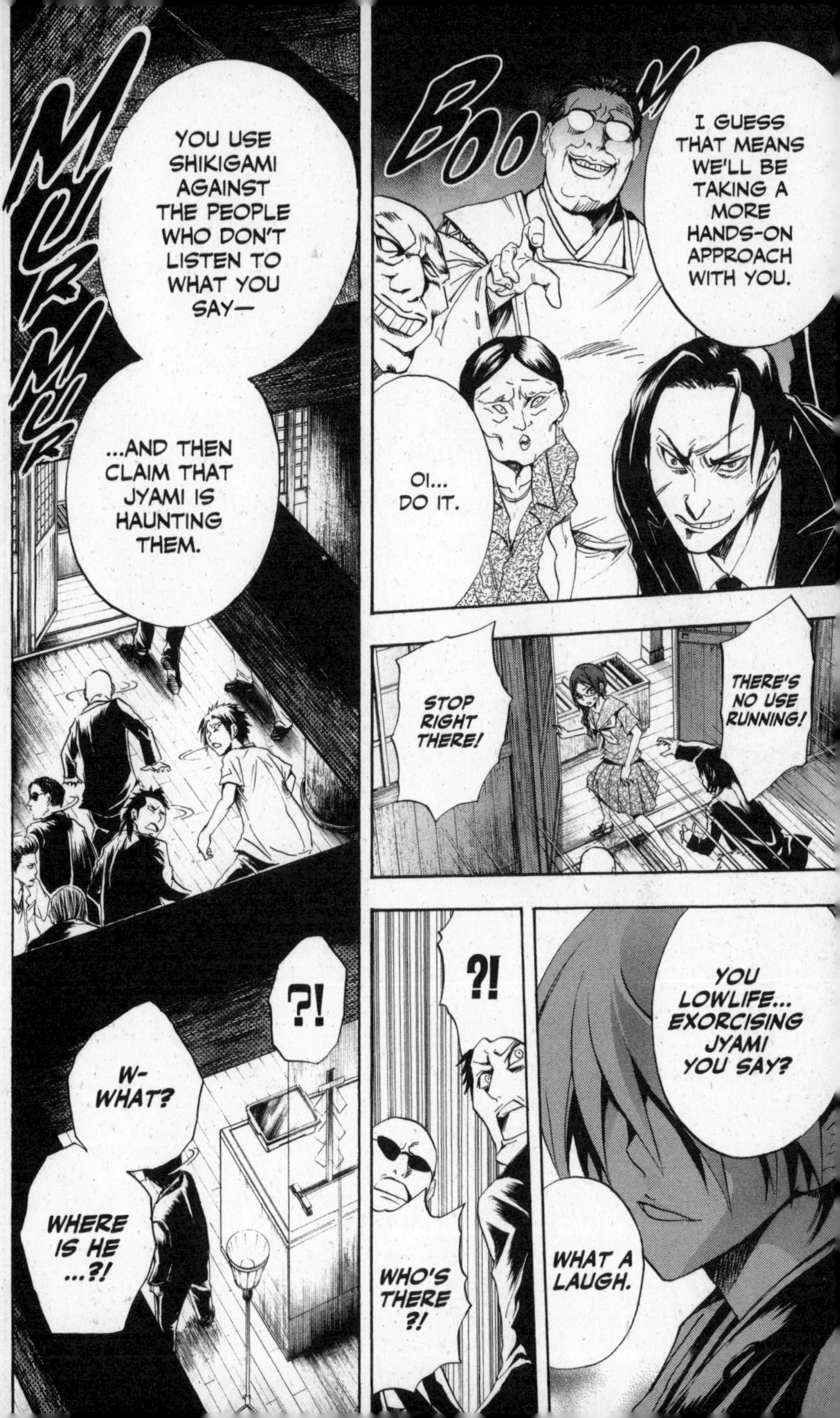
I GUESS THAT MEANS WE'LL BE TAKING A MORE HANDS-ON APPROACH WITH YOU.
BOOOM
OI... DO IT.
THERE'S NO USE RUNNING!
STOP RIGHT THERE!
YOU USE SHIKIGAMI AGAINST THE PEOPLE WHO DON'T LISTEN TO WHAT YOU SAY—
...AND THEN CLAIM THAT JYAMI IS HAUNTING THEM.
YOU LOWLIFE... EXORCISING JYAMI YOU SAY?
WHAT A LAUGH.
?!
WHO'S THERE ?!
?!
W- WHAT?
WHERE IS HE ...?!

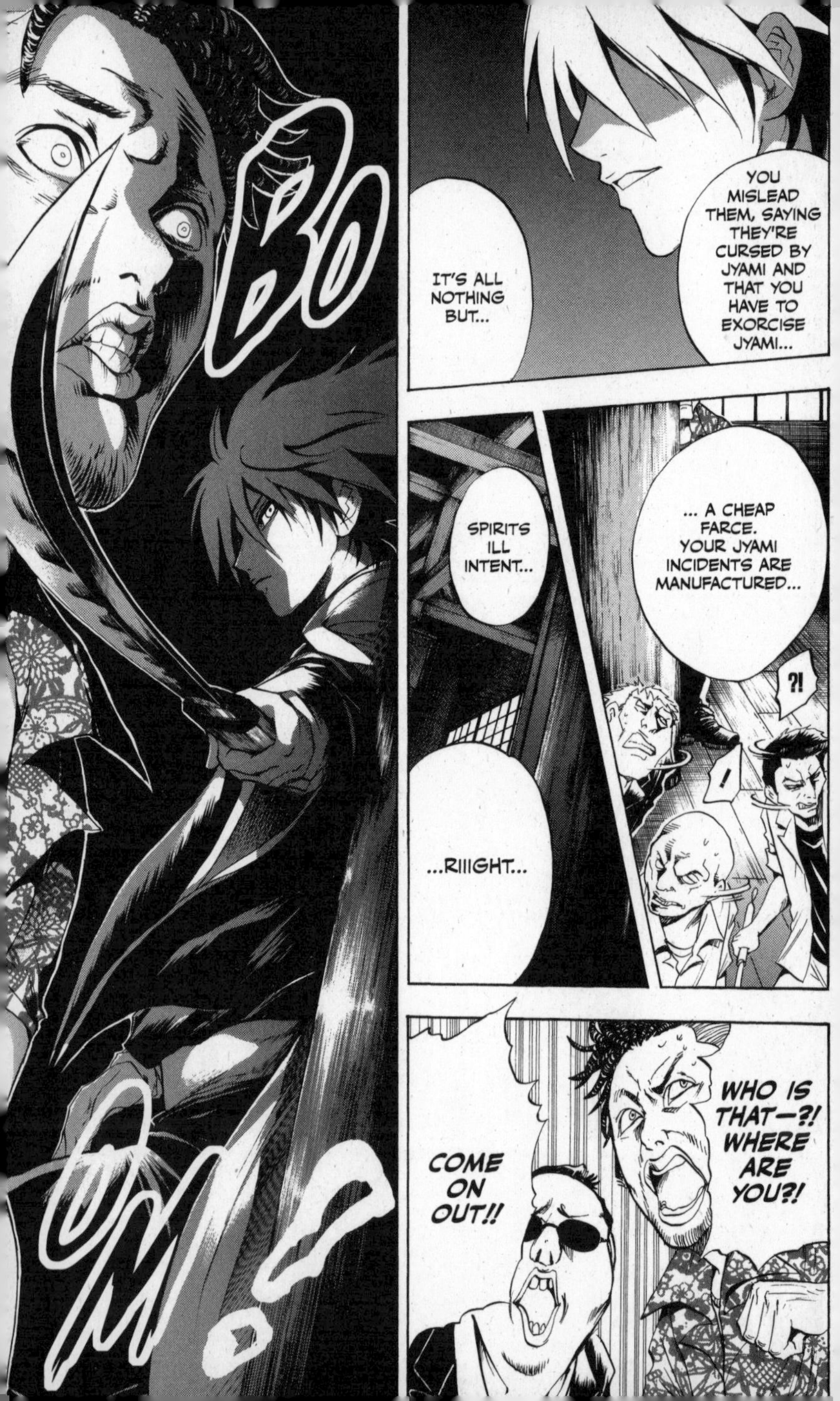
YOU MISLEAD THEM, SAYING THEY'RE CURSED BY JYAMI AND THAT YOU HAVE TO EXORCISE JYAMI...
IT'S ALL NOTHING BUT...
... A CHEAP FARCE. YOUR JYAMI INCIDENTS ARE MANUFACTURED...
?!
!
SPIRITS ILL INTENT...
...RIIIGHT...
WHO IS THAT—?! WHERE ARE YOU?!
COME ON OUT!!

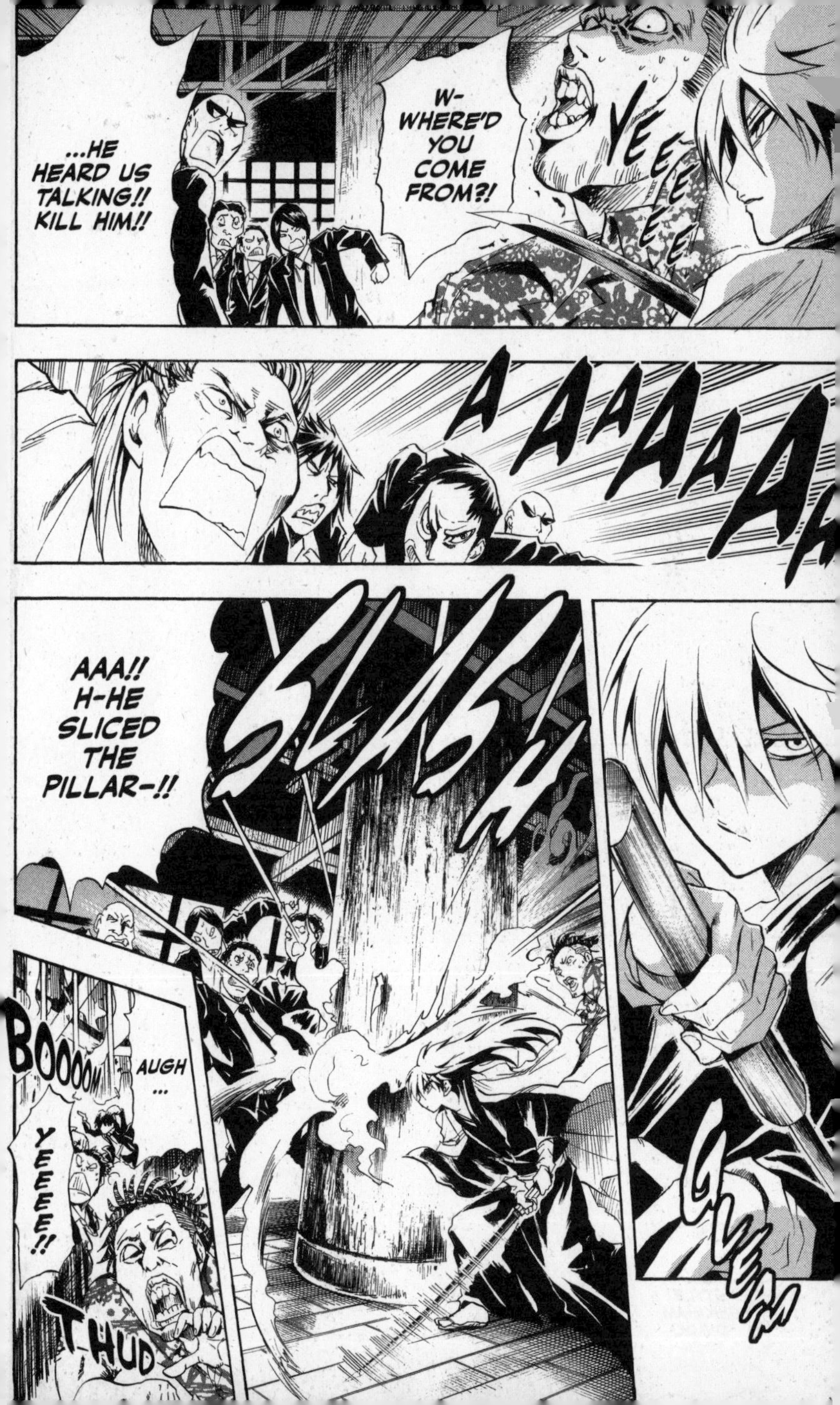

W-WHERE'D YOU COME FROM?!
YEEEEEE
...HE HEARD US TALKING!! KILL HIM!!
AAAAAAAH
SLASH
AAA!! H-HE SLICED THE PILLAR-!!
BOOOOM
AUGH ...
YEEEE!!
THUD

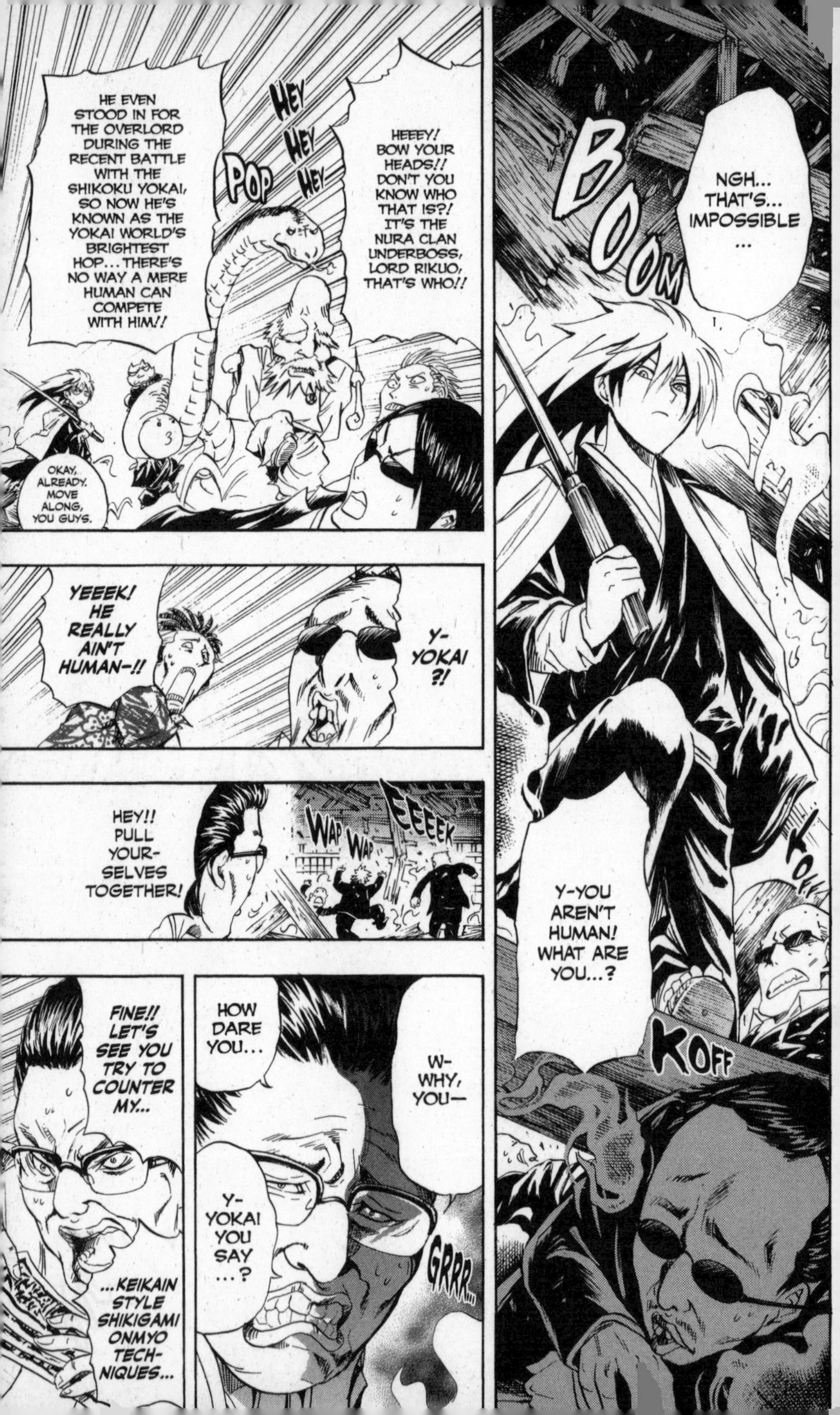
BOOM
NGH... THAT'S... IMPOSSIBLE...
KOFF
Y-YOU AREN'T HUMAN! WHAT ARE YOU...?
KOFF
HEY HEY HEY
POP
HEEEY! BOW YOUR HEADS!! DON'T YOU KNOW WHO THAT IS?! IT'S THE NURA CLAN UNDERBOSS, LORD RIKUO, THAT'S WHO!!
HE EVEN STOOD IN FOR THE OVERLORD DURING THE RECENT BATTLE WITH THE SHIKOKU YOKAI, SO NOW HE'S KNOWN AS THE YOKAI WORLD'S BRIGHTEST HOP... THERE'S NO WAY A MERE HUMAN CAN COMPETE WITH HIM!!
OKAY, ALREADY. MOVE ALONG, YOU GUYS.
Y-YOKAI?!
YEEEK! HE REALLY AIN'T HUMAN-!!
EEEEK
WAP WAP
HEY!! PULL YOURSELVES TOGETHER!
HOW DARE YOU...
W-WHY, YOU—
Y-YOKAI YOU SAY...?
GRRR...
FINE!! LET'S SEE YOU TRY TO COUNTER MY...
...KEIKAIN STYLE SHIKIGAMI ONMYO TECHNIQUES...

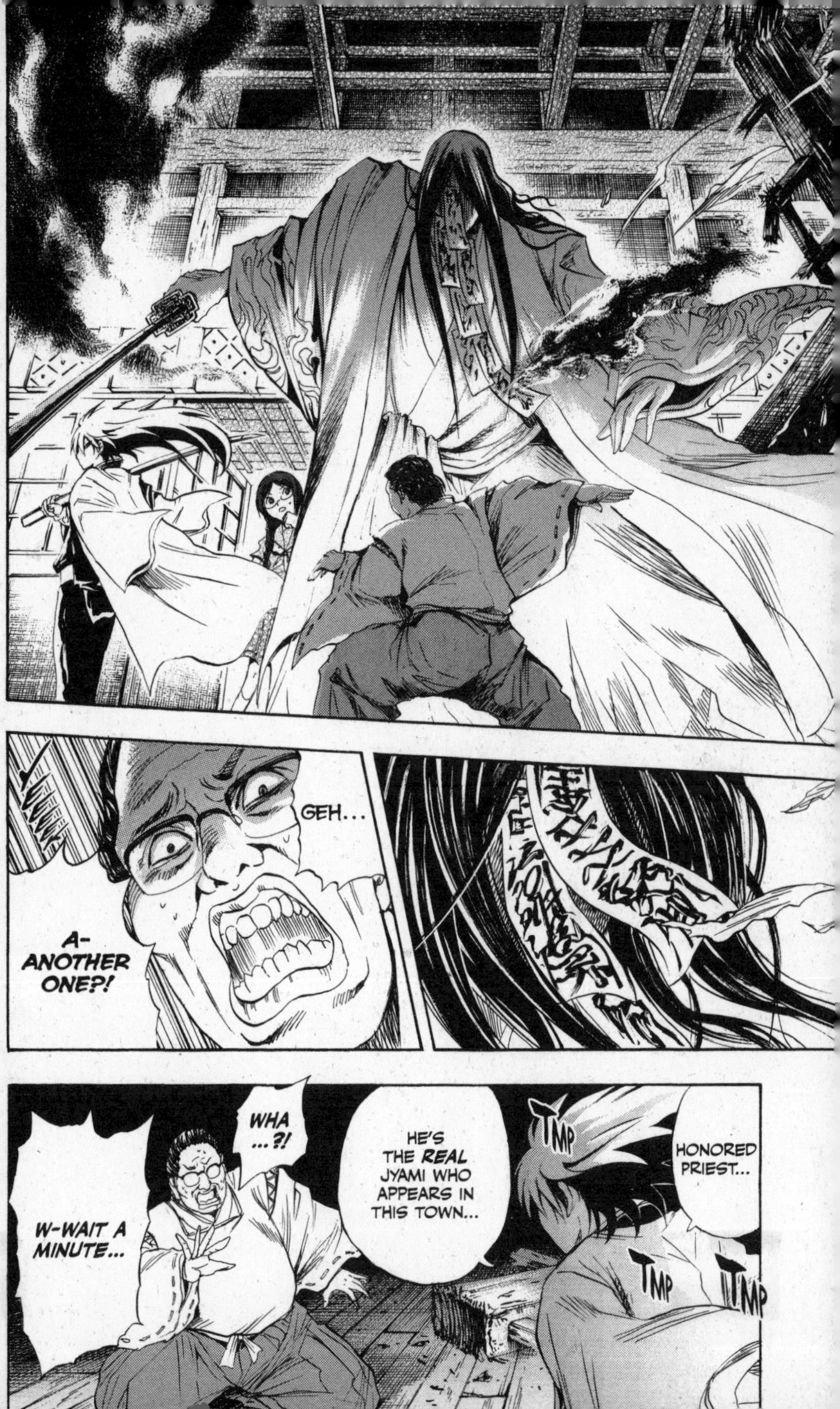
GEH...
A-ANOTHER ONE?!
HONORED PRIEST...
TMP
TMP
TMP
HE'S THE *REAL* JYAMI WHO APPEARS IN THIS TOWN...
WHA ...?!
W-WAIT A MINUTE...

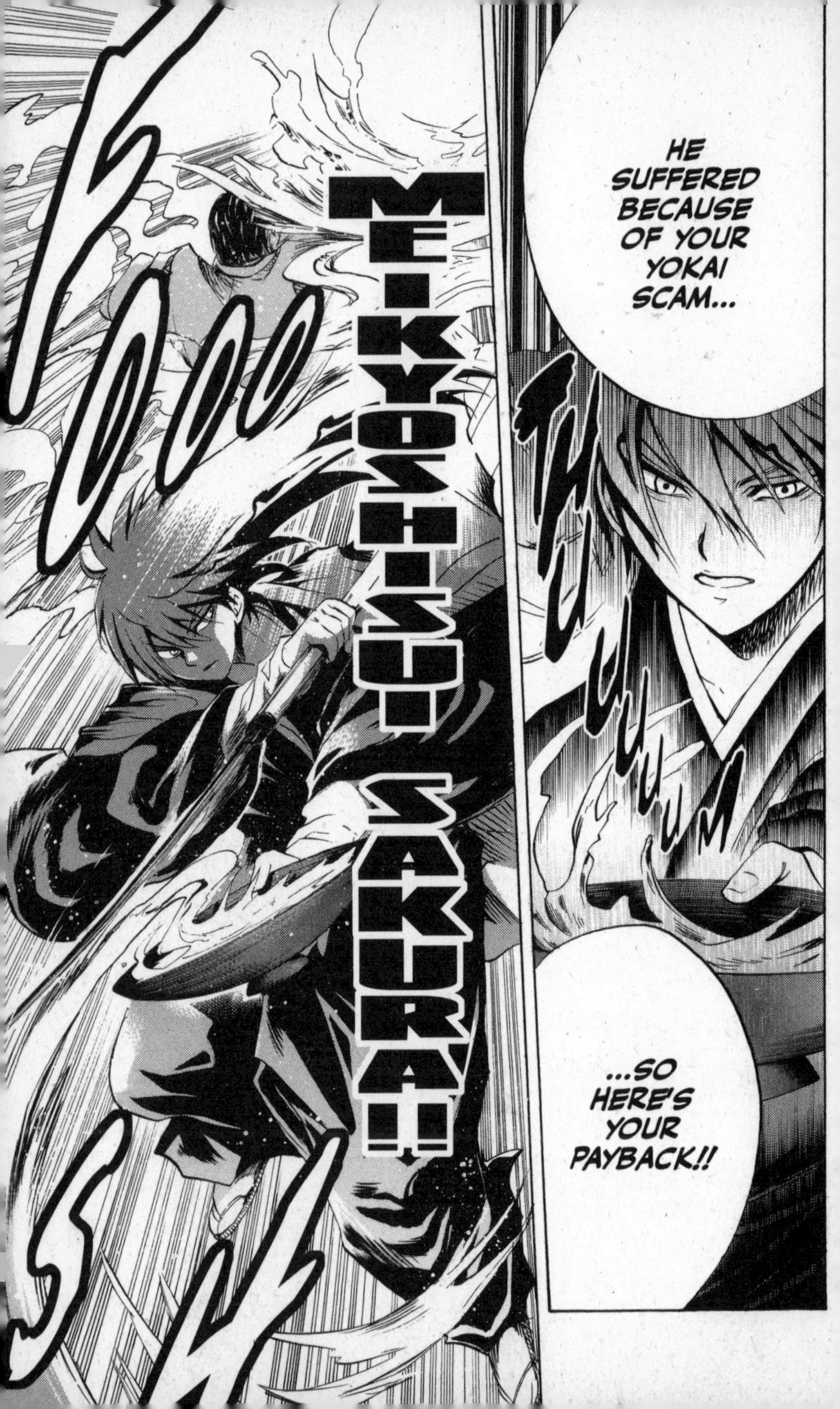
HE SUFFERED BECAUSE OF YOUR YOKAI SCAM...
...SO HERE'S YOUR PAYBACK!!
MEIKYOSHISUI SAKURA!!

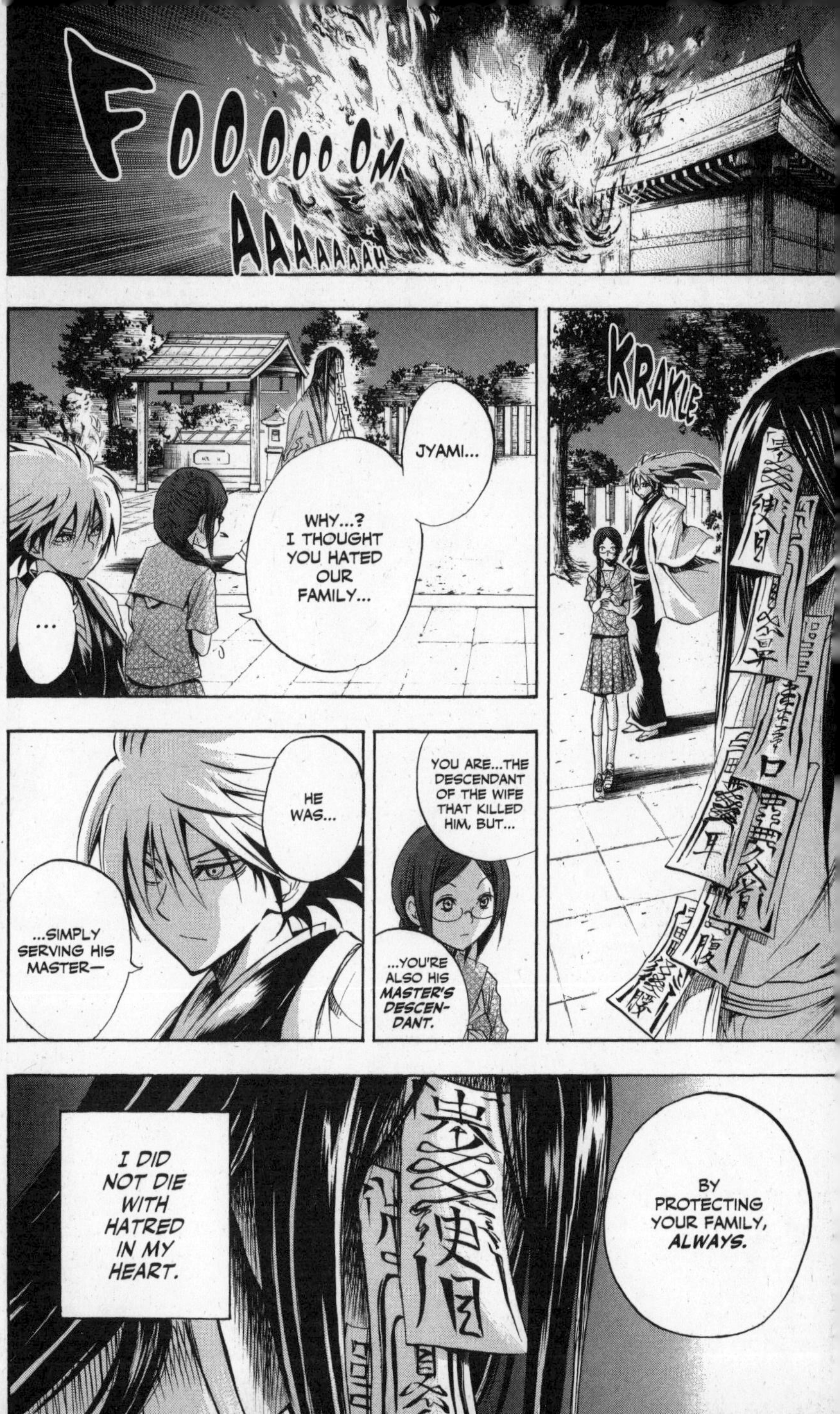
FOOOOOOM
AAAAAAAH
KRAKLE
JYAMI...
WHY...? I THOUGHT YOU HATED OUR FAMILY...
...
YOU ARE...THE DESCENDANT OF THE WIFE THAT KILLED HIM, BUT...
...YOU'RE ALSO HIS *MASTER'S DESCENDANT.*
HE WAS...
...SIMPLY SERVING HIS MASTER—
BY PROTECTING YOUR FAMILY, *ALWAYS.*
I DID NOT DIE WITH HATRED IN MY HEART.

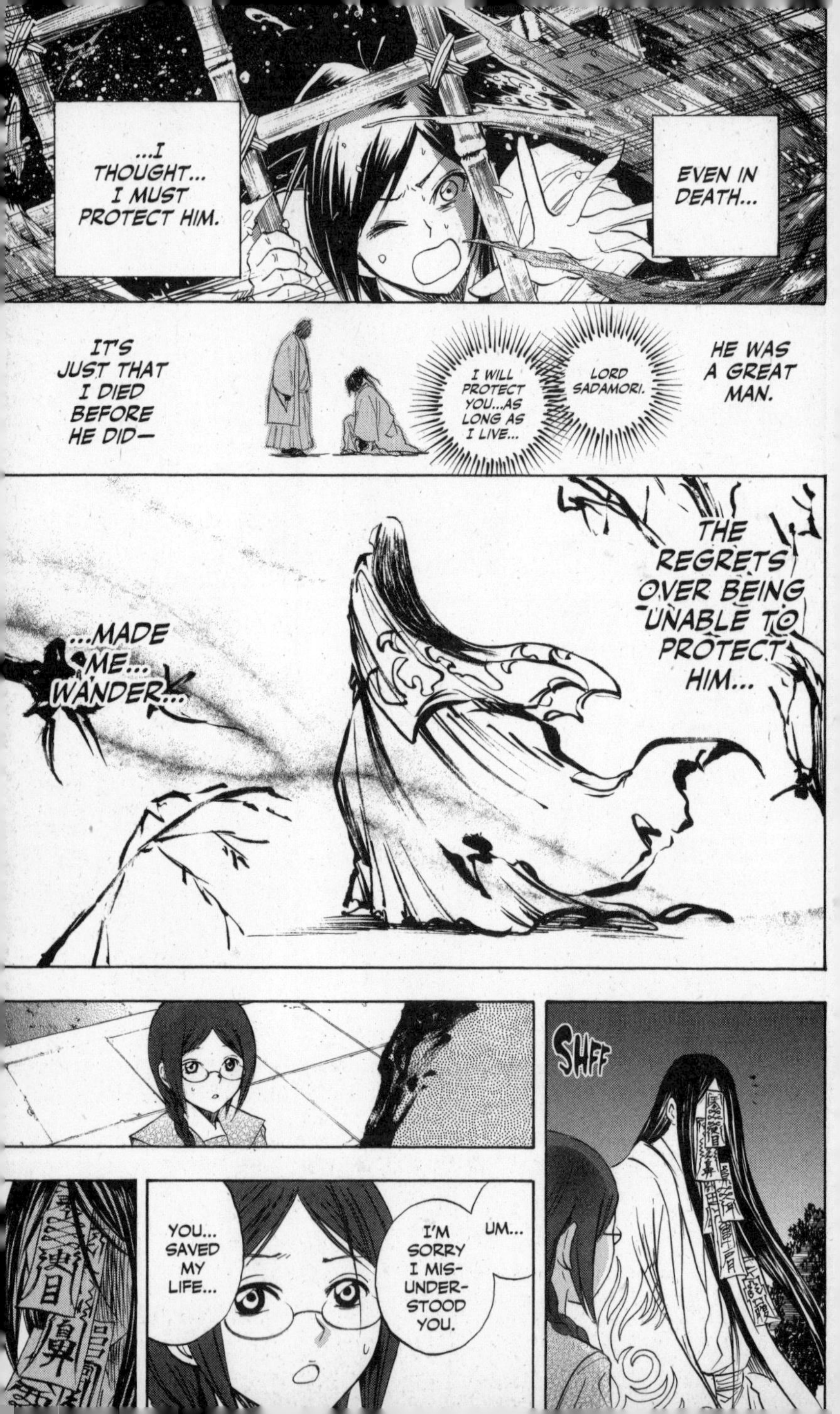
EVEN IN DEATH...
...I THOUGHT... I MUST PROTECT HIM.
HE WAS A GREAT MAN.
LORD SADAMORI.
I WILL PROTECT YOU...AS LONG AS I LIVE...
IT'S JUST THAT I DIED BEFORE HE DID—
THE REGRETS OVER BEING UNABLE TO PROTECT HIM...
...MADE ME... WANDER...
SHFF
UM...
I'M SORRY I MIS-UNDER-STOOD YOU.
YOU... SAVED MY LIFE...

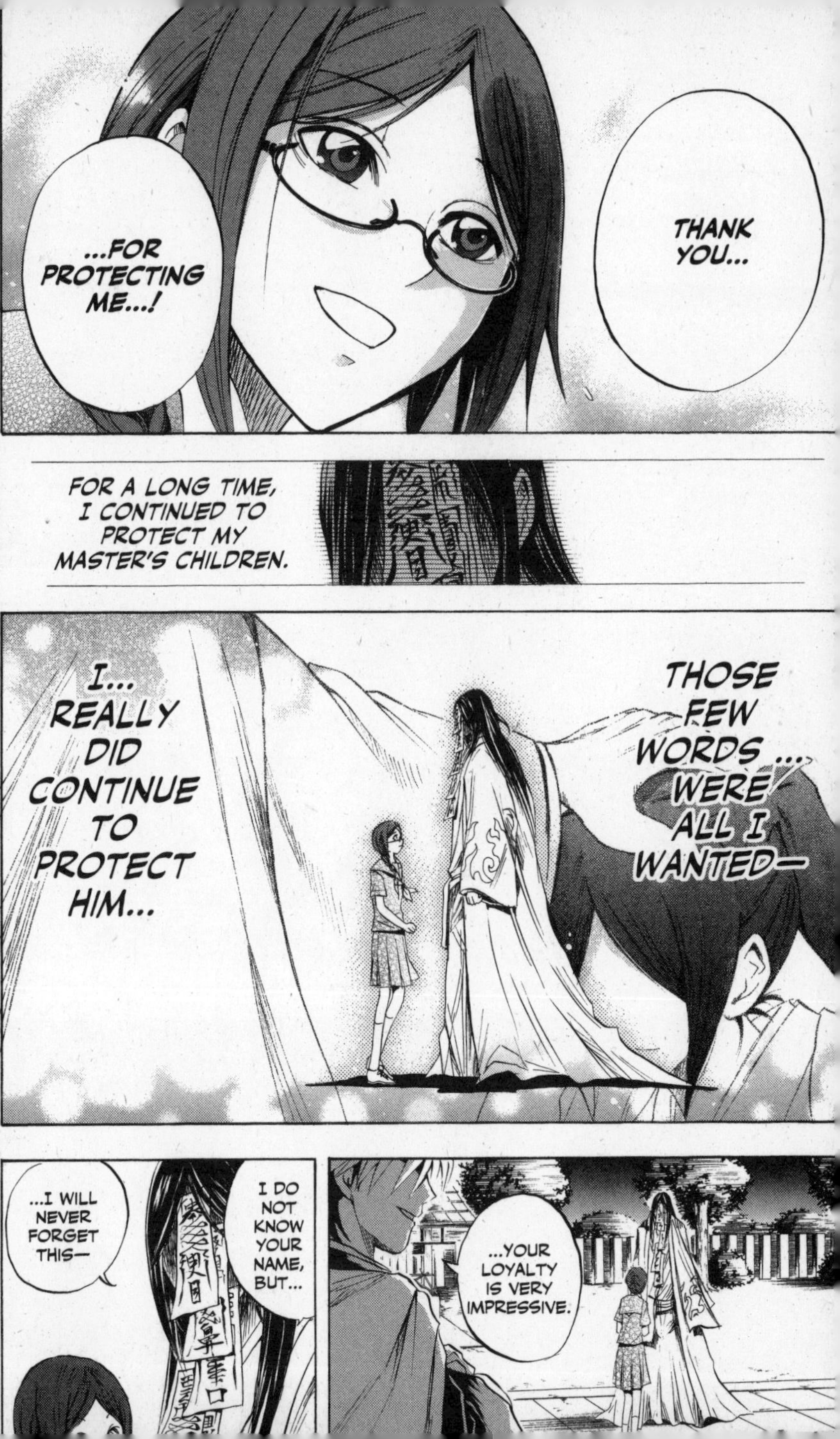
THANK YOU...
...FOR PROTECTING ME...!
FOR A LONG TIME, I CONTINUED TO PROTECT MY MASTER'S CHILDREN.
THOSE FEW WORDS ... WERE ALL I WANTED—
I... REALLY DID CONTINUE TO PROTECT HIM...
...YOUR LOYALTY IS VERY IMPRESSIVE.
I DO NOT KNOW YOUR NAME, BUT...
...I WILL NEVER FORGET THIS—

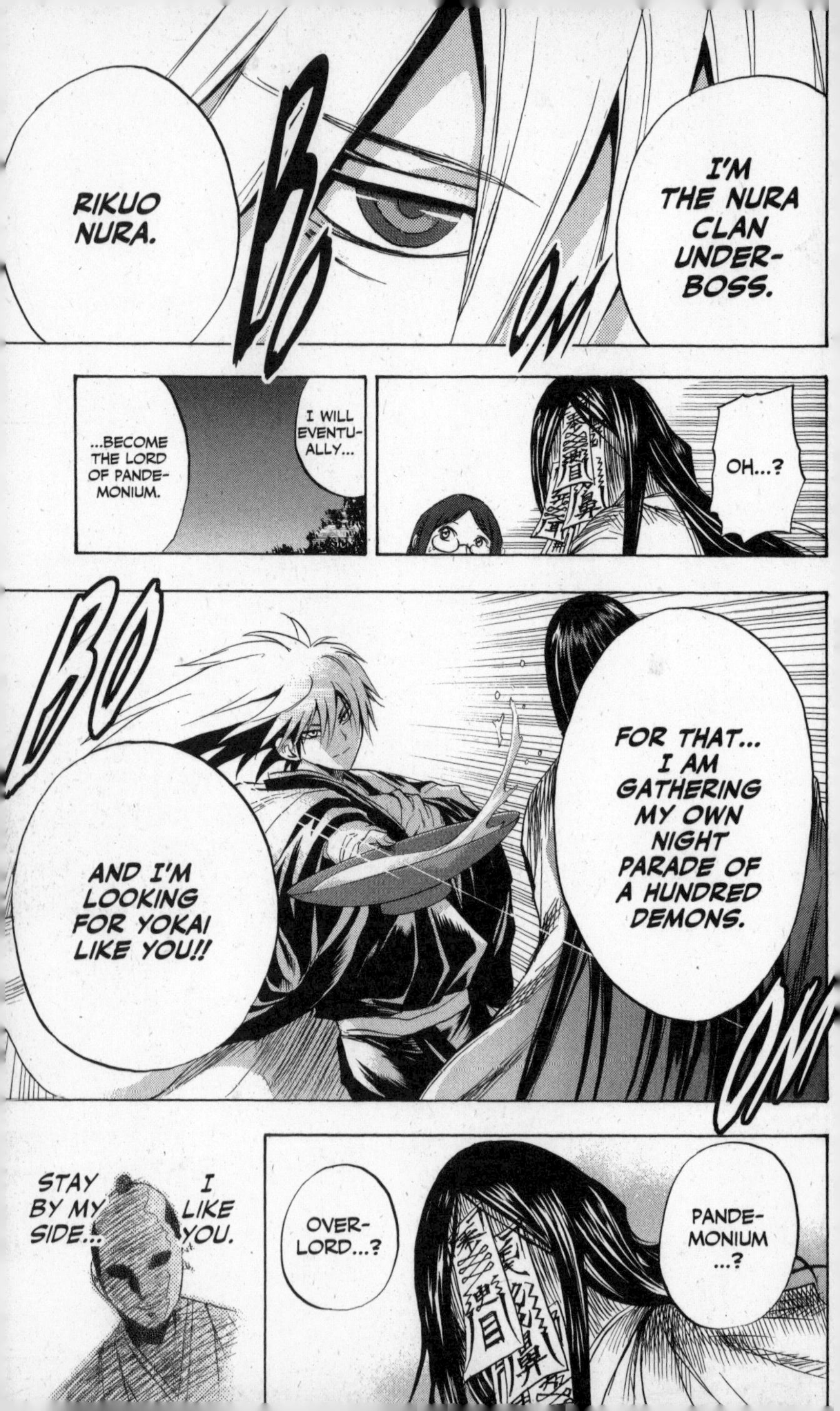
I'M THE NURA CLAN UNDER-BOSS.
RIKUO NURA.
OH...?
I WILL EVENTU-ALLY...
...BECOME THE LORD OF PANDE-MONIUM.
FOR THAT... I AM GATHERING MY OWN NIGHT PARADE OF A HUNDRED DEMONS.
AND I'M LOOKING FOR YOKAI LIKE YOU!!
PANDE-MONIUM ...?
OVER-LORD...?
I LIKE YOU.
STAY BY MY SIDE...

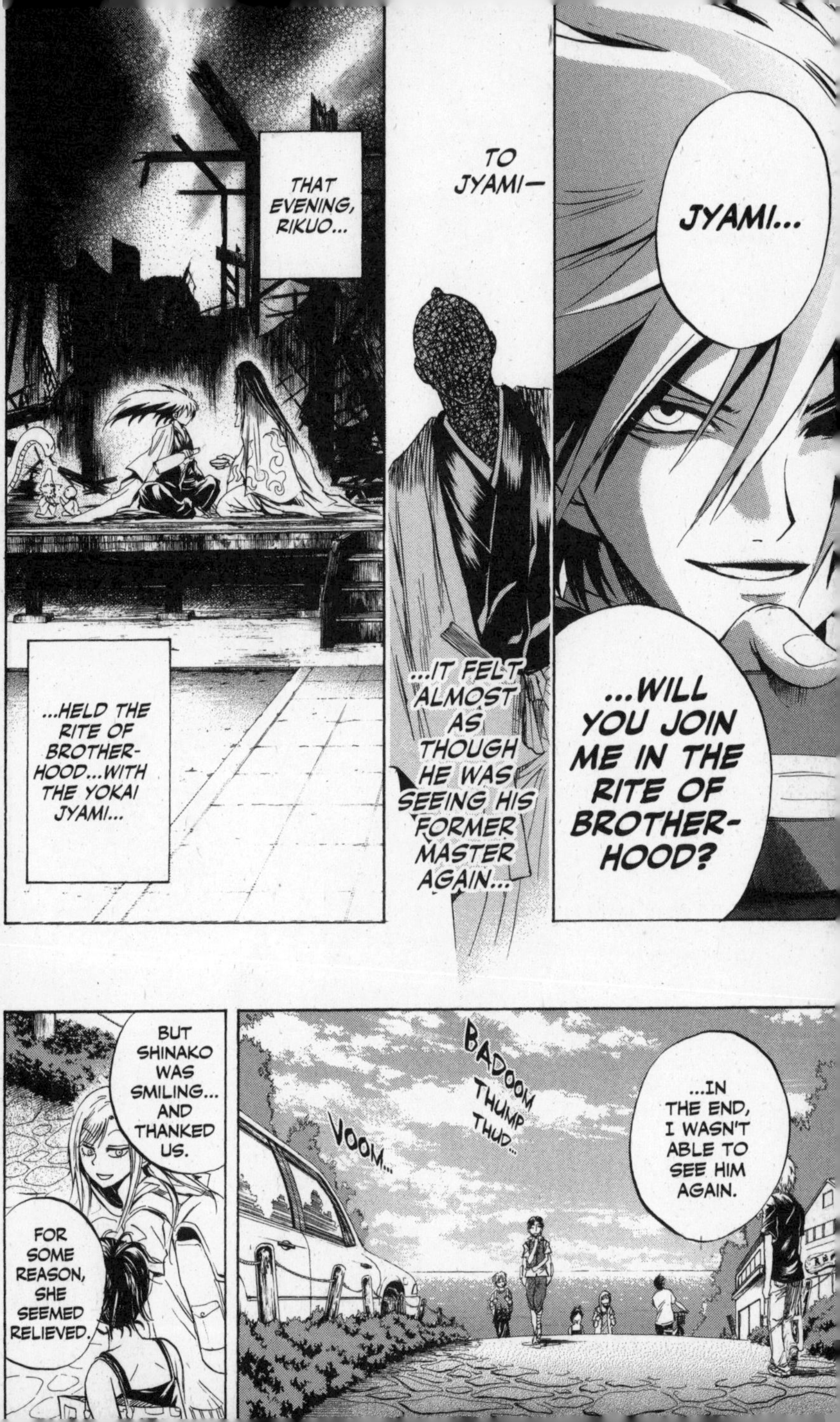
JYAMI...
...WILL YOU JOIN ME IN THE RITE OF BROTHER-HOOD?
TO JYAMI—
...IT FELT ALMOST AS THOUGH HE WAS SEEING HIS FORMER MASTER AGAIN...
THAT EVENING, RIKUO...
...HELD THE RITE OF BROTHER-HOOD...WITH THE YOKAI JYAMI...
...IN THE END, I WASN'T ABLE TO SEE HIM AGAIN.
BADOOM THUMP THUD...
VOOM...
BUT SHINAKO WAS SMILING... AND THANKED US.
FOR SOME REASON, SHE SEEMED RELIEVED.

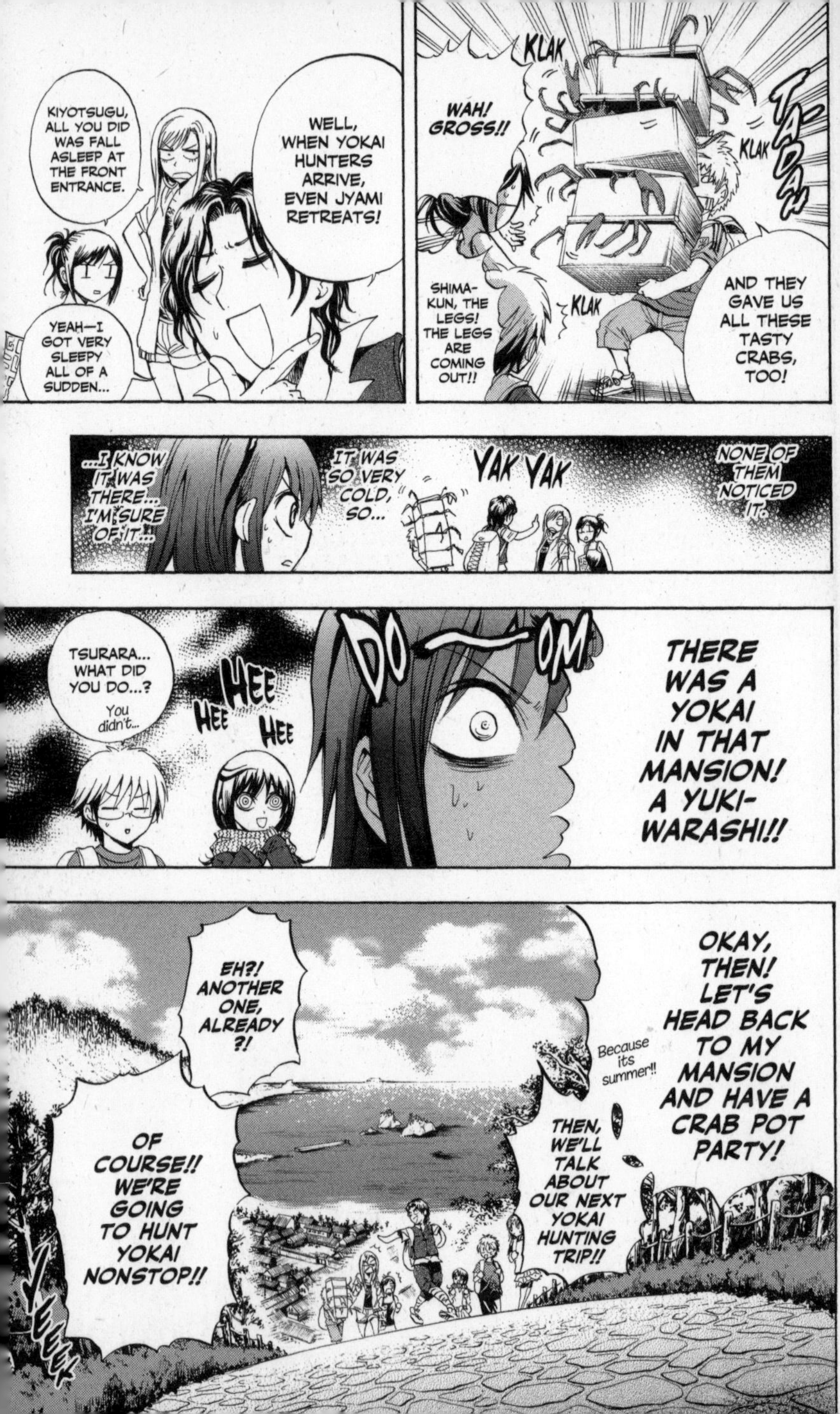
TA-DAH
KLAK
KLAK
WAH! GROSS!!
AND THEY GAVE US ALL THESE TASTY CRABS, TOO!
SHIMA-KUN, THE LEGS! THE LEGS ARE COMING OUT!!
KLAK
WELL, WHEN YOKAI HUNTERS ARRIVE, EVEN JYAMI RETREATS!
KIYOTSUGU, ALL YOU DID WAS FALL ASLEEP AT THE FRONT ENTRANCE.
YEAH—I GOT VERY SLEEPY ALL OF A SUDDEN...
NONE OF THEM NOTICED IT.
YAK YAK
IT WAS SO VERY COLD, SO...
...I KNOW IT WAS THERE... I'M SURE OF IT...
THERE WAS A YOKAI IN THAT MANSION! A YUKI-WARASHI!!
DO—OM
HEE HEE HEE
TSURARA... WHAT DID YOU DO...?
You didn't...
OKAY, THEN! LET'S HEAD BACK TO MY MANSION AND HAVE A CRAB POT PARTY!
Because its summer!!
THEN, WE'LL TALK ABOUT OUR NEXT YOKAI HUNTING TRIP!!
EH?! ANOTHER ONE, ALREADY?!
OF COURSE!! WE'RE GOING TO HUNT YOKAI NONSTOP!!
YEEEK

NURA: RISE OF THE YOKAI CLAN

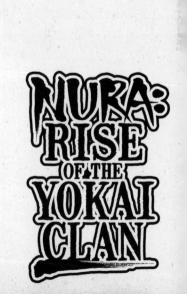

Act 51: Two Men of Justice

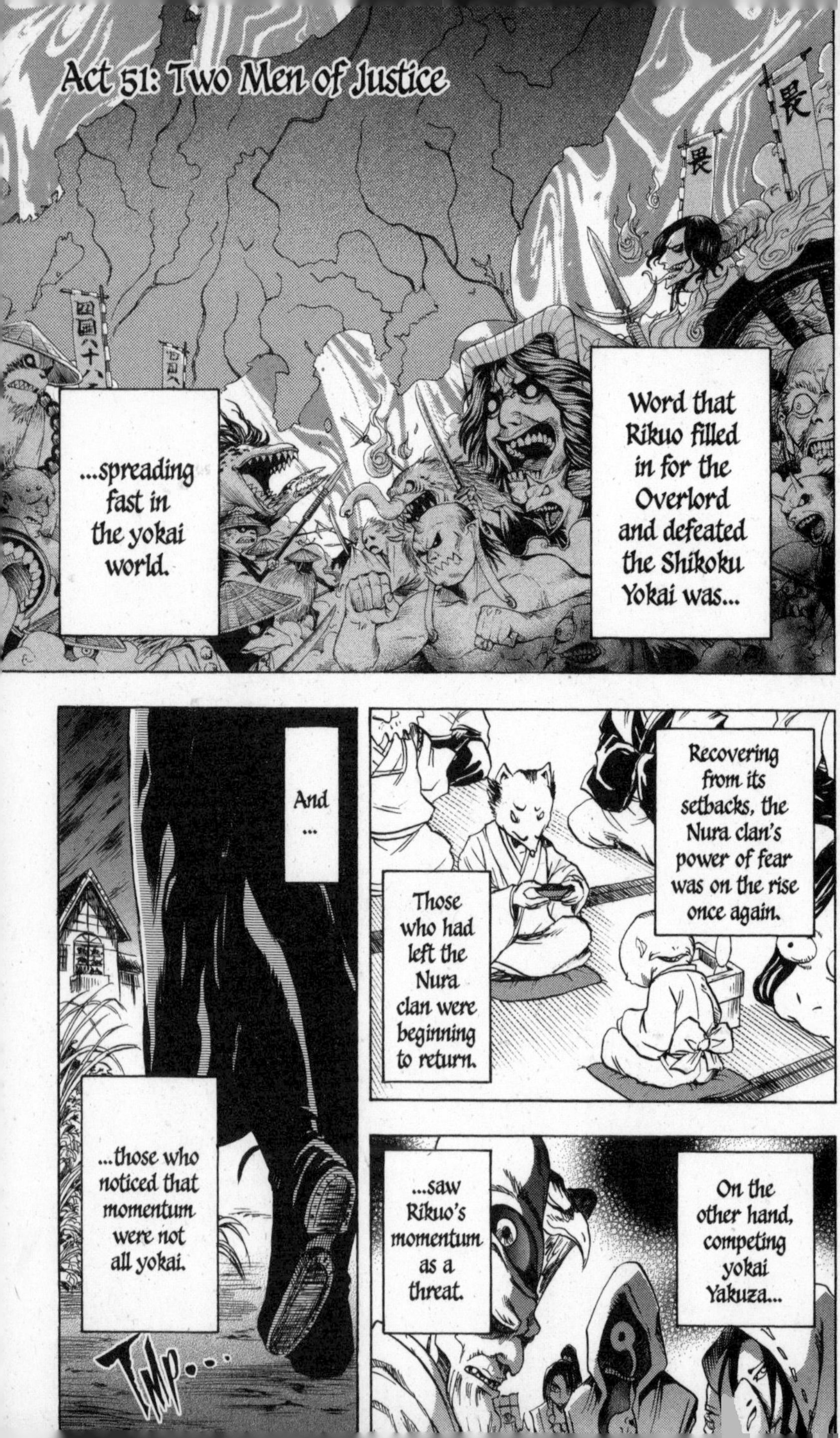
畏
畏
Word that Rikuo filled in for the Overlord and defeated the Shikoku Yokai was...
...spreading fast in the yokai world.
Recovering from its setbacks, the Nura clan's power of fear was on the rise once again.
Those who had left the Nura clan were beginning to return.
On the other hand, competing yokai Yakuza...
...saw Rikuo's momentum as a threat.
And ...
...those who noticed that momentum were not all yokai.
TMP...

Act 51: Two Men of Justice

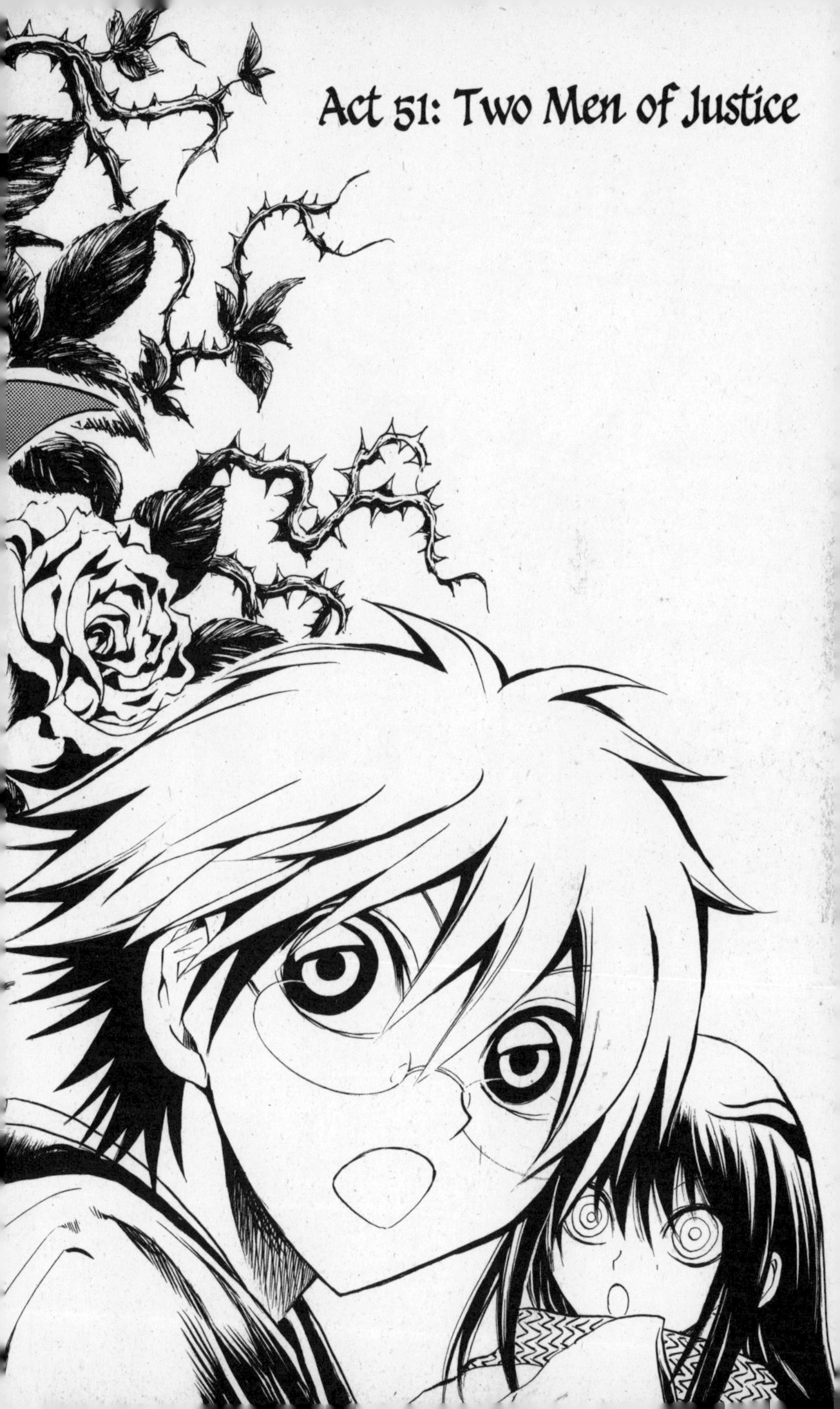

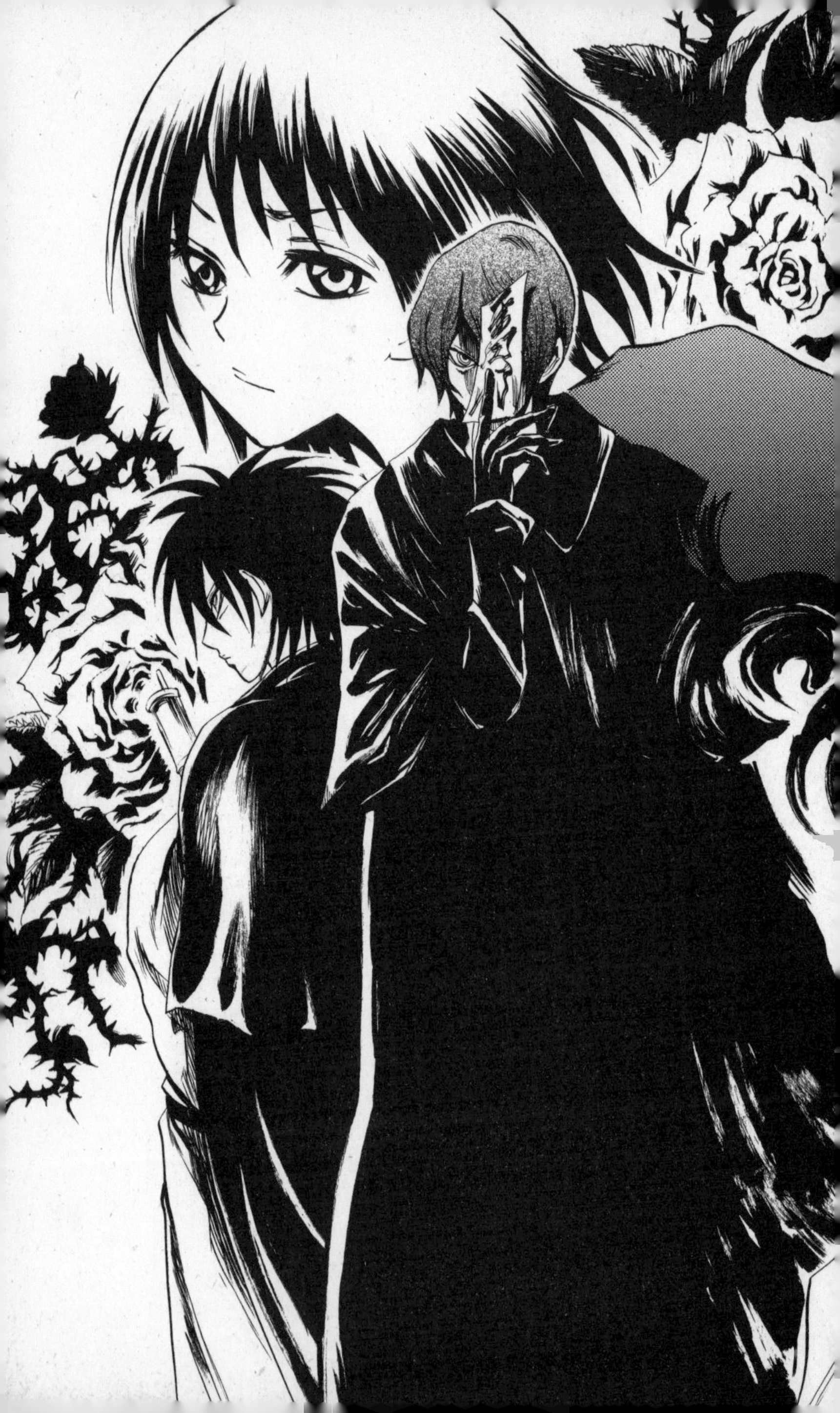

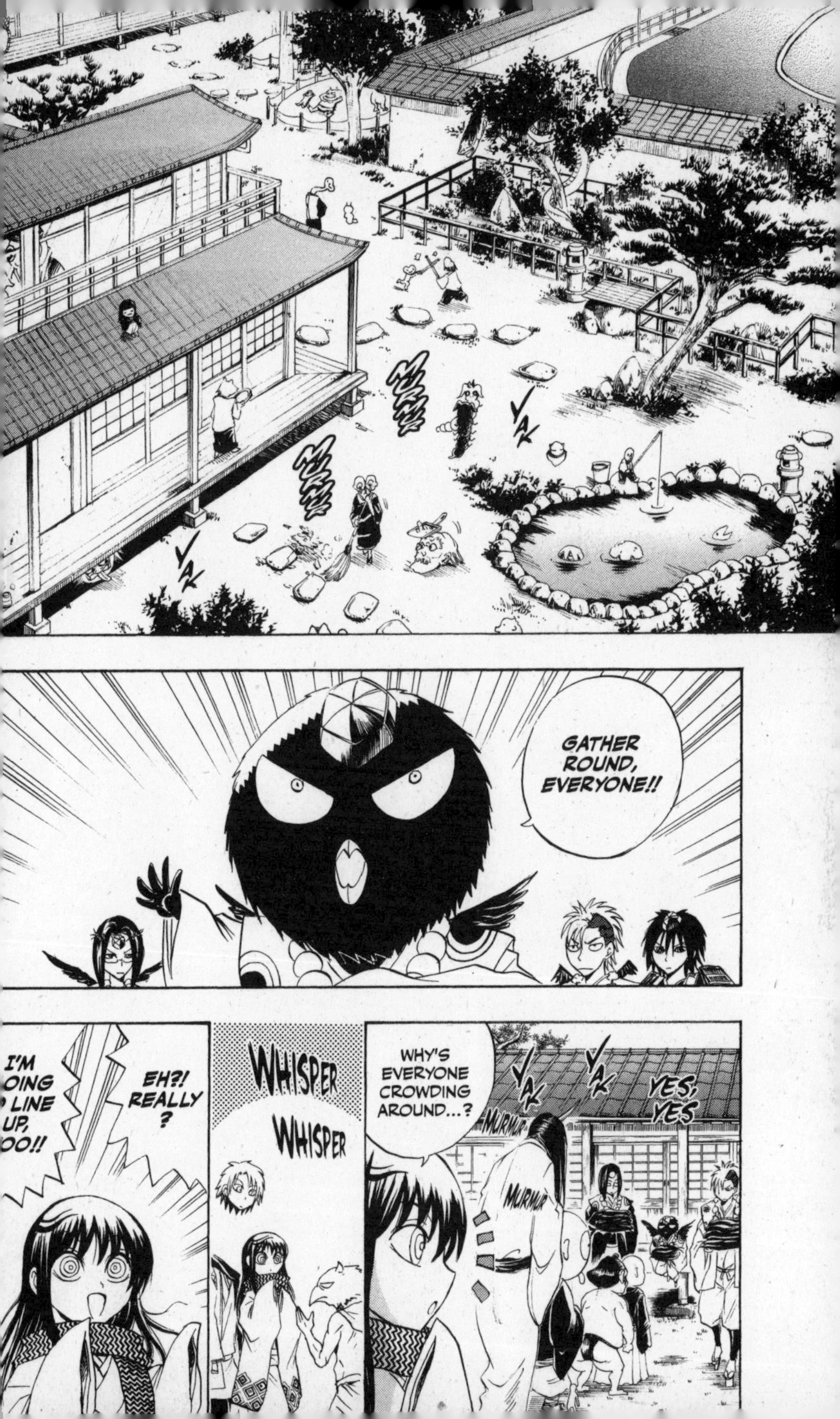
YAK
YAK
GATHER ROUND, EVERYONE!!
WHY'S EVERYONE CROWDING AROUND...?
YAK
YAK
YES, YES
MURMUR
MURMUR
WHISPER
WHISPER
EH?! REALLY?
I'M OING LINE UP, OO!!

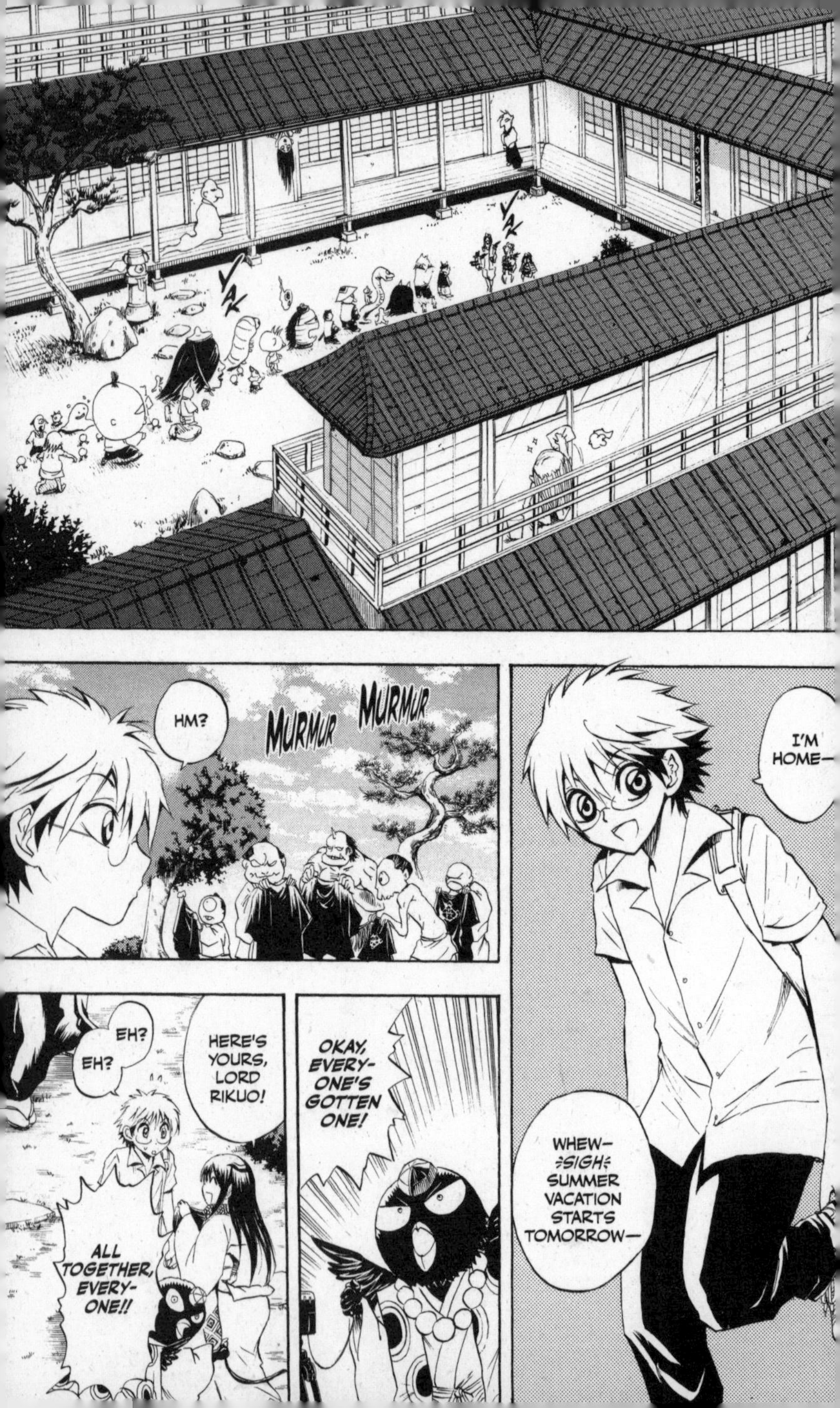
YAK
YAK
I'M HOME—
WHEW— *SIGH* SUMMER VACATION STARTS TOMORROW—
MURMUR
MURMUR
HM?
OKAY, EVERYONE'S GOTTEN ONE!
HERE'S YOURS, LORD RIKUO!
EH?
EH?
ALL TOGETHER, EVERYONE!!

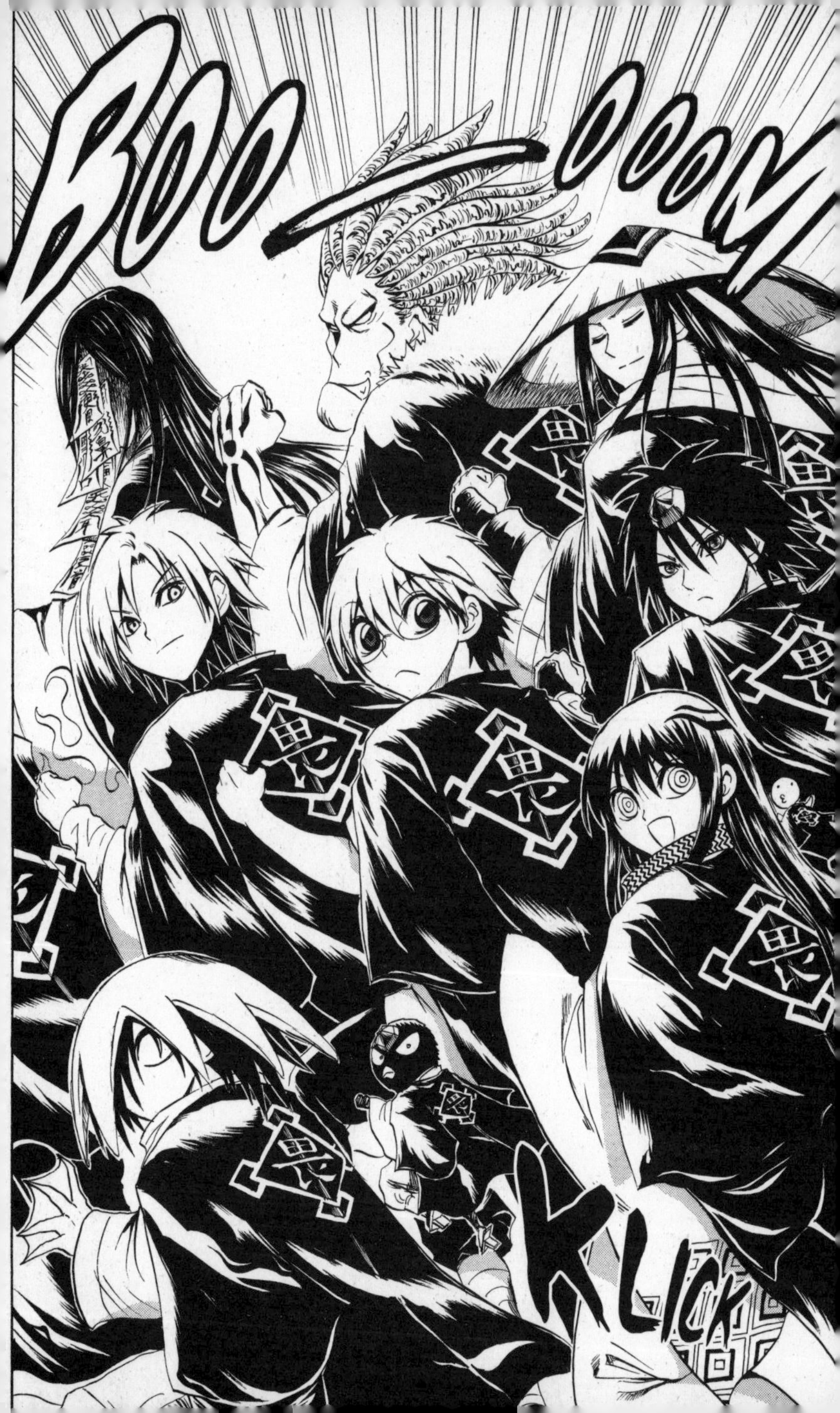
BOO—OOOM
KLICK

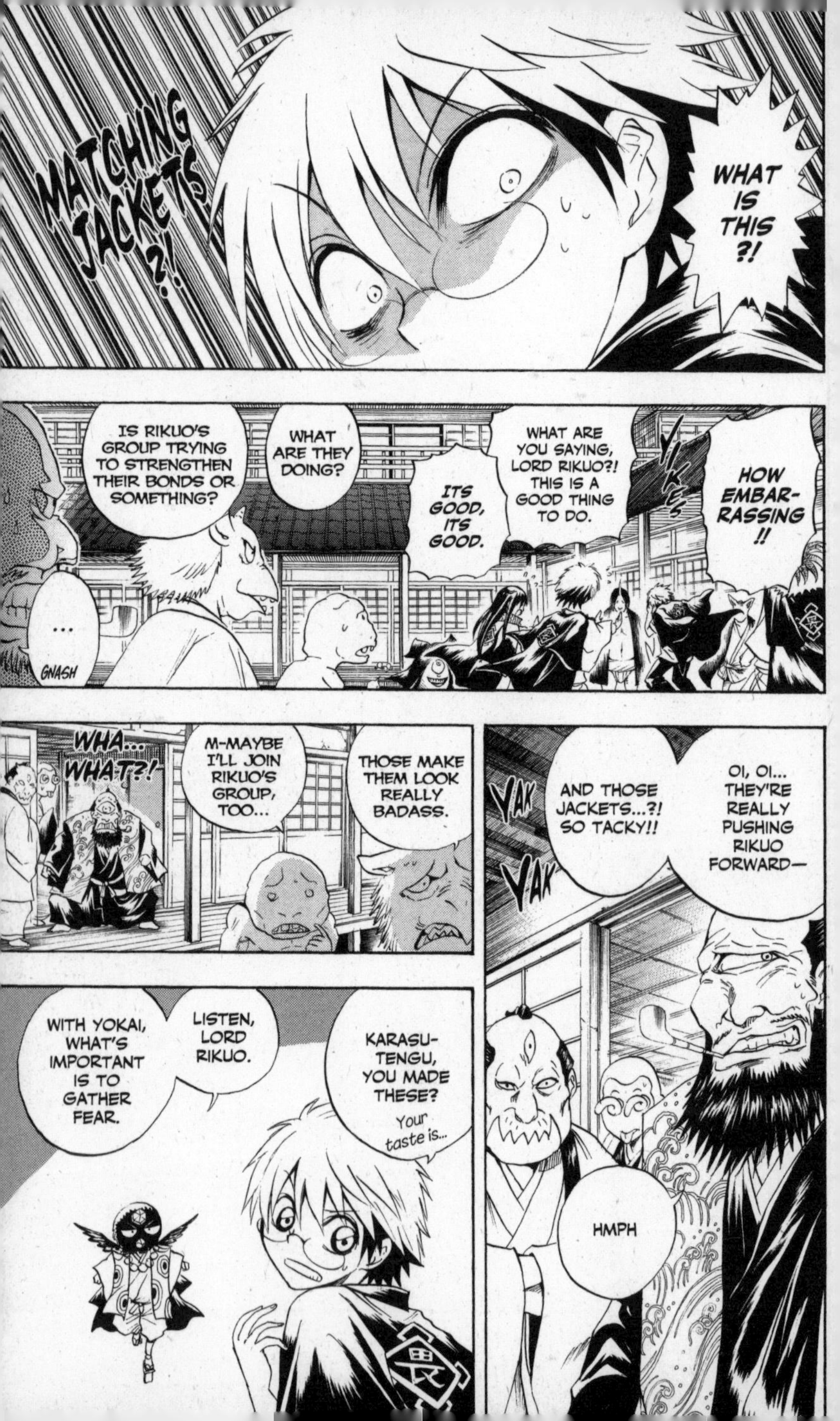
WHAT IS THIS ?!
MATCHING JACKETS ?!
HOW EMBARRASSING !!
YIKES
WHAT ARE YOU SAYING, LORD RIKUO?! THIS IS A GOOD THING TO DO.
ITS GOOD, ITS GOOD.
WHAT ARE THEY DOING?
IS RIKUO'S GROUP TRYING TO STRENGTHEN THEIR BONDS OR SOMETHING?
...
GNASH
OI, OI... THEY'RE REALLY PUSHING RIKUO FORWARD—
AND THOSE JACKETS...?! SO TACKY!!
YAK
YAK
HMPH
THOSE MAKE THEM LOOK REALLY BADASS.
M-MAYBE I'LL JOIN RIKUO'S GROUP, TOO...
WHA... WHAT?!
KARASU-TENGU, YOU MADE THESE?
Your taste is...
LISTEN, LORD RIKUO.
WITH YOKAI, WHAT'S IMPORTANT IS TO GATHER FEAR.

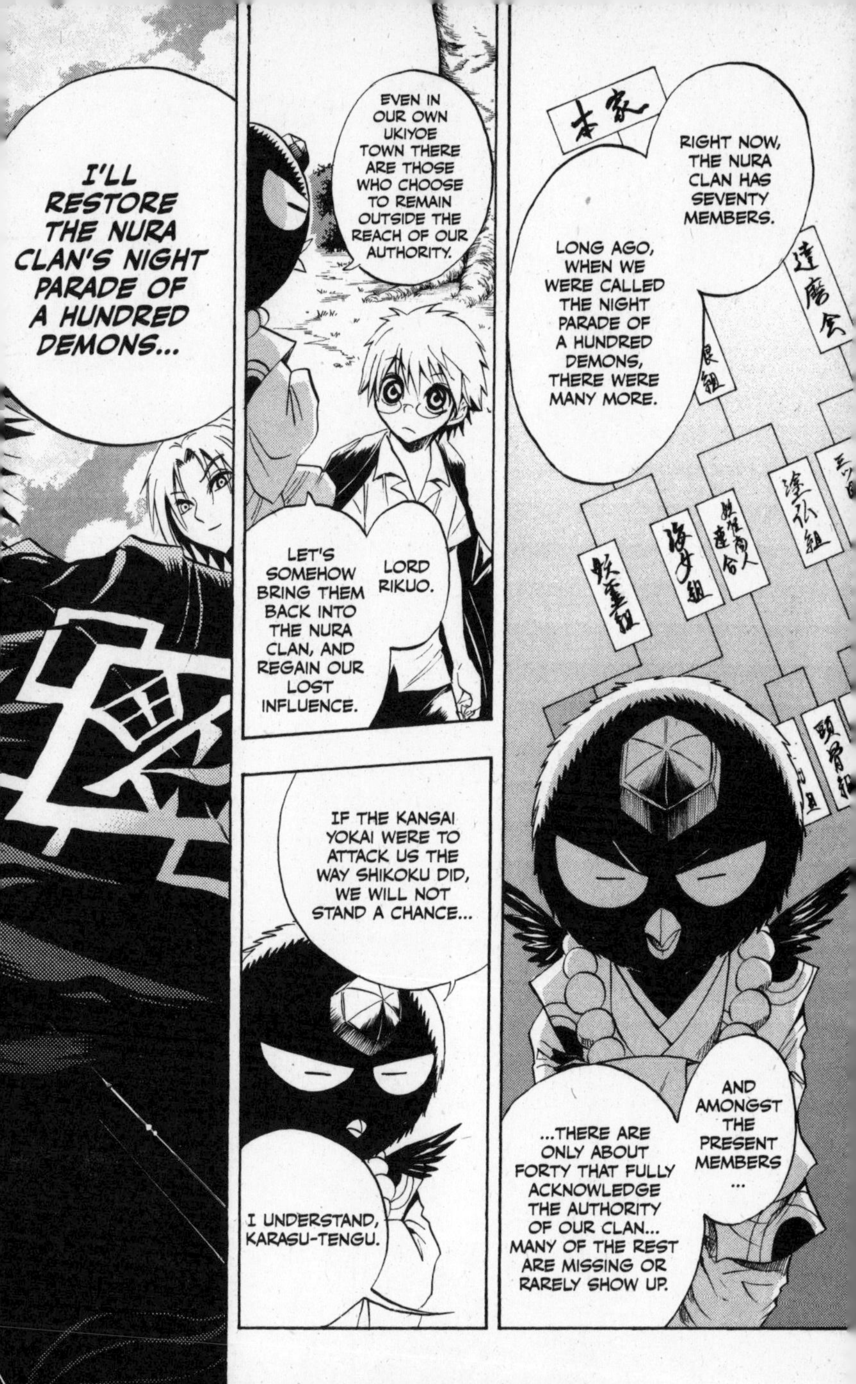
RIGHT NOW, THE NURA CLAN HAS SEVENTY MEMBERS.
LONG AGO, WHEN WE WERE CALLED THE NIGHT PARADE OF A HUNDRED DEMONS, THERE WERE MANY MORE.
本家
達磨会
AND AMONGST THE PRESENT MEMBERS...
...THERE ARE ONLY ABOUT FORTY THAT FULLY ACKNOWLEDGE THE AUTHORITY OF OUR CLAN... MANY OF THE REST ARE MISSING OR RARELY SHOW UP.
EVEN IN OUR OWN UKIYOE TOWN THERE ARE THOSE WHO CHOOSE TO REMAIN OUTSIDE THE REACH OF OUR AUTHORITY.
LORD RIKUO.
LET'S SOMEHOW BRING THEM BACK INTO THE NURA CLAN, AND REGAIN OUR LOST INFLUENCE.
IF THE KANSAI YOKAI WERE TO ATTACK US THE WAY SHIKOKU DID, WE WILL NOT STAND A CHANCE...
I UNDERSTAND, KARASU-TENGU.
I'LL RESTORE THE NURA CLAN'S NIGHT PARADE OF A HUNDRED DEMONS...

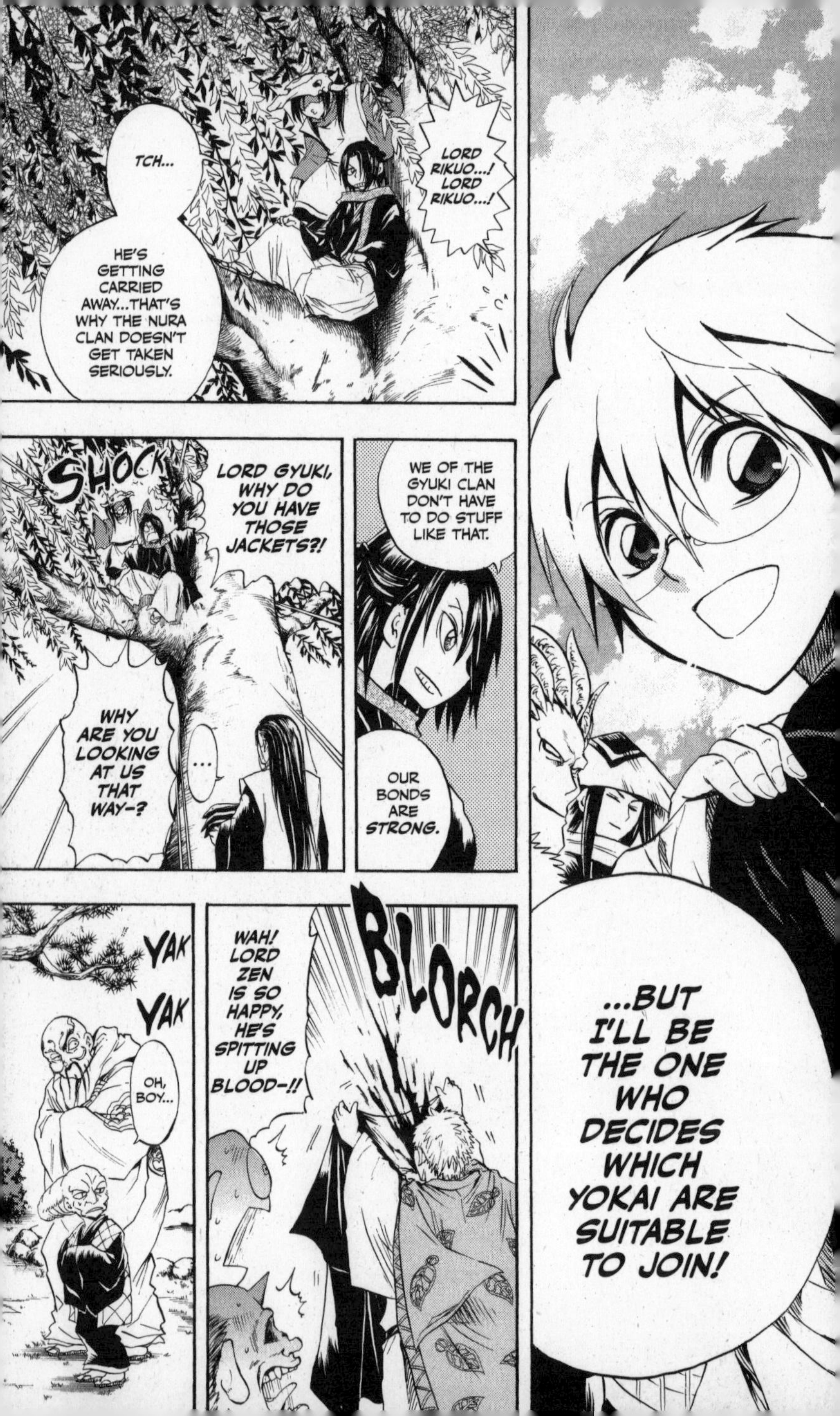
...BUT I'LL BE THE ONE WHO DECIDES WHICH YOKAI ARE SUITABLE TO JOIN!
LORD RIKUO...! LORD RIKUO...!
TCH...
HE'S GETTING CARRIED AWAY...THAT'S WHY THE NURA CLAN DOESN'T GET TAKEN SERIOUSLY.
WE OF THE GYUKI CLAN DON'T HAVE TO DO STUFF LIKE THAT.
OUR BONDS ARE STRONG.
SHOCK
LORD GYUKI, WHY DO YOU HAVE THOSE JACKETS?!
WHY ARE YOU LOOKING AT US THAT WAY-?
...
BLORCH
WAH! LORD ZEN IS SO HAPPY, HE'S SPITTING UP BLOOD-!!
YAK
YAK
OH, BOY...

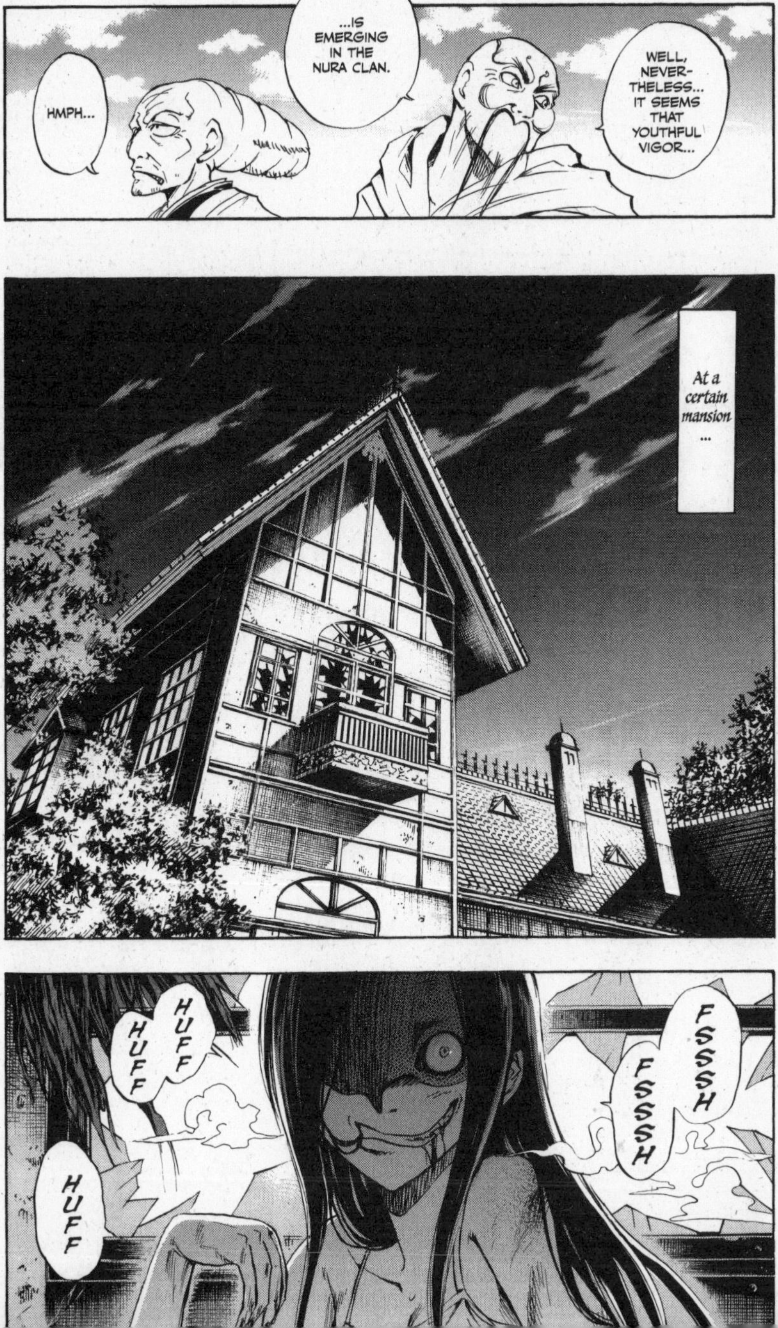
WELL, NEVER-THELESS... IT SEEMS THAT YOUTHFUL VIGOR...
...IS EMERGING IN THE NURA CLAN.
HMPH...
At a certain mansion ...
FSSSH
FSSSH
HUFF
HUFF
HUFF

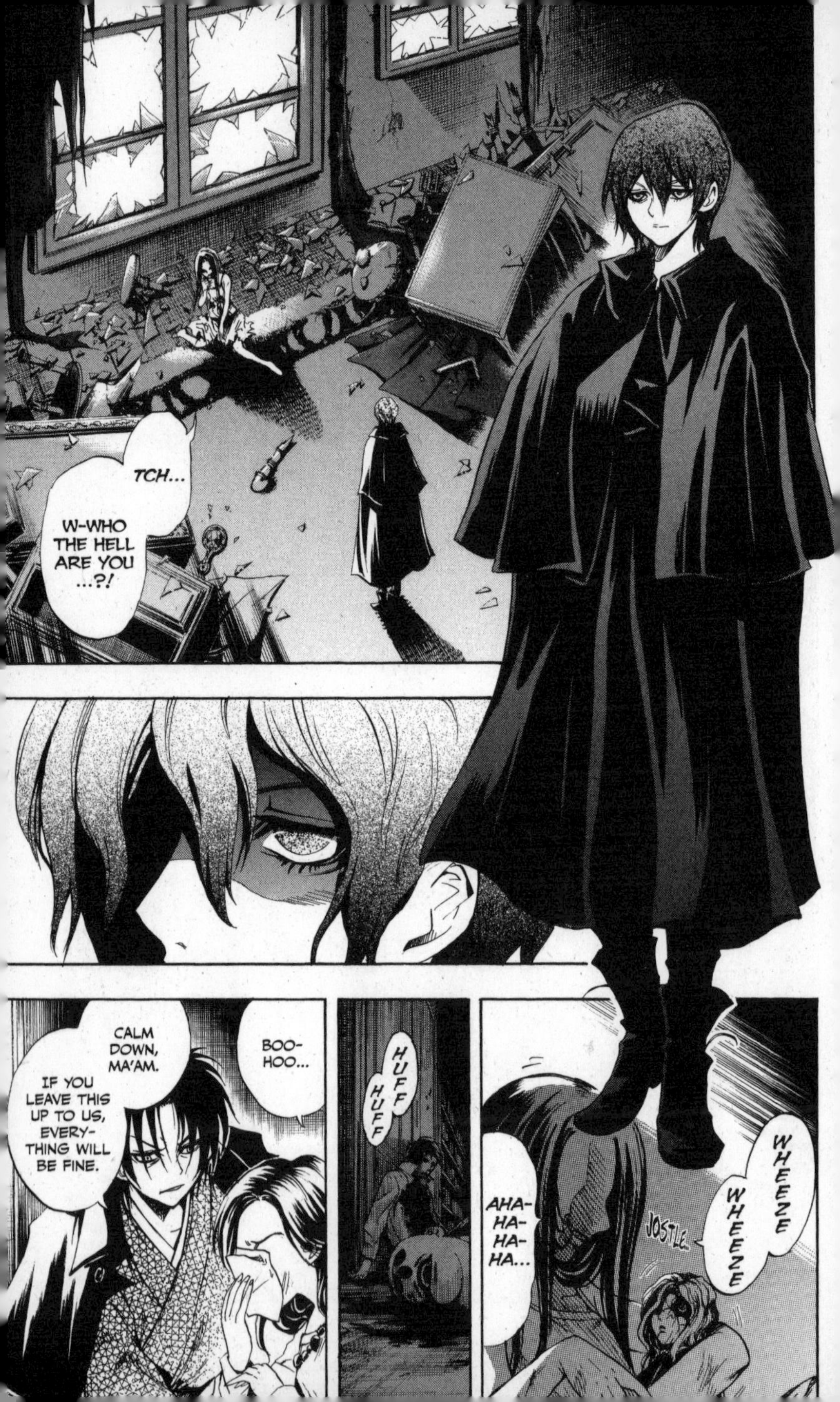
TCH...
W-WHO THE HELL ARE YOU ...?!
WHEEZE WHEEZE
JOSTLE
AHA-HA-HA-HA...
HUFF HUFF
BOO-HOO...
CALM DOWN, MA'AM.
IF YOU LEAVE THIS UP TO US, EVERY-THING WILL BE FINE.

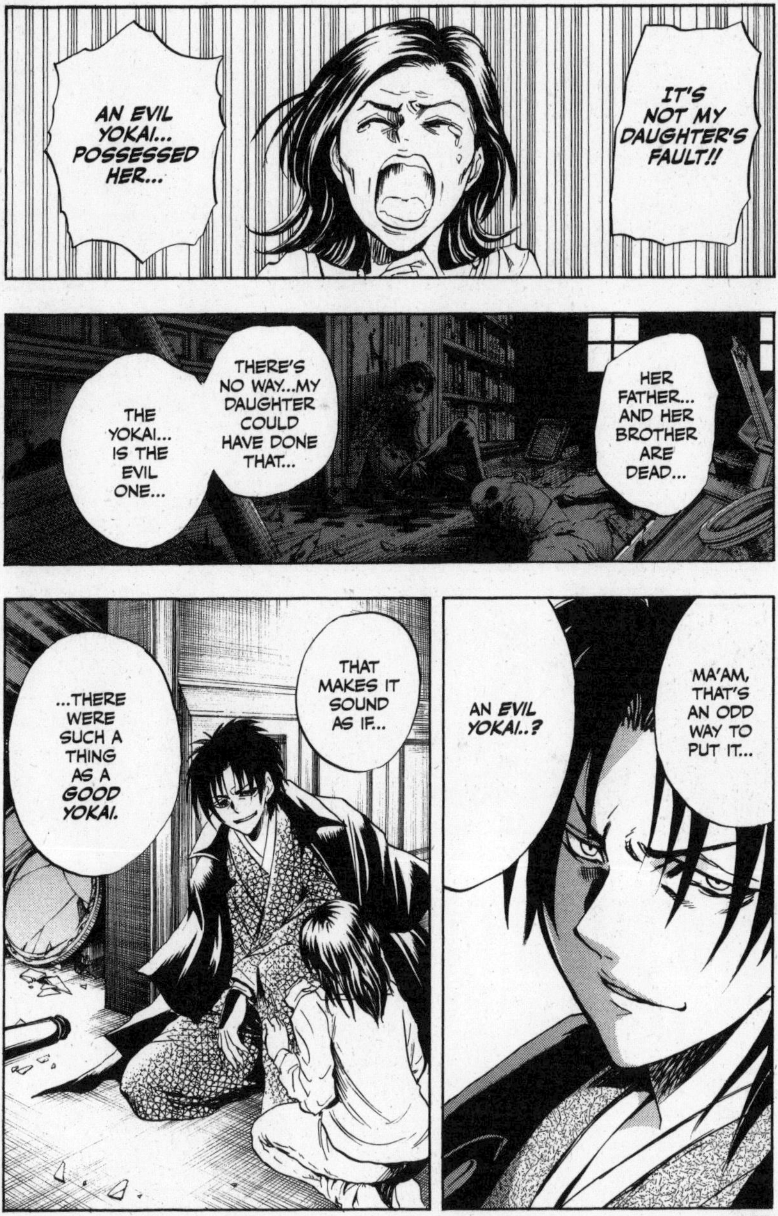
IT'S NOT MY DAUGHTER'S FAULT!!
AN EVIL YOKAI... POSSESSED HER...
HER FATHER... AND HER BROTHER ARE DEAD...
THERE'S NO WAY...MY DAUGHTER COULD HAVE DONE THAT...
THE YOKAI... IS THE EVIL ONE...
MA'AM, THAT'S AN ODD WAY TO PUT IT...
AN *EVIL* YOKAI..?
THAT MAKES IT SOUND AS IF...
...THERE WERE SUCH A THING AS A *GOOD* YOKAI.

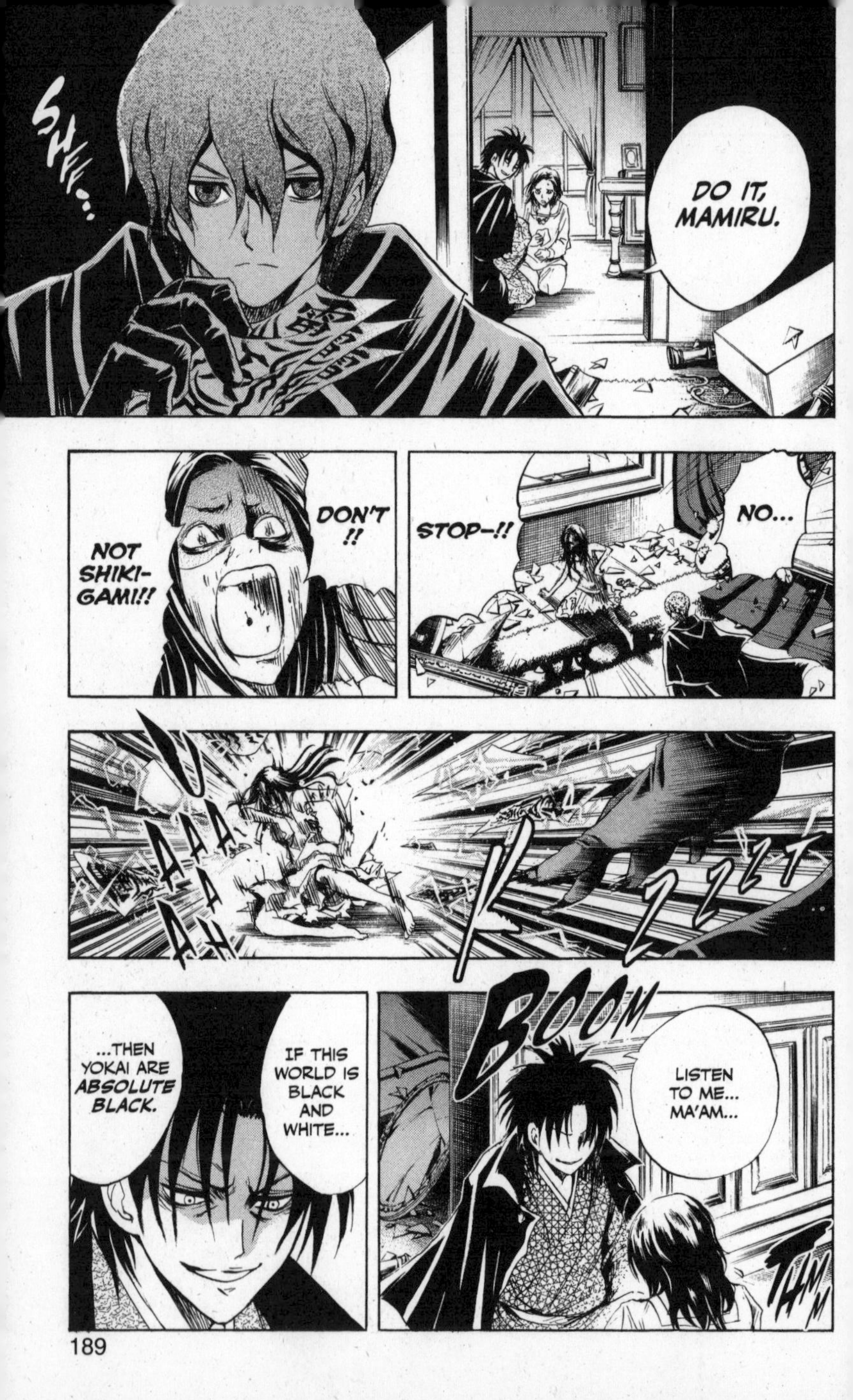
DO IT, MAMIRU.
SHFF...
NO...
STOP-!!
DON'T !!
NOT SHIKI-GAMI!!
ZZZZT
AAAAAH
BOOM
LISTEN TO ME... MA'AM...
THM
IF THIS WORLD IS BLACK AND WHITE...
...THEN YOKAI ARE ABSOLUTE BLACK.

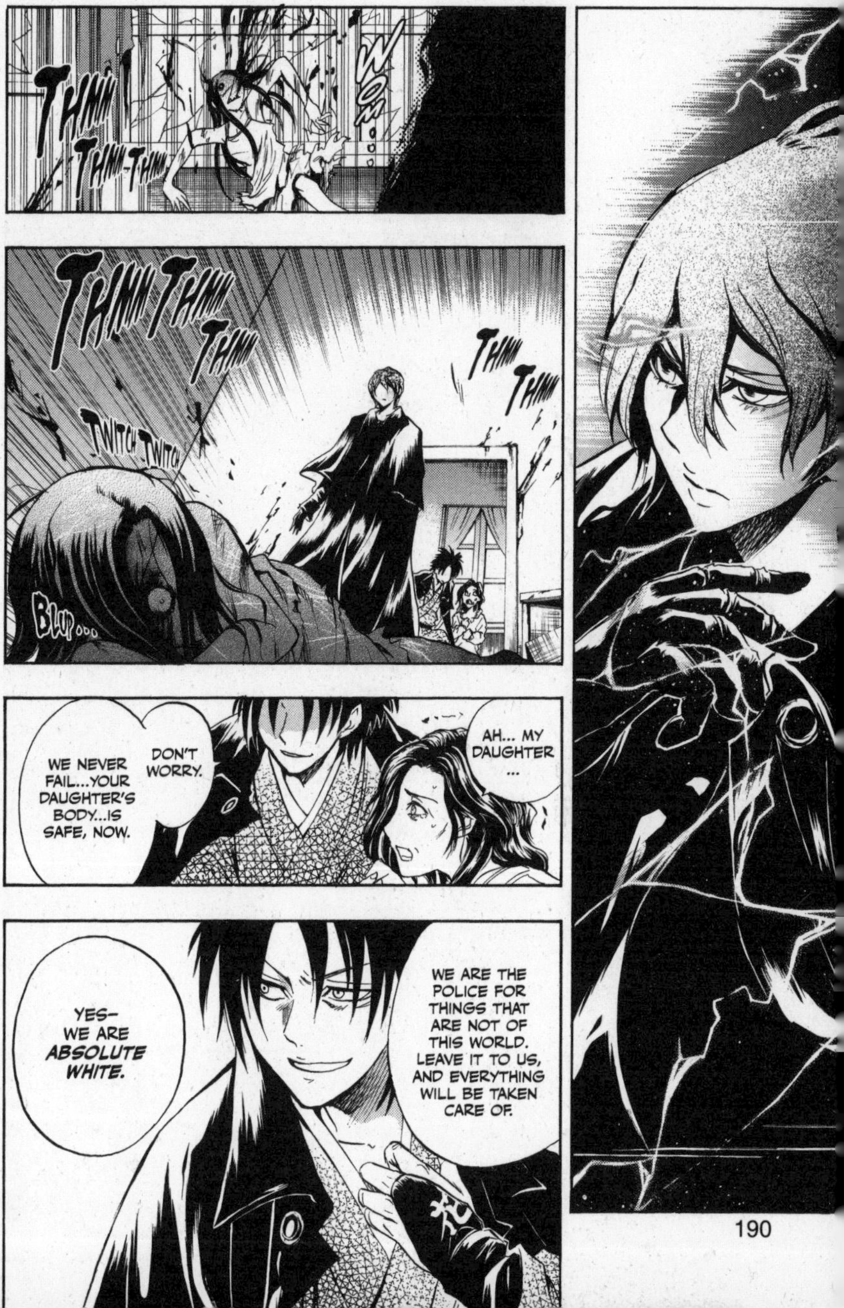
WOM...
THMM
THMM-THMM
THMM THMM
THMM
THMM
THMM
TWITCH TWITCH
BLUP...
AH... MY DAUGHTER ...
DON'T WORRY.
WE NEVER FAIL...YOUR DAUGHTER'S BODY...IS SAFE, NOW.
WE ARE THE POLICE FOR THINGS THAT ARE NOT OF THIS WORLD. LEAVE IT TO US, AND EVERYTHING WILL BE TAKEN CARE OF.
YES— WE ARE *ABSOLUTE WHITE.*

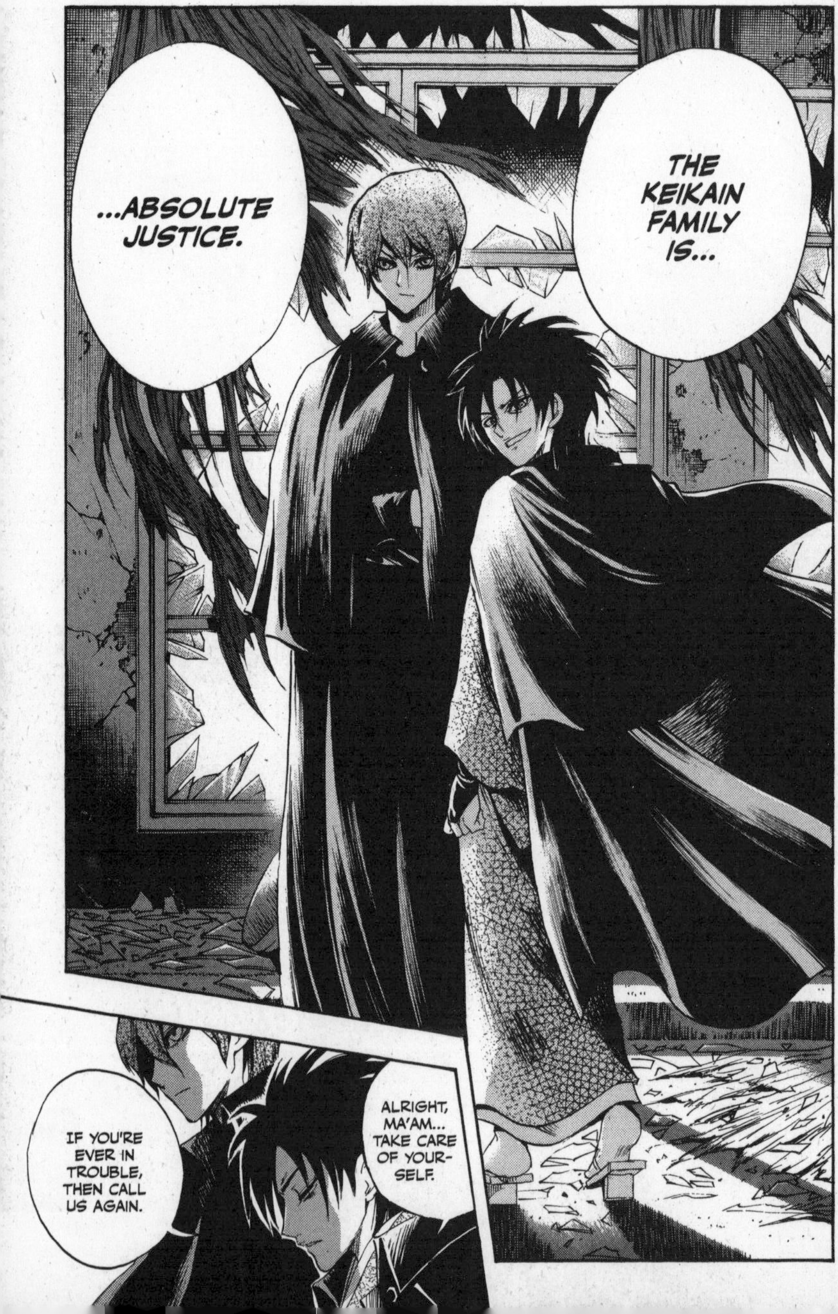
THE KEIKAIN FAMILY IS...
...ABSOLUTE JUSTICE.
ALRIGHT, MA'AM... TAKE CARE OF YOUR-SELF.
IF YOU'RE EVER IN TROUBLE, THEN CALL US AGAIN.

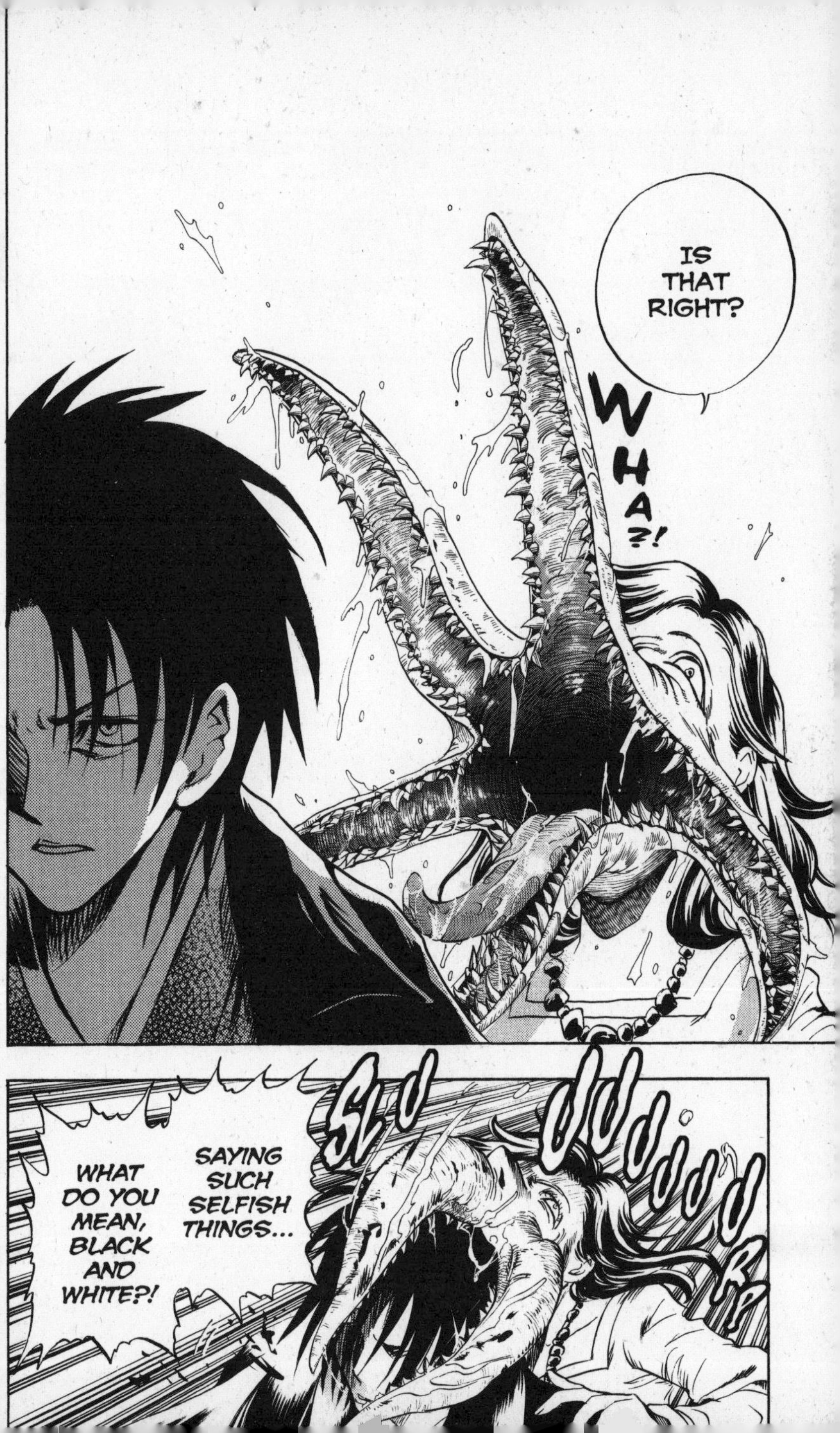
IS THAT RIGHT?
WHA?!
SAYING SUCH SELFISH THINGS...
WHAT DO YOU MEAN, BLACK AND WHITE?!

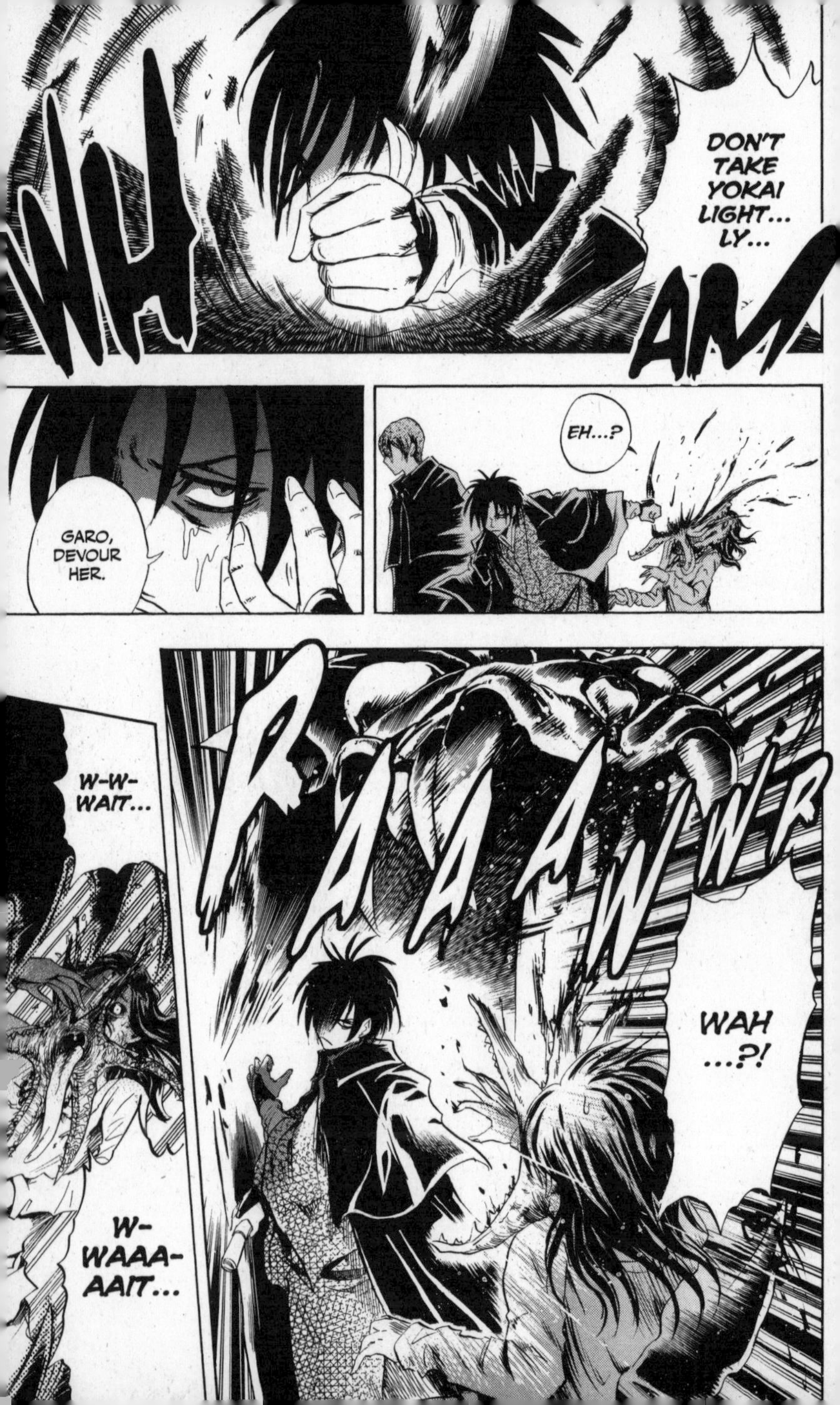
WHAM
DON'T TAKE YOKAI LIGHT... LY...
EH...?
GARO, DEVOUR HER.
RAAAWWR
WAH ...?!
W-W-WAIT...
W-WAAA-AAIT...

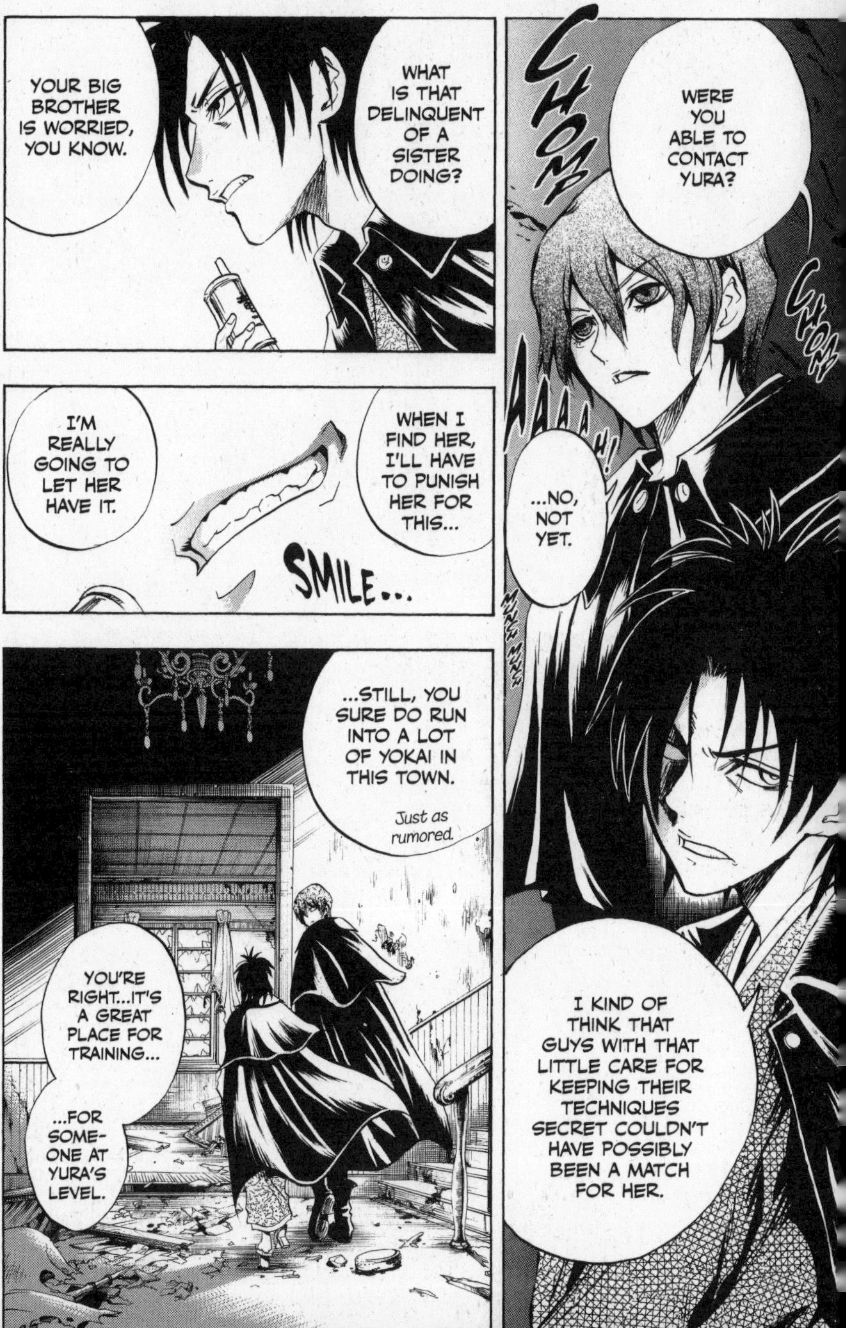

WERE YOU ABLE TO CONTACT YURA?
CHOMP
CHOMP
AAAAH!
...NO, NOT YET.
I KIND OF THINK THAT GUYS WITH THAT LITTLE CARE FOR KEEPING THEIR TECHNIQUES SECRET COULDN'T HAVE POSSIBLY BEEN A MATCH FOR HER.
WHAT IS THAT DELINQUENT OF A SISTER DOING?
YOUR BIG BROTHER IS WORRIED, YOU KNOW.
WHEN I FIND HER, I'LL HAVE TO PUNISH HER FOR THIS...
SMILE...
I'M REALLY GOING TO LET HER HAVE IT.
...STILL, YOU SURE DO RUN INTO A LOT OF YOKAI IN THIS TOWN.
Just as rumored.
YOU'RE RIGHT...IT'S A GREAT PLACE FOR TRAINING...
...FOR SOME-ONE AT YURA'S LEVEL.

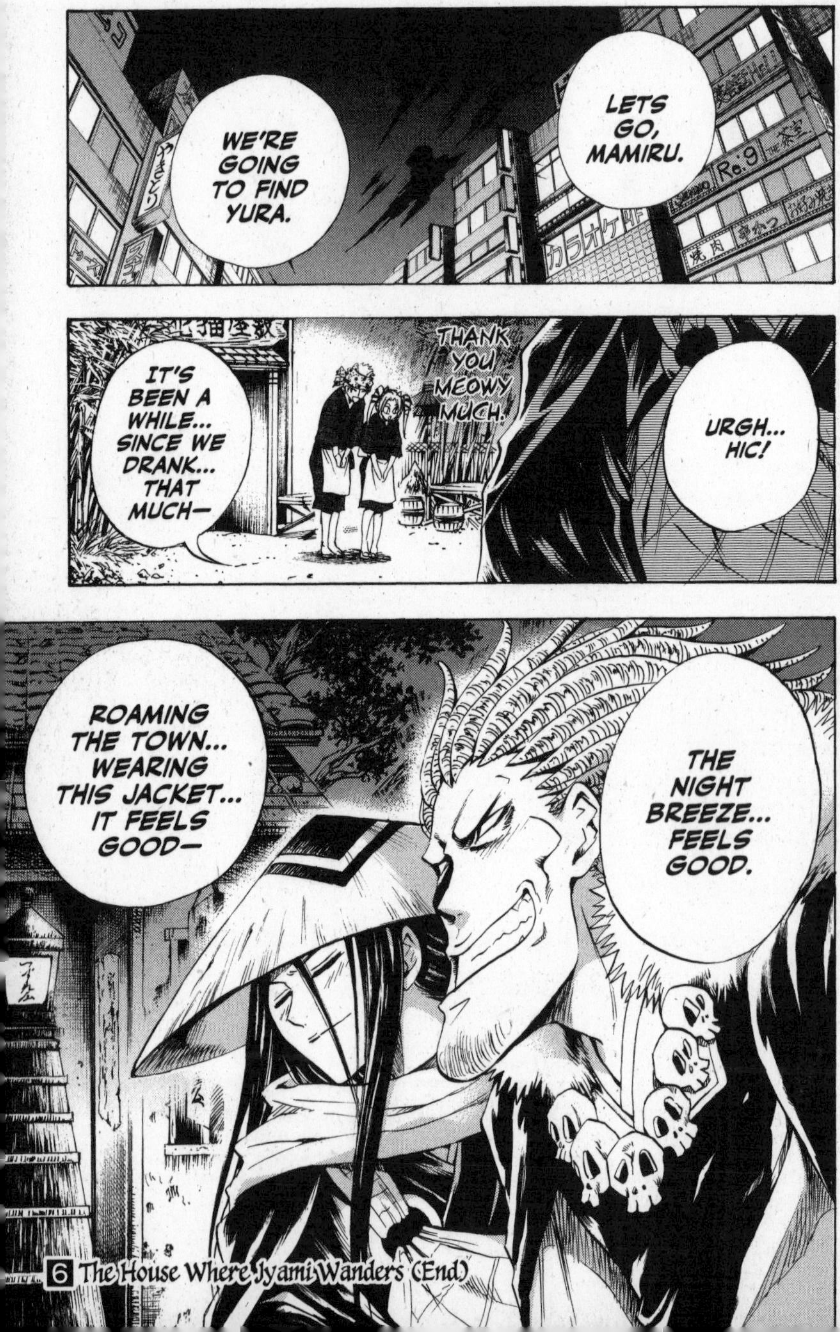
LETS GO, MAMIRU.
WE'RE GOING TO FIND YURA.
URGH... HIC!
THANK YOU MEOWY MUCH.
IT'S BEEN A WHILE... SINCE WE DRANK... THAT MUCH—
THE NIGHT BREEZE... FEELS GOOD.
ROAMING THE TOWN... WEARING THIS JACKET... IT FEELS GOOD—
6 The House Where Jyami Wanders (End)

NURARIHYON

Staff member Hidano made a Nurarihyon ambigram.

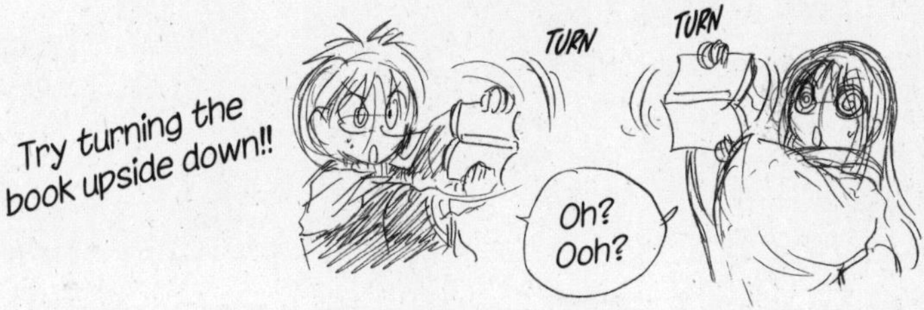

Try turning the book upside down!!
TURN
TURN
Oh? Ooh?

We want your questions and illustrations!!

Mailing Address:	**Nura Editor** **Viz Media** **P.O. Box 77010** **San Francisco, CA 94107**

***Please include your name, age, address and phone number in the letter. If you do not want to include your name, please use a handle or nickname. Letters and illustrations mailed to us will be stored for a certain period, but then later discarded. If you wish to keep a copy, please make one yourself before mailing it in. If you'd like to have your name and address remain anonymous, please indicate that in your letter.**

Bonus Story: Strange Tales of Ukiyoe Town

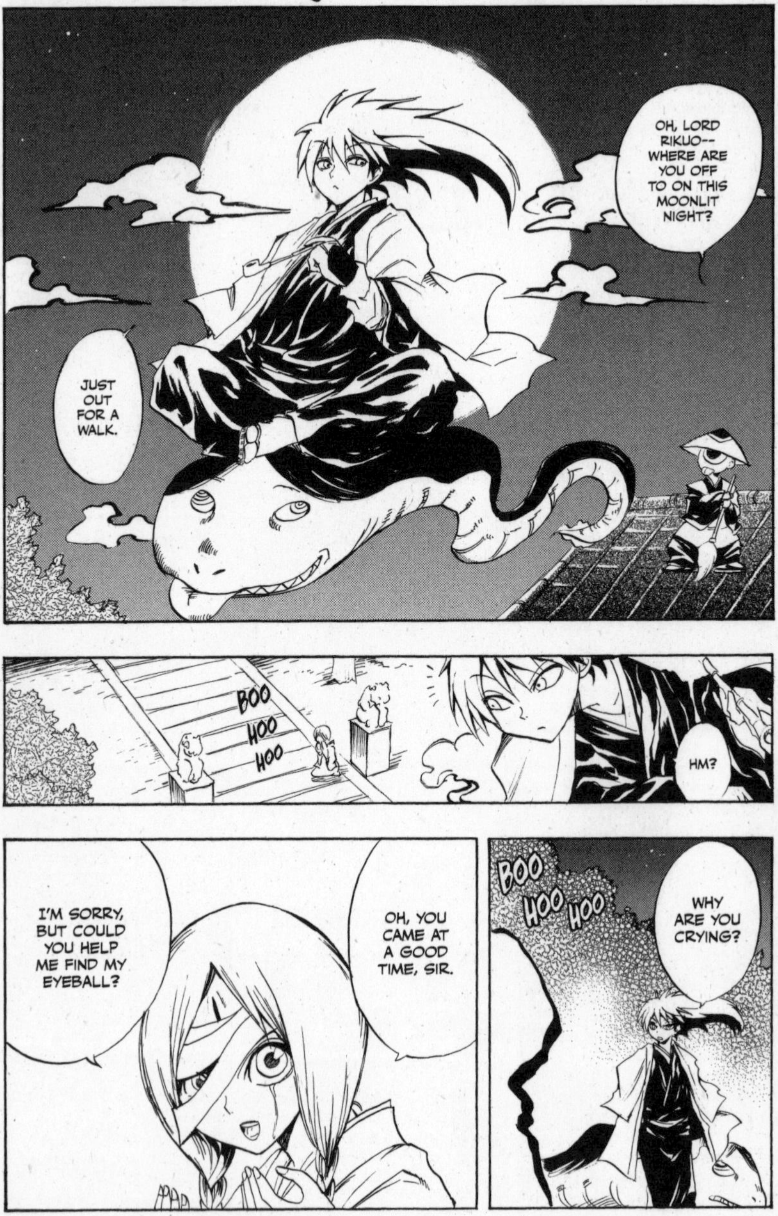

OH, LORD RIKUO-- WHERE ARE YOU OFF TO ON THIS MOONLIT NIGHT?
JUST OUT FOR A WALK.
BOO HOO HOO
HM?
BOO HOO HOO
WHY ARE YOU CRYING?
OH, YOU CAME AT A GOOD TIME, SIR.
I'M SORRY, BUT COULD YOU HELP ME FIND MY EYEBALL?

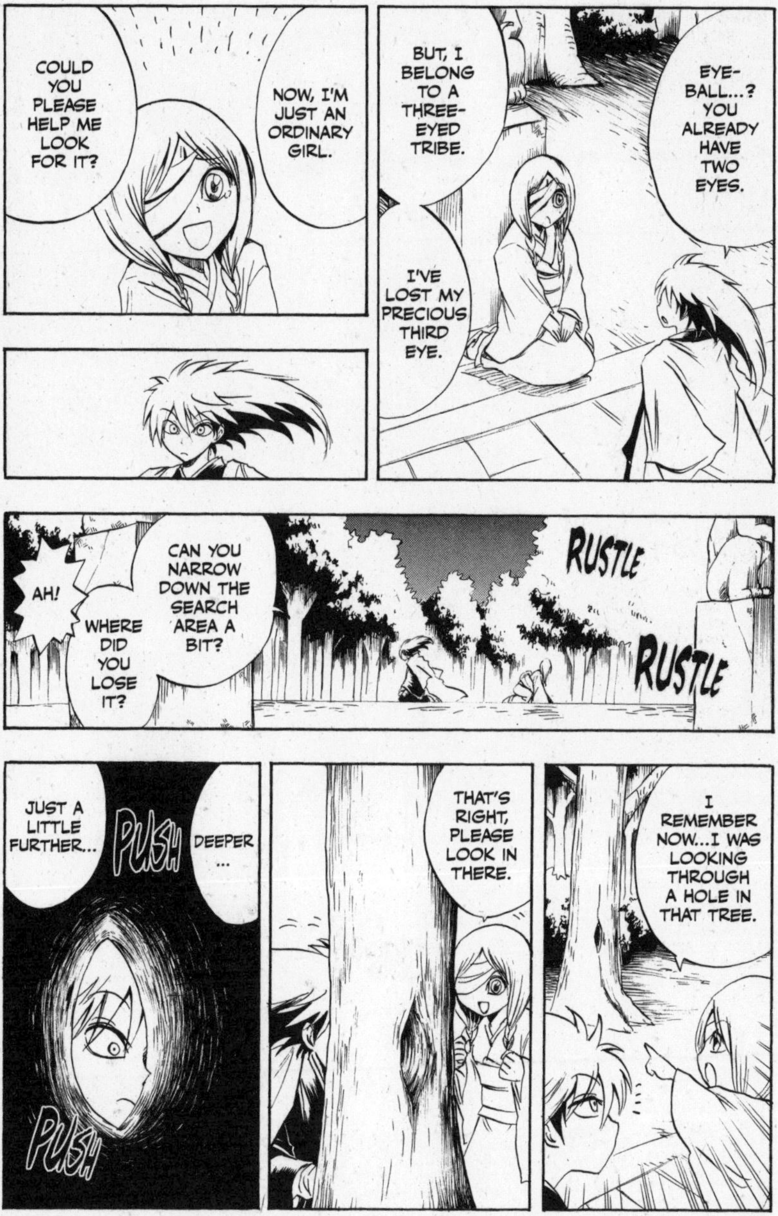
EYE-BALL...? YOU ALREADY HAVE TWO EYES.
BUT, I BELONG TO A THREE-EYED TRIBE.
I'VE LOST MY PRECIOUS THIRD EYE.
NOW, I'M JUST AN ORDINARY GIRL.
COULD YOU PLEASE HELP ME LOOK FOR IT?
RUSTLE
RUSTLE
CAN YOU NARROW DOWN THE SEARCH AREA A BIT?
WHERE DID YOU LOSE IT?
AH!
I REMEMBER NOW...I WAS LOOKING THROUGH A HOLE IN THAT TREE.
THAT'S RIGHT, PLEASE LOOK IN THERE.
DEEPER ...
PUSH
JUST A LITTLE FURTHER...
PUSH

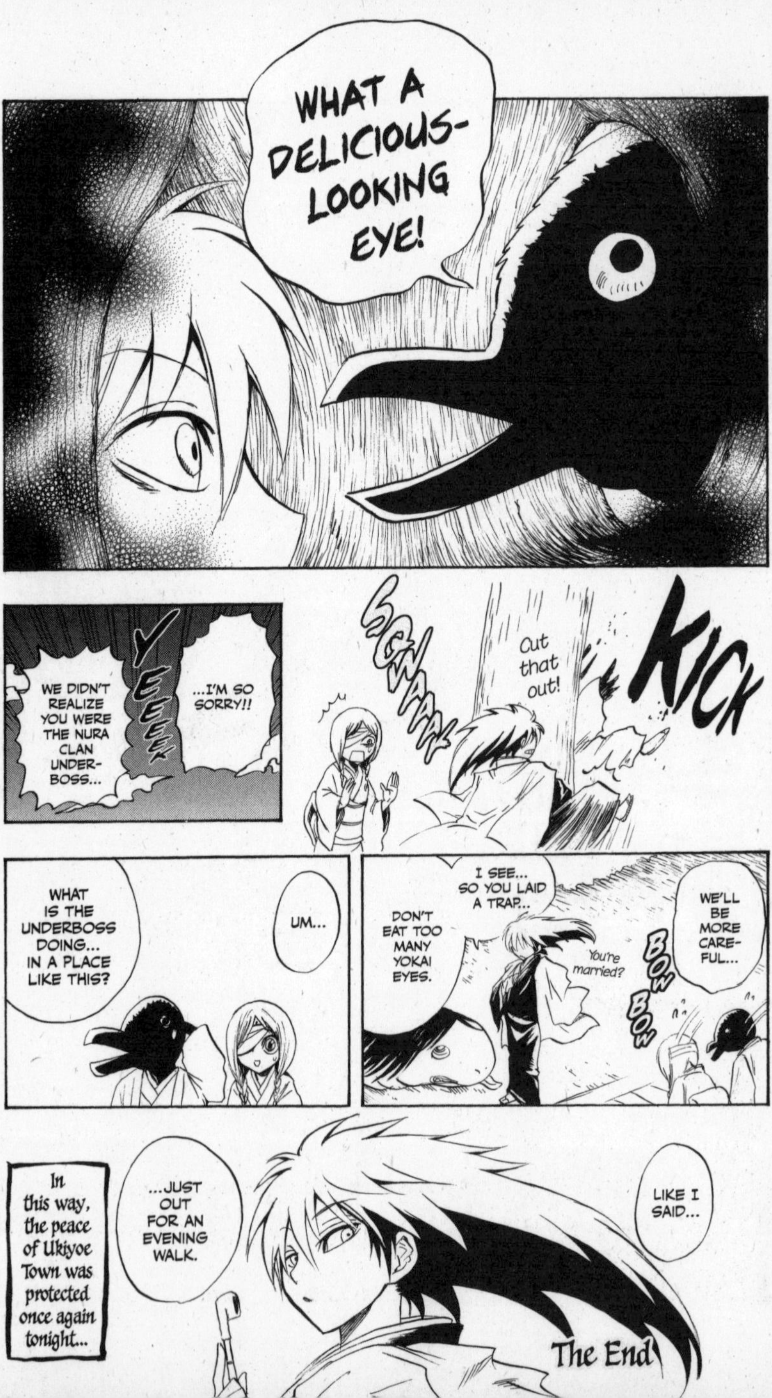
WHAT A DELICIOUS-LOOKING EYE!
KICK
Cut that out!
SQWAAAK
...I'M SO SORRY!!
YEEEEK
WE DIDN'T REALIZE YOU WERE THE NURA CLAN UNDER-BOSS...
WE'LL BE MORE CARE-FUL...
I SEE... SO YOU LAID A TRAP...
BOW BOW
You're married?
DON'T EAT TOO MANY YOKAI EYES.
UM...
WHAT IS THE UNDERBOSS DOING... IN A PLACE LIKE THIS?
LIKE I SAID...
...JUST OUT FOR AN EVENING WALK.
In this way, the peace of Ukiyoe Town was protected once again tonight...
The End

IN THE NEXT VOLUME...

THREE
KEIKAIN SIBLINGS

Rikuo encounters three siblings from the house of Keikain who come from a generations-long line of yokai hunters. Yura, the youngest of the trio, is not sure what to think of Rikuo and seems genuinely unconvinced as to whether he is friend or foe. But her brothers have other ideas. And the battle that ensues is epic!

AVAILABLE FEBRUARY 2012!